P.975.1
F 57
v. 3

LIBRARY OF
MUSKINGUM COLLEGE
New Concord, Ohio.

E 101
F 545
v. 2

THE
DISCOVERY OF AMERICA

*WITH SOME ACCOUNT OF ANCIENT AMERICA
AND THE SPANISH CONQUEST*

BY

JOHN FISKE

IN TWO VOLUMES

VOL. II.

Then I unbar the doors; my paths lead out
The exodus of nations; I disperse
Men to all shores that front the hoary main.
I too have arts and sorceries;
Illusion dwells forever with the wave.
I make some coast alluring, some lone isle
To distant men, who must go there or die.
EMERSON

BOSTON AND NEW YORK
HOUGHTON MIFFLIN COMPANY
The Riverside Press Cambridge

Copyright, 1892,
By JOHN FISKE.

All rights reserved

CONTENTS.

———

CHAPTER VII.

MUNDUS NOVUS.

3879

CHAPTER VIII.

THE CONQUEST OF MEXICO.

CHAPTER IX.

ANCIENT PERU.

CHAPTER X.

THE CONQUEST OF PERU.

CHAPTER XI.

LAS CASAS.

CHAPTER XII.

THE WORK OF TWO CENTURIES.

APPENDIX.

ILLUSTRATIONS.

———◆———

——◆——

CHAPTER VII.

MUNDUS NOVUS.

SOMETIMES in Wagner's musical dramas the introduction of a few notes from some leading melody foretells the inevitable catastrophe toward which the action is moving; as when in Lohengrin's bridal chamber the well-known sound of the distant Grail motive steals suddenly upon the ear, and the heart of the rapt listener is smitten with a sense of impending doom. So in the drama of maritime discovery, as glimpses of new worlds were beginning to reward the enterprising crowns of Spain and Portugal, for a moment there came from the north a few brief notes fraught with ominous portent. The power for whom destiny had reserved the world empire of which these southern nations — so noble in aim, so mistaken in policy — were dreaming stretched forth her hand, in quiet disregard of papal bulls, and laid it upon the western shore of the ocean. It was only for a moment, and long years were to pass before the consequences were developed. But in truth the first fateful note that heralded the coming English

supremacy was sounded when John Cabot's tiny
craft sailed out from the Bristol channel on a
bright May morning of 1497.

The story of the Cabots can be briefly told.
Less is known about them and their voyages than
one could wish.[1] John Cabot, a native

John Cabot.

of Genoa, moved thence to Venice,
where, after a residence of fifteen years, he was
admitted to full rights of citizenship in 1476.
He married a Venetian lady and had three sons,
the second of whom, Sebastian, was born in Venice some time before March, 1474. Nothing is
known about the life of John Cabot at Venice,
except that he seems to have been a merchant and
mariner, and that once in Arabia, meeting a car-
avan laden with spices, he made particular inquiries regarding the remote countries where such
goods were obtained. It is not impossible that
he may have reasoned his way, independently of
Columbus, to the conclusion that those countries
might be reached by sailing westward;[2] but there
is no evidence that such was the case. About
1490 Cabot moved to England with his family and
made his home in Bristol,[3] and he may have been

[1] The best critical discussion of the subject is that of M. Harrisse, *Jean et Sébastien Cabot*, Paris, 1882. Most of the author's
conclusions seem to me very strongly supported.

[2] This seems to be implied by the words of the late Dr. Charles
Deane : — "Accepting the new views as to 'the roundness of the
earth,' as Columbus had done, he was quite disposed to put them
to a practical test." Winsor, *Narr. and Crit. Hist.*, vol. iii. p. 1.
But is it not strange to find so learned a writer alluding to the
ancient doctrine of the earth's globular form as " new " in the time
of Columbus!

[3] M. d'Avezac's suggestion (*Bulletin de la Société de Géogra-*

one of the persons who were convinced at that time
by the arguments of Bartholomew Columbus.

Bristol was then the principal seaport of England, and the centre of trade for the Iceland fisheries.[1] The merchants of that town were
fond of maritime enterprise, and their ships had already ventured some distance
out upon the Atlantic. William of Worcester in-
forms us that in the summer of 1480 the wealthy
merchant John Jay and another sent out a couple
of ships, one of them of eighty tons burthen, commanded by Thomas Lloyd, "the most scientific
mariner in all England," in order to find "the island of Brazil to the west of Ireland," but after
sailing the sea for nine weeks without making any
discovery foul weather sent them back to Ireland.[2]
From a letter of Pedro de Ayala, one of the Spanish embassy in London in 1498, it would appear

The merchants of Bristol.

phie, Paris, 1872, 6ᵉ série, tom. iv. p. 44) that Columbus may have
consulted with Cabot at Bristol in 1477 seems, therefore, quite
improbable.

[1] See Hunt's *Bristol*, pp. 44, 137; Magnusson, *Om de Engelskes
Handel paa Island*, Copenhagen, 1833, p. 147.

[2] "1480 die jullij navis . . . et Joh[ann]is Jay junioris pon-
deris 80 doliorum inceperunt viagium apud portum Bristolliæ de
Kyngrode usque ad insulam de Brasylle in occidentali parte Hiber-
niæ, sulcando maria per . . . et . . . Thlyde [i. e. Th. Lyde =
Lloyd] est magister scientificus marinarius tocius Angliæ, et noua
venerunt Bristolliæ die lune 18 die septembris, quod dicta navis
velaverunt maria per circa 9 menses nec invenerunt insulam sed
per tempestas maris reversi sunt usque portum . . . in Hibernia
pro reposicione navis et mariniorum." *Itinerarium Willelmi de
Wyrcestre*, MS. in library of Corpus Christi College, Cambridge,
No. 210, p. 195, apud Harrisse, *op. cit.* p. 44. See also Fox-Bourne,
English Merchants, vol. i. p. 105. Though the Latin says nine
months, it is evident that only nine *weeks* are meant to be included
between "a day of July" and the 18th day of September.

that several expeditions, beginning perhaps as early as 1491, may have sailed from Bristol, at the instigation of John Cabot, in search of the imaginary islands of Brazil and Antilia.[1]

We are told that the news of the first voyage of Columbus was received by the Cabots and their English friends with much admiration.

Effects of the news from Columbus.

To have reached the coast of China by sailing westward was declared a wonderful achievement, and it was resolved to go and do likewise. On the 21st of January, 1496, the Spanish ambassador Puebla informed his sovereigns that "a person had come, like Columbus, to propose to the king of England an enterprise like that of the Indies." On the 28th of March the sovereigns instructed Puebla to warn Henry VII. that such an enterprise could not be put into execution by him without prejudice to Spain and Portugal.[2] But before this remonstrance arrived, the king had already issued letters patent, authorizing John Cabot and his three sons "to sail to the east, west, or north, with five ships carrying the English flag, to seek and discover all the islands, countries, regions, or provinces of pagans in whatever part of the world."[3] The expedition must return to the port of Bristol, and the king was to have one fifth of the profits. By implicitly excluding southerly

[1] Ayala to Ferdinand and Isabella, July 25, 1498; Harrisse, p. 329. The reader has doubtless already observed these fabulous islands on the Toscanelli map; see above, vol. i. p. 357.

[2] Ferdinand and Isabella to Puebla, March 28, 1496; Harrisse, p. 315.

[3] "Pro Johanne Cabot et filiis suis super Terra Incognita investiganda," March 5, 1496; Harrisse, p. 313.

courses it was probably intended, as far as possible, to avoid occasions for conflict with Spain or Portugal.

The voyage seems to have been made with a single ship, named the Matthew, or Matthews, after the evangelist, or perhaps after some English patron.[1] The crew numbered eighteen men. Sebastian Cabot may quite probably have accompanied his father. They sailed from Bristol early in May, 1497,[2] and discovered what was supposed to be the Chinese coast, "in the territory of the Grand Cham," on the 24th of June. By the end of July they had returned to Bristol, and on the 10th of August we find thrifty Henry VII. giving "to hym that founde the new isle" the munificent

John Cabot finds land supposed to be Cathay, June 24, 1497.

[1] Barrett, *History and Antiquities of Bristol*, 1789, p. 172. A contemporary MS., preserved in the British Museum, says that besides the flagship equipped by the king there were three or four others, apparently equipped by private enterprise : — "*In anno* 13 *Henr.* VII. This yere the Kyng at the besy request and supplicacion of a Straunger venisian, which [i. e. who] by a Cœart [i. e. chart] made hymself expert in knowyng of the world caused the Kynge to manne a ship w^t vytaill and other necessairies for to seche an Iland wherein the said Straunger surmysed to be grete commodities : w^t which ship by the Kynges grace so Rygged went 3 or 4 moo oute of Bristowe, the said Straunger beyng Conditor of the saide Flete, wheryn dyuers merchauntes as well of London as Bristow aventured goodes and sleight merchaundises, which departed from the West Cuntrey in the begynnyng of Somer, but to this present moneth came nevir Knowlege of their exployt." See Harrisse, p. 316. On page 50 M. Harrisse seems disposed to adopt this statement, but its authority is fatally impaired by the last sentence, which shows that already the writer had mixed up the first voyage with the second, as was afterwards commonly done.

[2] The date is often incorrectly given as 1494, owing to an old misreading of M. CCCC. XCIIII instead of M. CCCC. XCVII.

largess of £10 with which to celebrate the achievement.[1]

The news in England seems to have taken the
form that Cabot had discovered the isles of Brazil
and the Seven Cities, and the kingdom of the
Great Khan. A Venetian gentleman, Lorenzo
Pasqualigo, writing from London August 23, 1497,
says that "honours are heaped upon Cabot, he is
called Grand Admiral, he is dressed in silk, and
the English run after him like madmen."[2] It
seemed to Cabot that by returning to the point
where he had found land, and then proceeding somewhat to the southward, he
could find the wealthy island of Cipango,
and this time we do not hear that any
dread of collision with Spain prevailed upon the
king to discountenance such an undertaking. A
second expedition, consisting of five or six ships,
sailed from Bristol in April, 1498, and explored a
part of the coast of North America. In a despatch
dated July 25, Ayala told his sovereigns that its
return was expected in September. One of the
vessels, much damaged by stress of weather, took
refuge in an Irish port. When the others returned
we do not know, nor do we hear anything more
of John Cabot. It is probable that he sailed as
commander of the expedition, and it has been

John Cabot
and his son
Sebastian go
in search of
Cipango,
April, 1498.

---

[1] Harrisse, pp. 51, 59. "Fazi bona ziera," says Pasqualigo;
"pour s'amuser," says Harrisse, or, as one might put it, "to go
on a spree." It must be remembered that £10 then was equivalent to at least £100 of to-day. The king also granted to Cabot
a yearly pension of £20, to be paid out of the receipts of the Bristol custom-house.

[2] The letter is given in Harrisse, p. 322.

supposed that he may have died upon the voyage, leaving the command to his son Sebastian. It has further been supposed, on extremely slight evidence, that Sebastian may have conducted a third voyage in 1501 or 1503.

Sebastian Cabot married a Spanish lady, and seems to have gone to Spain soon after the death of Henry VII.[1] He entered the service of Ferdinand of Aragon October 20, 1512. In 1518 Charles V. appointed him Pilot Major of Spain; we shall presently find him at the congress of Badajoz in 1524; from 1526 to 1530 he was engaged in a disastrous expedition to the river La Plata, and on his return he was thrown into prison because of complaints urged against him by his mutinous crews. The Council of the Indies condemned him to two years of exile at Oran in Africa,[2] but the emperor seems to have remitted the sentence as unjust, and presently he returned to the discharge of his duties as Pilot Major. In 1548 he left the service of Spain and went back to England, where he was appointed governor of a company of merchants, organized for the purpose of discovering a northeast passage to China.[3] This enterprise opened a trade between England and Russia by way of the White Sea; and in 1556 the Muscovy Company received its charter, and Sebastian Cabot was appointed its governor. He seems to have died in London in 1557, or soon afterwards.

Later career of Sebastian Cabot.

[1] Peter Martyr, dec. iii. lib. vi. fol. 55.
[2] Navarrete, *Biblioteca maritima*, tom. ii. p. 699.
[3] Winsor, *Narr. and Crit. Hist.*, vol. iii. p. 6.

The life of the younger Cabot thus extended over
the whole of the period during which Europeans

Perplexities
caused by the
rapid accumu-
lation of geo-
graphical facts
in the six-
teenth cen-
tury.

were gradually awakening to the astounding fact that the western coasts
of the Atlantic were not the coasts of
Asia, but of a new continent, the existence of which had never been suspected
by any human being, except in the unheeded guess
of Strabo cited in a previous chapter.[1]   The sixty
years following 1497 saw new geographical facts
accumulate much faster than geographical theory
could interpret them, as the series of old maps
reproduced in the present volume will abundantly
show.   By the end of that time the revolution in
knowledge had become so tremendous, and men
were carried so far away from the old point of
view, that their minds grew confused as to the
earlier stages by which the change had been
effected.   Hence the views and purposes ascribed
to the Cabots by writers in the middle of the
sixteenth century have served only to perplex
the subject in the minds of later historians.   In
Ramusio's collection of voyages an anonymous
writer puts into the mouth of Sebastian Cabot
more or less autobiographical narrative, in which
there are almost as many blunders as lines.   In
this narrative the death of John Cabot is placed
before 1496, and Sebastian is said to have conducted the first voyage in that year.   It thus happened that until quite recently the discovery of

[1] See above, vol. i. p. 370.

[2] Ramusio, *Raccolta di Navigationi e Viaggi*, Venice, 1550,
tom. i.

the continent of North America was attributed to
the son, while the father was wellnigh forgotten.
It is to Ramusio's narrator, moreover, that we
owe the ridiculous statement — repeated by almost
every historian from that day to this — that the
purpose of the voyage of 1498 was the discovery
of a "northwest passage" to the coast of Asia!
As I shall hereafter show, the idea of a northwest
passage through or around what we call America
to the coast of Asia did not spring up in men's
minds until after 1522, and it was one of the consequences of the voyage of Magellan.[1] There is
no reason for supposing that Sebastian Cabot in
1498 suspected that the coast before him was anything but that of Asia, and it does not appear that
he contributed anything toward the discovery of
the fact that the newly found lands were part of a
new continent, though he lived long enough to become familiar with that fact, as gradually revealed
through the voyages of other navigators.

The slight contemporary mention, which is all
that we have of the voyages of the Cabots in 1497
and 1498, does not enable us to deter-   *What part of*
mine with precision the parts of the   *North Amer-*
                                          ica did the
North American coast that were vis-   *Cabots visit?*
ited.   We know that a chart of the first voyage
was made, for both the Spanish envoys, Puebla
and Ayala, writing between August 24, 1497, and
July 25, 1498, mentioned having seen such a
chart, and from an inspection of it they concluded
that the distance run did not exceed 400 leagues.
The Venetian merchant, Pasqualigo, gave the dis-

[1] See below, pp. 487–490.

tance more correctly as 700 leagues, and added
that Cabot followed the coast of the "territory of
the Grand Khan" for 300 leagues, and in returning saw two islands to starboard. An early tradition fixed upon the coast of Labrador as the
region first visited, and until lately this has been
the prevailing opinion.

The chart seen by the Spanish ministers in London is unfortunately lost. But a map engraved in
Germany or Flanders in 1544 or later,
and said to be after a drawing by Sebastian Cabot,[1] has at the north of what
we call the island of Cape Breton the legend
"*prima tierra vista*," i. e. "*first land seen;*" and
in this connection there is a marginal inscription,
Spanish and Latin, saying: — "This country was
discovered by John Cabot, a Venetian, and Sebastian Cabot, his son, in the year of our Saviour
Jesus Christ M. CCCC. XCIIII[2] on the 24th of June
in the morning, which country they called *prima
tierra vista*, and a large island near by they named
St. John because they discovered it on the same
day." Starting from this information it has been
supposed that the navigators, passing this St.
John, which we call Prince Edward island, coasted
around the gulf of St. Lawrence and passed out
through the strait of Belle Isle. The two islands

Map of 1544, attributed to Sebastian Cabot.

---

[1] It was discovered in 1843 in the house of a clergyman in Bava-
ria, and is now in the National Library at Paris. There is a beautiful facsimile of it in colours in Harrisse's *Jean et Sébastien Cabot*,
and it is described by M. d'Avezac, *Bulletin de la Société de Géographie*, 1857, 4ᵉ série, tom. xiv. pp. 268-270.

[2] This date is wrong. The first two letters after XC should be
joined together at the bottom, making a v.

seen on the starboard would then be points on the northern coast of Newfoundland, and a considerable part of Pasqualigo's 300 leagues of coasting would thus be accounted for. But inasmuch as the Matthew had returned to Bristol by the first of August, it may be doubted whether so long a route could have been traversed within five weeks.

If we could be sure that the map of 1544 in its present shape and with all its legends emanated from Sebastian Cabot, and was drawn with the aid of charts made at the time of discovery, its authority would be very high indeed. But there are some reasons for supposing it to have been amended or "touched up" by the engraver, and it is evidently compiled from charts made later than 1536, for it shows the results of Jacques Cartier's explorations in the gulf of St. Lawrence. Its statement as to the first landfall is, moreover, in conflict with the testimony of the merchant Robert Thorne, of Bristol, in 1527,[1] and with that of two maps made Testimony of Robert Thorne. at Seville in 1527 and 1529, according to which the "prima tierra vista" was somewhere on the coast of Labrador. It must be remembered, too, that John Cabot was instructed to take northerly and westerly courses, not southerly, and an important despatch from Raimondo de Soncino, in London, to the Duke of Milan, dated December 18, 1497, describes his course in accordance with these instructions. It is perfectly definite and altogether probable. According to this account Cabot sailed from Bristol in a small ship, manned by eighteen per-

[1] Hakluyt, *Principall Navigations*, vol. i. p. 216.

sons, and having cleared the western shores of Ireland, turned northward, after a few days headed for Asia, and stood mainly west till he reached "Terra Firma," where he planted the royal standard, and forthwith returned to England.[1] In other words, he followed the common custom in those days of first running to a chosen parallel, and then following that parallel to the point of destination. Such a course could hardly have landed him anywhere save on the coast of Labrador. Supposing his return voyage simply to have reversed this course, running south-easterly to the latitude of the English channel and then sailing due east, he may easily have coasted 300 leagues with land to starboard before finally bearing away from Cape Race. This view is in harmony with the fact that on the desolate coasts passed he saw no Indians or other human beings. He noticed the abundance of codfish, however, in the waters about Newfoundland, and declared that the English would no longer need to go to Iceland for their fish. Our informant adds

Cabot's course, as described by Soncino.

---

[1] "Cum uno piccolo naviglio e xviii persone se pose ala fortuna, et partitosi da Bristo porto occidentale de questo regno et passato Ibernia più occidentale, e poi alzatosi verso il septentrione, comenció ad navigare ale parte orientale [i. e. toward eastern Asia], lassandosi (fra qualche giorni) la tramontana ad mano drita, et havendo assai errato, infine capitoe in terra ferma, dove posto la bandera regia, et tolto la possessione per questa Alteza, et preso certi segnali, se ne retornato." See Harrisse, p. 324. The phrase "havendo assai errato" is rendered by Dr. Deane "having wandered about considerably" (Winsor, *Narr. and Crit. Hist.*, iii. 54), but in this context it seems to me rather to mean "having wandered sufficiently far [from Europe]," i. e. having gone far enough he found Terra Firma.

that Master John, being foreign-born and poor, would have been set down as a liar had not his crew, who were mostly Bristol men, confirmed everything he said.

With regard to the coasts visited in the expedition of 1498 our sole contemporary authority is the remarkable map made in 1500 by the La Cosa's Biscayan pilot, Juan de La Cosa, who map, 1500. had sailed with Columbus on his first and second voyages. So far as is known, this is the earliest map in existence made since 1492, and its importance is very great.[1] Las Casas calls La Cosa the

[1] A copy of the western sheet of this celebrated map, sketched upon a reduced scale after the copy in Humboldt's *Examen critique*, forms the frontispiece to the present volume. The original was found and identified by Humboldt in the library of Baron Walckenaer in 1832, and after the death of the latter it was bought April 21, 1853, at an auction sale in Paris, for the queen of Spain against Henry Stevens, for 4,020 francs. It is now to be seen at the Naval Museum in Madrid. It was made by La Cosa at Puerto Santa Maria, near Cadiz, at some time between June and October, in the year 1500 (see Leguina, *Juan de la Cosa*, Madrid, 1877, p. 70). It is superbly illuminated with colours and gold. Its scale of proportions, remarkably correct in some places, is notably defective in others. The Newfoundland region is properly brought near to the papal meridian of demarcation, and what we call Brazil is cut by it; which may possibly indicate that La Cosa had heard the news of Cabral's discovery, presently to be noticed, which reached Lisbon late in June. The Azores and Cape Verde islands are much too far west. The voyages of which the results are distinctly indicated upon the map are the first three of Columbus, the two of the Cabots, that of Ojeda (1498–99), and that of Pinzon (1499–1500), and, as we shall presently see, the map gives very important and striking testimony regarding the first voyage of Vespucius. The coast-lines and islands marked by La Cosa with names and flags represent results of actual exploration so far as known to La Cosa or exhibited to him by means of charts or log-books. The coast-lines and islands without names represent in general his unverified theory of the situation.

best pilot of his day.   His reputation as a cartographer was also high, and his maps were much
admired.   The map before us was evidently drawn with honesty and care.   It
represents the discoveries of the Cabots
as extending over 360 leagues of coast,
or about as far as from the strait of
Belle Isle to Cape Cod, and the names
from "Cabo de Ynglaterra" to "Cabo Descubierto" are probably taken from English sources.   But
whether the coast exhibited is that of the continent within the gulf of St. Lawrence, or the
southern coast of Newfoundland with that of Nova
Scotia, is by no means clear.[1]   The names end

The Cabot
voyages prob-
ably ranged
from Labra-
dor, through
the gulf of St.
Lawrence, and
perhaps as far
as Cape Cod.

Of the northern island " Frislanda " he must probably have been
told by Columbus, for he could not have known anything of the
Zeno narrative, first made public in 1558.   In the middle of the
west side of the map is a vignette representing Christopher (the
Christ-bearer) wading through the waters, carrying upon his
shoulders the infant Christ or Sun of Righteousness, to shine upon
the heathen.   At the bottom of the vignette is the legend "Juan
de la cosa la fizo en el puerto des^{ta} mr^a en año de 1500."   The
original is five feet nine inches long by three feet two inches
wide, and is a map of the world.   The full-sized facsimile published by M. Jomard (in his *Monuments de la géographie*, pl. xvi.)
is in three elephant folio sheets, of which the frontispiece to this
volume represents the third, or western.   The hypothetical coast-
line of Brazil, at the bottom, is cut off square, so that the map
may be there attached to a roller; and beyond the cut-off this
same coast-line is continued on the first, on eastern sheet, as the
coast of Asia east of the Ganges.   In the opinion of most geographers of that time, the situation of Quinsay (Hang-chow) in
China would come a little to the west of the westernmost English
flagstaff.

[1] The former view, which is that of Humboldt, is perhaps the
more probable.   See Ghillany, *Geschichte des Seefahrers Ritter
Martin Behaim*, Nuremberg, 1853, p. 2.   The latter view is held
by Dr. Kohl (*Documentary History of Maine*, vol. i. p. 154), who

near the mouth of a large river, which may very probably be meant for the St. Lawrence, and beyond the names we see two more English flags with the legend, "Sea discovered by Englishmen." Inasmuch as it would be eminently possible to sail through the gulf of St. Lawrence without becoming aware of the existence of Newfoundland, except at the strait of Belle Isle (which at its narrowest is about ten miles wide), one is inclined to suspect that the "Isla de la Trinidad" may represent all that the voyagers saw of that large island. It is worthy of note that on the so-called Sebastian Cabot map of 1544 Newfoundland does not yet appear as a single mass of land, but as an archipelago of not less than eleven large islands with more than thirty small ones. By this time the reader is doubtless beginning to have "a realizing sense"

---

identifies "Cabo de Ynglaterra" with Cape Race. To me it seems more likely that Cabo de Ynglaterra is the promontory just north of Invuktoke inlet on the coast of Labrador, and that the island to the right of it (Ysla Verde) is meant for Greenland. If, then, Isla de la Trinidad is the northern extremity of Newfoundland and the river by Cabo Descubierto is the St. Lawrence, we have a consistent and not improbable view. In spite of the two additional flags, the coast to the left of the St. Lawrence is evidently hypothetical; the next river is probably meant for the Hoang-ho in China (called by Polo the Caramoran; see Yule's *Marco Polo*, ii. 104–106), and the "sea discovered by the English" was probably supposed to be the Yellow Sea.

There is no good ground for the statement that Sebastian Cabot sailed as far south as Florida. "The remark of Peter Martyr, in 1515, about Cabot's reaching on the American coast the latitude of Gibraltar, and finding himself then on a meridian of longitude far enough west to leave Cuba on his left, is simply absurd, dilemmatize it as you will. Such a voyage would have landed him near Cincinnati." Stevens, *Historical and Geographical Notes*, p. 35.

of the fact that the work of discovering America was not such a simple and instantaneous affair as is often tacitly assumed.

The second voyage of the Cabots was regarded in England as a failure, for the same reason that the later voyages of Columbus were regarded with diminishing interest in Spain, because there was much outlay and little profit. Whatever there was to be found on these tantalizing coasts, it surely was not golden Cathay. The inhospitable shores of Labrador offered much less that was enticing than the balmy valleys of Hispaniola. Furs do not seem as yet to have attracted attention, and although the unrivalled fisheries were duly observed and reported, it was some time before the Bristol merchants availed themselves of this information, for they considered the Iceland fisheries safer.[1] There was thus little to encourage the cautious Henry VII. in further exploration. In 1505 he made a contract with some sailors from the Azores for a voyage to "the New-found-land," and one item of the result may be read in an account-book of the treasury: — "To Portyngales that brought popyngais and catts of the mountaigne with other Stuf to the Kinges grace, 5 l."[2] In the reign of Henry VIII., and in one and the same year, 1527, we find mention of two voyages from Portsmouth, the one conducted by John Rut, in the Samson and the Mary of

Why the Cabot voyages were not followed up.

Voyage of John Rut, 1527.

[1] Hunt's *Bristol*, p. 137.

[2] Harrisse, *Jean et Sébastien Cabot*, pp. 142, 272.

Guilford, the other by a certain Master Grube, in the Dominus Vobiscum, the latter being perhaps the most obscure of all the voyages of that century. I suspect that the two voyages were identical and the reports multifarious.[1] Rut's expedition was undertaken, at the instance of Robert Thorne, of Bristol, for the purpose of finding a route to Cathay. It encountered vast icebergs; the Samson was lost with all its crew, and the Mary "durst not go no further to the northward for fear of more ice;" so after reaching Cape Race and the bay of St. John's she returned to England.[2]

We hear of no further enterprises of this sort during the reign of Henry VIII. The lack of interest in maritime discovery is shown by the very small number of books on such matters published in England, — only twelve before 1576.[3] We may suppose that public attention was for the time monopolized by the struggles of the Reformation, and, even had the incentives to western voyages been much stronger than they seem to have been, there was serious risk of their leading to diplomatic complications with Spain. The government of Charles V. kept a lynx-eyed watch upon all trespassers to the west of Borgia's meridian.[4] It was not until the Protestant England of Elizabeth had come to a life and death grapple with

Change in the situation between the reign of Henry VIII. and that of Elizabeth.

---

[1] See Harrisse, *op. cit.* p. 294.

[2] Hakluyt, *Principall Navigations*, vol. iii. p. 129; *Purchas his Pilgrimes*, vol. iii. p. 809; Fox-Bourne, *English Merchants*, vol. i. p. 159; De Costa, *Northmen in Maine*, pp. 43–62.

[3] Winsor, *Narr. and Crit. Hist.*, vol. iii. pp. 199–208.

[4] See Harrisse, *op. cit.* p. 146.

Spain, and not until the discovery of America had advanced much nearer to completion, so that its value began to be more correctly understood, that political and commercial motives combined in determining England to attack Spain through America, and to deprive her of supremacy in the colonial and maritime world. Then the voyages of the Cabots assumed an importance entirely new, and could be quoted as the basis of a prior claim, on the part of the English crown, to lands which it had discovered. In view of all that has since happened, as we see these navigators coming upon the scene for a moment in the very lifetime of Columbus, and setting up the royal standard of England upon a bit of the American coast, we may well be reminded of the phrase of prophetic song that heralds a distant but inevitable doom.

La Cosa's map shows that definite information of the Cabot voyages and their results had been sent to Spain before the summer of 1500. Similar information was possessed in Portugal, and the enterprising King Emanuel (who had succeeded John II. in 1495) was led to try what could be accomplished by a voyage to the northwest. Some of the land visited by the Cabots seemed to lie very near Borgia's meridian; perhaps on closer inspection it might be found to lie to the east of it. There can be little doubt that this was one of the leading motives which prompted the voyages of the brothers Cortereal. Into the somewhat vexed details of these expeditions it is not necessary for

Portuguese voyages to Labrador; the brothers Cortereal, 1500–1502.

our purposes to enter. The brothers Gaspar and Miguel Cortereal were gentlemen of high consideration in Portugal. Two or three voyages were made by Gaspar in the course of the years 1500 and 1501; and from the last voyage two of his ships returned to Lisbon without him, and he was never heard of again. On May 10, 1502, Miguel sailed with three caravels in search of his brother; and again it happened that two of the ships returned in safety, but the commander and his flagship never returned. The incidents of the various voyages are sadly confused; but it seems clear that the coasts visited by Gaspar Cortereal were mainly within the region already explored by the Cabots, from Labrador perhaps as far south as the bay of Fundy. He probably followed the eastern shores of Newfoundland, and crossed over to Greenland. He brought home wild men (*homines silvestres*) and white bears, as well as a gilded sword-hilt and some silver trinkets of Venetian manufacture which the natives had evidently obtained from the Cabots.[1] The coast which he had followed, or part of it, was declared to lie to the east of the papal meridian and to belong to Portugal. A despatch dated October 17, 1501, recounting these facts, was sent to Ercole d' Este, Duke of Ferrara, by his agent or envoy, Alberto Cantino,

[1] These voyages are ably discussed by M. Harrisse, *Les Corte-Real et leurs voyages au Nouveau Monde*, Paris, 1883; see also the accounts in Peschel's *Geschichte des Zeitalters der Entdeckungen*, 2e aufl., Stuttgart, 1877; Kunstmann, *Die Entdeckung Amerikas*, Münich, 1859; Lafitau, *Histoire des découvertes des Portugais dans le Nouveau Monde*, Paris, 1733, 2 vols. 4to; Winsor, *Narr. and Crit. Hist.*, vol. iv. pp. 1-4, 12-16.

then resident in Lisbon. An elaborate map, concerning which we shall presently have more to say, was made for Cantino at a cost of twelve golden

The Cantino map, 1502.

ducats, and carried by him to Italy in the autumn of 1502. This map is now preserved in the Biblioteca Estense at Modena.[1] On it we see the papal meridian cutting through Brazil, and we see the outer coast of Newfoundland laid down to the east of the meridian and

[1] The rude sketch here presented gives no idea whatever of the fulness of detail and the gorgeous beauty of this remarkable map. A full-sized facsimile of the western portion, 3 feet 5¾ inches in width by 3 feet 2½ inches in height, in the original colours, is to be found in the portfolio accompanying M. Harrisse's work on the Cortereals. The continents are given in a soft green, the islands in rich blues and reds. Flags in their proper colours mark the different sovereignties, from that of the Turks at Constantinople to that of the Spaniards near Maracaibo. The two tropics are in red, the equator in gold, and the papal line of demarcation in a brilliant blue. Africa is characterized by a hilly landscape in pale blues and greens, a castellated Portuguese fortress, native huts, negroes in jet black, birds of various hue, and a huge lion-headed figure in brown and gold. A circular structure called "Tower of Babilonja" appears in Egypt, while Russia is marked by a pile of characteristic architecture suggestive of Moscow. Newfoundland, placed to the east of the papal meridian and labelled "Terra del Rey de Portugall," is decked out with trees in green and gold. The Brazilian coast — the southern part of which is given from hearsay, chiefly from the third voyage of Vespucius, who returned to Lisbon September 7, 1502 (as is proved, among other things, by its giving the name of the Bay of All Saints, discovered in that voyage) — is adorned with tall trees in green, gold, and brown, among which are interspersed smaller trees and shrubs in various shades of blue, and three enormous paroquets intensely red, with white beaks and claws, and divers wing and tail feathers in blue, buff, and gold. The ocean is of an ivory tint, and the lettering, sometimes gothic sometimes cursive, is in black and red. Every detail speaks for the intense and loving interest felt in this kind of work.

labelled " Land of the King of Portugal." The
southern extremity of Greenland is also depicted
with remarkable clearness. The islands afterwards known as West Indies, heretofore known

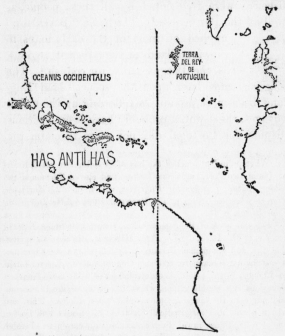

Sketch of part of the Cantino map, 1502.

simply as Indies, here appear for the first time as
Antilles (*has Antilhas*).

Portuguese sailors were prompt in availing themselves of the treasures of the Newfoundland fisheries. By 1525 a short-lived Portuguese colony
had been established on Cape Breton island.[1] But,

---

[1] Souza, *Tratado das Ilhas Novas*, p. 5 ; Harrisse, *Jean et Sébastien Cabot*, p. 76.

as the name of that island reminds us, the Portuguese had sturdy rivals in this work. As early as 1504 that spot was visited by Breton, Norman, and Basque sailors, and from that time forth the fisheries were frequented by all these people, as well as the Portuguese.[1] The name "Baccalaos,"

The New-foundland fisheries — Baccalaos.

applied on most of the early maps to Newfoundland or the adjacent regions, is the Basque name for codfish.[2] The English came later upon the scene. Had England been more prompt in following up the Cabot voyages, there would probably have been a serious dispute, for Portugal did not cease to claim the

[1] When John Rut reached the bay of St. John, August 3, 1527, he found two Portuguese, one Breton, and eleven Norman ships fishing there. *Purchas his Pilgrimes*, vol. v. p. 822 ; Harrisse, *Jean et Sébastien Cabot*, p. 75 ; Brown, *History of the Island of Cape Breton*, p. 13.

[2] See the book of the Jesuit father, Georges Fournier, *Hydrographie*, 2ᵉ éd., Paris, 1667. Peter Martyr is mistaken in saying that the land was named Baccalaos (by Sebastian Cabot) because it was the native name for codfish. Gomara's account, as rendered by Richard Eden, in 1555, is entertaining : — " The newe lande of Baccalaos is a coulde region, whose inhabytantes are Idolatours and praye to the sonne and moone and dyuers Idoles. They are whyte people and very rustical, for they eate flesshe and fysshe and all other things rawe. Sumtymes also they eate man's flesshe priuily, so that their Cacique have no knowledge thereof [!]. The apparell, both of men and women, is made of beares skynnes, although they have sables and marternes, not greatly estemed because they are lyttle. Sum of them go naked in sommer and weare apparell only in wynter. The Brytons and Frenche men are accustomed to take fysshe in the coastes of these lands, where is found great plenty of Tunnies which the inhabytauntes caul Baccalaos, whereof the land was so named. . . . In all this newe lande is neyther citie nor castell, but they lyue in companies lyke heardes of beastes." *The First Three English Books on America*, Birmingham, 1885, p. 345.

sovereignty of Newfoundland, on the ground that
it lay to the east of the papal meridian, and in
those days it was not easy to disprove this assumption.[1] But the question was swallowed up in the
events of 1580, when Spain conquered and annexed Portugal; and it was not long after that
time that the inability of the Spaniards to maintain their mastery of the sea left the wealth of
these fisheries to be shared between France and
England.

While these northern voyages are highly interesting in their relations to the subsequent work of
English colonization, nevertheless in the history of
the discovery of the New World they occupy but
a subordinate place. John Cabot was probably
the first commander since the days of the Vikings
to set foot upon the continent of North As links in the
America, yet it would be ridiculous to chain of discovery, the
compare his achievement with that of northern
voyages were
Columbus. The latter, in spite of its far less important than
admixture of error with truth, was a the southern.
scientific triumph of the first order. It was Columbus who showed the way across the Sea of
Darkness, and when once he had stood that egg
upon its end it was easy enough for others to follow.[2] On the other hand, in so far as the dis-

[1] The reader will observe the name of Cortereal upon Newfoundland as an island on Sebastian Münster's map of 1540; as
an archipelago on Mercator's map of 1541; and as part of the
mainland on Lok's map of 1582. See below, pp. 499, 153, 525.

[2] The anecdote of Columbus and the egg is told by Benzoni,
Historia del Mondo Nuovo, Venice, 1572, p. 12. It belongs to the
class of migratory myths, having already been told of Brunel-

covery of America was completed when it was made known to Europeans that what Columbus had found was not Asia, but a New World, the northern voyages had absolutely nothing to do with its completion. The causal sequence of events, from Columbus to Magellan, which brought out the fact that a New World had been discovered, would not have been altered if the voyages of the Cabots had never been made. It was only by voyages to the south that the eyes of Europeans could be opened to the real significance of what was going on. Our attention is thus directed to the famous navigator who, without himself understanding the true state of the case, nevertheless went far toward revealing it. The later voyages of Vespucius began to give a new meaning to the work of Columbus, and prepared the way for the grand consummation by Magellan.

Amerigo Vespucci [1] was born at Florence on

leschi, the great architect who built the dome of the cathedral at Florence about 1420. As Voltaire says, in this connection, "La plupart des bons mots sont des redites." *Essai sur les Mœurs*, .tom. iii. p. 351.

[1] Amerigo, Amerrigo, Merigo, Morigo, Almerico, Alberico, Alberigo; Vespucci, Vespucy, Vespuchy, Vespuche, Vesputio, Vespulsius, Espuchi, Despuchi; latinized Americus Vespucius. *Amerigo* is an italianized form of the old German *Amalrich* (not Emmerich), which in mediæval French became *Amaury*. It means "the steadfast" ("celui qui endure des labeurs"). See Humboldt, *Examen critique*, tom. iv. pp. 52–57. This derivation would naturally make the accent fall upon the penult, *Amerígo, Americus;* and thus light seems to be thrown upon the scanning of George Herbert's verses, written in 1631, during the Puritan exodus: —

> "Religion stands on tip-toe in our land,
> Readie to passe to the American strand."
> *The Church Militant*, 235.

the 18th of March, 1452 (N. S.). He was the
third son of Anastasio Vespucci and Lis-
abetta Mini. The family was old and
respectable, and had been wealthy. Anastasio was a notary public. His brother Giorgio
Antonio was a Dominican monk, an accomplished
Hellenist in those days of the Renaissance, and a
friend of the martyr Savonarola. One of Amerigo's brothers, Antonio, studied at the university
of Pisa. The second, Jerome, engaged in some
business which took him to Palestine, where he
suffered many hardships. Amerigo was educated
by his uncle, the Dominican, who seems to have
had several youth under his care ; among these
fellow-students was the famous Piero Soderini,
afterward gonfaloniere of Florence from 1502 to
1512.[1] Amerigo acquired some knowledge of
Latin and was sufficiently affected by the spirit of
the age to be fond of making classical quotations,
but his scholarship did not go very far. At some
time, however, if not in his early years, he acquired
an excellent practical knowledge of astronomy, and
in the art of calculating latitudes and longitudes he
became an expert unsurpassed by any of his contemporaries.[2] After his school days were over, he
was taken into the great commercial house of the

Early life of Americus Vespucius.

[1] See Guicciardini, *Storia Fiorentina*, cap. xxv.; Trollope's *History of the Commonwealth of Florence*, vol. iv. pp. 294, 337.

[2] See the testimony of Sebastian Cabot and Peter Martyr, and
Humboldt's remarks in connection therewith, in *Examen critique*,
tom. iv. pp. 144, 183, 191 ; tom. v. p. 36. Considering his strong in-
clination for astronomical studies, one is inclined to wonder whether
Vespucius may not have profited by the instruction or conversation of his fellow-townsman Toscanelli. How could he fail to
have done so ?

Medici, and seems to have led an uneventful life at Florence until he was nearly forty years of age.[1] He devoted his leisure hours to the study of geography, and was an eager collector of maps, charts, and globes. On one occasion he paid 130 golden ducats for a map made in 1439 by Gabriel de Valsequa.[2] He also became an expert map-maker himself,[3] and along with such tastes one

[1] What little is known of the early life of Vespucius is summed up in Bandini, *Vita e lettere di Amerigo Vespucci*, Florence, 1745. The only intelligent modern treatise on the life and voyages of this navigator is Varnhagen's collection of monographs — *Amerigo Vespucci: son caractère, ses écrits (même les moins authentiques), sa vie et ses navigations*, Lima, 1865; *Le premier voyage de Amerigo Vespucci définitivement expliqué dans ses détails*, Vienna, 1869; *Nouvelles recherches sur les derniers voyages du navigateur florentin, et le reste des documents et éclaircissements sur lui*, Vienna, 1869; *Postface aux trois livraisons sur Amerigo Vespucci*, Vienna, 1870; *Ainda Amerigo Vespucci: novos estudos e achegas especialmente em favor da interpretacão dada á sua la viagem em* 1497–98, Vienna, 1874. These are usually bound together in one small folio volume. Sometimes the French monographs are found together without the Portuguese monograph. Varnhagen's book has made everything else antiquated, and no one who has not mastered it in all its details is entitled to speak about Vespucius. In the English language there is no good book on the subject. The defence by Lester and Foster (*Life and Voyages of Americus Vespucius*, New York, 1846) had some good points for its time, but is now utterly antiquated and worse than useless. The chapter by the late Sydney Howard Gay, in Winsor's *Narrative and Critical History*, vol. ii. chap. ii., is quite unworthy of its place in that excellent work; but its defects are to some extent atoned for by the editor's critical notes.

[2] In 1848 this map " was still in the library of Count de Montenegro at Palma, in the island of Majorca." Harrisse, *Bibliotheca Americana Vetustissima, Additions*, p. xxiii. It is the only relic of Vespucius to which we can point as existing in the present century.

[3] " I repayred to the byshoppe of Burges [Fonseca] beinge the chiefe refuge of this nauigation. As wee were therfore secretly

can easily see how there was a latent love of adventure which it only required circumstances to bring out. He seems in these earlier years, as throughout his life, to have won and retained the respect of all who knew him, as a man of integrity and modesty, quiet, but somewhat playful in manner, mild and placable in temper, and endowed with keen intelligence. He seems to have been of middle height, and somewhat brawny, with aquiline features and olive complexion, black eyes and hair, and a mouth at once firm and refined.

The Medici had important business interests in Spain, and at some time between the midsummer of 1489 and the end of 1491 they sent Vespucius to Barcelona as their confidential agent. He took with him several young Florentines who had been placed under his care, and among them his own nephew, Giovanni (afterwards spanished into Juan) Vespucci, a very capable youth who accompanied him in some if not all his voyages, and lived to be regarded as one of the most accomplished navigators and cosmographers of the age.[1] Early in 1493 Americus seems

Vespucius goes to Spain.

togyther in one chamber, we had many instrumentes perteynynge to these affayres, as globes and many of those mappes which are commonly cauled the shipmans cardes, or cardes of the sea. Of the which, one was drawen by the Portugales, whereunto Americus Vesputius is sayde to have put his hande, beinge a man moste experte in this facultie and a Florentyne borne; who also vnder the stipende of the Portugales hadde sayled towarde the south pole." Peter Martyr, *Decades of the Newe Worlde*, Eden's translation, 1555, dec. ii. lib. x.

[1] "The younge Vesputius is one to whom Americus Vesputius his vncle left the exact knowledge of the mariners facultie, as it were by inheritance after his death, for he was a very expert mais-

to have formed some sort of connection with the
Florentine commercial house of Juanoto Berardi,
at Seville.[1] This Berardi, who had been domiciled
in Spain for more than nine years and was a friend
of Columbus, was employed by the crown in fitting out ships for the Atlantic voyages. On the
9th of April, 1495, we find him signing a contract
engaging to furnish twelve vessels with an aggre-
gate burthen of 900 tons, and to have four of them
ready that same month, four more in June, and
the rest in September.[2] We shall presently find
this contract quite interesting and its date eloquent. In, December of that same year Berardi
died, and we find Vespucius taking his place and
fulfilling what remained to be fulfilled of the contract and sundry obligations growing out of it.
From the above facts the statement, often made,
that Vespucius took part in fitting out the second
voyage of Columbus is quite probable. He can

ter in the knowledge of his carde, his compasse, and the eleuation
of the pole starre with all that perteineth therto. . . . Vesputius
is my verye familyar frende, and a wyttie younge man in whose
coompany I take great pleasure, and therefore vse hym often-
tymes for my geste." *Id.*, dec. iii. lib. v.

[1] " Vostra Mag. sapra, come el motiuo della venuta mia in
questo regno di Spagna fu p⸢ tractare mercatantie : & come se-
guissi in q'sto proposito circa di quattro anni : nequalli uiddi &
connobbi edisuariati mouime'ti della fortuna ; . . . deliberai *las-
ciarmi della mercantia* & porre elmio fine in cosa piu laudabile &
ferma : che fu che midisposi dandare a uedere parte del mondo,
& le sue marauiglie." *Lettera di Amerigo Vespucci delle isole
nuouamente trouate in quattro suoi viaggi,* — written to Soderini
from Lisbon, September 4, 1504 ; primitive text reprinted in Varnhagen, Lima, 1865, p. 35.

[2] See the document in Varnhagen, p. 93 ; Navarrete, tom. ii.
pp. 159–162.

hardly have failed to become acquainted with Columbus in the summer of 1493, if he had not known him before. The relations between the two seem always to have been most cordial;[1] and after the Admiral's death his sons seem to have continued to hold the Florentine navigator in high esteem.

Our information concerning Americus Vespucius, from the early part of the year 1496 until after his return from the Portuguese to the Spanish service in the latter part of 1504, rests primarily upon his two famous letters; the one addressed to his old patron Lorenzo di Pier Francesco de' Medici (a cousin of Lorenzo the Magnificent) and written in March or April, 1503, giving an account of his third voyage:[2] the other addressed to his old school-fellow Piero Soderini and dated from Lisbon, September 4, 1504, giving a brief account of four voyages which he had made under various commanders in the capacity of astronomer or pilot.[3]

His letters to Medici and Soderini.

---

[1] See the Admiral's letter to his son Diego, dated February 5, 1505, in Navarrete, tom. i. p. 351.

[2] The earliest Latin and Italian texts are given in Varnhagen, pp. 9-26.

[3] The primitive Italian text and the famous Latin version presently to be noticed are given in Varnhagen, pp. 33-64.

Varnhagen prints three other letters, attributed to Vespucius, which have been often quoted. They are all addressed to Lorenzo di Pier Francesco de' Medici: — 1. relating to the second voyage, and dated July 18, 1500, first published in 1745 by Bandini; it is unquestionably a forgery, not older than the seventeenth century, and has done much to bemuddle the story of Vespucius; 2. dated from Cape Verde, June 4, 1501, while starting on the third voyage, first published in 1827 by Baldelli; the document itself is not original, but I am inclined to think it may perhaps be made

These letters, for reasons presently to be set forth, became speedily popular, and many editions were published, more especially in France, Germany, and Italy. It is extremely improbable that proof-sheets of any of these editions could ever have been read by the author, and it is perfectly clear that if his eye ever rested at any time upon the few strange errors of editing and proof-reading which were destined to embroil and perplex his story in the minds of future generations, he could not possibly have foreseen or dimly surmised what wretched complications were going to flow from the slight admixtures of error in the printed text. For Americus died, as Columbus had died, without ever having suspected the real significance of the discoveries in which he had been concerned.

The letter to Soderini gives an account of four voyages in which the writer took part, the first two in the service of Spain, the other two in the service of Portugal. The first expedition sailed from Cadiz May 10, 1497, and returned October 15, 1498, after having explored a coast so long as to seem unquestionably that of a continent. This voyage, as we shall see, was concerned with parts of America

The four voyages described in the letters : — First voyage.

up from genuine notes or memoranda; 3. relating to the third voyage, and dated 1502, first published in 1789 by Bartolozzi. I do not regard it as genuine, but as it adds nothing to what is contained in the genuine letters, the point is of no great importance.

A Spanish letter from Vespucius to Cardinal Ximenes is published by Augusto Zeri, in his *Tre Lettere di Colombo e Vespucci,* Rome, 1881; but it has no reference to the questions discussed in the present chapter.

not visited again until 1513 and 1517. It discovered nothing that was calculated to invest it with much importance in Spain, though it by no means passed without notice there, as has often been wrongly asserted. Outside of Spain it came to attract more attention, but in an unfortunate way, for a slight but very serious error in proof-reading or editing in the most important of the Latin versions caused it after a while to be practically identified with the second voyage, made two years later. This confusion eventually led to most outrageous imputations upon the good name of Americus, which it has been left for the present century to remove.

The second voyage of Vespucius was that in which he accompanied Alonso de Ojeda and Juan de La Cosa, from May 20, Second voyage. 1499, to June, 1500. They explored the northern coast of South America from some point on what we would now call the north coast of Brazil, as far as the Pearl Coast visited by Columbus in the preceding year; and they went beyond, as far as the gulf of Maracaibo. Here the squadron seems to have become divided, Ojeda going over to Hispaniola in September, while Vespucius remained cruising till February.

In the autumn of 1500, or early in 1501, at the invitation of King Emanuel of Portugal, Vespucius transferred his services to that country. His third voyage was from Third voyage. Lisbon, May 14, 1501, to September 7, 1502. He pursued the Brazilian coast as far as latitude 34° S., and ran thence S. E., as far as the island of

South Georgia. I shall presently show why it
was that such a voyage, into this wholly new part
of the world, excited public curiosity even more
keenly than those of Columbus and Gama, and
how curiously but naturally it led to the placing
of the name " America " upon the map.

In a fourth voyage, from June 10, 1503, to
Fourth   June 18, 1504, Vespucius, with Gon-
voyage.   zalo Coelho, undertook to follow the
Brazilian coast to its end or until they should
find some passage into the Indian ocean. This
expedition met with disasters, and after reaching
latitude 23° S., Vespucius returned to Lisbon without accomplishing anything.

In the autumn of 1504 Americus returned to the
                 service of Spain with the rank of cap-
Later voyages.   tain and a salary of 30,000 maravedis.
He went on two more voyages, in company with
La Cosa, in 1505 and 1507, for the exploration of
the gulf of Urabá and the coasts adjoining. It
seems to have been early in 1505 that he married a Spanish lady, Maria Cerezo, and became le-
gally domiciled at Seville. On the 22d of March,
1508, because of the growing interest in voyages
to the Indies and the increasing number of squadrons equipped for such a purpose, the government
created the highly responsible office of Pilot Major
of Spain. It was to be the duty of this officer to
institute and superintend examinations for all candidates for the position of pilot, to judge of their
proficiency in practical astronomy and navigation,
and to issue certificates of competence to the successful candidates. Such work involved the es-

tablishment and supervision of regular methods of training in nautical science. The pilot major was also general inspector of maps, globes, and sailing charts, and he was expected to provide for the compilation of a "Carta Padron Real," or authoritative government map, which was to be revised and amended with reference to new information brought home by pilots from the Indies year after year.[1] On the 6th of August, 1508, this important office was conferred upon Vespucius, with a salary of 75,000 maravedis. It was but a short time that Americus lived to discharge the duties of pilot major. After his death, which occurred at Seville, February 22, 1512, he was succeeded in that office by Juan Diaz de Solis, who in turn was succeeded by Sebastian Cabot.

Vespucius appointed pilot major of Spain.

His death.

In view of the Egyptian darkness that has heretofore enveloped, and in the popular mind still surrounds, the subject of Americus Vespucius and his voyages, it has seemed advisable to complete the mere outline of the events of his life before entering into discussion, in the hope of showing where the truth is to be found and how the mistakes have been made. The reader will find it convenient to bear in mind this simple outline sketch while I now return to the consideration of the first and second voyages, and point out how the mystery that has so long surrounded them has

[1] The official document describing the duties and powers of the pilot major is given in Navarrete, *Coleccion de viages,* tom. iii. pp. 299–302.

LIBRARY OF
MUSKINGUM COLLEGE
New Concord, Ohio.

been in great part cleared away and seems likely erelong to be completely dispelled.

First we must note the character of our primary and only detailed authority for the events of all four voyages, the letter from Vespucius to Soderini, dated Lisbon, September 4, 1504. Observe that this is not a formal or official document; it is not a report from a naval commander or the conductor of a scientific expedition to the head of his department. It is the business of such official reports to give names and incidents, dates and distances, and all relevant statistical information, with the greatest possible fulness and precision; and if there is any noticeable deficiency in this regard, we are entitled to blame the writer. With informal letters written to one's friends the case is very different. If Vespucius, in sending to his old schoolmate a cursory account of his adventures during seven years past, failed to mention sundry details which it annoys and puzzles us not to know, we have no business to find fault with him. He had a perfect right to tell his story in his own way. He was writing to a friend, not posing for posterity. Some querulous critics have blamed him for not mentioning the names of his commanders, as if he were intending to convey a false impression of having commanded in these voyages himself. No such impression is conveyed to the reader, however, but quite the contrary. On the first voyage Americus describes himself as invited by King Ferdinand to " assist " in the enterprise; as to his position in the second voyage there is no im-

The letter from Vespucius to Soderini.

plication whatever; as to the third and fourth he expressly mentions that he served under other captains. His whole letter shows plainly enough that on his most important voyages he went in the capacity of "astronomer." During the latter half of the fifteenth century, as voyages were extending farther and farther into unknown stretches of sea, it became customary to sail with such an officer on board. Each ship had its captain, its " master " (or mate), and its pilot; and for the squadron, besides its captain-general, and its chief pilot, expert in the knack and mystery of navigation, there was apt to be (whenever it was possible to find one) a person well skilled in the astrolabe, fertile in expedients for determining longitude, and familiar with the history of voyages and with the maps and speculations of learned geographers. Sometimes there was a commander, like Columbus, who combined all these accomplishments in himself; but in the case of many captains, even of such superb navigators as Pinzon and La Cosa, much more in the case of land-lubbers like Bastidas and Ojeda, it was felt desirable to have the assistance of a specialist in cosmography. Such was evidently the position occupied by Vespucius; and occasions might and did arise in which it gave him the control of the situation, and made the voyage, for all historical purposes, his voyage.

It is certainly much to be regretted that in the narrative of his first expedition Vespucius did not happen to mention the name of the chief commander. If he had realized what a world of trouble

He went on his earlier voyages in the capacity of astronomer.

one little name, such as Pinzon, would have saved
us he would doubtless have obliged us by doing so.
However, as already observed, he was writing not
for us, but for his friend, and he told Soderini
only what he thought would interest him. In his
preface Americus somewhat playfully apologizes
for presuming to intrude upon that magistrate's
arduous cares of state with so long a letter. He
accordingly refrains from giving professional details, except in stating latitudes and longitudes and
distances run, and even here he leaves gaps and
contents himself with general statements that to
us are sometimes far from satisfactory. He also
gives very few proper names of places, either those
supposed to be current among the natives, or those
applied by the discoverers. But of such facts
as would be likely to interest Soderini he gives
plenty. He describes, with the keen
zest of a naturalist, the beasts, birds,
and fishes, the trees, herbs, and fruits,
of the countries visited ; their climates, the stars
in their firmament, the personal appearance and
habits of the natives, their food and weapons, their
houses and canoes, their ceremonies and their
diversity of tongues. Such details as these proved
intensely interesting, not only to Soderini, but to
many another reader, as was shown by the wide
circulation obtained by the letter when once it had
found its way into print. In an age when Pope
Leo X. sat up all night reading the " Decades " of
Peter Martyr, curiosity and the vague sense of
wonder were aroused to the highest degree, and
the facts observed by Vespucius — although told

Character of
his descrip-
tions.

in the hurried and rambling style of an offhand
epistle — were well adapted to satisfy and further
to stimulate these cravings. But for the modern
investigator, engaged upon the problem of determining precise localities in tropical America, these
descriptions are too general. They may sometimes be made to apply to more than one region,
and we are again reminded of the difficulty which
one finds in describing a walk or drive over country roads and making it intelligible to others without the aid of *recognized proper names.* The
reader will please note these italics, for it is an
error in proper names that has been chiefly responsible for the complicated misunderstandings that
have done such injustice to Vespucius.

In the letter to Lorenzo de' Medici, written
about April, 1503, reference is made to The *Quattro*
a book, or group of three pamphlets, *Giornate,* the
which Vespucius had already written, Vespucius.
giving a definite and detailed account of his voyages. He tells Lorenzo that the pamphlet describing the third voyage is now in the hands of
the King of Portugal, and he hopes it will soon be
returned to him. He hopes at some future day,
when more at leisure, to utilize these materials in
writing a treatise on cosmography, in order that
posterity may remember him and that God's crea-
tive work in a region unknown to the ancients
may be made known. If God shall spare his life
until he can settle down quietly at Florence, he
hopes then, with the aid and counsel of learned
men, to be able to complete such a book.[1] But

[1] "Vt si quando mihi ocium dabitur possim omnia hec singu-

just now he is about to start on a fourth voyage,
the results of which will probably need to be
added to the book. In the letter to Soderini, written seventeen months later, after the return from
the fourth voyage, Americus refers more than once
to this book, under the title "Four Journeys"
(*Quattro Giornate*). It is not yet published, he
says, because he needs more time to revise it ; in
this narrative everything will be minutely described.[1] It is thus quite clear why Vespucius
was not more explicit in his letters ; and we can
also well understand how his arduous duties as
pilot major of Spain would delay the publication
of his book until discourteous death[2] overtook
him. Unfortunately, while versions of the hastily
written letters, intended only for the moment,
have survived, the manuscript of the carefully
written book, so conscientiously withheld until it
could be perfected, has perished.[3]

laria atque mirabilia colligere, et vel geographie vel cosmographie
librum conscribere : ut mei recordatio apud posteros vivat, & omnipotentis dei cognoscatur tam immensum artificium in parte pris-
cis ignotum, nobis autem cognitum. . . . Patriam & quietem re-
petere conabor, vbi & cum peritis conferre : & ab amicis id opus
proficiendum confortari et adjuvari valeam." Varnhagen, p. 25.

[1] "In questa gente, & in loro terra conobbi & uiddi tanti de loro
costumi & lor modi di uiuere, che no' curo di allargharmi in epsi :
perche sapra V. M. come in ciascuno delli miei uiaggi ho notate le
cose piu marauigliose : & tutto ho ridocto in un uolume in stilo di
geografia : & le intitulo LE QUATTRO GIORNATE : nella quale
opera sicontiene le cose p₁ minuto & per anchora no' sene data
fuora copia, perche me necessario conferirla." Varnhagen, p. 45.

[2] "Morte villana ; " see Dante, *Vita Nuova*, viii., and Professor Norton's charming version.

[3] One hesitates to say too positively about any book that it has
perished. Things have such queer ways of turning up, as for instance Aristotle's treatise on the government of Athens, after its

As for the letters themselves, the manuscripts are nowhere forthcoming, and until lately it has been maintained that none of the printed texts are originals, but that all are reprints from a primitive text that has been lost. Of the letter to Soderini the version which has played the most important part in history is the Latin one first published at the press of the little college at Saint-Dié in Lorraine, April 25 (vij Kl' Maij), 1507. We shall presently have more to say about the remarkable book in which this version appears; suffice it here to observe that it was translated, not from an original text, but from an intermediate French version, which is lost. Of late years, however, we have detected, in an excessively rare Italian text, the original from which the famous Lorraine version was ultimately derived. Of this little book M. Harrisse was able in 1872 to mention four copies as still existing, — one in the Palatine library at Florence, one in the library of the Marquis Gino Capponi in that city, one in the British Museum, and one purchased at Havana in 1863 by the eminent Brazilian historian, Francisco Adolpho de Varnhagen, Viscount de Porto Seguro. This last-named copy had once been in the Cartuja at Seville, and it was bound in

The Latin version (1507) of the letter to Soderini.

Recent discovery of the primitive Italian text, 1505-06.

Rip Van Winkle slumber of two thousand years. Of a certain copy of Oviedo's first folio (Toledo, 1526) M. Harrisse observes: "The only other copy which we know of this extremely rare book is in Havana, and was found in a Madrid butcher's stall, as the illiterate dealer in meat was tearing it to wrap a sirloin of beef which a pretty *manola* had just purchased." *Notes on Columbus,* New York, 1866, p. 13.

vellum together with a tract of St. Basil, printed at
Florence by the printer Gian Stefano di Carlo di
Pavia, for the publisher Pietro Pacini, of Pescia, in
1506. From the manner in which the edges of the
leaves were gnawed it was evident that the two
tracts had been within the same cover for a great
length of time. Closer examination showed that
they were printed from the same font of type; and
a passage in Girolamo Priuli's diary, dated July 9,
1506, says that the voyages of Vespucius have already been printed.[1] If we were absolutely sure
that this statement refers to this edition, it would
settle its date beyond all question; but as there is
no other edition ever heard of or known to have
existed to which it can possibly refer, the circum-
stantial evidence becomes exceedingly strong.
Moreover the language of this text is a corrupt
Italian, abounding in such Spanish and Portuguese words and turns of expression as Vespucius
would have been likely, during fourteen years of
residence in the Iberian peninsula and of association with its sailors, to incorporate into his every-
day speech. This fact is very significant, for if a
book thus printed in Florence were a translation
from anything else, its language would be likely
to be the ordinary Italian of the time, not a jar-
gon salted with Atlantic brine. Altogether it
seems in the highest degree probable that we have
here the primitive text, long given up for lost, of

---

[1] "Questa navigazione, e la natura delle persone, e li viaggi, e
li venti, e tutto sono in stampa notati con gran intelligenza."
Foscarini, *Letteratura veneziana*, Padua, 1752, p. 179.

Lettera di Amerigo vespucci delle isole nuonamente trouate in quattro suoi viaggi.

Facsimile of title-page of the original Italian edition of the letter from Vespucius to Soderini, published at Florence, 1505–06.

the ever memorable letter from Vespucius to his former schoolmate Soderini.[1]

If now we compare this primitive text with the Latin of the Lorraine version of 1507, we observe that in the latter one proper name — the Indian name of a place visited by Americus on his first voyage — has been altered.   In the original it is *Lariab ;* in the Latin it has become *Parias.* This looks like an instance of injudicious editing on the part of the Latin translator, although, of course, it may be a case of careless proof-reading.   Lariab is a queer-looking word.   It is no wonder that a scholar in his

Change of the Indian name Lariab into the Indian name Parias in the Latin version of 1507 ; original source of all the calumny against Americus.

---

[1] The title of this edition is *Lettera di Amerigo Vespucci delle isole nuouamente trouate in quattro suoi viaggi,* sixteen unnumbered leaves in quarto. It is No. 87 in Harrisse's *Bibliotheca Americana Vetustissima,* New York, 1866, where the date 1516 is conjecturally assigned it; but that date is clearly wrong, as M. Harrisse has since recognized. In the *Additions* (Paris, 1872) to his great work he is inclined to adopt Varnhagen's date, 1505–1506, and considers it "almost certain " that this text was the original source of the Lorraine Latin version published April 25, 1507. M. d'Avezac is of the same opinion; see his *Martin Waltzemüller,* p. 46. For the whole argument, see Varnhagen, *Amerigo Vespucci,* pp. 27–31. This primitive text is reproduced, page for page and line for line, with all its typographical peculiarities and its few quaint wood cuts, by Varnhagen. Mr. Quaritch (*Rough List,* No. 111, April 16, 1891, p. 52) says there are five copies extant. He bought one for £524 at the sale of the late Dr. Court's library at Paris in 1884 ; and it is now, I believe, in the library of Mr. C. H. Kalbfleisch, of New York. From this original Mr. Quaritch published in 1885 a facsimile reproduction, which may be bought for five guineas, and an English translation, price two guineas and a half ; so that now for the first time since the discovery of America an English reader not thoroughly at home in Italian thickly interlarded with Spanish and Portuguese can see for himself what Vespucius really said.

study among the mountains of Lorraine could make nothing of it. If he had happened to be acquainted with the language of the Huastecas, who dwelt at that time about the river Panuco, — fierce and dreaded enemies of their southern neighbours, the Aztecs, — he would have known that names of places in that region were apt to end in *ab* (Tanlajab, Tancuayalab, Tancuallalab),[1] very much as English names of towns are apt to end in *ham* and Persian names of countries in *stan*. But as such facts were quite beyond our worthy translator's ken, we cannot much blame him if he felt that such a word as Lariab needed doctoring. Parias (Paria) was known to be the native name of a region on the western shores of the Atlantic, and so Lariab became Parias. As the distance from the one place to the other is more than two thousand miles, this little emendation shifted the scene of the first voyage beyond all recognition, and cast the whole subject into an outer darkness where there has since been much groaning and gnashing of teeth.

Another curious circumstance came in to confirm this error. On his first voyage, shortly before arriving at Lariab, Vespucius saw an Indian town built over the water, "like Venice." He counted forty-four large wooden houses, "like barracks," supported on huge tree-trunks and communicating with each other by bridges that could be drawn

How the "little wooden Venice" aided and abetted the error.

---

[1] Orozco y Berra, *Geografía de lengoas y carta etnográfica de México*, p. 289; Varnhagen, *Le premier voyage de Vespucci*, p. 20.

up in case of danger. This may well have been a village of communal houses of the Chontals on the coast of Tabasco ; but such villages were afterwards seen on the gulf of Maracaibo, and one of them was called Venezuela,[1] or "Little Venice," a name since spread over a territory nearly twice as large as France. So the amphibious town described by Vespucius was incontinently moved to Maracaibo, as if there could be only one such place, as if that style of defensive building had not been common enough in many ages and in many parts of the earth, from ancient Switzerland to modern Siam. Such "little Venices" might once have been seen near the mouth of the Amazon, and there is now, or has lately been, a similar town named Bodegas, on the coast of Ecuador, near Guayaquil.[2]

Thus *in spite of the latitudes and longitudes distinctly stated by Vespucius in his letter*, did Lariab and the little wooden Venice get shifted from the gulf of Mexico to the northern coast of South America. Now there is no question that Vespucius in his second voyage, with Ojeda for captain, did sail along that coast, visiting the gulfs of Paria and Maracaibo. This was in the

The charge that Vespucius feigned to have discovered the coast of Paria in 1497.

---

[1] The name occurs in this place on La Cosa's map, which thus confirms the common statement that Ojeda found such a village on his first voyage (Vespucius's second) in 1499. Ojeda at first called the gulf "the lake of St. Bartholomew," because he discovered it on the 24th of August ; some years afterward he spoke of it as "gulf of Venice" (*golfo de Venecia*). See Navarrete, *Coleccion*, tom. iii. p. 8.

[2] Varnhagen, *Le premier voyage de Vespucci*, p. 13.

summer of 1499, one year after a part of the same coast had been visited by Columbus. Hence in a later period, long after the actors in these scenes had been gathered unto their fathers, and when people had begun to wonder how the New World could ever have come to be called America instead of Columbia, it was suggested that the first voyage described by Vespucius must be merely a clumsy and fictitious duplicate of the second, and that he invented it and thrust it back from 1499 to 1497, in order that he might be accredited with the "discovery of the continent" one year in advance of his friend Columbus. It was assumed that he must have written his letter to Soderini with the base intention of supplanting his friend, and that the shabby device was successful. This explanation seemed so simple and intelligible that it became quite generally adopted, and it held its ground until the subject began to be *critically* studied and Alexander von Humboldt showed, about sixty years ago, that the first naming of America occurred in no such way as had been supposed.

The date 1497 had nothing whatever to do with the naming of America.

As soon as we refrain from projecting our modern knowledge of geography into the past, as soon as we pause to consider how these great events appeared to the actors themselves, the absurdity of this accusation against Americus becomes evident. We are told that he falsely pretended to have visited Paria and Maracaibo in 1497, in order to claim priority over Columbus in the discovery of "the continent." What continent?

When Vespucius wrote that letter to Soderini, in 1504, neither he nor anybody else suspected that what we now call America had been discovered. The only continent of which there could be any question, so far as supplanting Columbus was concerned, was Asia. But in 1504 Columbus was generally supposed to have discovered the continent of Asia, by his new route, in 1492. In that year and in 1494, taking the two voyages together, he had sailed more than a thousand miles along the coast of Cuba without detecting its insular character. As the history of that time has always, until very lately, been written, we have been told that the insularity of Cuba was first revealed by Sebastian de Ocampo, who circumnavigated it in 1508. If this opinion were correct, Americus could not possibly have undertaken to antedate Columbus with his figure 1497; it would have been necessary for him to feign a voyage earlier than the autumn of 1492. As I shall presently show, however, Americus probably did know, in 1504, that Cuba was an island, inasmuch as in 1497–98 he had passed to the west of it himself, touching the coasts of both Yucatan and Florida! If this view is correct, then he did visit what we now know to have been the continent of America, but which he supposed to be the continent of Asia, a year in advance of Columbus, and of course the accusation against him falls to the ground. From this dilemma there seems to be no escape.

The perplexity surrounding the account of the first voyage of Vespucius is therefore chiefly due

Absurdity inherent in the charge.

to the lack of intelligence with which it has been read. There is no reason whatever for imagining dishonesty in his narrative, and no reason for not admitting it as evidence on the same terms as those upon which we admit other contemporary documents. The court presumes the witness to be truthful until adequate reason has been alleged for a contrary presumption. What, then, are we to conclude in the case of this voyage of 1497 ?

The evidence that no such voyage was made in that year *along the Pearl Coast* is as strong as it is possible for negative evidence to be; indeed it seems unanswerable. We have seen how Columbus, owing to his troubles with rebellious Spaniards and the machinations of his enemy Fonseca, was deprived of his government of Hispaniola, and how he ended his days in poverty and neglect, vainly urging King Ferdinand (as acting regent of Castile) to reinstate him in the dignities and emoluments which had been secured to him by solemn compact under the royal seal in April, 1492. The right to these dignities and emoluments was inherited by his eldest son, Don Diego Columbus, and that young man was earnest in pressing his claims. He urged that Ovando should be recalled from Hispaniola and himself duly installed as viceroy of the Indies, with his percentage of the revenues accruing from Hispaniola, the Pearl Coast, and such other regions as his father had discovered. Whether these claims of Diego would ever have received any recognition, except for one fortunate circumstance, may be doubted. Diego seems to have

inherited his father's good fortune in winning the
hearts of aristocratic ladies. He had lived in the
royal household since he was taken there as a page
in 1492, and in 1508 he married a princess, Maria
de Toledo, whose paternal grandmother was sister
to the mother of Ferdinand the Catholic.[1] The
next year Ovando was recalled from Hispaniola,
and Diego, accompanied by his bride and many
people from the court, went out and assumed the
government of the Indies.[2] The king, however,
was not prepared to admit the full claims of Diego
Columbus to a percentage on the revenues without interposing every obstacle in his power. It
was understood that the matter must be adjusted
by litigation ; and in 1508, the year of his marriage, Diego brought suit against the
crown of Castile, in the fiscal court of
that kingdom, for the full restitution of
rights and emoluments wrongfully withheld from
the heir of the Admiral Don Christopher Columbus. This suit dawdled along for several years,
as such suits are apt to do. Various pleas in
abatement of Diego's demands were presented by
the crown. At length in 1513 a plea was put in
which invested the case with fresh interest, insomuch that Diego came home from Hispaniola to
give it his personal care. The king had taken it
into his head to subject the Admiral's claims as
discoverer to a critical examination, in the hope of
paring them down to as small a figure as possible.

His lawsuit against the crown.

[1] See Harrisse, *Christophe Colomb*, tom. ii. p. 247.

[2] Herrera, dec. i. cap. vii. p. 189; Oviedo, *Historia general de
las Indias*, tom. i. p. 97.

An inquiry was accordingly instituted in 1513, and renewed in 1515, in order to define by a judicial decision how much Columbus had discovered and how far the work of other navigators might properly be held to diminish his claims to originality. Observe that the question at issue was not as to " who discovered America." It was a question of much narrower and more definite import, and the interest felt in it by both parties to the suit was mainly a pecuniary interest. The question was : — in just what islands and stretches of " terra firma " in the Indies was Diego Columbus entitled to claim a share in the revenues on the strength of his father's discoveries ? What might have been done by other Spanish navigators, outside of the regions visited by Christopher Columbus, was quite irrelevant ; the Columbus family could have no claim upon such regions. The investigation, therefore, was directed chiefly upon three points : — 1. great pains were taken to bring out all the facts relating to the discovery of the rich Pearl Coast ; 2. much less attention was given to the Admiral's last voyage along Honduras and Veragua ; and 3. some attempt was made to see if his merit in first pointing out the way to the Indies could be diminished by proof of indispensable aid rendered by Martin Alonso Pinzon and others.

The great judicial inquiry — the *Probanzas.*

These interrogatories and answers, which were published in the great work of Navarrete under the general title of *Probanzas*,[1] are simply invaluable for the light which they throw upon the

[1] Navarrete, *Coleccion de viages*, tom. iii. pp. 538–615.

biography of Columbus and some of the more minute details in the history of the time. With regard to the alleged voyage of Vespucius (*as along the Pearl Coast*) in 1497 they are quite conclusive. Nearly a hundred witnesses were examined under oath, including Alonso de Ojeda himself, who made the voyage along that coast in 1499, when he had with him Juan de La Cosa, Americus Vespucius, and other pilots.[1] Ojeda was a friend of Fonseca and an enemy of Columbus. In his voyage of 1499 he used a copy of a chart, furnished him by Fonseca, which had been made by Columbus the year before and sent by him to the sovereigns. At the time of the *Probanzas*, Vespucius and La Cosa were both in their graves and could not be summoned as witnesses, but Ojeda's testimony was positive and explicit that Columbus was the discoverer of the Pearl Coast. Now if his own pilot, Vespucius, had visited that coast in 1497, Ojeda could not have failed to know the fact, and he would have been only too glad to proclaim it. If such a fact could have been established, it would at once have settled the question as to the Pearl Coast in favour of the king, and there would have been no need of the elaborate but weak and unsuccessful arguments to which the crown lawyers had recourse. The result of the inquiry was overwhelmingly in favour of Columbus ; and from beginning to end

It proves that Vespucius did not discover the Pearl Coast in 1497.

[1] "En este viage que este dicho testigo trujo consigo á Juan de la Cosa, piloto, e Morigo Vespuche, e otros pilotos." Navarrete, tom. iii. p 544.

not an interrogatory nor an answer, either on the part of Diego or on the part of the crown, betrayed the faintest glimmering of a consciousness that anybody had ever made, *or that anybody had ever professed to have made*, a voyage along the Pearl Coast before 1498.

This fact has been commonly and rightly regarded as decisive. It makes it morally certain that Vespucius did not visit Paria or Maracaibo or the coast between them in 1497. But it contains another implication which seems to have passed without notice. *It makes it equally certain that Vespucius had never professed to have made such a voyage.*

It proves, with equal force, that he never professed to have done so.

At the beginning of the *Probanzas*, in 1513, the Italian letter from Vespucius to Soderini had been in print at least seven years; the Latin version, which made it accessible to educated men all over Europe, had been in print six years, and was so popular that it had gone through at least six editions. We can hardly suppose the letter to have been unknown in Spain; indeed we know that one copy of the Italian original was in Spain in 1513 in the possession of Ferdinand Columbus, who bought it in Rome in September, 1512, for five *cuattrini*.[1] From 1508 until his death in February, 1512, Americus held one of the highest positions in the Spanish marine. Now if the Pilot Major of Spain had ever made any public pretensions which in any way tended to invalidate the claim of Diego Columbus, that his father had first discovered the Pearl Coast, can we for a moment

[1] Harrisse, *Fernand Colomb*, p. 11.

suppose that at just that time, with such a lawsuit
impending, the king would not have heard of
those pretensions and used them for all they were
worth? It is not supposable. · The fact that
neither party to the suit knew of such claims on
the part of Americus proves *not only that they
were unfounded, but that they had never been
made*. It shows that contemporary Spaniards,
familiar with the facts and reading the narrative
of his voyages, did not understand the first one as
referring to the Pearl Coast, but to an entirely different region.

It was M. Varnhagen who first turned inquiry

The landfall
on the first
voyage of Ves-
pucius was
near Cape
Honduras.

on this subject in the right direction.
Where does Vespucius *say* that he went
on his first voyage? He says that he
started May 10, 1497, from Cadiz and
ran to the Grand Canary, the distance of which
from Lisbon he calls 280 leagues. We thus find
the length of the league used by Vespucius and
get a scale wherewith to measure his distances.
That run is not likely to have been made in less
than seven days, and as he staid eight days more
at the Grand Canary, he must have started thence
about May 25. After a run of 37 (or 27) days [1]
he made land in a direction about west-southwest
from the Canaries and distant 1,000 leagues, in
latitude 16° N. and longitude 75° W. from the
meridian of the Grand Canary. If we suppose
this land to have been Cape Honduras, the latitude, about which Vespucius was least likely to be
mistaken, is exactly right; his distance by dead

[1] See below, p. 87, note.

reckoning is somewhat too small, probably because he failed to allow for the acceleration due to the westward current in the Caribbean sea; and his longitude is scarcely 5° in excess, a very moderate error for those days. The northern coast of Honduras not only thus suits the conditions of the case,[1] but makes the subsequent details of the voyage consistent and intelligible. Having taken a correct start by simply following the words of Vespucius himself, from a primitive text, without reference to any preconceived theories or traditions, M. Varnhagen finds, from further analysis of the narrative, that he sailed around Yucatan, and found his aquatic village of communal houses,[2] his little wooden Venice, on the shore of Tabasco. Thence, after a fight with the natives in which a few tawny prisoners[3] were captured and carried on board the caravels, Vespucius seems to have taken a straight course to the Huasteca country by

[1] The entrance to the gulf of Maracaibo is about 12° N. by 52° W. from Canaries; Paria, at the other end of the Pearl Coast, is about 11° N. by 44° W. from Canaries; so that no point on that coast can by any possibility be intended by Vespucius.

[2] In a single house Vespucius found 600 people, and in one place he estimated the population of 13 houses as about 4,000, or rather more than 300 to a house. These figures are eminently probable.

[3] They were of medium stature, and well proportioned, with reddish skin like a lion's: — " Sono di mediana statura, molto ben proportionati: le lor carni sono di colore che pende in rosso come pelle di lione." *Lettera* (ed. 1505–1506), fol. a. iii. recto. Varnhagen, p. 37. He notes their ornaments of gorgeous feathers, their hammocks, and their " paternostrini che fanno dossi di peschi," i. e. " paternosters made of fish-bones " (fol. a. iv. verso), meaning strings analogous to *quipus* and to wampum-belts. See below, p. 299.

Tampico, without touching at points in the region subject or tributary to the Aztec confederacy.

The "province of Lariab."

This Tampico country was what Vespucius understood to be called Lariab.

He again gives the latitude definitely and correctly as 23° N.,[1] and he mentions a few interesting circumstances. He saw the natives roasting a dreadfully ugly animal, "like a serpent, [dragon?] only it had no wings." It was about the

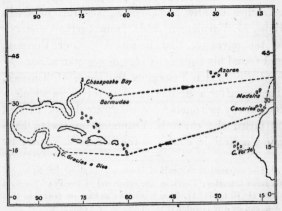

First voyage of Vespucius (with Pinzon and Solis, 1497–98).

size of a kid, half as long again as a man's arm, with a hard skin of various hues, a snout and face like a serpent's, and a saw-like crest running from the top of its head down the middle of its back and on to the upper part of its tail. The sailors

[1] It is just 2,400 miles distant, as the crow flies, from Paria, the region with which it has so long been stupidly identified. This has been preëminently one of the cases mentioned by Bishop Berkeley, in which commentators first kick up a dust and then wonder why they cannot see through it!

saw many of these creatures, and were afraid to
touch them lest they might have a ven-
omous bite, but the natives esteemed   Roasted
  iguanas and
them as delicacies. This is an excellent   fish patties.
description of the iguana, the flesh of which is to
this day an important article of food in tropical
America.[1] These Huastecas also made cakes or

[1] "Doue uede'mo che arrostiuano un certo animale ch' pareua
un serpe'te, saluo ch' no' teneua alia, & nella apparenza ta'to
brutto, che molto cimarauiglia'mo della sua fiereza: Anda'mo
cosi p. le lor case, o uero tra bacche & haua'mo molti di questi
serpe'te uiui, & eron legati pe piedi . . . : eron di tanto fiero
aspecto, che nessuno di noi no' ardiua di torne uno, pensando, ch'
eron uenenosi: sono di grandeza di uno cauretto & di lu'gheza
braccia uno & mezo: te' gono epiedi lunghi & grossi & armati co'
grosse unghie: tengono la pelle dura, & sono di uarii colori:
elmuso & faccia tengon di serpe'te: & dal naso simuoue loro una
cresta come una segha, che passa loro p. elmezo delle schiene
infino alla sommita della coda: in co'clusione gligiudica'mo serpi
& uenenosi, segli ma'giauano." *Lettera*, fol. a. v. recto. Varnhagen, p. 43. Compare the description in the *Century Diction-
ary:* — "It attains a length of five feet or more, and presents a
rather formidable appearance, but is inoffensive unless molested;
. . . its flesh is much used for food. The tail is very long, com-
pressed, and tapering; a row of scales along the back is developed into a serrate crest or dorsal ridge; the head is covered with
scaly plates; . . . its coloration is variegated with brownish, green-
ish, and yellowish tints." Yet this well-known animal has sorely
puzzled the commentators. It is not easy to imagine, says Navarrete (tom. iii. p. 225), what kind of a serpent this could have been,
as big as a kid, and with wings and feet (*y que tenian alas y pies*),
and he is inclined to set it down as "one of Vespucio's many absurdities" (*uno de los muchos absurdos de Vespucio en sus relaciones*). Apparently Navarrete could not read his own text correctly when a chance was offered for a fling at poor old Vespucius,
for that text (on the very same page ! !) reads "only it did NOT
have wings" (*solo que no tenia alas*) ! Why should Vespucius
have taken the pains to say that it had no wings ? It probably
indicates that he had only a literary acquaintance with serpents,
and dimly confused them with dragons.

patties out of small fish, which they kneaded up
with a sort of pastry and baked upon red-hot coals.
The Spaniards tasted them and found them good.[1]
The people were enemies of those whom the Spaniards had found in the " little Venice " over on the
Tabasco shore, and when it was observed that
some of the latter were shackled prisoners on
board the caravels,[2] the white men were forthwith
greeted as friends.   The Indians received them
most hospitably, and under their escort twenty-
three of the mariners, among whom Vespucius was
one, made a journey some eighteen leagues inland,
to see what could be found in that country.   They
visited several villages, composed of communal
houses.   In one of these villages, described as well

Navarrete's remark is a fair specimen of the mingled dulness
and flippancy with which commentators have been wont to treat the
great Florentine sailor, — finding it easier to charge him with absurdities than patiently to ascertain his meaning.   Even Mr. Lester, in a different temper from Navarrete, thinks that "the navigator has perhaps drawn somewhat upon his imagination in his
description of this animal" (*Life of Americus Vespucius*, p. 129).
Yet, as we have here seen, his description is strictly accurate, and
I cite it in illustration of the general faithfulness of his narrative.
— As for the flesh of the ugly reptile, I do not find any mention
of it among the 1,394 dishes described by Alessandro Filippini, of
Delmonico's, in his interesting book, *The Table*, New York, 1889;
but one fancies that it might be so treated as to commend itself
to epicures, even as the peerless terrapin, of which one of our
British cousins is said to have declared, "Upon my word, it's not
so nasty as it looks!"   I have been told that the flavour of the
iguana reminds one of spring chicken.

[1] " Proua'molo, & troua'mo che era buono."   Compare some of
the Mexican dishes mentioned below, p. 268.

[2] They were expert swimmers and thought nothing of jumping
overboard and striking out for the shore, even when it was several
leagues distant and out of sight; so that all those whom the Spaniards had not put in irons had escaped.

peopled, the number of such houses was but nine.
Lions and panthers (i. e. probably pumas and
ocelots) were seen, but neither horse, ass, nor cow,
nor any kind of domesticated animal.[1] It was a
populous country, with no end of rivers,[2] and an
astonishing quantity of birds of most brilliant
plumages. The people were struck dumb with
amazement at the sight of the white strangers, and
when they had so far recovered themselves as to
ask the latter whence they came, the Spaniards
gave them to understand that they came from beyond the sky.

After leaving this country of Lariab the ships
kept still to the northwest for a short
distance, and then followed the windings
of the coast for 870 leagues,[3] frequently
landing and doing petty traffic with the natives.

Coasting to Florida and around it.

---

[1] " No te'ghono caualli ne muli, ne co' reuerentia asini, ne cani,
ne di sorte alcuna bestiame peculioso, ne uaccino : ma sono ta'ti
li altri animali che te'ghono & tucti sono saluatichi, & di nessuno
siseruono per loro seruitio, che no' siposson contare." *Lettera*,
fol. b. i. recto. Varnhagen, p. 45.

[2] " Questa terra e populatissima, & di gente piena, & dinfiniti
fiumi." *Id.* The whole description agrees with Tampico.

[3] According to the most obvious reading of the text they sailed
N. W. for 870 leagues, but this would be impossible upon any
theory of the voyage : — " Partimo di questo porto : la prouincia
sidice Lariab : & nauiga'mo allungo della costa sempre a uista
della terra, tanto che corre'mo dessa 870 leghe tutta uia uerso el
maestrale," etc. *Lettera*, fol. b. i. verso. Varnhagen, p. 46.
Does *tuttavia* here mean " always," or " still " ? For the equivalent Spanish *todavia* the latter meaning is the more primary and
usual. M. Varnhagen supposes that the words " tutta uia uerso
el maestrale " belong in the writer's mind with " partimo di
questo porto ; " so that the sense would be, " we sailed from this
port still to the N. W., and we followed the coast always in sight
of land until we had run 870 leagues " (*Le premier voyage de*

They bought a little gold, but not much. Here
the letter hurries over the scene somewhat
abruptly. It was not likely that Soderini would
be particularly interested in the shape of these
strange coasts, and as for red Indians, much had
already been said about them in the earlier part of
the letter. So we are brought quickly to the end
of the journey. After traversing the 870 leagues
of crooked coast the ships found themselves in "the
finest harbour in the world." It was in June,
1498, thirteen months since they had started from
Spain. The ships were leaky and otherwise dilapidated, no discoveries of abundant gold or spices
or jewels, calculated to awaken enthusiasm, had
been made, and the men were tired of the voyage.
It was therefore unanimously agreed[1] to beach and
repair the ships, and then return home. They
spent seven-and-thirty days in this unrivalled harbour, preparing for the home voyage, and found
the natives very hospitable. These red men
courted the aid of the white strangers. On some
islands a hundred leagues or more out at sea there
lived a fierce race of cannibals, who from time to

Vespucci, p. 22). If the style of Vespucius were that of a correct
and elegant writer, such a reading would be hardly admissible,
but as his style was anything but correct and elegant, perhaps it
may pass. Or perhaps N. W. may have been carelessly substi-
tuted for N. E., as would have been easy if signs were used in the
manuscript instead of words like *maestrale* and *greco*. Then it
would mean that the *general* direction after leaving Lariab was
N. E. Upon any possible supposition there is a blunder in the
statement as it appears in the printed text.

[1] "Acchorda'mo di comune consiglio porre le nostre naui
amonte, & ricorrerle per stancharle, che faceuano molta acqua,"
etc. fol. b. i. verso.

time in fleets of canoes invaded the coasts of the
mainland and carried off human victims by the
score. Here a source of profit for the Spaniards
was suggested; for Columbus, as we shall hereafter
see,[1] had already set the example of kidnapping
cannibals, and it was coming to be a recognized
doctrine, on the part of the Spanish government,
that it was right for people "guilty of that unnat-
ural crime" to be sold into slavery. The expedition with which Vespucius was sailing The Bermu-
weighed anchor late in August, taking das.
seven of the friendly Indians for guides, on condition that they should return to the mainland in
their own canoes. The Indians were glad to go
on these terms and witness the discomfiture of
their enemies. After a week's voyage they fell in
with the islands, some peopled, others uninhabited,
evidently the Bermudas,[2] 600 miles from Cape
Hatteras as the crow flies. The Spaniards landed
on an island called Iti, and had a brisk fight with
a large body of the cannibals, who defended themselves manfully, but could not withstand firearms.
More than 200 prisoners were taken, seven of
whom were presented to the seven Indian guides.
Taking a large canoe from the island, these
friendly barbarians paddled away westward, "right
merry and marvelling at our power."[3] "We also

[1] See below, p. 433.

[2] When these islands were rediscovered in 1522 they were entirely depopulated, — an instance, no doubt, of the frightful thoroughness with which the Spanish kidnappers from Hispaniola had
done their work during the interval.

[3] "Sene tornarono allor terra molto allegri, marauiglia'dosi
delle nostre forze." If they ever succeeded in getting home, one
does not need to be told of the lurid fate of the captives.

set sail for Spain, with 222 prisoners, slaves; and arrived in the port of Cadiz on the 15th day of October, 1498, where we were well received and sold our slaves. This is what happened to me in this my first voyage that may be most worth telling."[1]

The words of Vespucius are too vague to enable us, without help from other sources, to determine the situation of that "finest harbour in the world," where the expedition made its last halt before striking eastward into the Atlantic. So much depends upon the quantity of allowance to be made for tacking and for the sinuosities of the coast-line, that it is impossible to say with any confidence to what point a run of 870 leagues from Tampico would have brought the ships. It is clear that they must have sailed between Cuba and Florida, and must have taken their final start from some point on the Atlantic coast of what is now the United States. The conditions of the case seemed at first to M. Varnhagen to point to the waters of the Chesapeake, but he was afterward inclined to

[1] "Noi alsi facemo uela p. Spagna con 222 prigioni schiaui: & giugnemo nel porto di Calis adi 15 doctobre 1498 doue fumo ben riceuuti & uende'mo nostri schiaui. Questo e, quello che miacchadde in questo mio primo uiaggio di piu notabile." Fol. b. ii. verso. It was a dreadful number of slaves to pack away in four caravels, and 22 has been suggested as a more probable figure. Perhaps so; mistakes in numerals are easy and frequent. The annals of the slave trade, however, give grewsome instances of what human greed can do. "De nos jours encore," observes Varnhagen, "que la traite des nègres est presque entièrement supprimée, nous avons vu aborder au Callao, venant de Chine, dans un seul navire, quelques cents Coolies: plus de la dixième partie de ces Coolies avait péri à bord, pendant le traversée."

designate Cape Cañaveral on the Florida coast as
the final point of departure for the cannibal islands
which apparently must have been the Bermudas.[1]
But, as Mr. Hubert Bancroft suggests, it is hard
to imagine what port near Cape Cañaveral could
have been called the best harbour in the world, except "by a navigator little familiar with good har-
bours." I shall presently point to some reasons for
believing that capes Charles and Cañaveral were
probably the northern and southern limits between
which the final departure was taken. Meanwhile
another and more important question claims our
attention.

We have hitherto been considering only the
statements of Vespucius himself in an informal letter. It has been urged, with reference to the credibility of these statements, that there is no contemporary allusion whatever to such a voyage, either
in books of history or in archives.[2] There is
strong reason for believing that this sweeping assertion is far from correct, and that contemporary allusions have not been found
simply because scholars have sought
them in the wrong quarter. With their

*Why critics
have found no
contemporary
allusions to
this voyage.*

backs turned upon Lariab they have been staring

---

[1] Varnhagen, *Amerigo Vespucci*, Lima, 1865, p. 99, and chart
at the end; *Le premier voyage de Vespucci*, Vienna, 1869, p. 30.

[2] "It should first of all be noted that the sole authority for a
voyage made by Vespucci in 1497 is Vespucci himself. All contemporary history, other than his own letters [it should be *letter*],
is absolutely silent in regard to such a voyage, whether it be history in printed books, or in the archives of those kingdoms of
Europe where the precious documents touching the earlier expeditions to the New World were deposited." S. H. Gay, in Winsor,
Narr. and Crit. Hist., ii. 137.

PRINCIPAL SPANISH AND PORTUGUESE VOYAGES SOUTH OF TROPIC OF CANCER.

N. B. — *Portuguese in Italics.*

NO.	NAME.	DATE.	PLACE.
1	Columbus I.	Aug. 3, 1492 — March 15, 1493.	Several Bahamas ; Cuba and Haytí, north coasts.
2	Columbus II.	Sept. 25, 1493 — June 11, 1496.	Several lesser Antilles ; Jamaica ; Cuba and Haytí, south coasts.
3	Pinzon and Solis, Vespucius I.	May 10, 1497 — Oct. 15, 1498.	North coast of Honduras, gulf of Mexico, Florida, Bermudas.
4	*Gama.*	*July 8, 1497 — July 10, 1499.*	*West coast of Hindustan via Cape of Good Hope.*
5	Columbus III.	May 30, 1498 — Nov. 25, 1500.	Trinidad, Paria, and Pearl Coast as far west as Cubagua.
6	Ojeda, La Cosa, Vespucius II.	May 16, 1499 — June, 1500.	From some point on north coast of Brazil to Paria and westward to Maracaibo, and to Cape de la Vela.
7	Pinzon.	Dec., 1499 — Sept., 1500.	Brazilian coast at about 8° S., and thence northwestward.
8	Lepe.	Jan. — June, 1500.	Brazilian coast to about 10° S.
9	*Cabral.*	*March 9, 1500 — July, 1501.*	*Brazilian coast from about 12° to 16° 30′ S., thence via Cape of Good Hope to Hindustan.*
10	Bastidas, La Cosa.	Oct., 1500 — Sept., 1502.	From Pearl Coast westward to Puerto Bello on isthmus of Darien.
11	*Nuno Manuel ? Vespucius III.*	*May 14, 1501 — Sept. 7, 1502.*	*Brazilian coast from 5° to 34° S., thence to South Georgia island, 54° S.*
12	Columbus IV.	May 11, 1502 — Nov. 7, 1504.	From Cape Honduras eastward and southward to gulf of Darien.

13	Coelho, Vespucius IV.	June 10, 1503 — June 18, 1504.	Brazilian coast, Vespucius to about 23° S., Coelho to about 40° S.
14	Christovão Jaques.	1503.	Brazilian and Patagonian coasts to about 52° S.
15	La Cosa, Vespucius V.	May — Dec., 1505.	Search for a strait in gulf of Darien and Atrato river.
16	Almeida.	1506.	Ceylon.
17	La Cosa, Vespucius VI.	March — Nov., 1507.	Further explorations about Darien.
18	Pinzon and Solis.	June 29, 1508 — Oct., 1509.	Brazilian coast, etc., to about 40° S.
19	Ocampo.	1508.	From Hayti circumnavigated Cuba.
20	Sequeira.	1509.	Malacca.
21	Abreu and Serrano.	1512.	The Spice Islands (Moluccas) by eastward route.
22	Ponce de Leon.	1513.	Florida.
23	Solis.	1516.	Search for a strait at river La Plata.
24	Andrade.	1517.	First voyage of European ships to China.
25	Córdova.	1517.	Rediscovery and circumnavigation of Yucatan.
26	Grijalva.	1518.	Exploration of gulf of Mexico.
27	Cortes.	1519.	March into Mexico.
28	Magellan, Elcano.	Sept. 20, 1519 — Sept. 8, 1522.	The Spice Islands (Moluccas) by westward route, circumnavigating the globe.

at Paria, and might have gone on staring to eternity without seeing what was all the time behind them. So, too, one might look long into narratives and archives, and look in vain for a "voyage of Vespucius," for it was customary to speak of a voyage by the name of the commanding officer, and the language of Vespucius distinctly implies that in this voyage of 1497 he was not the commander; he was chosen by King Ferdinand "to go with the ships and *assist* in the work of discovery."[1] Let us, then, turn our faces toward Lariab,

There are such contemporary allusions.

and see if contemporary documents know anything about a voyage into the gulf of Mexico earlier than those of Ocampo in 1508 and Ponce de Leon in 1513. We find at once a remarkable and significant group of allusions, both in narratives and in archives, to such a voyage, undertaken by no less a person than Vicente Yañez Pinzon, captain of the little ship Niña in the first voyage of Columbus. Associated with Pinzon, and probably second in command, was another consummate sailor, Juan Diaz de Solis, who in 1512 succeeded Vespucius as pilot major of Spain.

The date commonly assigned to this voyage of Pinzon and Solis is 1506. The figure rests upon the single unsupported statement of Antonio de Herrera, whose great work was published in 1601.[2]

[1] "Che fu, chel Re don Ferrando di Castiglia haue'do a mandare quattro naui a discoprire nuoue terre uerso loccidente fu-electo per sua alteza che io fussi in essa flocta per adiutare a discoprire." *Lettera*, fol. a. ii. recto. Varnhagen, p. 35.

[2] Herrera, *Historia general de los hechos de los Castellanos en las islas i tierra firme del Mar Oceano*, Madrid, 1601, 4 vols. in quarto.

For events that happened in the time of Ferdinand and Isabella, this book cannot be cited as of original authority. It is a compilation of priceless value, but not without grave defects. Mr. Hubert Bancroft is quite right in saying that we find in it "evidences everywhere of inexperience and incompetent assistance. Now that we have before us many of the sources of Herrera's material, we can see that his notes were badly extracted and compiled in a bungling manner; so much so that in addition to the ordinary errors, from which to some extent the most carefully executed work cannot be expected to be wholly free, there are many and serious discrepancies and contradictions for which there is no excuse, the cause being simply carelessness." [1]

Antonio de Herrera.

Now Herrera tells us that when it had been made known in Castile what the Admiral had discovered afresh, Pinzon and Solis made up their minds to go and further pursue the route which he had taken; and from the Guanajos islands on the northern coast of Honduras they sailed westward and passed the Golfo Dulce [2] without seeing it, but they gave the name of Navidad to what is now known as the bay of Honduras. Thence they discovered the mountains (or lands) of *Caria* and a considerable part of Yucatan. But *as there was nobody who followed up that discovery*, nothing more was known about

His account of the first voyage of Pinzon and Solis.

---

[1] *History of Central America*, San Francisco, 1882, vol. i. p. 317.

[2] For the position of the Golfo Dulce, see the map of the region around Tuzulutlan, below, p. 466. It is simply the deep inlet at the head of the bay of Honduras.

those coasts until the whole of New Spain was discovered [in 1517–19] from Cuba. The principal object of these navigators, Pinzon and Solis, adds Herrera, was, through a spirit of rivalry with the Admiral, to discover land and to pass beyond what he had discovered.[1]

---

[1] The passage in Herrera is somewhat confused and involved, from the wrong connection in which he conceived it; but when once we have fathomed the confusion under which he laboured, it is remarkable how nearly right he was in the principal items of his statement: — "Sabido en Castilla lo que havia descubierto de nuevo el Almirante, Juan Diaz de Solis i Vincente Yañez Pinzon determinaron de ir à proseguir el camino que dejaba hecho, i fueron à tomar el hilo desde las islas de los Guanajos i volver de ellas à levante; pero navegaron desde las dichas islas hácia el poniente hasta el parage de el Golfo Dulce, aunque no lo vieron, porque está escondido; reconocieron la entrada que hace la mar entre la tierra que contiene el Golfo, i la de Yucatan que es como una grande ensenada, ó baia, que asi llaman los marineros. . . . Y como vieron aquel rincon grande que hace la Mar entre dos Tierras, la una que está à la mano esquierda teniendo las espaldas à Oriente, que es la costa que contiene el Puerto de Caballos, i adelante de él el Golfo Dulce: i la otra de mano derecha, la costa del reino de Iucatan, parecióles gran baia, i por esto la llamaron ia gran Baia de Navidad, desde donde descubrieron las sierras [tierras?] de Caria; bolvieron al Norte, i descubrieron mucha parte de el reino de Yucatan, pero como despues no huvo nadie, que prosiguiese aquel Descubrimiento, no se supo mas, hasta que se descobrió todo lo de Nueva España desde la isla de Cuba, i estos Descubridores principalmente pretendian descubrir tierra por emulacion del Almirante, i pasar adelante de lo que él habia descubierto" (dec. i. lib. vi. cap. 17). *Pretendian* here does not mean "pretended," but "undertook" or "attempted." The allusion to *sierras de Caria* has always been felt to be puzzling, as no mountain-chains are known which it seems to fit. The expression is evidently taken by Herrera from Pinzon's testimony in the *Probanzas*, in which occur several other names now unintelligible, such as the countries of *Camarona*, *Chabaca*, and *Pintigron*, which Pinzon says he visited after turning northward from Honduras, but to which we have no further clue. The lapse into oblivion of

In this statement Herrera understands the voyage of Pinzon and Solis to have been consequent upon the news of what Columbus had discovered in his fourth voyage (1502–1504); and this opinion is evidently based upon his interpretation of the testimony of Pinzon himself and other sailors in the *Probanzas*. It is a very natural way in which to read that testimony if we have nothing but the text itself to guide us; and if Herrera made a mischievous mistake we cannot blame him. There are the strongest reasons for believing that he did make such a mistake, and that this voyage of Pinzon and Solis was made, not in consequence of the fourth voyage of Columbus, but in consequence of the news of what he had discovered in 1494 in the course of his second voyage.

Herrera got the date wrong—1506 instead of 1497.

In the first place the evidence collected by Navarrete seems to prove conclusively that Pinzon did not go upon any voyage of discovery between the end of the year 1504 and June 29, 1508. A voyage for him was indeed contemplated as early as February or April, 1505, but it was not a voyage in the direction of Honduras, nor had it any reference to the fourth voyage of Columbus. On the contrary, as we shall hereafter see, it was a direct consequence of the fourth voyage of Vespucius. Its object was

Pinzon did not go on any voyage in 1506.

so many names known to the first navigators is just what we might expect in the case of a voyage which was not followed up for twenty years (cf. Nos. 3, 25, 26 in my table of voyages). We shall presently have a similar illustration in the names upon a part of the Cantino map.

the further exploration of the Brazilian coast south of the tropic of Capricorn, and while it was planned early in 1505, the fear of complications with Portugal prevented such an expedition from sailing until the summer of 1508. During that interval we keep coming upon documents that prove the presence of Pinzon in Spain; and it is not for a moment to be supposed that while thus concerned in this enterprise he could have been at the same time engaged in a long voyage into the gulf of Mexico.[1]   We have no alternative but to suppose that Herrera's date of 1506 for Pinzon's Honduras voyage is a mistake, and that he ought to have made it consequent, not upon the fourth, but upon the second, voyage of Columbus.

It was all the more easy to make such a mistake since the farthest point reached by Columbus upon the southern coast of Cuba in June, 1494, was not far from the point whence he crossed from Cuba to Honduras in July, 1503. If he had kept

[1] We find Pinzon in Spain receiving a payment of 10,000 maravedis, February 28, 1505 (Navarrete, *Coleccion*, iii. 112); he is appointed to command a fortress in San Juan de Porto Rico, March 14, 1505 (iii. 112); the king wishes to consult with Pinzon and Vespucius about a projected voyage, May 17, 1505 (iii. 302); Pinzon wants a lawsuit settled, as it is hindering his departure on a voyage, September 28, 1505 (iii. 113); he is in Spain, busy on work on which he has evidently been engaged for a good while, August 23, 1506 (iii. 294); on September 15, 1506, the officers of the Casa de la Contratacion inform the king that the expedition will not be able to sail before February, 1507 (iii. 321); by that time the growl from Portugal has become so audible that the expedition is for the time abandoned and the ships used for other purposes (*id.*). These documents evidently relate to one and the same voyage, and they leave no place for a voyage to Honduras and the gulf of Mexico.

straight ahead in the former voyage and left the
coast of Cuba, he would have crossed to Honduras
very much as in the latter voyage. It is not
strange, then, that in the mind of Herrera, as perhaps even in the *report* of the *Probanzas* upon
which Herrera seems to have relied, the two voyages should have got more or less mixed together.

Assuming, then, that Pinzon's first voyage was
consequent upon news received from Columbus in
1494, and that it was the voyage upon which
Vespucius describes himself as having sailed in
May, 1497, we can understand sundry statements
in early historians of the Discovery, that have
heretofore been unintelligible.   Peter Testimony of
Martyr, in a passage written before Peter Martyr.
1508, says: — "For there are many which affirme
that they haue sayled rownd abowt Cuba. But
whether it bee so or not, or whether enuyinge the
good fortune of this man [Columbus] they seeke
occasions of querelinge ageynste hym, I cannot
judge. But tyme shall speake, which in tyme appoynted, reuealeth both truth and falsehod." [1]   In
another place Martyr says that Vicente Yañez
sailed about Cuba, which had hitherto, because of
its great size, been regarded as continent; and
having found that this is an island, he went on and
struck upon other lands to the west of it. [2]   Again

---

[1] "Neque enim desunt qui se circuisse Cubam audeant dicere.
An hæc ita sint, an invidia tanti inventi occasiones quærant in
hunc virum, non dijudico: tempus loquetur, in quo verus judex
invigilat." Martyr, dec. i. lib. vi. As Humboldt says, this last
clause shows conclusively that the passage was written before
Ocampo's voyage in 1508.

[2] "Vicentius Annez . . . Cubam, a multis ad ea usque tem-

Gomara says that three years before Columbus
visited the coast of Honduras that coast
had been discovered by Pinzon and Solis.[1]   Gomara's three years should be
five, but the main fact is the fact of priority, which
is again expressly affirmed by Oviedo (in 1526–
35): — "Some persons have attributed the discovery of the bay of Honduras to Don Christopher
Columbus, the first Admiral, saying that he discovered it.   But that is not true; for it was discovered by the pilots Vicente Yañez Pinzon, Juan
Diaz de Solis, and Pedro de Ledesma, with three
caravels, and that was before Vicente Yañez had
discovered the river Amazon,"[2] in other words,
before January, 1500.   This explicit and definite
testimony from a contemporary first-hand authority is not lightly to be set aside.

Testimony of
Gomara and
Oviedo.

There can be little doubt that Oviedo, Gomara,
Martyr, Herrera, and the witnesses in the tenth
section of the *Probanzas*, in their various refer-

---

pora ob suam magnitudinem continentem putatam, circuivit. . . .
Vicentius Annez cognito jam experimento patenti Cubam esse insulam, processit ulterius et terras alias ad occidentem Cubæ offen-
dit."   *Id.*, dec. ii. lib. vii.

[1] "Descubrió Christoual Colon treziĕtas y setĕta leguas de
costa, que ponen de rio grande de Higueras al Nŏbre de Dios, el
año de mil y quinientos y dos; dizen empero algunos q̃ tres años
ante lo auian andado Vicente Yañez Pinzon y Juan Diaz de Solis,
q̃ fueron grandíssimos descubridores."   Gomara, *Historia general
de las Indias*, Antwerp, 1554, cap. lv. fol. 63 recto.

[2] "Algunos atribuyen al Almirante primero, Don Christoval
Colon, diciendo que él lo descubrió.   Y no es así; porque el golfo
de Higueras lo descubrieron los pilotos Vicente Yañez Pinzon ó
Johan Diaz de Solis ó Pedro de Ledesma, con tres caravelas, antes
que el Vicente Yañez descubriese el rio Marañon."   Oviedo, *Historia general de las Indias*, Madrid, 1851, tom. ii. p. 140.

ences to the voyage of Pinzon and Solis, are all
referring to the first voyage described by Vespucius in his letter to Söderini, — a voyage which
achieved the first discovery of Honduras, with
parts of the coasts of Mexico and Florida, and
which first revealed to some persons the insularity
of Cuba. Here the map made in 1500 by La Cosa
becomes quite interesting. It will be remembered that this able navigator was with Columbus
on that memorable occasion in June, 1494, when
all hands solemnly subscribed to the belief that
Cuba was part of the Asiatic continent.[1] On that

---

[1] This affair, so grotesque according to modern notions, is usually misrepresented; e. g. "Columbus voyaged for India, thought
his first landing was there, and forced his crew to swear they
thought so too by threatening to cut out their tongues." (Prof.
J. D. Butler, in a very meritorious paper on "The Naming of
America," in *Transactions of Wisconsin Academy of Sciences*,
1874, vol. ii. pp. 203–219.) The passage in Henry Stevens's *Hist.
and Geog. Notes*, p. 12, to which the writer refers, does not justify
such a statement. Stevens simply says "caused his captains, his
pilots, his master of charts [La Cosa], and all his sailors to sign a
declaration under oath, that they believed Cuba to be part of the
continent of Asia near Mangi." The notary's original document,
preserved in the Archives of the Indies at Seville (printed in Navarrete, tom. ii. pp. 143–149), does not indicate that in this "caus-
ing" there was either any force or any threat used. The officers
and men were asked to state their dissenting views if they had
any. Nobody seems to have had any, and there is no reason for
supposing that anybody signed the declaration reluctantly. The
formal provision, that if any one should afterward deny that on
this occasion he had expressed the opinion written down in the
document he should have the tip of his tongue slit (as was often
done to liars), was simply a bit of genuine mediævalism, about
equivalent to the solemn imprecations of modern children: "Huck
Finn and Tom Sawyer wishes they may drop down dead in their
tracks if they ever tell of this and rot," as Mark Twain so
faithfully puts it. For the owlish gravity with which some modern writers use this incident in evidence of the Admiral's alleged

occasion, La Cosa declared that he had never heard
of an island with 335 leagues length of coast from

Cuba repre-
sented as an
island on La
Cosa's map,
1500.

east to west, and that from the contour
of this coast, as well as its apparently
interminable length, he had no sort of
doubt that it was the mainland.   We
have no reason for supposing that La Cosa did not
mean precisely what he said.   Yet upon his famous
map, of which a sketch is prefixed to the present
volume, Cuba is distinctly represented as an island.   On the north of it the left-hand flagstaff
marks the westernmost point reached by Columbus
and La Cosa in 1492; on the south we read *C.
Bien Espera*, the "Cape of Good Hope" where
in 1494 La Cosa and his comrades all testified that
to the best of their knowledge and belief they were
on the coast of Asia; and just to the south of this
cape we see a few small islands whereunto the
map-maker's fancy has added a goodly archipelago
of bigger ones.   The shore on the west of these
islands Columbus called Evangelista, deeming it
"fraught with good tidings" for him when he
should come that way again.   On the map we see
"Abangelista," albeit written too far to the west.
Then Cuba is terminated by a western coast-line
all the way around from the archipelago to the flagstaff, — a coast-line which, as even an unpractised
eye may see, is drawn not from exploration, but
from theory or from hearsay.   On the original map

"deceitfulness" and weakness of character, the proper answer is
a peal of Homeric laughter. I have described the affair above,
vol. i. pp. 476, 477, with as much seriousness as I think it de-
serves.

this western coast-line is abruptly cut off with a
dash of green paint.[1] This means to my mind
that when La Cosa drew the map, between June
and October, 1500, he had been informed of, or
brought to believe in, the insularity of Cuba, but
had not seen a chart of its western extremity.
Where did he get his information? The answer
is obvious. He had just returned from that voyage on the Pearl Coast with Ojeda (the second voyage of Vespucius) in which he and Vespucius were
associated as pilots. Evidently the latter had told
him of the discovery of a passage between Cuba
and the mainland two years before, but had not
shown him his charts, which very likely were then
in the hands of Bishop Fonseca. Hence it appears that the continental coast-line opposite Cuba
was drawn not wholly from theory, but partly from
hearsay. The protruding land at the words "Mar
Oceanuz" and below may indicate that La Cosa

[1] Hence the late Henry Stevens suggested that La Cosa did not
intend to be understood as representing Cuba as an island, but
only meant to show that his own definite knowledge did not go
beyond the archipelago on the south and the flagstaff on the
north. (*Historical and Geographical Notes*, London, 1869, p. 13.)
But if that was all that he meant to show, why did he separate
Cuba from the mainland at all? The mere fact of the separation indicates a knowledge of something to the west of "Abangelista," though confessedly a dim knowledge. At least it indicates
a decided change of opinion since 1494; otherwise La Cosa would
not only have made the western end of Cuba flare like the outline
of a trumpet, but beyond the flagstaff it would have trended
strongly to the northward and become continuous with the mainland. At the archipelago it would have been prolonged indefinitely to the southwest, and there would have been nothing of
that vague but unmistakable suggestion of the gulf of Mexico
which La Cosa cannot have got from any other source than the
first voyage of Vespucius.

had heard something about Florida, but having no drawings to guide him, had pictured it to himself as a big promontory rather than a peninsula.

The striking suggestion thus afforded by the map of La Cosa is confirmed with overwhelming force by that of Alberto Cantino already mentioned in The Cantino map, 1502. connection with the voyages of the brothers Cortereal. This map was made in Portugal by some cartographer unknown, at the order of Alberto Cantino, who carried it to Italy in the autumn of 1502, and sent it to Ercole d' Este, Duke of Ferrara. It had reached the duke, or was on its way to him, November 19, 1502, as we know from Cantino's letter of that date written at Rome. It has been carefully preserved, and since 1868 has been accessible in the Biblioteca Estense at Modena; but it is only within the past ten years that scholars have begun to wake up to its importance.

The Cantino map,[1] which gives both Hayti and Cuba, not only represents the latter as an island, What it proves concerning Florida. terminated on the west by a *hypothetical* coast, but goes on to depict a considerable portion of the coast-line of the United States, including both sides of the peninsula

[1] A sketch showing the relative positions was given above on page 21. This sketch of the Florida coasts I have copied from the full-sized facsimile published in 1883 by M. Harrisse, and have taken pains to reproduce with accuracy the details of the coast-line. Off the southwestern coast the original has a group of islands which I have omitted in order to get room for the names. One cannot do all that one would like on so small a page. These islands may be seen on the other sketch just mentioned. On the original map the coasts end abruptly just where they touch my border, at "Rio de las Palmas" and "Costa del Mar Vaano."

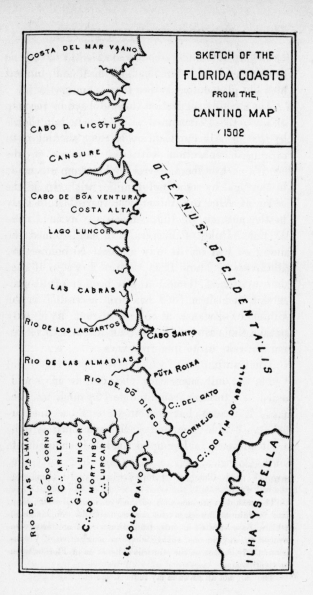

SKETCH OF THE
FLORIDA COASTS
FROM THE
CANTINO MAP
1502

COSTA DEL MAR VẶANO

CABO D. LICÕTU

CANSURE

CABO DE BÕA VENTURA
COSTA ALTA

LAGO LUNCOR

LAS CABRAS

RIO DE LOS LARGARTOS

CABO SANTO

RIO DE LAS ALMADIAS

PŪTA ROIXA

RIO DE. DÕ DIEGO

C∴ DEL GATO

CORNEJO

C∴ DO FIN DO ABRILL

OCEANUS OCCIDENTALIS

ILHA YSABELLA

RIO DE LAS PALMAS
RIO DE CORNO
C∴ ARLEAR
G∴DO LURCOR
C∴ DO MORTINBO
C∴ LURCAR
EL GOLFO BAVO

LIBRARY OF
MUSKINGUM COLLEGE
New Concord, Ohio.

of Florida, and all this is depicted as a *visited* coast, with sundry details of bay and headland, upon which are placed twenty-two local names. A few of these names have been distorted beyond recognition by the Portuguese draughtsman, but their original form is unquestionably Spanish and not Portuguese. The names furnish absolute proof that this part of the map was copied from a Spanish map [1] by a person not familiar with Spanish, and furthermore that this copyist was a Portuguese. These names, like fossils from an age extinct, are eloquent in their silence. As I shall presently show, they had ceased to be understood before the rediscovery of Florida by Ponce de Leon in 1513; the continuity of tradition was broken off short. All this means that THIS PORTION OF THE UNITED STATES COAST WAS VISITED AND MAPPED BY SPANISH MARINERS BEFORE NOVEMBER, 1502, AND THAT THE VOYAGE IN WHICH THIS WAS DONE WAS NOT FOLLOWED UP.

It is not only clear that the Cantino map was copied or compiled from an older Spanish map or maps; it is also clear that it was not based upon the map of La Cosa, but upon some entirely different authority. For upon the northern coast of South America, where La Cosa has forty-five names [2] and Cantino twenty-nine, only three of

---

[1] The mistakes are mistakes of the eye, not of the ear; they stand for misread letters, not for misheard sounds. M. Harrisse, in his work on the Cortereals, demonstrates that no Portuguese voyages, nor any *recorded* voyage whatever, except that of Vespucius in 1497–98, will account for this delineation of Florida upon the Cantino map.

[2] They are not all given in my reduced sketch.

these names agree on the two maps. It therefore
appears that the Cantino map, while it represents
knowledge gained at some length of time before the
autumn of 1502, also gives testimony that is independent, and not a mere repetition of the testimony
of La Cosa.

It is worth our while here to follow out a little
further some of the relations of this map to the
cartography of that time. The original
from which it was made exercised much
more influence than that of La Cosa,
which does not seem to have been engraved or extensively copied. In the edition of
Ptolemy published at Strasburg in 1513 there is
a remarkable map, made before 1508 [1] by Martin

*Waldseemül-
ler's map, the
Tabula Terre
Nove, made
before 1508.*

[1] "Charta autem Marina, quam Hydrographiam vocant, per
Admiralem quondam serenissimi Portugaliæ [Castellæ?] regis
Ferdinandi, cæteros denique lustratores verissimis peragrationi-
bus lustrata: ministerio Renati dum vixit, nunc pie mortui Ducis
illustrissimi Lotharingiæ liberius prælographationi tradita est,"
etc., *anglicè,* "The sailing chart, or Hydrography, as it is called,
rectified by means of very exact navigations made by a former
Admiral of the most gracious King Ferdinand of Portugal [Cas-
tile?], and thereafter by other explorers, was liberally given to be
engraved by the care of the most illustrious René, in his lifetime
Duke of Lorraine, now deceased," etc. Avezac, *Martin Waltzemüller,* p. 153; cf. Lelewel, *Géographie du Moyen Age,* tom. ii.
pp. 157–160; Humboldt, *Examen critique,* tom. iv. p. 109. As
René died in 1508, this is perhaps the earliest *engraved* map now
extant showing portions of America, though the map made by
Johann Ruysch and published in the edition of Ptolemy issued at
Rome, August 13, 1508 (see below, p. 114), may have been en-
graved earlier. The Waldseemüller map, known by its title
Tabula Terre Nove, seems to have been made after an original
chart obtained from Portugal by Duke René in 1504 (see Har-
risse, *Bibliotheca Americana Vetustissima,* p. 108). The "former
Admiral" above mentioned is probably Columbus, and calling
Ferdinand "king of Portugal" was a mere slip of the pen. It

Waldseemüller, a geographer of whom we shall have more to say hereafter. This map, known as *Tabula Terre Nove*, has been a puzzle to scholars, but a long step is taken toward understanding it when we learn that it was made from an original chart which found its way from Portugal into Lorraine in 1504, and when we furthermore see that this original must have been the same that was followed by Cantino's draughtsman. This is proved by the identity in names, of which the following list, containing all the names upon the Florida coasts, is sufficiently striking: —

CANTINO.	TABULA TERRE NOVE.	MEANINGS.
	lago de loro,	parrot lake.
Rio de las palmas,	Rio de la parmas,	river of palms.
rio do corno,	rio de como,	{ dogwood river ? { r. *corvo*, crow river ? }
C. arlear,	C. arlear,	?
G. do lurcor,	G. dolivor,	?
C. do mortinbo,		?
C. lurcar,	C. lurcar,	?
el golfo bavo,		?
C. do fim do abrill,	C. doffim de abril,	cape of the end of April.
cornejo,	comello,	dogwood ?
Rio de do diego,		river of Don Diego.
C. del gato,	C. de lago,	cape of the cat.
puta Roixa,	ponta royal,	{ red point ? { p. *Bayxa*,[1] low point ? }
Rio de las almadias,	rio de las amadias,	river of canoes.
Cabo Santo,	C. Santo,	holy cape.
Rio de los largartos,	rio de los garlartos,	river of lizards, or alligators.
las cabras,	la cablas?	?
lago luncor,	lago luncor,	l. *luengo*, long lagoon ?
Costa alta,	Costa alta,	high coast.
Cabo de boa ventura,	C. de bonauentura,	cape of good fortune.
Cansure,	Camnor,	?
Cabo d. licotu,	C. del itontir,	*C. del encontro*,[1] cape of meeting ?
Costa del mar vaano,	C. del mar usiano,	{ coast { cape ? } of the ocean sea.

has often been called "The Admiral's Map," but that phrase is misleading. It represents, as the editors say, the results of voyages made by Columbus, "and thereafter by other explorers;" but it is not likely that it emanated from Columbus. It leads us much more directly back to Vespucius.

[1] I am indebted for these two suggestions to M. Harrisse, *Les Corte-Real*, pp. 89, 90.

Of the twenty-two names on Cantino's coasts of Florida, nineteen are thus repeated in the later map. Originally Spanish, these names have on the Portuguese map in a few instances been deformed beyond recognition; on the Lorraine map the deformity is generally carried a little farther, as we might expect. There can be no doubt that, so far as the delineation of Florida is concerned, the two maps are drawn from the same source. Observe the conclusions to which this fact carries us. As the history of the Discovery of America has usually been written, Florida was first visited by Ponce de Leon on Easter Sunday, 1512; and a superficial observer might not be surprised at seeing the Florida coasts laid down on a map first published in 1513; perhaps, too, it might not occur to him that the peculiar names on these coasts are not derived from the explorations that began with Ponce de Leon. But now, while on the one hand it has lately been proved that Ponce de Leon did not see Florida until Easter Sunday, 1513,[1] on the other hand the map of the 1513 Ptolemy was certainly made before 1508, and the comparison with the Cantino map proves it to have been drawn from an original as old as 1502, and probably older. It follows, therefore, with the force of absolute demonstration, that the coasts of Florida were explored and the insularity of Cuba detected before 1502. There is no possible escape from this conclusion.

The Florida coasts were visited by Spaniards before 1502.

[1] See Peschel, *Geschichte des Zeitalters der Entdeckungen*, p. 521; Kohl, in *Documentary History of Maine*, vol. i. p. 240; Winsor, *Narr. and Crit. Hist.*, ii. 233.

But this is not the whole story. Our facts show that while Florida was visited at that·early date, and while for the moment the discovery attracted enough attention, among cartographers at least, to leave its indelible impression upon more than one map, nevertheless it soon ceased to occupy attention and became forgotten, so that the names it left behind became a source of worry and confusion for map-makers. Because Florida (as yet without a name) purported to be a piece of continent, and because until after 1508 most people believed Cuba to be a piece of continent, the old maps used to mix them together without rhyme or ·reason; and the perplexity was increased by the fact that the true Cuba was often called Isabella. Sometimes the island appeared under the latter designation, while the name Cuba was placed upon the Florida peninsula; sometimes the two were fused into one, because while geographers found both countries mentioned or drawn upon maps, they knew only of the one as being actually visited, and hence tried to correct the apparent error. For example, in Johann Ruysch's map, 1508, to the west of Hispaniola we see an island abruptly cut off with the scroll marked C, upon which is the legend, "the ships of Ferdinand, king of Spain, have come as far as here." [1] Now this might be meant for Cuba, and the two ends of the scroll might be intended to mark the two farthest points reached by Columbus in 1492 and 1494; or it may be meant for Florida, partially capsized, — an accident not uncommon in early

How the old map-makers were puzzled.

[1] See below, p. 114.

maps, — and the scroll may simply show what
Ruysch was able to gather from the original of
the Cantino map. That the latter is probably the
true explanation is indicated by the names:[1] — at
the eastern point we have *C. de Fundabril*, and,
going thence to the right, *Corveo* (for *Cornejo*)
and *C. Elicontii* (for *C. de licontu*); going to the
left, we have *Culcar* (for *C. arlear*) and then
Lago del Oro. This seems to show what Ruysch
had in mind. On the other hand, on Stobnicza's
map, 1512, which was in part derived from the
Cantino source, we see the islands of "Spagnolla"
and "Isabella" rudely drawn in much the same
outline as in the *Tabula Terre Nove*, but the name
"Isabella" has taken refuge upon the mainland.[2]

These examples show that the geographers of
that time had more facts set before them than they
were able to assimilate. In some directions a
steady succession of voyages served to
correct imperfections in theory and to
attach certain names permanently to certain localities. But the facts relating to the gulf
of Mexico and Florida remained indigestible because from fifteen to twenty years elapsed before
the earliest voyage in those waters was followed
up and the first crude impressions made definite.
The names applied to those coasts soon sank into
oblivion, and when the actors in that generation
had all passed from the scene, the very memory of
the voyage itself was lost, the maps which it in-

Why they were thus puzzled.

---

[1] There is not room enough for them on my reduced sketch of
this map.

[2] See below, p. 178.

spired slept unheeded in the gloom of great libraries, the only literary document describing it was wrongly referred to a very different voyage, and the illustrious writer of that document became the target for all manner of ignorant abuse.

There is little room for doubt that the first voyage of Vespucius was made just as he describes it in his own sea-faring dialect. No other source is known from which those Florida coasts, depicted with their long-forgotten names upon the Cantino and Waldseemüller maps, can possibly have come. We must either admit that Americus Vespucius circumnavigated the Florida peninsula before 1502, or we must *invent* some voyage, never heard of and never mentioned by anybody, in which that thing was done; and as the latter alternative is not likely to commend itself to sensible minds, we are driven to the former.[1] But if Vespucius

The voyage of Vespucius in 1497-98 is the only voyage on record that explains the Cantino map.

[1] " De toutes les expéditions maritimes du xve siècle, celle-ci [the first voyage of Vespucius] est la seule qui cadre avec les configurations géographiques que l'on relève sur la carte de Cantino." Harrisse, *Les Corte-Real*, p. 107. In a footnote to this passage M. Harrisse is strongly tempted to believe that the Portuguese map which Peter Martyr saw in Bishop Fonseca's office, " whereunto Americus Vesputius is sayde to have put his hande," was the very prototype of the map made in Lisbon for Cantino. Yet M. Harrisse finds a difficulty in supposing that the voyage which inspired the Cantino map was made before 1500. If it had been, he thinks the Florida coasts would have been delineated and studded with names on La Cosa's map. Since La Cosa, when he made his map, had just been for a year in company with Vespucius, why had not the latter put him in possession of all the facts recorded upon the Cantino map, if he knew them ? To M. Harrisse this difficulty seems so formidable that he is actually disposed to *invent* a voyage between 1500 and 1502 in order to account for the Cantino map ! *Les Corte-Real*, p. 151. To my mind the

made this voyage before November, 1502, then he must have made it exactly when he says he did, in 1497–98, for we can trace him through the whole intervening period and know that he was all the time busy with other things.

To return, then, to the beginning, and sum up the case, it seems to me that things must have happened about as follows: —

It was in the course of the year 1494 that Ferdinand and Isabella began to feel somewhat disappointed at the meagre results obtained by Columbus. The wealth of Cathay and Cipango had not been found, the colonists, who had expected to meet with pearls and gold growing on bushes, were sick and angry, Friar Boyle was preaching that the Admiral was a humbug, and the expensive work of discovery was going on at a snail's pace. Meanwhile Vicente Yañez Pinzon and other bold spirits were grumbling at the monopoly granted to Columbus and begging to be allowed to make ventures for themselves. Now in this connection several documents preserved in the Archives of the Indies at Seville are very significant. On the 9th of April, 1495, the sovereigns issued their letter of credentials to Juan Aguado, whom they were about sending to Hispaniola to inquire into the charges

How it came about that Vespucius and Pinzon made this voyage in 1497.

difficulty does not exist. La Cosa's map seems to me — as I have already observed — to show just the knowledge which he must have gained from conversation with Vespucius without seeing a chart of the Florida coast; and I see no reason why Vespucius must necessarily have carried such a chart with him on a voyage to the Pearl Coast, or why he should have been anxious to impart all the details of his professional experience to a brother pilot.

against Columbus.[1] On that very same day they signed the contract with Berardi, whereby the latter bound himself to furnish twelve vessels, four to be ready at once, four in June, and four in September. On the next day they issued the decree throwing open the navigation to the Indies and granting to all native Spaniards, on certain prescribed conditions, the privilege of making voyages to the newly found coasts. On the 12th they instructed Fonseca to put Aguado in command of the first four caravels.[2] All these acts were coherent parts of a settled policy which the sovereigns were then pursuing. Under the permission of April 10, says Gomara, quite a number of navigators sailed, some at their own expense, others at the expense of the king; all hoped to acquire fame and wealth,

[1] The reader may like to see the form of this sort of letter, which so often carried dismay to explorers, worthy and unworthy, in the New World: — " El Rey é la Reina: Caballeros y Escuderos y otras personas que por nuestro mandado estais en las Indias, allá vos enviamos á Juan Aguado, nuestro Repostero, el cual de nuestra parte vos hablará. Nos vos mandamos que le dedes fe y creencia. De Madrid á nveve de Abril de mil y cuatrocientos y noventa y cinco años. — Yo EL REY. — Yo LA REINA. — Por mandado del Rey é de la Reina nuestros Señores — HERNAND ALVAREZ." Las Casas, *Hist. de las Indias,* tom. ii. p. 110; *anglicè:* —

THE KING AND THE QUEEN:

Cavaliers, Esquires, and other persons, who by our command are in the Indies, we send you thither Juan Aguado, our Gentleman of the Chamber, who will speak to you on our part. We command that you give him faith and credence. From Madrid the ninth of April, one thousand four hundred and ninety-five.

I THE KING: I THE QUEEN.

By command of the King and Queen, our Lords,

HERNAND ALVAREZ.

Brief but comprehensive!

[2] Navarrete, *Coleccion,* tom. ii. pp. 159–169.

but since for the most part they only succeeded in ruining themselves with their discovering, their voyages were forgotten.[1]

The delays in fitting out such expeditions were apt to be many and vexatious. Of the twelve caravels which Berardi was to furnish, the first four started off in August, with Aguado in command. The second squadron of four, which was to have been ready in June, was not yet fully equipped in December, when Berardi died. Then Vespucius, representing the house of Berardi, took up the work and sent the four caravels to sea February 3, 1496. They were only two days out when a frightful storm overtook and wrecked them, though most of the crews were saved.[2] The third squadron of four caravels was, I believe, that which finally sailed May 10,

The three Berardi squadrons.

[1] "Entendiendo quan grandissimas tierras eran las que Christoval Colon descubria, fueron muchos á continuar el descubrimiento de todas; unos á su costa, otros á la del Rey, y todos pensando enriquecer, ganar fama y medrar con los Reyes. Pero como los mas dellos no hizieron sino descubrir y gastarse, no quedó memoria de todos, que yo sepa," etc. Gomara, *Historia general de las Indias*, Saragossa, 1553, fol. 50.

[2] These particulars are from memoranda in MS., extracted by Muñoz from account-books in the Casa de Contratacion at Seville. See Irving's *Columbus*, vol. iii. p. 397. Irving and Navarrete had access to the documents of Muñoz, and Navarrete (tom. iii. p. 317), in speaking of a payment made from the treasury on January 12, 1496, observes that Vespucius "went on attending to everything until the armada was despatched from San Lucar," i. e. February 3, 1496. Humboldt strangely interpreted this statement as meaning that Vespucius fitted out the third expedition of Columbus, and was thus kept in Spain till May 30, 1498 (*Examen critique*, tom. iv. p. 268). This ingenious *alibi*, often quoted as proving the impossibility of a voyage anywhere by Vespucius in 1497, is not sustained.

1497.   While it was getting ready Vicente Yañez
Pinzon returned from the Levant, whither he had
been sent on important business by the sovereigns
in December, 1495.[1] Columbus, who had returned to Spain in June, 1496, protested against
what he considered an invasion of his monopoly,
and on June 2, 1497, the sovereigns issued a decree which for the moment was practically equivalent to a revocation of the general license accorded
to navigators by the decree of April 10, 1495.[2]
Observe that this revocation was not issued until
after the third squadron had sailed! The sovereigns were not going to be baulked in the little
scheme which they had set on foot two years before, and for which they had paid out, through
Vespucius, so many thousands of maravedis.[3] So
the expedition sailed, with Pinzon in chief command and Solis second, with Ledesma for one of
the pilots, and Vespucius as pilot and cosmographer.

The course taken and the coasts visited have
already been sufficiently indicated. The landfall

[1] Navarrete, tom. iii. p. 75.

[2] Navarrete, tom. ii. p. 201.

[3] Vespucius speaks of the expedition as sailing in the service of
King Ferdinand. He does not say "their highnesses," or "Los
Reyes," the sovereigns, but mentions only the king, and this
agrees with Gomara's expression above quoted, "some at their
own expense, others at the expense of the king," and also with
the expression of the pilot Ledesma in his testimony in the *Probanzas*, "por mandado de S. A." (Navarrete, tom. iii. p. 558).
On the other hand Pinzon, in his testimony, says "por mandado
de SS. AA." (which he would not have been likely to say, by the
way, if he had been referring to events of the year 1506, after the
queen's death). On the whole it seems not unlikely that this was
especially Ferdinand's venture.

was undoubtedly upon the northern coast of Honduras,[1] points on the coasts of Yucatan and Tabasco were visited, then a
straight run was made to Tampico, and
thence the coast was followed to some

How far north
did Vespucius
follow the
coast of the
United States?

[1] It was a very common custom to name newly-discovered
places after the saint upon whose day they were discovered.
When you see a saint's name on a cape or bay, it is good ground
for a presumption that the name was given by some explorer who
first visited it on that saint's day. When you see *Navidad* it
generally means Christmas, but not unfrequently June 24, the
Nativity of John the Baptist. When Herrera tells us that Pinzon
and Solis discovered the bay of Honduras and named it "Baia de
Navidad," it affords a strong presumption that it was discovered
on St. John's day. The ships, as we have seen, probably started
May 25 from the Grand Canary, whence a run of 27 days would
bring their landfall at or near Cape Honduras on June 21. Three
more days would enable them to recognize the water to the west
of that point as a great bay. But the primitive text of Vespucius says the landfall occurred after 37 days. As the figure is
given in Arabic numerals there is a good chance for error. Curiously enough, the Latin version of 1507 says "viginti septem
vix elapsis diebus," i. e. "after barely twenty-seven days." Is
this a mistake, or an emendation suggested to the Latin translator by some outside source of information? The latter, I suspect. With the trade wind nearly dead astern, and with the
powerful westward current in the Caribbean sea, the quicker run
is the more probable, and it fits the name *Navidad*. The reader
will remember that this same June 24, 1497, was the date of John
Cabot's landfall on the northeastern coast of North America. If
the Latin figure is correct, Vespucius probably saw "the continent" two or three days before Cabot. The question may have
interest for readers fond of such trifles. It is really of no consequence what navigator — after the genius of Columbus had
opened the way — happened to be the first to see land which we
have since come to know as part of the coast-line of a continental
system distinct from the Old World. Nor has the question a
historic interest of any sort; for, as we shall see, considerations
of "priority" connected with this voyage of 1497 had nothing
whatever to do with the naming of America.

point on the Atlantic coast of the United States
which may perhaps be determined if any one can
succeed in interpreting the details of the Cantino
map. If the latitudes on the *Tabula Terre Nove*
were given with any approach to correctness, it
would be helpful in deciding this point; but they
are hopelessly wrong. Though Vespucius was in
·all probability the original source of this part of
the map, it is impossible that he should ever have
given such latitudes. It is pretty clear that the
data must have been "amended" by Waldseemüller
to suit some fancy of his own. The Pearl Coast
is not far out of place, but Hispaniola is more
than five degrees too far north and above the tropic
of Cancer; the tip of Florida comes in 35°, which
is ten degrees too far north; and for aught we know
the error may go on increasing to the top of the
map. The latitude assigned to "C. del mar usi-
ano" is 55°, the latitude of Hopedale on the coast
of Labrador! That is of course absurd. But if
we turn back to the Cantino sketch of Florida and
suppose the *proportions* of the sailing chart from
which it was taken to have been fairly preserved,
we may give a sort of definiteness to our guessing.
As a starting-point, what is the "River of Palms"?
M. Varnhagen thinks it is the Mississippi,[1] and
if we were to adopt that scale it would throw the
"Costa del mar vaano" as far north as Long
Island. But I suspect that M. Varnhagen is mistaken. This "River of Palms" may be seen in
the same place upon the *Tabula Terre Nove*, and
farther to the left, a little above the 30th parallel,

[1] Varnhagen, *Amerigo Vespucci*, p. 98.

we see the delta-like mouth of a much larger river, which strongly suggests the Mississippi. Although it is tilted too far to the left and the coastline is incorrectly drawn, such things are what we expect to find in these old maps. It seems to me that this is the Mississippi, and that the river of the palms or palmettos is the Appalachicola, while the lake of the parrots may be St. Andrew's bay or Santa Rosa bay. With the scale thus reduced the "Costa del mar vạano" *Perhaps as far as the Chesapeake.* (which should probably be "Cabo del mar oceano") may very probably represent Cape Hatteras. If this was the point reached by Vespucius, as he says, in June, 1498, we can easily understand the significance of the name "Cape of the end of April,"[1] applied to the extremity of Florida.

The reader must not attach to these suggestions an importance which I am far from claiming for them. The subject is a difficult one, and stands much in need of further clues, which perhaps may yet be found. The obscurity in which this voyage has so long been enveloped is due chiefly to the fact that it was not followed up till many years had elapsed, and the reason for this neg- *Why the voyage was not followed up.* lect impresses upon us forcibly the impossibility of understanding the history of the Discovery of America unless we bear in mind

[1] On St. Bernard's day, August 20, Vespucius was very likely at the Bermudas, and Mr. Hubert Bancroft (*Central America*, vol. i. p. 106) suggests that "the Bermudas may have been the archipelago of San Bernardo, famous for its fierce Carib population, but generally located off the gulf of Urabá." This seems not unlikely.

all the attendant circumstances.   One might at first suppose that a voyage which revealed some 4,000 miles of the coast of North America would have attracted much attention in Spain and have become altogether too famous to be soon forgotten.   Such an argument, however, loses sight of the fact that these early voyagers were not trying to "discover America."   There was nothing to astonish them in the existence of 4,000 miles of coast-line on this side of the Atlantic.   To their minds it was simply the coast of Asia, about which they knew nothing except from Marco Polo, and the natural effect of such a voyage as this would be simply to throw discredit upon that traveller.   So long a stretch of coast without any great and wealthy cities did not answer at all to his descriptions. It may seem strange that Pinzon and Solis did not come upon pyramidal temples and other evidences of semi-civilization on the coast of Yucatan, as Hernandez de Cordova did in 1517; but any one who has sailed along coasts in various weathers knows well how easy it is for things to escape notice at one time which at another time fairly jump at your eyes.   As will be shown in the next chapter, it was such sights in 1517, after Cuba had been colonized by Spaniards, that turned the drift of exploration into the gulf of Mexico.   Not happening to catch sight of such things in 1497, and nowhere finding an abundance of gold

It was not a commercial success.

or jewels or spices, the voyagers did not regard their expedition as much of a success, and there is no reason why people in Spain should have so regarded it.   If King Ferdinand

made an especial venture on this occasion, he probably took no pleasure in recollecting the fact or
having it recalled to him. Indeed, the tone of
Vespucius, in this part of his letter to Soderini, is
not at all that of a man exulting in the consciousness of having taken part in a great discovery.
He says that they did not find anything of profit
in that country, except some slight indications of
gold; but he suggests that perhaps they might have
done better if they had understood the languages
of the natives. The general impression left by the
letter is that but for the capture of as many slaves
as they could crowd into their four caravels, they
would have returned home without much to show
for their labours.

It is plain, then, that the 1497 voyage of Pinzon
and Solis was not followed up for precisely the
same reason that prevented the voyages *All eyes were*
of the Cabots from being followed up. *turned toward*
the Indian
There was no prospect of immediate *ocean.*
profit, and, moreover, public attention was absorbed in another direction. All eyes were turned
to the south, and for a good reason, as I had occasion to observe in the preceding chapter, in connection with the declining reputation of Columbus. In July, 1499, Vasco da Gama returned
to Lisbon from Hindustan, with ships laden with
the riches of the East. The fame of this achievement for the time threw Columbus quite into the
shade. The glories of Cipango and Cathay seemed
unsubstantial, like promissory notes thrice renewed, when Portugal stepped blithely into the
foreground jingling the hard cash. Interest in the

eastern coast of Asia for the moment died away.
The great object was to get into the Indian ocean,
and come as nearly as possible to the rich countries
visited by Gama.   Spain could not go east of the
papal meridian; she must go to the west and seek
the vaguely rumoured strait of Malacca, which was
supposed to be somewhere to the south of Honduras.   Nothing more was done in the gulf of
Mexico for twenty years, and the first voyage
made by Spaniards in those waters was probably
seldom talked of.

We have already seen that the fourth voyage
of Columbus was a direct response to the voyage
of Gama.   It was an attempt to get from
Probable in-
fluence of the
first voyage
of Vespucius
upon the
fourth of Co-
lumbus.
the Atlantic into the Indian ocean.   If
the view here taken of the first voyage
of Vespucius be correct, Columbus must
have known its results in 1502, for he
took with him Pedro Ledesma, who had been one
of the pilots in that voyage.   Perhaps the Admiral
may have selected him for that very reason.
Ledesma would naturally tell Columbus that he
had sailed through the passage between Cuba and
Yucatan, and found a continental coast which led
him ultimately far to the north of the tropic of
Cancer.   Columbus would thus see that Cuba,
though not a part of the continent as he had supposed, was nevertheless close by it; that a voyage
upon the coast of that continent would, as he had
supposed, only lead him northward; and that he
was not likely in the latitude of Cuba to find a
channel westward through Asia into the Indian
ocean.   With his general view of the situation

thus confirmed in spite of the insularity of Cuba, Columbus had no motive for steering west; and the prompt decisiveness with which from the Queen's Gardens he steered across open sea straight for Cape Honduras and there turned eastward is to my mind a strong indication that he was well informed as to what his friend Americus had seen to the west of that cape. But for such definite information would he not have hugged the coast of Cuba? and when he had thus passed his "Cape of Good Hope" and reached the end of the island, with no land in sight before him in any direction, would not a natural impulse have carried him westward into the gulf of Mexico?

The fourth voyage of Columbus was not the first response made by Spain to the voyage of Gama. The first response was entrusted to Vicente Yañez Pinzon, the way having been indicated by the second voyage of Vespucius, in company with Ojeda and La Cosa, in the summer of 1499. The voyage of Ojeda was instigated by Bishop Fonseca, with some intention of taking out of the hands of Columbus the further exploration of the coast upon which valuable pearls had been found. The expedition sailed May 16, 1499, from Cadiz, ran down to the Cape Verde islands, crossed the equator, and sighted land on the coast of Brazil in latitude 4° or 5° S., somewhere near Aracati. Vespucius gives a good account of this half-drowned coast.[1] Thence the ships ran a few

[1] The landfall on this voyage has been commonly placed on the coast of Surinam, about 600 miles eastward from Trinidad. This

leagues to the southeast, probably to see whether the shore seemed to be that of an island or a continent. Finding progress difficult against the equatorial current, they turned about and ran northwest as far as Cayenne, thence to Paria, and so on to Maracaibo and to Cape de la Vela. From

is because Ojeda, in his testimony in the *Probanzas*, did not allude to any place farther east than Surinam. But this negative evidence is here of small value. In a second voyage, in 1502, Ojeda had trespassed upon Portuguese territory, and had been censured and heavily fined for so doing (Navarrete, tom. ii. p. 430). Evidently in giving his testimony, in 1513, Ojeda thought it prudent to give the Portuguese a wide berth, and as there was no occasion for his saying that he had been on the coast of Brazil, he said nothing about it. The account of Vespucius is clear and straightforward. It is true that Mr. Hubert Bancroft says, "his account in the different forms in which it exists is so full of blunders that it could throw but little light upon the subject" (*Central America*, vol. i. p. 113). When Mr. Bancroft says this, he of course has in mind the spurious letter published in 1745 by Bandini, in which Vespucius is supposed to give to his friend Lorenzo di Pier Francesco de' Medici an account of his second voyage. The MS. of this letter which professes to be an original, and by which Bandini was deceived, is at Florence, in the Biblioteca Riccardiana, MS. No. 2112. Neither the paper nor the ink is older than the seventeenth century, the handwriting is not that of Vespucius, the language is a very different Italian from that which he used, and the pages swarm with absurdities. (See Varnhagen's paper in *Bulletin de la société de géographie*, avril, 1858.) Nothing except the blundering change of *Lariab* to *Parias* has done so much to bemuddle the story of Vespucius as this letter which some clever scamp was kind enough to write for him after he had been more than a hundred years under the sod. It is curious to see the elaborate arguments to which Humboldt was driven, in his *Examen critique*, tom. v., because he did not begin at the beginning, with textual criticism of sources, and so accepted this epistle as genuine. The account of Ojeda's voyage in the third volume of Irving's *Columbus*, from its mixing the first and second voyages of Vespucius, is so full of blunders as to be worse than worthless to the general reader.

this point Ojeda, with part of the little squadron, went over to Hispaniola, and arrived there on the 5th of September. Ojeda's visit to that island was made in no friendly spirit toward Columbus, but there is good reason for believing that the Admiral or some of his people learned the particulars of Ojeda's route across the ocean and his landfall. Early in October two caravels were sent from San Domingo to Spain, and probably carried such information as to determine the route to be taken by Pinzon. That gallant captain started in December, and followed in the track of Vespucius and Ojeda, but went a little farther to the south, losing sight of the pole-star and Second voyage of Pinzon. finally striking the coast of Brazil near the site of Pernambuco, in latitude 8° S. Our accounts of this voyage [1] are meagre, and it does not appear just why Pinzon turned northward from that point. While crossing the equator from south to north, with no land in sight, he found the sea-water fresh enough to drink. Full of wonder at so strange a thing he turned in toward the coast and entered the mouth of the greatest river upon the earth, the Amazon, nearly a hundred miles wide and sending huge volumes of fresh water more than a hundred miles out into the sea. After proceeding as far as

---

[1] Manuel de Valdovinos, one of the witnesses in the *Probanzas*, says that he went on this voyage with Pinzon *the* SECOND *time that he* (Pinzon) *went to make discoveries* (" la segunda vez que fué á descubrir," Navarrete, tom. iii. p. 552). This might mean that his first voyage was the one with Columbus in 1492, but in accordance with the general usage of these speakers, the phrase refers to him as for the second time in command, so that his first voyage must have been that of 1497-98.

the Pearl Coast and Hispaniola, and losing two of his ships in a hurricane, Pinzon returned to Spain in September, 1500. When he arrived he found that his fellow-townsman Diego de Lepe had set sail just after him, in January, with two caravels, and had returned in June, after having doubled Cape San Roque and followed the Brazilian coast to latitude 10° S., or thereabouts, far enough to begin to recognize its southwesterly trend.[1]

Affairs now became curiously complicated. King Emanuel of Portugal intrusted to Pedro Alvarez de Cabral the command of a fleet for Hindustan, to follow up the work of Gama and establish a Portuguese centre of trade on the Malabar coast. This fleet of thirteen vessels, carrying about 1,200 men, sailed from Lisbon March 9, 1500. After passing the Cape Verde islands, March 22, for some reason not clearly known, whether driven by stormy weather or seeking to avoid the calms that were apt to be troublesome on the Guinea coast, Cabral took a somewhat more westerly course than he realized, and on April 22, after a weary progress averaging less than 60 miles per day, he found himself on the coast of Brazil not far beyond the limit reached by Lepe. It was easy enough thus to

Cabral crosses the Atlantic accidentally.

[1] From June, 1499, to April, 1500, Pero Alonso Niño and Cristoval Guerra made a voyage to the Pearl Coast and acquired much wealth, but as it contributed nothing to the progress of discovery I have not included it in my list.

The voyage of Rodrigo de Bastidas, with La Cosa for pilot, from October, 1500, to September, 1502, was also in its main intent a voyage for pearls and gold, but it completed the discovery of the northern coast of what we now know to be South America, from Cape de la Vela to Puerto Bello on the isthmus of Darien.

cross the ocean unintentionally, for in that latitude the Brazilian coast lies only ten degrees west of the meridian of the Cape Verde islands, and the southern equatorial current, unknown to Cabral, sets strongly toward the very spot whither he was driven. Approaching it in such a way Cabral felt sure that this coast must fall to the east of the papal meridian. Accordingly on May day, at Porto Seguro in latitude 16° 30′ S., he took formal possession of the country for Portugal, and sent Gaspar de Lemos in one of his ships back to Lisbon with the news.[1] On May 22 Cabral weighed anchor and stood for the Cape of Good Hope. As the fleet passed that famous headland the angry Genius of the Cape at last wreaked his vengeance upon the audacious captain who had dared to reveal his secret. In a frightful typhoon four ships were sunk, and in one of them the gallant Bartholomew Dias found a watery grave.

Cabral called the land he had found Vera Cruz, a name which presently became Santa Cruz; but when Lemos arrived in Lisbon with the news he had with him some gorgeous paroquets, and among the earliest names on old maps of the Brazilian coast we find "Land of Paroquets" and "Land of the Holy Cross." The land lay obviously so far to the east that Spain could not deny that at last there was something for Portugal out

[1] See Gandavo, *Historia da provincia Santa Cruz a vulgarmente chamamos Brazil*, Lisbon, 1576, cap. i. ; Riccioli, *Geographia et Hydrographia*, Venice, 1671, lib. iii. cap. 22 ; Barros, *Asia*, dec. i. lib. v. cap. 2 ; Macedo, *Noções de Corographia do Brasil*, Rio de Janeiro, 1873 ; Machado, *Memoria sobre o descobrimento do Brasil*, Rio de Janeiro, 1855.

in the "ocean sea." Much interest was felt at
Lisbon. King Emanuel began to prepare an ex-

Vespucius passes into the service of Portugal. pedition for exploring this new coast, and wished to secure the services of some eminent pilot and cosmographer familiar with the western waters. Overtures were made to Americus, a fact which proves that he had already won a high reputation. The overtures were accepted, for what reason we do not know, and soon after his return from the voyage with Ojeda, probably in the autumn of 1500, Americus passed from the service of Spain into that of Portugal.

The remark was made long ago by Dr. Robertson, that if Columbus had never lived, and the

America would have been discovered without Columbus. chain of causes and effects at work independently of him had remained unchanged, the discovery of America would not long have been postponed.[1] It would have been discovered by accident on April 22, 1500, the day when Cabral first saw the coast of Brazil. All other navigators to the western shores of the Atlantic since 1492 were successors of Columbus; not so Cabral. In the line of causal sequence he was the successor of Gama and Dias, of Lançarote and Gil Eannes, and the freak of wind and wave that carried him to Porto Seguro had no connection with the scientific triumph of the great Genoese.

This adventure of Cabral's had interesting consequences. It set in motion the train of events

---

[1] Robertson, *History of America*, book ii. Harrisse makes a similar remark in the preface to his *Christophe Colomb*.

which ended after some years in placing the name
"America" upon the map. On May 14, 1501,
Vespucius, who was evidently principal pilot and
guiding spirit in this voyage under unknown

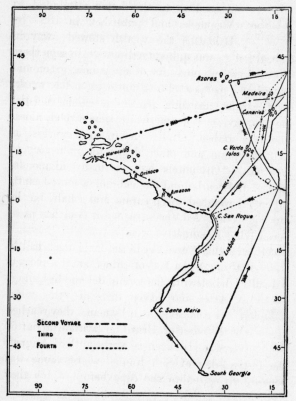

Second, Third, and Fourth Voyages of Vespucius.

skies, set sail from Lisbon with three caravels.
It is not quite clear who was chief captain, but M.
Varnhagen has found reasons for believing that

it was a certain Don Nuno Manuel.[1] The first halt was made on the African coast at Cape Verde, the first week in June; and there the explorers met Cabral on his way back from Hindustan.

Vespucius meets Cabral at Cape Verde.

According to the letter attributed to Vespucius and published in 1827 by Baldelli,[2] the wealth stowed away in Cabral's ships was quite startling. "He says there was an immense quantity of cinnamon, green and dry ginger, pepper, cloves, nutmegs, mace, musk, civet, storax, benzoin, porcelain, cassia, mastic, incense, myrrh, red and white sandalwood, aloes, camphor, amber," Indian hemp and cypress, as well as opium and other drugs too numerous to mention. "Of jewels he saw many diamonds, rubies, and pearls, and one ruby of a most beautiful colour weighed seven carats and a half, but he did not see all."[3] Verily, he says, God has prospered King Emanuel.

After leaving Cape Verde the little fleet had to struggle through the belt of calms, amid a perpetual sultry drizzle with fierce thunder and lightning.

On his third voyage Vespucius explores the coast of Brazil,

After sixty-seven days of "the vilest weather ever seen by man" they reached the coast of Brazil in latitude about 5° S., on the evening of the 16th of August, the festival-day of San Roque, whose name was accordingly given to the cape before which they

[1] Varnhagen, *Nouvelles recherches sur les derniers voyages du Navigateur Florentin*, Vienna, 1869, p. 9.

[2] If not itself genuine, it is very likely based on genuine memoranda.

[3] Major, *Prince Henry the Navigator*, p. 412; see the document in Varnhagen, *Amerigo Vespucci*, p. 81.

dropped anchor.   From this point they slowly followed the coast to the southward, stopping now and
then to examine the country.   In some places the
inhabitants were ferocious Indians, who received
them with showers of arrows, but fled in terror
from firearms.[1]   In other places they found the
natives disposed to be friendly, but "wicked and
licentious in their manner of living,
more like the style of the Epicureans <small>and meets with canni-</small>
than that of the Stoics.   All their women <small>bals.</small>
are in common, and they have neither kings . nor

[1] " There were two in the shippe which toke vpon them to
vewe the lande, and learne what spyces and other commodities
might be had therein.   They were appoynted to returne within
the space of fiue daies at the vttermost.   But when eyght dayes
were now paste, they whiche remayned in the shippes heard yet
nothing of theyr returne : wher as in the meane time great mul-
titudes of other people of the same lande resorted to the Sea
syde, but could by no meanes be allured to communicacion.
Yet at the length they broughte certaine women, which shewed
themselues familier towarde the Spaniardes [i. e. Portuguese].
Wherupon they sent forth a young man, beyng very strong and
quicke, at whom as the women wondered, and stode gazing on
him and feling his apparell, there came sodenynly a woman downe
from a mountayne, bringing with her secretely a great stake,
with which she gaue him such a stroke behynde that he fell dead
on the earth.   The other womenne foorthwith toke hym by the
legges, and drewe him to the mountayne, whyle in the mean
tyme the men of the countreye came foorth with bowes and
arrowes, and shot at oure men.   But the [Portuguese] discharge-
ing foure pieces of ordenaunce agaynst them, droue them to
flighte.   The women also which had slayne the yong man, cut
hym in pieces euen in the sight of the [Portuguese], shewing
them the pieces, and rosting them at a greate fyre.   The men
also made certayn tokens, wherby they declared that not past
viii. daies before they had in lyke maner serued other christian
men.   Wherfore ye [Portuguese] hauinge thus sustayned so gre-
uous iniuries vnreuenged, departed with euil wyl." Eden's
Treatise of the Newe India, London, 1553.

temples nor idols. Neither have they commerce or money; but they have strife among them and fight most cruelly and without any order. They also feed on human flesh. I saw one very wicked wretch who boasted, as if it were no small honour to himself, that he had eaten three hundred men. I saw also a certain town, in which I staid about twenty-seven days, where salted human flesh was suspended from the roofs of the houses, even as we suspend the flesh of the wild boar from the beams of the kitchen, after drying and smoking it, or as we hang up strings of sausages. They were astonished to hear that we did not eat our enemies, whose flesh they say is very appetizing, with dainty flavour and wondrous relish." [1] The climate and landscape pleased Americus much better than the people. He marvelled at the temperate and balmy atmosphere, the brilliant plumage of the birds, the enormous trees, and the aromatic herbs, endowed by fancy with such hygienic virtues that the people, as he understood them to say, lived to be a hundred and fifty years old. His thoughts were of Eden, like those of Columbus on the Pearl Coast. If the terrestrial paradise is anywhere to be found on the earth, said Vespucius, it cannot be far from this region.

So much time was given to inspecting the country and its inhabitants that the progress of the ships was slow. It was not until All Saints day, the first of November, that they reached the bay in latitude 13° S., which is

The Bay of All Saints.

[1] See the letter to Medici, in Varnhagen, *Amerigo Vespucci*, p. 19.

still known by the name which they gave it, Bahia
de Todos Santos.[1] On New Year's day, 1502,
they arrived at the noble bay where fifty-four
years later the chief city of Brazil was founded.
They would seem to have mistaken it Change of di-
for the mouth of another huge river, rection near
the mouth of
like some that had already been seen in La Plata.
this strange world; for they called it Rio de Janeiro (river of January).[2] Thence by February 15
they had passed Cape Santa Maria, when they left
the coast and took a southeasterly course out into
the ocean. Americus gives no satisfactory reason
for this change of direction; such points were probably reserved for his book. Perhaps he may have
looked into the mouth of the river La Plata, which
is a bay more than a hundred miles wide; and the
sudden westward trend of the shore may have led
him to suppose that he had reached the end of the
continent. At any rate, he was now in longitude
more than twenty degrees west of the meridian

[1] The misreading of this name, in which the *h* was changed into
d, gave rise to one of the funniest absurdities known to geography. *A Bahia de Todos Santos* became *La Badia de Todos Santos* (Latin, *Abbatia Omnium Sanctorum*); so the *Bay* became an
Abbey, supposed to exist on that barbarous coast ! ! The reader
may see this name, given very distinctly, upon the Ruysch map,
and also (if his eyes are sharp) on the *Tabula Terre Nove.*

Mr. Winsor (*Narr. and Crit. Hist.*, viii. 373) attributes the discovery of the Bahia de Todos Santos to Christovão Jaques in
1503. But that is impossible, for the name occurs in that place
on the Cantino map. Vespucius arrived in Lisbon September 7,
1502; so that I believe we can fix the date of that map at between September 7 and November 19, 1502.

[2] Varnhagen, p. 110; the name is sometimes attributed to Mar-
tino de Sousa, 1531, but that is improbable. See Winsor, *Narr.
and Crit. Hist.*, viii. 390.

of Cape San Roque, and therefore unquestionably out of Portuguese waters.   Clearly there was
no use in going on and discovering lands which
could belong only to Spain.   This may account, I
think, for the change of direction.   New lands
revealed toward the southeast might perhaps come
on the Portuguese side of the line.   Americus was
already somewhat farther south than the Cape of
Good Hope, and nearer the antarctic pole than any
civilized man had ever been before, except Bartholomew Dias.   Possibly he may also have had
some private notion of putting Ptolemy's theory of
antarctic land to the test.   On the part of officers
and crews there seems to have been ready acqui-
escence in the change of course.   It was voted that
for the rest of the voyage Americus should assume
the full responsibility and exercise the chief command; and so, after laying in food and fresh water
enough to last six months, they started for realms
unknown.

The nights grew longer and longer until by
April 3 they covered fifteen hours.   On that day
the astrolabe showed a southern latitude of 52°.   Before night a frightful
storm overtook our navigators, and after
four days of scudding under bare poles, land hove
in sight, but no words of welcome greeted it.   In
that rough sea the danger on such a coast was appalling, all the more so because of the fog and
sleet.   It was the island of South Georgia, in latitude 54° S., and about 1,200 miles east from Tierra
del Fuego.   Captain Cook, who rediscovered it in
January (midsummer), 1775, called it the most

wretched place he had ever seen on the globe. In comparison with this scarped and craggy island, covered down to the water's edge with glaciers, Cook called the savage wastes of Tierra del Fuego balmy and hospitable. Struggling gusts lash the waves into perpetual fury, and at intervals in the blinding snow-flurries, alternated with freezing rains, one catches ominous glimpses of tumbling ice-floes and deadly ledges of rock. For a day and a night while the Portuguese ships were driven along within sight of this dreadful coast, the sailors, with blood half frozen in their veins, prayed to their patron saints and made vows of pilgrimage. As soon as the three ships succeeded in exchanging signals, it was decided to make for home. Vespucius then headed straight N. N. E., through the huge ocean, for Sierra Leone, and the distance of more than 4,000 miles was made — with wonderful accuracy, though Vespucius says nothing about that — in thirty-three days. At Sierra Leone one of the caravels, no longer seaworthy, was abandoned and burned; after a fortnight's rest ashore, the party went on in the other two ships to the Azores, and thence after some further delay to Lisbon, where they arrived on the 7th of September, 1502.

Return to Lisbon, Sept. 7, 1502.

When we remember how only sixty-seven years before this date the dauntless Gil Eannes sailed into the harbour of Lisbon amid deafening plaudits over the proud news that in a coasting voyage he had passed beyond Cape Bojador, there is something positively startling in the progress that had been achieved.

Historical importance of this voyage.

Among all the voyages made during that eventful
period there was none that as a feat of navigation
surpassed this third of Vespucius, and there was
none, except the first of Columbus, that outranked
it in historical importance.   For it was not only a
voyage into the remotest stretches of the Sea of
Darkness, but it was preëminently an incursion
into the antipodal world of the southern hemisphere.   Antarctic cold was now a matter of positive experience, no less than arctic cold.[1]   Still
more remarkable was the change in the aspect of
the starry heavens.   Voyages upon the African
coast had indeed already familiarized Portuguese
sailors with the disappearance of the pole-star below the northern horizon, and some time before
reaching the equator one could see the majestic
Southern Cross.[2]   But in this course from Lisbon
to South Georgia Vespucius sailed over an arc of
93°, or more than one fourth the circumference of
the globe.   Not only the pole-star, but the Great

---

[1] Vespucius might well have said, in the words of the great
Spanish epic : —

> Climas passé, mudé constelaciones,
> Golfos inavegables navigando,
> Estendiendo, Señor, vuestra corona
> Hasta la austral frigida zona.
>
> Ercilla, *Araucana*, xxxvii.

[2] In Ptolemy's time the Southern Cross passed the meridian of
Alexandria at an altitude of 6° 54′ above the horizon ; to-day,
owing to the precession of the equinoxes, it is 3° below the horizon in that place.   See Humboldt, *Examen critique*, tom. iv. p.
321.   The sight of it was familiar to Christian anchorites in
Egypt in the days of St. Athanasius, and to Arab sailors in the
Red Sea in the Middle Ages, whence Dante may have got his
knowledge of it.   It finally passed out of sight at Alexandria
about A. D. 1340.   Cadamosto observed it in 1454 from the river
Gambia.

Bear, the Swan, and the larger part of the constellations visible from Lisbon sank out of sight; Castor and Pollux, Arcturus and the An Antarctic World. Pleiades, were still visible, but in strange places, while over all the sky ahead twinkled unknown stars, the Milky Way changed its shape, and the mysterious Coalsacks seemed to beckon the voyager onward into realms of eternal sleet and frost. Our Florentine navigator was powerfully affected by these sights. The strange coast, too, which he had proved to extend at least as far south as the Cape of Good Hope, arrested his attention in a very different way from the coasts of Honduras and Florida. In these there was nothing to startle one out of the natural belief that they must be parts of Asia, but with the Brazilian shore it was otherwise. A coast of continental extent, beginning so near the meridian of the Cape Verde islands and running southwesterly to latitude 35° S. and perhaps beyond, did not fit into anybody's scheme of things. None of the ancient geographers had alluded to such a coast, unless it might be supposed to be connected with Why Vespucius thought it was a "new world." the Taprobane end of Mela's Antichthones, or with Ptolemy's Terra Incognita far to the east and southeast of Cattigara. In any case it was land unknown to the ancients, and Vespucius was right in saying that he had beheld there things by the thousand which Pliny had never mentioned.[1] It was not strange that he

[1] "Et certe credo quod Plinius noster millesimam partem non attigerit generis psitacorum reliquarumque auium, necnon & animalium que in iisdem regionibus sunt, cum tanta facierum atque colorum diuersitate quod consumate picture artifex Poli-

should call it a NEW WORLD, and in meeting with this phrase, on this first occasion in which it appears in any document with reference to any part of what we now call America, the reader must be careful not to clothe it with the meaning which it wears in our modern eyes. In using the expression "New World" Vespucius was not thinking of the Florida coast which he had visited on a former voyage, nor of the "islands of India" discovered by Columbus, nor even of the Pearl Coast which he had followed after the Admiral in exploring. The expression occurs in his letter to Lorenzo de' Medici, written from Lisbon in March or April, 1503, relating solely to this third voyage. The letter begins as follows: —

"I have formerly written to you at sufficient length [1] about my return from those new His letter to Lorenzo. countries which in the ships and at the expense and command of the most gracious King

cletus in pingendis illis deficeret. Omnes arbores ibi sunt odorate : et singule ex se ginnum vel oleum vel liquorem aliquem emittunt. Quorum proprietates si nobis note essent non dubito quin humanis corporis saluti forent, & certe si paradisus terrestris in aliqua sit terre parte, non longe ab illis regionibus distare existimo." Varnhagen, p. 21. In this charming passage the great sailor, by a slip of the memory, got one of his names wrong. It was not the sculptor Polycletus, but the painter Polygnotus that he really had in mind.

[1] Several allusions in the letter indicate that Vespucius had written to Lorenzo soon after his return, announcing that fact and promising to send him his journal of the voyage. He was unable to fulfil this promise because the King of Portugal kept the journal and Vespucius felt delicate about asking him for it. At last, in the spring of 1503, before starting on another long voyage, our navigator wrote this brief letter to his old friend, giving him "just the main points," though he had not yet recovered his journal.

of Portugal we have sought and found. It is
proper to call them a new world."

Observe that it is only the new countries visited
on this third voyage, the countries from Cape San
Roque southward, that Vespucius thinks it proper
to call a new world, and here is his reason for so
calling them: —

"Since among our ancestors there was no knowledge of them, and to all who hear of the affair it
is most novel. For it transcends the ideas of the
ancients; since most of them say that beyond the
equator to the south there is no continent, but
only the sea which they called Atlantic, and if any
of them asserted the existence of a continent there, •
they found many reasons for refusing to consider
it a habitable country. But this last voyage of
mine has proved that this opinion of theirs was
erroneous and in every way contrary to the facts,
since in those southern regions I have found a continent more thickly inhabited by peoples and animals than our Europe, or Asia, or Africa, and
moreover a climate more temperate and agreeable
than in any other region known to us; as you will
understand below when I write you briefly just the
main points, and [describe] the most remarkable
things that were seen or heard by me in this new
world, — as will appear below." [1]

[1] I give here in parallel columns two of the earliest texts of
this very interesting and important paragraph: —

Latin text of 1504.	Italian version in Venetian dia-lect, Vicenza, 1507.
"Superioribus diebus satis ample tibi scripsi de reditu meo ab novis illis regionibus quas et classe et impensis	"Li passati zorni assai am-plame'te te scrissi de la mia retornata de q̇lli noui paese: iquali & cu' larmata & cu'

This expression "Novus Mundus," thus occurring in a private letter, had a remarkable career.

et mandato istius serenissimi Portugalio Regis perquisivimus & invenimus. Quasque novum mundum appelare licet. Quando apud maiores nostros nulla de ipsis fuerit habita cognitio & audientibus omnibus sit nouissima res. Et enim hec opinionem nostrorum antiquorum excedit: cum illorum maior pars dicat vltra lineam equinotialem et versus meridiem non esse continentem, sed mare tantum quod Atlanticum vocauere et si qui eorum continentem ibi esse affirmauerunt, eam esse terram habitabilem multis rationibus negauerunt. Sed hanc eorum opinionem esse falsam et veritati omnino contrariam, hec mea ultima nauigatio declarauit, cum in partibus illis meridianis continentem invenerim frequentioribus populis & animalibus habitatam quam nostram Europam, seu Asiam, vel Africam, et insuper aerem magis temperatum et amenum quam in quauis alia regione a nobis cognita: prout inferius intelliges vbi succincte tantum rerum capita scribemus, et res digniores annotatione et memoria que a me vel vise vel audite in hoc nouo mundo fuere: vt infra patebit."

lespese & coma'dame'to de q.sto Serenissimo Re de portogallo hauemo cercato & retrouato: i q.li nouo mondo chiamare ne sta licito p. ch' ap.sso de imazori n.ri niuna de q.lli estata hauta cognitio'e: & a tuti q.lli che aldira'no sera nouissime cose: imperoche q.sto la oppinione de li n.ri antiq. excede: co'cio sia che d' q.lli la mazor p.te dica ultra lalinea eq.notiale: & uerso el mezo zorno no' esser co'tinente: Ma el mare solame'te: elqual Atala'tico ha'no chiamato: E si qual che uno de q.lle co'tinente li esser ha'no affirmato: q.lla esser terra habitabile per molte rasione ha'no negato. Ma questa sie oppinione esser falsa & alauerita ogni modo co'traria: Questa mia ultima nauigatione he dechiarato: co' ciosia che in quelle parte meridionale el co'tinente io habia retrouato: de piu frequenti populi & a'i'ali habitata de la n.ra Europa: o uero Asia: o uero Affrica: & ancora laere piu temperato & ameno: che in que banda altra regione de nui cognosciute: come de sotto intenderai: Doue breuamente solamente de la cose icapi scriueamo: & le cose piu degne de annotatio'e & de memoria: le qual da mi: o uero uiste: o uero audite in questo nouo mo'do foreno: como de sotto sera'no manifeste."

Early in June, 1503, about the time when Americus was starting on his fourth voyage, Lorenzo died. By the beginning of 1504, a Latin version of the letter was printed and published, with the title "Mundus Novus." The letter translated into Latin and published by the architect Giocondo. It is a small quarto of only four leaves, with no indication of place or date; but on the verso of the last leaf we are informed that "The interpreter Giocondo translated this letter from the Italian into the Latin language, that all who are versed in the Latin may learn how many wonderful things are being discovered every day, and that the temerity of those who want to probe the Heavens and their Majesty, and to know more than is allowed to know, be confounded; as notwithstanding the long time since the world began to exist, the vastness of the earth and what it contains is still unknown." [1] This rebuke to some of the audacious speculators of the time is quite in the clerical vein, and we are not surprised to learn that "the interpreter Giocondo" [2] was a Dominican friar. He was Giovanni Giocondo, of Verona, the eminent mathematician, the scholar who first edited Vitruvius, and himself an architect famous enough to be intrusted with the building of the dome of St. Peter's during part of the interval between Bramante and Michael Angelo. [3] From

[1] For an account of this and the other early editions of *Mundus Novus*, see Harrisse, *Bibliotheca Americana Vetustissima*, pp. 55–88, and *Additions*, pp. 16–21, 26.

[2] "Iocūdus interpres" becomes, in the hands of the Venetian translator of 1507, "el iocondo interprete," *anglicè* "the jocund interpreter"!!

[3] Symonds, *Renaissance in Italy*, vol. ii. p. 429, vol. iii. p. 91.

1499 to 1507 Giocondo was living in Paris, engaged in building the bridge of Notre Dame, which is still standing.[1] Of all the thousands who pass over it from day to day, how many have ever dreamed of associating it with the naming of America? This Giocondo, who is now positively known to have been the one that translated the letter of Vespucius,[2] was on terms of intimacy with the Medici family at Florence and also with Soderini. There would be nothing strange, therefore, in a manuscript copy of a brief but intensely interesting letter finding its way into his hands from this quarter. I can find no indication that any *printed* Italian text preceded this Latin version, and am disposed to believe that Giocondo made it directly from a manuscript copy of the original letter. The first edition of Giocondo's version was clearly one of those that were published in Paris late in 1503 or early in 1504. At that time Ves-

---

[1] Sauval, *Histoire et recherches des antiquités de Paris*, Paris, 1724, tom. i. p. 230; Tiraboschi, *Letteratura italiana*, Florence, 1809, tom. vi. pp. 128, 203, 1144–1150.

[2] Walter Lud, *Speculum Orbis*, Strasburg, 1507, fol. iii. This little tract, of only four leaves folio, has been of priceless value in clearing up many of the unjust and absurd aspersions against Vespucius. One of the only two copies known to be now in existence was discovered in 1862 by my old and much esteemed friend Henry Stevens, who was the first to point out its importance. After trying in vain to place it in some American library, Mr. Stevens showed it to Mr. Major, and it found a place in that greatest of all treasure-houses for the materials of American history, the British Museum. It is one of the most precious documents in the world. See Stevens, *Historical and Geographical Notes*, p. 35; Avezac, *Martin Waltzemüller*, pp. 60–67; Harrisse, *Bibliotheca Americana Vetustissima*, No. 49. The other copy is in the Imperial library at Vienna.

pucius, on the coast of Brazil, and Columbus, on the coast of Jamaica, were alike contending against the buffets of adverse fortune. People in Europe, except the few persons directly concerned with their enterprises, took little heed of either of these mariners. The learned Giocondo, if interrogated about their doings, would probably have replied that Columbus had arrived at the eastern coast of Asia by sailing westward, and that Vespucius had disclosed the existence of an Inhabited World in the south temperate zone and in a new and untried direction. It surely would not have occurred to Giocondo that the latter achievement came into competition with the former or tended in any way to discredit it.

The little four-leaved tract, "Mundus Novus," turned out to be the great literary success of the day. M. Harrisse has described at least eleven Latin editions probably published in the course of 1504, and by 1506 not less than eight editions of German versions had been issued. Intense curiosity was aroused by this announcement of the existence of a populous land beyond the equator and UNKNOWN (could such a thing be possible?) TO THE ANCIENTS !! One of the early Latin editions calls for especial mention, by reason of its title and its editor. Instead of the ordinary "Mundus Novus" we find, as an equivalent, the significant title "De Ora Antarctica," concerning the Antarctic Coast lately discovered by the King of Portugal. This edition, published at Strasburg in 1505, was edited by "Master Ringmann Philesius," a somewhat pale

Great interest felt in "Mundus Novus."

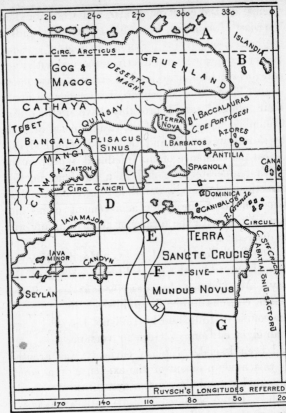

Universalior Cogniti
Johann Ruysch's Map of the World, published August

[1] A reduction of a part of the original map, in Ruysch's conical projection, may be seen in Winsor, *Narr. and Crit. Hist.*, iv. 8. As that projection would be puzzling to most readers, I have reduced it to Mercator's. An English translation of the various legends upon the map is here subjoined: —

A. "Here the ship's compass loses its property, and no vessel with iron on board is able to get away."

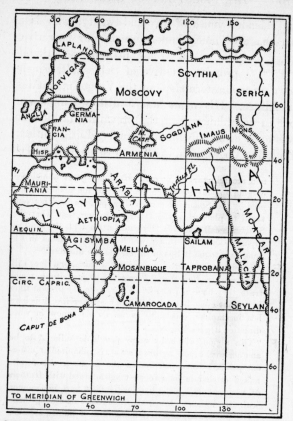

Orbis Tabula.
13, 1508, reduced to Mercator's projection.[1]

B. "This island was entirely burnt in 1456." [See above, vol.
i. p. 242.]

C. "The ships of Ferdinand, king of Spain, have come as far
as here." [See above, p. 80.]

D. "Marco Polo says that 1,400 miles eastward from the
port of Zaiton there is a very large island called Cipango,
whose inhabitants are idolaters, and have their own king,

and slender youth of two-and-twenty, who is a
personage of much importance in our narrative.

Matthias
Ringmann. He was a young man of remarkable
promise, a native of Schlestadt, a little
town on the eastern slope of the Vosges mountains
in Alsace. His name was Matthias Ringmann,
but in accordance with the prevailing fashion he
was more commonly known by a dog-Latin epithet,
Philesius Vogesigena, in allusion to his birth-place.

and are tributary to no one. Here is a great abundance
of gold and all sorts of gems. But as the islands discovered by the Spaniards occupy this spot, we have not ventured to place this island here, thinking that what the
Spaniards call Spagnola [Hispaniola, Hayti] is the same as
Cipango, since the things which are described as in Cipango are found in Spagnola, besides the idolatry."

E. "Spanish sailors have come as far as here, and they call
this country a New World because of its magnitude, for in
truth they have not seen it all nor up to the present time
have they gone beyond this point. Wherefore it is here
left incomplete, especially as we do not know in what
direction it goes."

F. "This region, which by many people is believed to be
another world (*alter terrarum orbis*), is inhabited at different points by men and women who go about either quite
naked or clad in interwoven twigs adorned with feathers
of various hues. They live for the most part in common,
with no religion, no king; they carry on wars among themselves perpetually and devour the flesh of human captives.
They enjoy a wholesome climate, however, and live to be
more than 140 years old. They are seldom sick, and then
are cured merely by the roots of herbs. There are lions
here, and serpents, and other horrid wild beasts. There
are mountains and rivers, and there is the greatest abundance of gold and pearls. The Portuguese have brought
from here brazil-wood and quassia."

G. "Portuguese mariners have examined this part of this
country, and have gone as far as the 50th degree of south
latitude without reaching its southern extremity."

He acquired an early reputation by his graceful Latin verses, which sparkled with wit and could sting if the occasion required it. In 1504 Ringmann was in Paris, studying at the college of Cardinal Lemoine, and there he seems to have become acquainted with Fra Giocondo and with the letter of Vespucius, a new edition of which he presently brought out at Strasburg. Thus in its zigzag career the Italian letter sent by its writer from Lisbon to Florence was first turned into Latin and printed at Paris, with its phrase "New World" lifted up from the text and turned into a catching title, by the friar Giocondo, and thereupon a friend of this accomplished friar sent it into Alsace, and into a neighbourhood where the affair was soon to enter into a new stage of development.

We shall the better understand that further stage if we pause to illustrate, by means of two or three early maps, just what the phrase "New World" meant to the men who first used it. A glance at my sketch of Martin Behaim's globe [1] will assure the reader that in the old scheme of things there was no place for such a coast as that which Americus had lately explored. Such a coast would start to the east of Behaim's 330th meridian, a little below the equator, and would run at least as far south as the southern extremity of Behaim's island of "Candyn." Nobody had ever dreamed of inhabited land in such a place. What could it be? What could be said of its relations to Asia? Two contrasted opinions are revealed by

What did the phrase " New World " originally mean ?

Oceanic and continental theories.

[1] See above, vol. i. p. 422.

the old maps. As in the days of Ptolemy and
Mela, we again see a dry theory confronted by a
wet theory. Some supposed the "Land of the
Holy Cross" to be a southeasterly projection from
the vast continental mass of Asia; others conceived
it as an island of quasi-continental dimensions lying
to the southeast of Asia, somewhat in the position
actually occupied by Australia. This theory is
most vividly presented on the map of the world by
Ruysch's map, Johann Ruysch, in the edition of Ptol-
1508. emy published at Rome in 1508. This
is the earliest *published* map that shows any parts
of America, and it is the first such map that was
engraved, except perhaps the *Tabula Terre Nove*.
It exhibits a study of many and various sources of
information, and is a very interesting sketch of the
earth's surface as conceived at that time by a truly
learned geographer. In the eastern half of his
map Ruysch is on a pretty firm ground of knowledge as far east as the Ganges. The relative
position of Sailam (Ceylon) is indicated with a fair
approach to correctness. Taprobana (Ptolemy's
Ceylon) has now become a different island, apparently Sumatra; and both this island and Malacca
are carried more than a thousand miles too far to
the south, probably from associations with Ptolemy's Cattigara land. Curiously enough, Ceylon
(Seylan) reappears in latitude 40° S. as the very
tip end of Asia. Coming now to the western half
of the map, we find Sumatra reappearing as "Iava
Minor," and Java itself as "Iava Major" wildly
out of place. Ciamba (Cochin China), Mangi and
Cathay (southern and northern China) are given,

after Marco Polo, with tolerable correctness; but Bangala (Bengal) is mixed up with them on the coast of the Plisacus Sinus (Yellow Sea). Gog and Magog, from the Catalan map of 1375, are separated only by a great desert from Greenland, which is depicted with striking correctness in its relations to Gunnbjörn's Skerries (at B) and Iceland, as well as to Terra Nova (probably Labrador) and I. Baccalauras (Newfoundland). The voyages of the Cortereals are recognized in the name *C. de Portogesi*. In rather startling proximity comes the Barbadoes. The island which terminates with the scroll C probably represents the Florida of the Cantino map, with which this of Ruysch is demonstrably connected by the droll blunder "Abatia ōniū sāctorū" on the Brazilian coast. There is no mistaking Spagnola (Hayti), which Ruysch is still inclined (in legend D) to identify with Cipango. The fabulous Antilia is in the same longitude as upon Behaim's globe. If now, contrasting Ruysch with Behaim, we observe the emergence of the "Land of the Holy Cross, or New World" from the Atlantic ocean, in place of the fabulous St. Brandan's isle, we cannot fail to see in a moment what was the most huge and startling feature that had been added to the map of the world during the interval between 1492 and 1507. And this emergence of land from an unknown deep was due chiefly to the third voyage of Vespucius, for the short extent of Pearl Coast explored by Columbus in 1498 was not enough to impress men's minds with the idea of a great continent detached from Asia.

So far as "Mundus Novus" is concerned, I have called Ruysch's map an exponent of the wet or oceanic theory. In its northern portion, however, where Greenland and Labrador are joined to China, we have the continental or dry style of theorizing, very much

The Lenox globe, cir. 1510.

Western half of the Lenox globe, cir. 1510.

after the fashion of Claudius Ptolemy. For an extreme illustration of the oceanic style of interpretation we must look to the Lenox globe, which was discovered in Paris about forty years ago, and afterward found its way into the library of Mr. James Lenox, of New York. This is a copper globe, about five inches in diameter, made in two sections which accurately fit together, making a spherical box; the line of junction forms the equator. The maker's name is unknown, but it is generally agreed that it must have been made in 1510 or early in 1511.[1] It is one of the earliest records of a reaction against the theory that it would be possible to walk westward from Cuba to Spain dry-shod. Here the new discoveries are all placed in the ocean at a good distance from the continent of Asia, and all except South America are islands. The land discovered by the Cabots appears, without a name, just below the Arctic circle, with a small vessel approaching it on the east. Just above the fortieth parallel a big sea monster is sturdily swimming toward Portugal. The sixtieth meridian west from Lisbon cuts through Isabel (Cuba) and Hayti, which are placed too far north, as on most of the early maps. If we compare the position of these islands here with the imaginary Antilia on Ruysch's map, we shall have no difficulty in understanding how they came to be called Antilles. A voyage of about 1,000 miles westward, from Isabel, on this Lenox globe, brings us to Zipangri (Japan), which occupies the position actually belonging to Lower California. Immediately southeast of Japan begins a vast island or quasi-continent, with the name "Terra do Brazil" at its northwestern extremity. The general name of this

---

[1] There is a description of the Lenox globe by Dr. De Costa, in *Magazine of American History*, September, 1879, vol. iii. pp. 529–540.

whole portion of the earth is "Mundus Novus" or
"Terra Sanctæ Crucis." The purely hypothetical
character of the western coast-line is confessed by
the dots. The maker knew nothing of the existence of the Pacific ocean and nothing of South
America except the northern and eastern coasts;
he had no means of proving that it did not extend
as solid land all the way to Asia; but his general
adherence to the wet theory, i. e. his general disposition to imagine water rather than land in the
unknown regions, led him to give it a western
boundary. He would probably have called it a
vast island in the Atlantic ocean. Observe that
the eastern coast seems to be known as far as latitude 50° S. and beyond, and a notable eastward
twist at the extremity seems intended to include
the ice-bound coast where Vespucius turned back
in 1502.

The Ruysch map and the Lenox globe illustrate
sufficiently the various views of those who were inclined to imagine the region we call South America
as separated from Asia by water. In the globe
we have an extreme instance of oceanic theory, in
Ruysch a kind of compromise. Now for an instance of the opposite or continental theory we
cannot do better than cite a very remarkable globe,
made, indeed, a quarter of a century later than
Ringmann's edition of the "Mundus Novus," but
retaining the earlier views in spite of more recent
discoveries. This globe was made in
The globe of
Orontius Fi-   1531, by Oronce Fine, better known as
næus, 1531.   Orontius Finæus, a native of Dauphiny,
professor of mathematics in the Collège Royal de

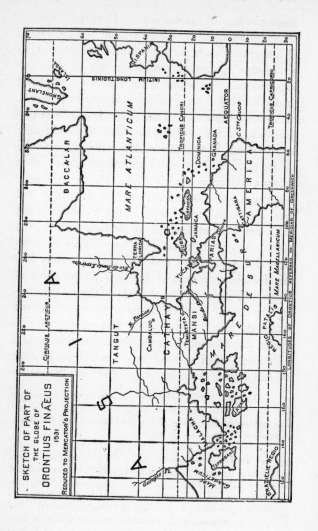

SKETCH OF PART OF
THE GLOBE OF
ORONTIUS FINÆUS
1531
REDUCED TO MERCATOR'S PROJECTION

France. In his mathematics Orontius, though clever, was decidedly unsound;[1] but his knowledge of geography was extensive and minute. One of the chief points of interest in his globe is the conservatism with which it presents a geographical theory derived from Ptolemy and dovetails into it the new discoveries.[2] This makes it excellent testimony to the views of the continentalists, if I may so call them, in the time of Ruysch's map and the Lenox globe. The reader must bear in mind that before Orontius made his globe, Mexico had been discovered and conquered, the Pacific ocean had been discovered and crossed, the Peruvian coast had been explored as far as latitude 10° S., the North American coast had been followed from Labrador to Florida, and Portuguese sailors had found their way around Malacca to the coast of China. Yet so far was Orontius from assimilating the unwieldy mass of facts so rapidly thrust before the mind, that we find him unable to surrender the preconceived theory — common to him with many other geographers — which made what we call South America a huge peninsula jutting

[1] He believed that he had discovered how to square the circle and trisect angles, "ce qui est un peu scandaleux de la part d'un professeur du Collège Royal de France," says Delambre, *Astronomie du Moyen Age*, p. 400.

[2] A double-hearted map representing this globe, with northern and southern hemispheres each on a polar projection, was published in Grynæus, *Novus Orbis*, Paris, 1531. It is reproduced by Henry Stevens, in his *Historical and Geographical Notes*, London, 1869. Stevens also gives a reduction of it to Mercator's projection, after which I have made my simplified sketch. For the sake of clearness I have omitted many details which have nothing whatever to do with the purpose for which it is here cited.

out southeasterly from Asia. This, I say, was the dry or Ptolemaic way of conceiving the position of "Mundus Novus," as Ruysch's was the wet or Mela-like way of conceiving it.

Starting now from the prime meridian and from the top of the map, we may observe that Orontius has a fairly good idea of the relations between Greenland and Baccalar (Labrador-Newfoundland). Florida and the northern part of the gulf of Mexico are quite well depicted. Observe the positions of the Rio de Santo Espiritu (the Mississippi), the R. Panuco, and the Rio de Alvarado, as well as of Temisteta (the city of Mexico); they are given with a fair approach to correctness. But observe also that these places are supposed to be in China, and there is Cambaluc (Peking) about 1,000 miles distant from the city of Mexico, slightly to west of north! As for Parias (i. e. Lariab), which the early maps sometimes correctly place by the river Panuco, but which is oftener confounded with Paria and placed near the island of Grenada, the worthy Orontius makes a compromise, and it stands here for what we call Central America. And now we come to the most instructive feature of the map. The Mexican peninsula being represented as part of Asia, the "Mundus Novus," here called AMERICA, is represented as a further offshoot from Asia. But this is not all. In the theory of Orontius America is evidently a part of the Terra Incognita by which Ptolemy imagined Asia to be joined to Africa, enclosing the Indian ocean. This is proved by

The name Cattigara shows that " America " was supposed to be part of Ptolemy's Terra Incognita in the southern hemisphere.

the position of the name CATTIGARA, which occurs
in the same latitude at the easternmost verge of
Ptolemy's world; and it is further illustrated by
the bits of antarctic continent labelled "Regio
Patalis" and "Brazielie Regio" (!) peeping up
from the lower border. The "Mare Magellanicum," or Pacific ocean, was to the mind of Orontius only a huge gulf in a landlocked Indian ocean!
This notion of an antarctic continent coming well
up into the southern temperate zone may be seen
upon many maps, and it survived into the seventeenth century.[1] It was probably a reminiscence
of both Ptolemy and Mela, of Ptolemy's Terra
Incognita and Mela's Antichthon or Opposite-
Earth. Mela's idea that Taprobane, or some such
point eastward in Asia, formed an entrance to this
antipodal world[2] was very nearly in harmony with
the suggestion, upon Ptolemy's map, that one might
go thither from Cattigara.[3] In this southern
world, according to Mela's doctrine of the zones,
the course of things was quite contrary to that with
which we are familiar. Shadows fell to the south,

---

[1] See for example the maps of Agnese, 1536, and Gastaldi,
1548, below, pp. 496, 497. On the great influence of Ptolemy and
Mela in the sixteenth century, there are some good remarks in
Thomassy, *Les Papes géographes et la cartographie du Vatican*,
Paris, 1852.

[2] See above, vol. i. p. 308.

[3] Orontius was not alone in identifying the New World with
Ptolemy's Cattigara land. The name recurs upon old maps, as
e. g. the French mappemonde of about 1540, now in the British
Museum. It is given in Winsor, *Narr. and Crit. Hist.*, viii. 389.
In this map, made after the discovery of Peru had had time to
take effect, the name Cattigara is simply pushed southward into
Chilian territory.

it was summer in December and winter in June, and the cold increased as you went southward. Mela had even heard that somewhere out in "India," on the way toward this mysterious region, the Greater and Lesser Bears disappeared from the sky.[1] In the Middle Ages there was more or less discussion as to the possible existence of such an antipodal world as Mela had described; and among the clergy there was a strong disposition to condemn the theory on the ground that it implied the existence of a race of men cut off (by an impassable torrid zone) from the preaching of the gospel. The notion of this fiery zone was irretrievably damaged when the Portuguese circumnavigated Africa; it was finally demolished by the third voyage of Vespucius. Many things seen upon that voyage must have recalled Mela's antipodal world with startling vividness. It is true that the characteristics of the southern temperate zone had been to some extent observed in Africa. But to encounter them in a still greater degree and in the western ocean on the way to Asia, upon the coast of a vast country which no one could call by name, was quite another affair. That it did not fail to suggest Ptolemy's Terra Incognita is proved by the position of Cattigara and the general conception of the Indian ocean upon the globe of Orontius; and for those who preferred Mela's wet theory it was fair to suppose

Mela's antipodal world.

[1] *De Situ Orbis*, lib. iii. cap. 7; probably a misunderstanding of the very different statement reported by Strabo (ii. 1, § 19), that in the southern part of India the Greater and Lesser Bears are seen to set.

that the "Mundus Novus" as given upon Ruysch's map was the entrance to that geographer's antipodal world. From a passage interpolated in the Latin text of the Nuremberg Chronicle (1493) we learn that this supposed antipodal world in the southern hemisphere was sometimes called "Quarta Pars."[1] Europe, Asia, and Africa were the three parts of the earth, and so this opposite region, hitherto unknown, but mentioned by Mela and indicated by Ptolemy, was the Fourth Part. We can now begin to understand the intense and wildly absorbing interest with which people read the brief story of the third voyage of Vespucius,[2] and we can see

It was sometimes called "Quarta Pars."

---

[1] " Extra tres ptes orb: qrta ē ps trāsocceanū īteriore ī meridie q sol' arderibˢ nob' incognita ē: ī cuiˢ finibˢ antipodes fabulose habitare dicuntur." Harrisse, *Bibliotheca Americana Vetustissima*, p. 40.

[2] When we remember how much theological discussion there had been with regard to an antipodal world beyond the equator, we can appreciate the startling effect of the simple right-angled triangle with which Americus illustrated the statement that he had sailed over an arc of 90° from Lisbon to a point where the zenith corresponded to Lisbon's horizon: — " Igitur ut dixi ab Olysippo, unde digressi sumus, quod ab linea equinoctiali distat gradibus trigintanouem semis nauigavimus vltra lineam equinoctialem per quinquaginta gradus qui simul juncti efficiunt gradus circiter nonaginta, que summa eam quartam partem obteniat summi circuli, secundum veram mensure rationem ab antiquis nobis traditam, manifestum est nos nauigasse quartam mundi partem. Et hac ratione nos Olysippum habitantes citra lineam equinoctialem gradu trigesimo nono semis in latitudine septentrionali sumus ad illos qui gradu quingentesimo habitant vltra eandem lineam in meridionali latitudine angulariter gradus quinque in linea transuersali : et vt clarius intelligas : Perpendicularis linea que dum recti stamus a puncto celi imminente vertici nostro dependet in caput nostrum : illis ᾱependet in datus [*read* latus] vel in costas. Quo fit vt nos simus in linea recta : ipsi vero in

that in the nature of that interest there was nothing
calculated to bring it into comparison with the
work of Columbus. The two navigators were not
regarded as rivals in doing the same thing, but as
men who had done two very different things; and
to give credit to the one was by no means equivalent to withholding credit from the other.

The last point which we are called upon to observe in the Orontius globe is the occurrence of the
name AMERICA in place of the *Mundus* Successive
Novus of the Ruysch map and the steps in the
naming of
Lenox globe. Thus in about a quarter America.
of a century the first stage in the development
of the naming of America had been completed.
That stage consisted of five distinct steps: 1.
Americus called the regions visited by him beyond

linea transuersa, et species fiat trianguli orthogoni, cujus vicem
linee tenemus cathete ipsi autem basis et hipotenusa a nostro
ad illorum pretenditur verticem : vt in figura patet.

Mundus Novus, 1504, apud Varnhagen, p. 24. The Venetian
version introduces the above paragraph with the heading,—
" Forma dela quarta parte de la terra retrouata."

the equator a " new world " because they were unknown to the ancients; 2. Giocondo made this
striking phrase *Mundus Novus* into a title for his
translation of the letter, which he published at
Paris while the writer was absent from Europe
and probably without his knowledge;[1] 3. the
name Mundus Novus got placed upon several maps
as an equivalent for Terra Sanctæ Crucis, or what
we call Brazil; 4. the suggestion was made that
Mundus Novus was the Fourth Part of the earth,
and might properly be named America, after its
discoverer; 5. the name America thus got placed
upon several maps as an equivalent for what we
call Brazil, and sometimes came to stand alone as
an equivalent for what we call South America,
but still signified ONLY A PART OF THE DRY LAND
BEYOND THE ATLANTIC TO WHICH COLUMBUS HAD
LED THE WAY.   We have described the first three
of these steps, and it is now time to say something
about the fourth and fifth.

René II., de Vaudemont, reigning Duke of Lorraine, and titular King of Sicily and Jerusalem —
the "blue-eyed gentle René" who with the aid of
stout Swiss halberds overthrew Charles the Bold
at Nancy in 1477 — was an enthusiastic
patron of literature and the arts, and at
his little town of Saint-Dié, nestling in one of
those quiet valleys in the Vosges mountains which
the beautiful tales of Erckmann-Chatrian have in-

René II. of
Lorraine.

---

[1] Since Vespucius was so careful to withhold his book from the
press until he could have leisure to revise it, I am inclined to believe that if he had known what Giocondo was doing he would
not have been pleased.

vested with imperishable charm, there was a college.
The town had grown up about a Benedictine monastery founded in the seventh century by St. Deodatus, bishop of Nevers. Toward the end of the
tenth century this monastery was secularized and
its government placed in the hands of a collegiate
chapter of canons under the presidency of a mitred
prelate whose title was Grand Provost. The
chapter was feudal lord of the neigh- The town of
bouring demesnes, and thus as the pop- Saint-Dié.
ulation increased under its mild rule there grew up
the small town in whose name *Deodatus* suffered
contraction into *Dié*.[1] It is now a place of some
8,000 inhabitants, the seat of a bishopric, and
noted for its grain and cattle markets, its fine linen
fabrics, and its note-paper. From the lofty peaks
that tower above the town you can almost catch
sight of Speyer where Protestantism first took its
name, while quite within the range of vision come
Strasburg, associated with the invention of printing, Freiburg with that of gunpowder, and Vau-
couleurs in the native country of the Maid of Orleans. The college of Saint-Dié was curiously
associated with the discovery of America, for it
was there that toward 1410 the Cardinal Pierre
d'Ailly wrote his "Imago Mundi," the book which
so powerfully influenced the thoughts of Columbus.
At the end of that century there were several eminent men among the canons, as Pierre de Blarru,
author of the local heroic poem the Walter Lud.
"Nancéide," Jean Basin de Sendacour,
of whom we shall have more to say presently, and

---

[1] Avezac, *Martin Waltzemüller*, p. 12.

Duke René's secretary, Walter Lud. Under the auspices of the latter a printing press was set up at Saint-Dié about the year 1500, and so many learned men came to the college that Pico della Mirandola wondered how such a society could ever have been brought together in so obscure a town. One of the lights of this little society was the brilliant and witty young Ringmann, who returned from Paris in 1505 and accepted a professorship of Latin at Saint-Dié. About the same time an-

Martin Wald-seemüller.

other young man of three-and-twenty or so, named Martin Waldseemüller,[1] a native of Freiburg in the Breisgau, was appointed professor of geography at Saint-Dié, and an intimate friendship sprang up between him and Ringmann. The latter had acquired while at Paris, and probably through his acquaintance with Fra Giocondo, a warm admiration for Vespucius, and published, as we have already seen, in 1505 a Latin version of the letter to Medici, under the title "De Ora Antarctica."

Now Vespucius wrote his second epistle, the one to Soderini giving a brief account of his four voyages, at Lisbon, September 4, 1504, and Soderini

French version of the letter of Americus to Soderini.

had a certified MS. copy of it made February 10, 1505.[2] From that magistrate's hands it afterward passed into those of the publisher Pacini, for whom it was printed at Florence before July 9, 1506.

---

[1] The family name seems to have been Waltzemüller, but he always preferred to write it Waldseemüller. He was more commonly known by his literary name Hylacomylus.

[2] Varnhagen. *Amerigo Vespucci*, p. 30.

From this Italian original, of which I have mentioned five copies as still existing, somebody made a French version of which no copy is now to be found. Walter Lud tells us that a copy of this French version was obtained directly from Portugal for the little group of scholars at Saint-Dié. This copy could not have come from Vespucius himself, who before February 10, 1505, had left Portugal forever, and on the 5th of that month was making a friendly visit to Columbus at Seville. There is nothing to indicate the existence of any personal relations or acquaintanceship between Vespucius and any of the people at Saint-Dié.

The French version of the letter to Soderini arrived at Saint-Dié just as Lud and Ringmann and Waldseemüller had matured their plans for a new edition of Ptolemy, revised and amended so as to include the results of recent discovery. The strong interest felt in geographical studies during the latter half of the fifteenth century was shown in the publication of six Latin editions of Ptolemy between 1472 and 1490.[1] Before 1506 the rapid progress of discovery had made all these editions antiquated, and our friends at Saint-Dié proposed to issue one that should quite throw into the shade all that had gone before.[2] Walter Lud, who was blessed with a long purse, undertook to defray the expenses; Wald-

The proposed new edition of Ptolemy.

[1] At Bologna, 1472; Vicenza, 1475; Rome, 1478 and 1490; Ulm, 1482 and 1486; all except that of Vicenza provided with engraved maps. Avezac, *Martin Waltzemüller*, p. 23.

[2] Just at the same time another little group of scholars at Vienna were similarly at work on a new edition of Pomponius Mela.

seemüller superintended the scientific part of the
work and Ringmann the philological part, for the
sake of which he made a journey to Italy and obtained from a nephew of the great Pico della Mirandola an important manuscript of the Greek
text. Duke René, who was much interested in the
scheme, gathered rare data from various quarters
and seems to have paid for the engraving of Waldseemüller's map entitled *Tabula Terre Nove*,
The French
version of the
letter turned
into Latin. which was to accompany the new edition. Early in 1507 Waldseemüller
had finished a small treatise intended as
an introduction to the more elaborate work which
he was embodying in the edition of Ptolemy, and
it was decided to print this treatise at once on the
college press. Just in the nick of time Duke
René handed over to the professors the letter of
Vespucius in its French version, which he had
lately obtained from Portugal. It was forthwith
turned into Latin by the worthy canon Jean Basin
de Sendacour, who improved the situation by ad-
dressing his version to his enlightened sovereign
René instead of Soderini, thus bemuddling the
minds of posterity for ever so long by making
Vespucius appear to address the Duke of Lorraine
as his old schoolmate![1]

This Latin version, containing that innocent but

[1] The error has been furthered by the abbreviation *vostra Mag.*
i. e. "your Magnificence," the proper form of address for the
chief magistrate of Florence. It has been misread "your Majesty," a proper form of address for René, who was titular King
of Sicily and Jerusalem. Now that we know how it happened,
it is curious to see Humboldt struggle with the subject in his
Examen critique, tom. iv. pp. 108, 113, 166.

baneful blunder of *Parias* instead of *Lariab*, the source of so much misunderstanding and so much unjust aspersion, was appended to Waldseemüller's little treatise, along with some verses by Ringmann in praise of the great Florentine navigator. The book, entitled "Cosmographie Introductio," was first published at Saint-Dié on the 25th of April, 1507. The only copy of this edition known to exist at present was picked up for a franc on one of the Paris quays by the geographer Jean Baptiste Eyriès; upon his death in 1846, it was bought at auction for 160 francs by Nicolas Yéméniz, of Lyons; upon the death of Yéméniz in 1867, it was bought for 2,000 francs; and it may now be seen in the Lenox Library at New York.[1] Three other editions were published in 1507, concerning which there is no need of entering into particulars.[2] The copy in the library of Harvard University, which I have now before me, was published August 29, 1507, — a little quarto of fifty-two leaves.[3] Mr. Winsor mentions eighteen or twenty copies of it as still in existence, but in 1867 a copy was sold for 2,000 francs, the same price paid that year for the first edition; in 1884 a copy in Munich was held at 3,000 marks, equivalent to 750 dollars.

The Cosmographie Introductio.

In this rare book occurs the first suggestion of the name AMERICA. After having treated of the division of the earth's inhabited surface into three

[1] Winsor, *Narr. and Crit. Hist.*, ii. 166.

[2] They are described in Avezac, *Martin Waltzemüller*, pp. 28–59; Harrisse, *Bibl. Amer. Vetust.*, pp. 89–96; *Additions*, pp. 29–34; and more briefly mentioned in Winsor, *loc. cit.*

[3] It is No. 46 in Harrisse, *Bibl. Amer. Vetust.*

parts — Europe, Asia, and Africa — Waldseemüller
speaks of the discovery of a Fourth Part, and the
passage is of so much historic interest that instead
of a mere transcription the reader will doubtless
prefer to see a photograph of that part of the page
in our Harvard copy.[1]   It is as follows: —

Nunc vero & heç partes sunt latius lustratæ / &
alia quarta pars per Americũ Vespuuium(vt in se
quentibus audietur)inuenta est:quã non video cur
quis iure vetet ab Americo inuentore sagacis inge
nij viro Amerigen quasi Americi terram/siuç Ame
ricam dicendam:cum & Europa & Asia a mulieri
bus sua sortita sint nomina.Eius situ & gentis mo
res exbis binis Americi nauigationibus quç sequũ
tur liquide intelligi datur.

Or, in English: — "But now these parts have
been more extensively explored and another fourth

The sugges-
tion that
Quarta Pars
should be
called *Amer-
ica.*

part has been discovered by Americus
Vespucius (as will appear in what follows): wherefore I do not see what is
rightly to hinder us from calling it
Amerige or America, i. e. the land of Americus,
after its discoverer Americus, a man of sagacious
mind, since both Europe and Asia have got their
names from women.[2]   Its situation and the man-

[1] It is somewhat reduced to fit my narrower crown octavo page.
The book contains another passage in which America is mentioned as part of Mela's antipodal world.

[2] I suppose Waldseemüller was thinking of the passage where
Herodotus (iv. 45) speaks of Europe, Asia, and Libya (i. e. the
little known to him) as all one land, and cannot imagine why
three names, *and women's names especially*, should have been bestowed upon it.   In this connection Herodotus calls Asia the

ners and customs of its people will be clearly understood from the twice two voyages of Americus
which follow."

wife of Prometheus. Hesiod (*Theog.*, 359) makes her a daughter
of Oceanus and Tethys. Geographically the name seems to have
had an especial reference to a small district about the Caÿster
in Lydia (Æschylus, *Prometheus*, 411 ; Pindar, *Olymp.*, vii. 33).
In its most common Greek usage it meant Asia Minor, but by
the time of Herodotus it had already begun to be extended into
the dim vastness of continent behind that peninsula.

Much better known than the mythic personality of the female
Asia is that of Europa, daughter of Agenor (Hegesippus, *Fragm.*,
6), or of Tityos (Pindar, *Pyth.*, iv.), or of Phoroneus (see Preller,
Griechische Mythologie, ii. 37). This greater celebrity is due to
her escapade with Zeus, about which so many verses have been
written. Every reader remembers the exquisite picture in Ten-
nyson's *Palace of Art*. Less generally known are the charming
lines of Reynolds : —

> " We gathered wood flowers, — some blue as the vein
> O'er Hero's eyelid stealing, and some as white,
> In the clustering grass, as rich Europa's hand
> Nested amid the curls on Jupiter's forehead,
> What time he snatched her through the startled waves."
> *Garden of Florence*, London, 1821.

As for this Europa, Herodotus is sure that she never set foot in
Europe ; and as for Libya he knows nothing except that she was
a "native" woman. "However," he wisely concludes, "let us
quit these matters. We shall ourselves continue to use the names
which custom sanctions " (Rawlinson's *Herodotus*, vol. iii. p. 33).
There was really nothing like uniformity of tradition in the
mythical interpretations of these geographical names. Nor were
they always feminine, for in Eustathius (*Comm. in Dionys. Perieg.*,
170) we read of Europus, Asius, and Libyus. Of course all these
explanations got the cart before the horse ; the continents were not
named after the persons, but the persons were eponymous myths
invented to explain the names of the continents. Professor Rawlinson's opinion is highly probable, that both Europe and Asia are
Semitic words which passed to the Greeks from the Phœnicians.
Europe seems to be the Hebrew עֶרֶב, Assyrian *ereb*, Arabic
gharb (whence *Arab*), meaning "the setting" and "the west"
(cf. Latin *occidens*, Italian *ponente*); while *Asia* seems to be a

Such were the wingèd words but for which, as
M. Harrisse reminds us, the western hemisphere
might have come to be known as Atlantis, or Hes-

Why the west-
ern hemi-
sphere was not
named after
Columbus.

perides, or Santa Cruz, or New India, or
perhaps Columbia. There was not
much likelihood, however, of its getting
named after Columbus, because long
before the distinct and separate existence of the
western hemisphere was so much as suspected, the
names had taken root in its soil, and before that
time it would not have occurred to anybody to
name it after Columbus, for the sufficient reason
that it had two good names already, viz. "Asia"
and "the Indies." Separate islands and stretches
of coast received their local names, as Hispaniola
or Veragua, but no one thought of proposing a
new name for the whole western world.

participial form of Hebrew צָא, Assyrian *Azu*, meaning "the
rising" and "the east" (cf. Latin *oriens*, Italian *levante*). In
the days when Phœnicia ruled the wave, the sailors of Tyre and
Sidon probably called the opposite coasts of the Ægean sea
Europe and *Asia = west* and *east*, and the Greeks acquired the
habit of using these names, just as they acquired so many other
words and ideas from the Phœnicians. This seems to me downright common sense. — As for the name *Libya*, it strongly suggests λίψ (*lips*) or λίβα (*liba*), the southwest wind (Aristotle,
Meteorol., ii. 6, 7 ; cf. Theocritus, ix. 11), which the Romans called
Africus (Seneca, *Quæst. Nat.*, v. 16 ; Horat., *Epod.*, xvi. 22), and
which Italian sailors still call *Affrico*. The Greeks called it λίψ
(cf. λείβω) because it brought showers. According to this view
Libya was simply "the southwest country." The meaning of the
name *Africa* is very obscure. A conjecture, as plausible as any,
connects it with Hebrew פְּרָא and supposes it to have been
applied by the settlers of Carthage to the *nomadic* or barbarous
tribes in the neighbourhood (Mövers, *Die Phönizier*, ii. 402).
Originally confined to the region about Carthage, the name Africa
gradually superseded Libya as a name for that continent.

Why, then, it may be asked, did Waldseemüller propose America as a new name for the whole? The reply is, that he did nothing of the sort. We shall never understand what he had in mind until we follow Mr. Freeman's advice and free ourselves from the bondage of the modern map. Let us pursue for a moment the further fortunes of the work in which our friends of Saint-Dié were engaged. Upon the death of Duke René in 1508 the little coterie was broken up. Lud seems in some way to have become dissociated from the enterprise; Ringmann in that year became professor of cosmography at Basel,[1] and his untimely death occurred in 1511. Waldseemüller was thus left comparatively alone. The next edition of the *Cosmographiœ Introductio* was published at Strasburg in 1509, the work upon the Ptolemy was kept up, or resumed, with the aid of two jurists of that city, Jacob Aeszler and Georg Uebelin, and the book was at last published there in 1513. Among the twenty new maps in this folio volume is one to which we have had frequent occasion to refer, the *Tabula Terre Nove*, made for this edition of Ptolemy at the expense of Duke René and under the supervision of Waldseemüller, if not by his own hands, and engraved before 1508.[2] We must therefore regard this map and the text of the *Cosmographiœ Introductio* as expressions of opinion practically contemporaneous and emanating from the

[Sidenote: It was not the western hemisphere that was at first meant by America.]

[Sidenote: The new Ptolemy published at Strasburg, 1513.]

[1] Avezac, *Martin Waltzemüller*, p. 105.

[2] See above p. 77.

same man (or men, i. e. Waldseemüller and Ringmann). Now what do we find on this map? The
Brazilian coast is marked with local names derived
from the third voyage of Vespucius, but instead of
the general name America, or even Mundus Novus,

The inscrip-
tion upon
Waldseemül-
ler's map.

we have simply Terra Incognita; and
over to the left, apparently referring to
the Pearl Coast and perhaps also to
Honduras, we read the inscription: — "This land
with the adjacent islands was discovered by Columbus of Genoa by order of the King of Castile."[1]
The appearance of incompatibility between this
statement and the assertion that Vespucius discovered the Fourth Part has puzzled many learned
geographers.[2] But I venture to think that this incompatibility is only apparent, not real. Suppose
we could resuscitate those bright young men, Waldseemüller and Ringmann, and interrogate them!
I presume they would say: — "Bless you, dear
modern scholars, you know many things that we
did not, but you have clean forgotten some things
that to us were quite obvious. When we let fall
that little suggestion about naming the Fourth
Part after Americus, perhaps we were not so
fiercely in earnest as you seem to think. We were
not born of Hyrcanian tigers, but sometimes enliv-
ened our dry disquisitions with a wholesome laugh,
and so neat a chance for quizzing Europa and the
fair sex was not lost upon us. Seriously, how-

[1] " Hec terra cum adiacentib⁵ insulis inuenta est per Columbū
ianuensem ex mandato Regis Castellæ."

[2] As for instance Humboldt, *Examen critique*, tom. iv. pp. 118–
120; Avezac, *Martin Waltzemüller*, p. 154; Major, *Prince Henry
the Navigator*, p. 386.

ever, what did we do that was inconsistent or un-
fair? Did we not give Columbus the
credit for discovering exactly what he What Ring-
did discover, the Pearl and Honduras
coasts and the adjacent islands? And
did we not say of Americus that he had found the
Fourth Part, or Mundus Novus, *beyond the equator*, concerning which the ancients had no knowledge, but the existence of which was plainly indicated, in their different ways, by Ptolemy and
Mela? But you go on to ask was it not Columbus
that first showed the way to the Indies? To be
sure it was; we never denied it! Again you ask
if the Pearl Coast and the Mundus Novus were not
alike parts of South America. Our answer is that
when we were living on the earth nobody had
framed a conception of the distinct and integral
whole which you now call South America. We
knew that long stretches of strange coast had been
discovered here and there; and some of them interested us for one reason and some for another. It
was doubtless a thing more divine than human for
the Admiral Columbus to sail by the west to Asia
along the circumference of the Œcumene, but he
never supposed that he had thus found a new part
of the earth, nor did we. To sail across the torrid
zone and explore a new antipodal world that formed
no part of the Œcumene was a very different
thing, and it was this deed for which we properly
gave the credit to Americus; for did not the learned
and accurate Master Ruysch testify that voyagers
upon this antarctic coast had beheld the southern
pole more than 50° above the horizon, and yet had

seen no end to that country? We therefore acted according to our best lights, emphasizing, as we admit, that which appealed to us most forcibly. If we could have studied your nineteenth century globes we should have learned to express ourselves differently; but, bless you again, dear modern scholars, may not some of your own expressions run risk of being misunderstood after an equal lapse of time?"

If along with our two editors of Ptolemy we could also call back for a moment from the Undis-

Significant si-
lence of Fer-
dinand Colum-
bus.

covered Country that learned geographer, accomplished scholar, and devoted son, Ferdinand Columbus, and let him hear their explanation, I feel sure that he would promptly and heartily recognize its substantial correctness. Upon the point in question we already have Ferdinand's testimony, clothed in a silence more eloquent than any conceivable words. I have already remarked upon Ferdinand's superb library, of which the remnant of four or five thousand volumes is still preserved, — the Biblioteca Colombina at Seville. It will be remembered that he had a habit of marking and annotating his books in a way that is sometimes quite helpful to the historian. Now the number 1773 of Ferdinand's library is a copy of the *Cosmographiæ Introductio* in the edition published at Strasburg in 1509. His autograph note informs us that he bought it at Venice in July, 1521, for five *sueldos*.[1] As his death occurred in 1539, he had this book in his possession for eighteen years, and during a part

[1] Harrisse, *Christophe Colomb*, tom. ii. p. 370.

of this time he was engaged in preparing the
biography of his father. He was naturally very
sensitive about everything that in any way great
or small concerned his father's fame, and if any
writer happened to make statements in the slightest degree derogatory to his father's importance
or originality, Ferdinand would pause in his
narrative and demolish the offender if it took a
whole chapter to do it.[1] But his book makes no
allusion whatever to Waldseemüller or his suggestion of the name America or his allusion to Vespucius as the discoverer of Quarta Pars. Not so
much as a word had Ferdinand Columbus to say
on this subject! Still more, the book of Waldseemüller did not sleep on the shelf during those
eighteen years. Ferdinand read and annotated it
with fulness and care, but made no comment upon
the passage in question! This silence is absolutely
decisive. Here was the son of Columbus and for
some years the fellow-townsman of Americus at
Seville, the familiar friend of the younger Vespucius who had gone with his uncle on most if not
all his voyages, — can we for a moment suppose
that he did not know all that had been going on
among these people since his boyhood? Of course
he understood what voyages had been made and
where, and interpreted them according to the best

---

[1] See, for example, his refutation of Giustiniani's "thirteen
lies" in *Vita dell' Ammiraglio*, cap. ii.; and his attacks upon
Martin Pinzon and Oviedo, cap. x., xvi., xli. As M. Harrisse observes, "Lorsqu'il rencontre sur son chemin un rival de Christophe Colomb, ou un écrivain dont le récit semble devoir diminuer
l'importance du navigateur génois devant la posterité, il le vili-
pende sans pitié." *Fernand Colomb*, p. 141.

light of an age in which he was one of the fore-most geographers. His annotations show him to have been eminently clear-headed, accurate, and precise. It would be impossible to find a contemporary witness more intelligent or more certain to utter a sharp and ringing protest against any attempt to glorify Americus at the expense of his father. Yet against Waldseemüller's suggestion Ferdinand Columbus uttered no protest. He saw nothing strange in the statement that it was Americus who discovered the Quarta Pars, or in the suggestion that it should bear his name. Under the circumstances there is but one possible explanation of this. It proves that Ferdinand shared Waldseemüller's opinion, and that to the former as to the latter this Fourth Part meant something very different from what we mean when we speak of America or of the New World.[1]

[1] M. Harrisse (in his *Fernand Colomb*, Paris, 1872, pp. 141–145) uses the silence of the *Vita dell' Ammiraglio*, as an argument in support of his crotchet that the book was not written by Ferdinand (see above, vol. i. p. 340). His argument suffers severely from "bondage to the modern map." Referring to Waldseemüller, he says : — "On déclare d'abord que c'est Vespuce, *et non Christophe Colomb* [! ! the italicizing is mine : Waldseemüller says nothing of the sort], qui a découvert le Nouveau Monde ; ensuite on promet de le prouver ' ut in sequentibus audietur,' en publiant la relation de ses quatre voyages ; enfin, pour l'en récompenser, l'auteur propose de donner et donne en effet d'une manière indélébile à ces pays nouveaux le nom d'Amérique." It should be added that M. Harrisse, while calling Waldseemüller's book " ce méchant petit livre," does full justice to the integrity of Vespucius. In the argument just cited the reader will now be able to see that all its force is lost by its failure to seize the historical perspective ; it uses the phrase *Nouveau Monde* in its nineteenth century sense. As regards Ferdinand Columbus, its force is destroyed by the fact that his silence extends to his

What that Fourth Part really meant I believe I have now sufficiently explained. It is again defined for us most clearly and explicitly in the revised edition of Waldseemül- The Ptolemy of 1522. ler's Ptolemy published at Strasburg in 1522, three years after his death. This edition was completed by Lorenz Fries, and is usually known by his name. It uses the three names America, Mundus Novus, and Quarta Pars as synonymous and interchangeable; and in its map corresponding to the *Tabula Terre Nove*, but variously amended, it substitutes America for Terra Incognita about where the name Brazil would come on a modern map; while at the same time in the Venezuelan region it repeats the inscription stating that this coast and the neighbouring islands were discovered by Columbus.

It is not to be supposed that all map-makers at that day took just the same view of this or of any other obscure subject. Some thought Different conceptions of Mundus Novus. the Mundus Novus deserved its name because it was Ptolemy's unknown land beyond Cattigara, as the Orontius globe proves; some because it was of indefinite extent and reminded them of Mela's antipodal world, as we

---

copy of Waldseemüller's book. But indeed Las Casas, as will presently be shown, expressly declares that Ferdinand's book says nothing about the naming of America (*Historia de las Indias*, tom. ii. p. 396). — Among other books belonging to Ferdinand, in which the name America was adopted, or Vespucius mentioned as discoverer of Mundus Novus, were Walter Lud's *Speculum*, the 1518 edition of Pomponius Mela, the works of Johann Schöner, and the *Cosmographicus Liber* of Apianus (Harrisse, *op. cit.* p. 144). There is nothing to show that anything in them disturbed him.

LIBRARY OF
MUSKINGUM COLLEGE
New Concord, Ohio

may gather from Ruysch's map;[1] some simply because it was an enormous mass of land in an unexpected quarter.[2] When carefully placed, with strict reference to its origin, the name Mundus Novus, or its alternative America, is always equivalent to Brazil; but sometimes where the southern continent appears as a great island its position is so commanding as to make it practically the name of that island. This is the case with the earliest known map upon which the name America appears. This map was discovered about thirty years ago in

The map attributed to Leonardo da Vinci, cir. 1514.

Queen Victoria's library at Windsor Castle, in a volume of MS. notes and drawings by Leonardo da Vinci. There is much reason for regarding the map as the work of Leonardo, but this has been doubted.[3]

---

[1] " Terra etiam nova . . . a Vesputio nuper inventa, quam ob sui magnitudinem *Mundum novum* appellant, ultra æquatorem plus 35 gradibus, Vesputii observatione protendi cognita est, et *necdum finis inventus.*" Alberto Pighi Campense in 1520, apud Humboldt, *Examen critique*, tom. iv. p. 145. Compare the inscriptions E and G on Ruysch's map.

[2] " Sic si ad austrum spectes, magna pars terræ nostra tempestate explorata est, aut salte circumnavigata, quam Ptolemæus ut incognitam reliquit : ab Hispanis uero quum in orientem nauigio contendunt, obambulatur & circuitur, ut paulo post disseremus. Quin & in oceano occidentali fere nouus orbis nostris têporibus ab Alberico Vesputio & Christophoro Columbo, multisque aliis insignibus uiris inuentus est, qui non abs re quarta orbis pars nuncupari potest, etiam terra non sit tripartita, sed quadripartita, quum hæ Indianæ insulæ sua magnitudine Europam excedant, presertim ea quâ ab Americo primo inuentore Americam uocat." Sebastian Münster, *Tabulæ cosmographicæ*, apud Grynæus, *Novus Orbis*, Paris, 1832.

[3] The subject is elaborately discussed by Major, " Memoir on a Mappemonde by Leonardo da Vinci, being the earliest Map hitherto known containing the name of America," *Archæologia*,

It represents the oceanic theory in its extreme form and has some points of likeness to the Lenox globe. The northern continent is represented by the islands of Bacalar and Terra Florida, and the

Part of Leonardo da Vinci's map, cir. 1514 — earliest known map with the name "America."

latter name proves the date of the map to be subsequent to Ponce de Leon's discovery on Easter Sunday, 1513. Cipango, here spelled Zipugna, still hovers in the neighbourhood. The western

London, 1866, vol. xl. pp. 1–40. The sketch here given is reduced from Winsor (ii. 126), who takes it from Wieser's *Magalhães-Strasse.*

coast of the southern continent is drawn at random; and the antarctic land, the inevitable reminiscence of Ptolemy and Mela, protrudes as far as the parallel of 60° S.

In 1515 Johann Schöner, professor of mathematics at Nuremberg, made a globe upon which
America is drawn very much as upon Leonardo's map, with an inscription stating that the western coast is unknown; above corresponding to Mexico, is "Parias" in the true position of Vespucius's Lariab, and this is joined to the Florida (with no name) taken from Cantino and ending with a scroll, as in Ruysch, saying that what is beyond is unknown. Leonardo's antarctic land here comes up so as almost to touch America, and it bears the name "Brazilie Regio," reminding us of Orontius.

America on Schöner's first globe;

In 1520 Schöner made a second globe, which is still preserved at Nuremberg. Here the unnamed
Florida has taken the name "Terra de Cuba," though both globes also give the island. "Paria" still denotes Mexico, while "Terra Parius" appears for the true Paria on the Pearl Coast. America is expressly identified with the land discovered by Cabral; the legend between latitudes 10° and 20° S. is "America or Brasilia or Land of Paroquets." The antarctic land has here become "Brasilia Inferior." [1]

and on his second globe.

On the important map made by Baptista Agnese at Venice in 1536, the name America does not appear, but Mundus Novus and Brazil are placed

[1] Sketches of these two Schöner globes are given in Winsor, *Narr. and Crit. Hist.*, ii. 118, 119.

close together and south of the equator.[1]   And on
the map made by Sebastian Münster for
the 1540 Ptolemy, we read, a little below   *Various maps.*
the equator, "Novus Orbis, the Atlantic island
which they call Brazil and America." Below, to
the west of the river La Plata, we read "Die Nüw
Welt."[2] These are some of the exam-   The "New
ples which show that it was an essential   World" was
                                           not the west-
part of the conception of the "New   ern, but the
                                     southern
World," in the minds of the men who   world.
first used the expression, that it was *a world lying
south of the equator*. The opposition between
Old World and New World was not, as now, between the eastern and western hemispheres; the
opposition was between the northern hemisphere
and the southern; and as Columbus had not
crossed the equator in the course of his four voyages, he had never entered or seen what Waldseemüller and geographers generally during the first
half of the sixteenth century called the New
World.

But the course of time and the progress of discovery wrought queer changes in men's conception
of Mundus Novus and in the applica-   Extension of
tion of the name America. It was not   the name
                                       "America"
very difficult for such a euphonious   from Brazil to
                                       South Amer-
name to supplant its unwieldy syno-   ica.
nyms, Land of Paroquets and Land of the Holy
Cross.   Nor did it require much extension for it
to cover the whole southern continent soon after

---

[1] This map is given below, p. 496.

[2] This map, upon which we see also Cattigara, is given below,
pp. 498, 499.

the idea of that continent as an integral whole distinct from other wholes had once been conceived. The names of Paria and the Pearl Coast, Venezuela and Darien have remained upon the map to this day; but Terra Firma, the cumbrous name which covered the four, was easily swallowed up by America. Thus the name of the Florentine navigator came to be synonymous with what we call South America; and this wider meaning became all the more firmly established as its narrower meaning was usurped by the name Brazil. Three centuries before the time of Columbus the red dye-wood called brazil-wood was an article of commerce, under that same name, in Italy and Spain.[1] It was one of the valuable things that were brought from the East, and when the Portuguese found the same dye-wood abundant in those tropical forests that had seemed so beautiful to Vespucius, the name Brazil soon became fastened upon the country[2] and helped to set free the name America from its local associations.

[1] Muratori, *Antichità italiane*, tom. ii. pp. 894–899; Capmany, *Memorias sobre la antigua marina de Barcelona*, tom. ii. pp. 4, 17, 20; Humboldt, *Examen critique*, tom. 216–225. The name of the fabulous island *Brazil* or *Bresylle* in the ocean west of Ireland seems to be a case of accidental resemblance. It is probably the Gaelic name of an island in Irish folk-lore. See Winsor, *Narr. and Crit. Hist.*, i. 50.

[2] The Portuguese historian Barros declares that the substitution of such a name as Brazil for such a name as Holy Cross must have been the work of some demon, for of what account is this miserable wood that dyes cloth red as compared with the blood shed for our eternal salvation! — "Porém como o demonio per o final da Cruz perdeo o dominio que tinha sobre nós, mediante a Päixao de Christo Jesus consummada nella; tanto que daquella terra começou de vir o páo vermelho chamado Brazil, trabalhou

By 1540 South America had been completely circumnavigated, and it was possible to draw an outline map of its coast with a fair approach to accuracy. It was thus beginning to be known as a distinct whole, and the name America had gone far toward taking exclusive possession of it. That continent was by far the most imposing result of discovery in the western waters, and the next step was for its name to spread beyond its natural limits so as to cover adjacent and less known regions.[1] Now by 1540 men were just beginning to grasp the fact that the regions called New Spain, Terra Florida, and Baccalaos were different parts of one continent that was distinct from Asia. There was as yet no steadiness of thought on the subject. The wet theory, as shown in Leonardo da Vinci's map, had long since separated North America from Asia, but only by reducing it to a few islands. The dry theory, as shown in the Orontius globe, made it continental, but only by attaching it to

que este nome ficasse na boca do povo, e que se perdesse o de Sancta Cruz, como que importava mais o nome de hum páo que tinge pannos, que daquelle páo que deo tintura a todolos Sacramentos per que somos salvos, por o sangue de Christo Jesus, que nelle foi derramado," etc. Barros, *Decadas da Asia*, Lisbon, 1778, tom. i. p. 391.

[1] Peter Bienewitz (called Apianus), in his celebrated book published in 1524, clearly distinguishes Cuba, Hispaniola, etc., from America. They are islands lying near America, and their inhabitants have customs and ceremonies like those of the people of America : — "Habet autem America insulas udiacentes [adjacentes] q plurimas vt Parianã Insulam, Isabellam quo Cuba dicitur [sic] Spagnollam . . . Accolæ vero Spagnollæ insulæ loco panis vescuntur serpentibus maximis et radicibus. Ritus et cultus istarum circumiacentium Insularum par est Americæ accolarum cultui." *Cosmographicus Liber*, Landshut, 1524, fol. 69.

Asia. A combination of wet and dry theorizing was needed to bring out the truth. This combination was for a moment realized in 1541 by a man who in such matters was in advance of his age. Gerard Kaufmann, better known by his latinized name Mercator, was a native of East Flanders, born in 1512, the year in which Vespucius died.

Mercator was an able geographer and mathematician. He is now remembered chiefly for the important method of map projection called by his name, and for certain rules of navigation associated therewith and known as "Mercator's sailing." But he should also be remembered as the first person who indicated upon a map the existence of a distinct and integral western hemisphere and called the whole by the name America. Upon the gores for a globe which he made in 1541, Mercator represented the northern continent as distinct from Asia, and arranged the name America in large letters so as to cover both northern and southern continents, putting AME about on what we should call the site of the Great Lakes and RICA just west of the river La Plata.[1] This was a stride, nay a leap beyond what had gone before. We have only to contrast Mercator, 1541, with Agnese, 1536, and with Gastaldi, 1548, to realize what a startling innovation it was.[2] It was some time yet before Mercator's ideas prevailed, but his map enables us to see how the recognition of a

The name "America" first applied to the western hemisphere by Gerard Mercator, 1541.

[1] The sketch is reduced from Winsor, *Narr. and Crit. Hist.*, ii. 177.

[2] These two maps are given below, pp. 496, 497.

AME

BACCALEARUM REGIO

INS CORTEREALIS

ISLAND INS OLIM THYLE

HISPANIA MAJOR CAPTA ANNO 1530

HEPTAPOLIS

CORSO FLORES

GRACIOSA

FAIALO UEL PICO TERCERA S MICHAEB

O S MARIA

BARMUDA SIVE GARCA

ACORES INS

HISPANIA NOVA

ASPRO DEL SANCTO

FLERIDA

GUANAD

PORTUS OF MADERA

INS FORTUNATE NUNC CANARIE

IUCATANA

JOSEPHELLA

JAMAICA

CAMERCANE INSULE

NESPERIDES NUNC INS DE ANTON

TRINITATIS INS

PARIA

PERU NOVA CASTILIE

COSCO

B PABLO

C S CRUCIE

C S AUGUSTINI

RICA

A MULTIS HODIE NOVA INDIA DICTA

MARE PACIFICUM

FRETUM PATHAGONICUM SIVE MAGELLANICUM

Sketch of Gerard Mercator's map, 1541.

western hemisphere emerged and during the latter
half of the sixteenth century became more and
more distinct.[1] As this process went on and the
ideas of the ancient geographers lapsed into oblivion, the old contrast between north and south became superseded by the new contrast
between east and west. Thus the names
America and New World came to
awaken associations of ideas utterly
different from those amid which they originated.
If Waldseemüller had been told that a time would
arrive when such places as Baccalaos and his Cape-
of-the-end-of-April would be said to be in the New
World, he would have asked, in great amazement,
how could places in Asia and wholly within the
bounds of the ancient Œcumene have anything
whatever to do with the Quarta Pars! That time,
however, did arrive, and when it came the name
of America began to look like a standing denial of
the just rights of Columbus. It looked as if at
some time a question had arisen as to whose name
should be given to the western hemisphere, and as
if for some reason Americus was preferred to Columbus. When such a notion had got into men's
heads Americus was sure to be attacked. No
charge is easier to make than that of falsehood.
The sin of lying is common enough, and geography
is not the simplest of subjects. Hence most great
travellers, from Herodotus down, have for one reason or another been ignorantly accused of lying.

*Change of
meaning in the
names "New
World" and
"America."*

---

[1] See John Dee's map, 1580, below, p. 527; but Michael Lok's
map, 1582, shows in this respect a less advanced stage of development than Mercator's. See below, pp. 524, 525.

Never was such an accusation more completely the offspring of ignorance than in the case of Vespucius.

It was that precious blunder of "Parias" for "Lariab" that started the business, and it was aided by a slipshod expression of the Nuremberg professor, Johann Schöner. In a little tract published in 1515, probably as an accompaniment to his globe made in that year, Schöner alludes to "America, a new world and fourth part of the globe, named after its discoverer, Americus Vespucius, a man of sagacious mind, who found it in the year 1497." [1] This confusing the first voyage with the third was not ignorance, but downright carelessness, for inasmuch as on his globes Schöner placed "Parias" in Mexico and identi- Schöner's loose remarks. fied America with Brazil, he knew well enough that it was not in 1497, but in 1501 that Vespucius visited the Fourth Part. Eighteen years afterward Schöner made another bad slip when he said, though here again he knew better, that "Americus appointed a part of Upper India, which he supposed to be an island, to be called by his name." [2] There is nothing in the remark

---

[1] "America siue Amerigen nouus mundus : & quarta orbis pars : dicta ab eius inuêtore Americo Vesputio viro sagacis ingenii : qui eam reperit Anno domini. 1497. In ea sunt homines brutales," etc. Schöner, *Luculentissima quœdã terræ totius descriptio*, Nuremberg, 1515. For an account of this very rare book see Harrisse, *Bibl. Amer. Vetust.*, No. 80.

[2] "Americus Vesputius maritima loca Indiæ superioris ex Hispaniis navigio ad occidentem perlustrans, eam partem quæ superioris Indiæ est, credidit esse Insulam quam a suo nomine vocari instituit." Schöner, *Opusculum geographicum*, Nuremberg, 1533. Inasmuch as Schöner knew the *Cosmographiæ Introductio* he

which implies censure,[1] but it was probably this that led Las Casas, after 1552, to say that Americus had been accused of putting his name on the map, "thus sinfully failing toward the Admiral."

The situation, as misunderstood by Las Casas after 1550.

Las Casas had finally come back from America in 1547, and by 1552 had settled down quietly at Valladolid to work upon his great history. He was vexed at seeing the name America so commonly used,[2] knew that it was Waldseemüller and not Vespucius who "instituit," etc. But he was evidently a man of slovenly speech.

[1] It is commonly spoken of as a "charge" against Vespucius. Harrisse calls it "the first attempt to tarnish the reputation of the Florentine cosmographer" (*Bibl. Amer. Vetust.*, p. 65). Here again comes the fallacy of reading our modern ideas into the old texts. There is nothing whatever in Schöner's context to suggest that he attached any blame to Vespucius or saw any impropriety in the name. Indeed he had himself put it on his globes in 1515 and 1520, and done as much as anybody to give it currency.

[2] The suggestion of Waldseemüller as to the name America seems to have been first adopted in the anonymous *Globus Mundi*, Strasburg, 1509. The name was used by Joachim Watt (called Vadianus) in his letter to Rudolphus Agricola, Vienna, 1515, reprinted in his edition of Mela, Vienna, 1518. I have already alluded to its adoption by Leonardo da Vinci and Schöner and Fries. Peter Bienewitz (called Apianus) put the name America on his map published in 1520 (given in Winsor, ii. 183) and adopted it in his *Cosmographicus Liber*, Landshut, 1524; an abridgment of this book was published by Gemma Frisius at Ingoldstadt, 1529. Heinrich Loritz (called Glareanus) used the name in his *De geographia liber unus*, Basel, 1527; Sebastian Münster gave it further currency in his essay in Grynæus, *Novus Orbis*, Paris, 1532; and so again did Honter in his *Rudimenta Cosmographica*, Zurich, 1542. All these were very popular books and were many times reprinted; being in Latin they reached educated people everywhere, and some of them were translated into Spanish, Italian, German, Bohemian, English, French, etc. Sir Thomas More in his *Utopia* speaks of the voyages of Vespucius as "nowe in printe and abrode in euery mannes handes."

since by that time it had come to cover much ground that belonged especially to Columbus. Indeed there can be no doubt that by 1550 the greater exploit of having sailed west in order to get to the east was somewhat overshadowed by the lesser exploit of having revealed the continental dimensions of a mass of antipodal land unknown to the ancients. Vespucius was more talked about than Columbus. This aroused the generous indignation of Las Casas. A wrong seemed to have been done, and somebody must have been to blame. Las Casas read the Latin version of the letter to Soderini, appended to Waldseemüller's book, and could not imagine why Americus should write such a letter to Duke René or why he should address him as an old friend and schoolmate. But when he came to the place where Vespucius seemed to be speaking of Paria his wrath was kindled. Las Casas quotes the guilty sentence, and exclaims, "Americus tells us that he went to Paria on his first voyage, saying: *And that province is called by the people themselves Parias;* and then he made his second voyage with Ojeda," also to Paria.[1] The clause which I have italicized is the very clause in which the Latin version ignorantly substitutes

Effect upon Las Casas of the blundering substitution of "Parias" for "Lariab."

See Harrisse, *Bibl. Amer. Vetust.*, under the different years; Winsor, *Narr. and Crit. Hist.*, ii. 180–186 ; Varnhagen, *Nouvelles recherches*, pp. 19–24.

[1] "De haber llegado á Paria el Américo en este su primer viaje, él mismo lo confiesa en su primera navegacion, diciendo : *Et provincia ipsa Parias ab ipsis nuncupata est.* Despues hizo tambien con el mismo Hojeda la segunda navegacion," etc. **Las Casas**, *Historia de las Indias*, tom. ii. p. 273.

Parias for the *Lariab* of the original text; and the passage in which Las Casas quotes it is the documentary evidence upon which I am content to rest the statement with which I opened this long discussion, that it was this miserable alteration that made all the trouble. It at once riveted the attention of Las Casas upon the Pearl Coast, in spite of the explicit statement, on the same page and only nine lines above the name "Parias," that it was "under the tropic of Cancer, in latitude 23° N." Las Casas understood Vespucius to say that he had been at Paria in 1497, and found no difficulty in proving that this could not be true. Could it be that Americus intended to usurp honours which he knew to belong to the Admiral? If so, it was a great piece of wickedness, says Las Casas; still he admits that the fault may lie with the persons who printed the account of the four voyages.[1] For a while his strong love of fairness restrains the pen of Las Casas, but when at length he loses all patience with "these foreigners" who make maps and put the name America where they ought to put "Columba" [sic], he hastily includes Vespucius in his condemnation, and adds that he cannot conceive why Ferdinand Columbus, whom he *knows* to have had the book of the Vespucius voyages in his possession, did not take notice of this "theft and usurpation" by Americus of what be-

---

[1] "Y es bien aquí de considerar la injusticia y agravio que aquel Américo Vespucio parece haber hecho al Almirante, ó los que imprimieron sus cuatro navegaciones, atribuyendo á sí ó no nombrando sino á sí solo, el descubrimiento desta tierra firme," etc. *Op. cit.* tom. ii. p. 268.

longed to his illustrious father.[1] If Las Casas
had closely watched the gradual development of
the affair he would have understood Ferdinand's
silence, but as for half a century he had been
mostly in America, absorbed in very different
matters, the exaltation of Vespucius took him by
surprise and he was unable to comprehend it.

As the history of Las Casas remained in manuscript, it produced no immediate effect upon the
public mind. There were people still Herrera's
living between 1552 and 1561, as for ex- charge against
Vespucius,
ample Ramusio and Benzoni,[2] who were 1601.
probably competent to set Las Casas right. But
in 1601 all such people had passed away, and then
the charge against Vespucius was for the first
time published by Herrera, the historiographer of

[1] "Y maravíllome yo de D. Hernando Colon, hijo del misma
Almirante, que siendo persona de muy buen ingenio y prudencia,
y teniendo en su poder las mismas nauegaciones de Américo,
como lo sé yo, no advirtió en este hurto y usurpacion que Américo
Vespucio hizo á su muy ilustre padre." *Op. cit.* tom. ii. p. 396.
This reference to Ferdinand's book seems to prove that the remarks of Las Casas about Americus were written as late as 1552,
or later. Las Casas seems to have begun work on his history at
the Dominican monastery in San Domingo, somewhere between
the dates 1522 and 1530. He took it up again at Valladolid in
1552 and worked on it until 1561. His allusion to Ferdinand
Columbus was clearly made after the death of the latter in 1539,
so that this part of the book was doubtless written somewhere
between 1552 and 1561.

[2] At the end of the fifth chapter of his *Historia del Mondo
Nuovo*, Venice, 1565, Benzoni enumerates various men for whom
claims had been made that conflicted with the priority of Columbus in his discovery; he does not include Vespucius in the number. See the excellent remarks of Humboldt on Benzoni **and**
Ramusio, in his *Examen critique*, tom. iv. pp. 146–152.

Spain, who had used the manuscript of Las Casas.[1]
Herrera flatly accused Vespucius of purposely an-
tedating his voyage of 1499 with Ojeda to Paria,
in order to make it appear that he had found Terra
Firma before Columbus.   Then Herrera assumed
that Vespucius again accompanied Ojeda to Paria
on the second voyage of that cavalier, which began
in January, 1502.   This assumption displaced the
third voyage of Vespucius, who, it will be remembered, was in the harbour of Rio de Janeiro on
that New Year's day.   A doubt was thus raised
as to whether the third voyage was not a lie, and
so the tangle went on until one might well wonder
whether any of these voyages ever were made at
all !   Surely no poor fellow was ever so victimized
by editors and commentators as this honest Florentine sailor !   From the dire confusion into which
Herrera contrived to throw the subject it was no
easy task for scholars to emerge.   Where was the
Ariadne who could furnish a clue to such a labyrinth?   For two centuries and a half the assertion
that Vespucius had somehow contrived to cheat
people into the belief that he was the discoverer
of the western hemisphere was repeated by historians, proclaimed in cyclopædias,
preached about by moralists, and taught
to children in their school-books.   In
the queer lumber-garret of half-formed
notions which for the majority of mankind does duty as history this particular misty notion was, and is still, pretty sure to

The charge of
Herrera gave
rise to the
popular
notion that
Americus
contrived to
supplant Co-
lumbus.

[1] Herrera, *Historia de las Indias Occidentales*, Madrid, 1601,
tom. i. pp. 125–128, 131, 148, 224, 230.

be found. Until the nineteenth century scarcely anybody had a good word for the great navigator except Bandini, Canovai, and other Florentine writers. But inasmuch as most of these defenders simply stood by their fellow-countryman from the same kind of so-called "patriotic" motives that impel Scandinavian writers to attack Columbus, their arguments produced little impression; and being quite as much in the dark as their adversaries, they were apt to overdo the business and hurt their case by trying to prove too much. Until the middle of the present century the renewal of assaults upon Vespucius used to come in periodic spasms, like the cholera or the fashion of poke bonnets.[1] Early in this century the publication

[1] The latest and fiercest of these assaults was the little book of the Viscount de Santarem, *Recherches historiques, critiques, et bibliographiques sur Améric Vespuce et ses voyages*, Paris, 1842. For perverse ingenuity in creating difficulties where none exist, this book is a curiosity in the literature of morbid psychology. From long staring into mare's nests the author had acquired a chronic twist in his vision. What else can be said of a man who wastes four pages (pp. 53–56) in proving that Vespucius could not have been a schoolmate of the *first* René of Lorraine, who was born in 1410? and who is, or affects to be, so grossly ignorant of Florentine history as to find it strange (p. 63) that Vespucius should have been on friendly terms at once with Soderini and with a Medici of the younger branch? M. de Santarem's methods would have been highly valued by such sharp practitioners as Messrs. Dodson and Fogg: — "Chops! Gracious heavens! and tomato sauce!! Gentlemen, is the happiness of a sensitive and confiding female to be trifled away by such shallow artifices as these?" With arguments of this character M. de Santarem contrived to abolish all the voyages of Vespucius except the one with Ojeda. The only interest that can be felt to-day in this worthless book lies in the fact that an English translation of it was published in Boston in 1850, and is to be held responsible for the following outburst, at which no one would have been so

of many original documents seemed at first only to enhance the confusion, for it took time and patient

shocked as the illustrious author, if he had been properly informed : — "Strange that broad America must wear the name of a thief. Amerigo Vespucci, the pickle-dealer at Seville, who went out in 1499, a subaltern with Hojeda, and whose highest naval rank was boatswain's mate in an expedition that never sailed, managed in this lying world to supplant Columbus and baptize half the earth with his own dishonest name." Emerson, *English Traits*, Boston, 1856 (p. 148 of the Riverside edition, 1883).

Closely connected with these recurrent assaults have been more or less serious proposals from time to time to change the name of America, or of North America, or of the United States. In point of euphony the names suggested would hardly be an improvement, and they have often been of dubious historical propriety; e. g. *Cabotia*; or even *Sebastiana*, which would be honouring the son at the expense of the father; or *Alleghania*, but why should the Tallegwi monopolize it? I suppose Mr. Lewis Morgan might have approved of *Ganowania*, or perhaps *Hodenosaunia*, "country of the Long House." Early in the seventeenth century Pizarro y Orellana (*Varones ilustres del Nuevo Mundo*, Madrid, 1639, p. 51) expressed his disgust at the name of America, not because it was an injustice to Columbus, but because it was not aristocratic enough; the New World ought not to be named after anybody lower than royalty, and so he proposed to call it *Fer-Isabelica!* That would have been a nice name! Gentle reader, how would you like to be a Fer-Isabelican? Another sage Spaniard would have enshrined the memory of Charles V. in such an epithet as *Orbis Carolinus*. See Solórzano Pereyra, *De Indiarum Jure*, Leyden, 1672, lib. i. cap. 2. Late in the sixteenth century a learned Portuguese writer characterized the New World as Golden India, while he distinguished the eastern possessions of his nation as Aromatic India. See Gaspar Fructuoso, *Saudades da Terra*, Lisbon, 1590.

Speaking of *Alleghania* reminds me of the droll conceit of Professor Jules Marcou that the name America after all was not taken from Vespucius, but from a mountain range in Nicaragua, the Indian name of which was *Amerrique* or *Americ*, and which he imagines (without a morsel of documentary evidence) that Columbus must have heard on his fourth voyage! (See *Atlantic Monthly*, March, 1875, vol. xxxv. pp. 291–296.) According to

thinking to get so many new facts into the right connections.

At length the gigantic learning of Alexander von Humboldt was brought to bear on the subject, and enough was accomplished to vindicate forever the character of Americus. But owing to inadequate textual criticism, much still remained to be cleared up. Proceeding from the Latin text of 1507, and accepting the Bandini letter as genuine, Humboldt naturally failed to unravel the snarl of the first two voyages. Then came Varnhagen, who for the first time began at the very beginning by establishing the primitive and genuine texts from which to work. This at once carried the first voyage far away from Paria, and then everything began to become intelligible. Though scholars are not as yet agreed as to all of Varnhagen's conclusions, yet no shade of doubt is left upon the integrity of Vespucius.[1] So truth is strong and prevails at last.

The charge partly refuted by Humboldt; fully by Varnhagen.

this fancy, the name America should have been first applied to Nicaragua, whereas it was really first applied to Brazil and had been used for many a year before it extended across the isthmus of Darien. Speculation *à priori* is of little use in history, and a great many things that must have happened never did happen. If I were not afraid of starting off some venturesome spirit on a fresh wildgoose-chase, I would — well, I will take the risk and mention the elfish coincidence that, whereas Brazil, the original America, received its name from its dye-wood like that of the East Indies, there was a kind of this brazil-wood in Sumatra which the fourteenth century traveller Pegolotti calls AMERI, and along with it another and somewhat better kind which he calls COLOMBINO !!! See Yule's *Marco Polo*, vol. ii. p. 315.

[1] No competent scholar anywhere will now be found to dissent from the emphatic statement of M. Harrisse: — "After a dili-

One thing more was needed, and that was to make a comprehensive statement of the case entirely freed from "bondage to the modern map," — a statement interpreting the facts as they appeared in the first half of the sixteenth century to students of Ptolemy and Mela, and rigorously avoiding the error of projecting our modern knowledge into the past. I sincerely hope that in the present chapter I have kept clear of that error.

It has not been merely through a desire to do justice to the memory of a great navigator and worthy man that I have devoted so much space to this subject and made such large demands upon the reader's patience. It will at once be recognized, I think, that through such a discussion, more than through any mere narrative, are we made to realize what a gradual process of evolution the Discovery of America really was. We have now to follow that process into its next stage of advancement, and see how men came to the knowledge of a vast ocean to the west of Mundus Novus. We have here fortunately arrived at a region where the air is comparatively clear of controversial mists, and although we have to describe the crowning achievement in the records of maritime discovery, the story need not long detain us.

We may properly start by indicating the pur-

gent study of all the original documents, we feel constrained to say that there is not a particle of evidence, direct or indirect, implicating Americus Vespucius in an attempt to foist his name on this continent." *Bibliotheca Americana Vetustissima*, New York, 1866, p. 65.

pose of the fourth voyage of Americus; and here
we shall be helped by a tabular view
showing its position in the group of
voyages to which it belonged. The third
voyage of Columbus, in which he skirted
the Pearl Coast for a short distance, had

Causal se-
quence of
voyages from
the third of
Columbus to
that of Ma-
gellan.

revealed land which he had correctly interpreted
as continental, and it was land in an unexpected
position. His letter describing this voyage did not
obtain a wide circulation, and there is no reason
for supposing that it would have aroused public
attention to any great extent if it had. People's
ideas as to "continents" and "islands" in these
remote parts were, as we have seen, very hazy;
and there was nothing in this new land *north* of
the equator to suggest the idea of Quarta Pars or
Mundus Novus. But this voyage was followed up
next year by that of Ojeda with La Cosa and Vespucius, and it was proved that the Pearl Coast
opposed quite a long barrier to voyages in this
direction into the Indian ocean. The triumphant
return of Gama from Hindustan in midsummer
of 1499 turned all eyes toward that country.
Cathay and Cipango suffered temporary eclipse.
The problem for Spain was to find a route into the
Indian ocean, either to the west or to the east of
the Pearl Coast. Thus she might hope to find
riches in the same quarter of the globe where Portugal had found them. As the Spanish search
went on, it became in a new and unexpected way
complicated with Portuguese interests through the
discovery of a stretch of Brazilian coast lying east
of the papal meridian. Bearing these points in

mind, the reader will be helped by the following diagram in which some of the voyages already discussed are grouped with those which we are now about to consider. The numbers refer back to the numbers in my fuller table of voyages on pages 62, 63 above, and here as there the Portuguese voyages are distinguished by italics.

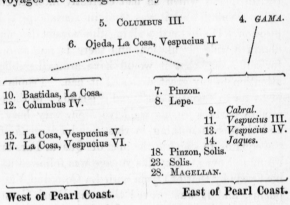

<table>
<tr><td></td><td>5. Columbus III.</td><td>4. Gama.</td></tr>
<tr><td></td><td>6. Ojeda, La Cosa, Vespucius II.</td><td></td></tr>
</table>

10. Bastidas, La Cosa. 12. Columbus IV.	7. Pinzon. 8. Lepe.	
		9. *Cabral.* 11. *Vespucius* III. 13. *Vespucius* IV. 14. *Jaques.*
15. La Cosa, Vespucius V. 17. La Cosa, Vespucius VI.	18. Pinzon, Solis. 23. Solis. 28. Magellan.	

West of Pearl Coast. | **East of Pearl Coast.**

While the voyages of Bastidas and Columbus between the Pearl Coast and Cape Honduras revealed no passage into the Indian ocean,

Voyages of Coelho and Jaques.

the voyages of Pinzon, Lepe, and Vespucius proved that from Paria to Cape San Roque, and thence southerly and southwesterly there extended a continuous coast as far as the latitude of the Cape of Good Hope. If this was Cattigara land, or part of Ptolemy's southern Terra Incognita, might it be possible to sail around it and enter the Indian ocean? Or might some passage be found connecting the waters on its opposite sides? If such a passage should be found, of course much interest would attach to its position, whether east or west of the papal meridian. It was to determine such points as these that two expeditions sailed from Portugal in 1503, the one commanded by Gonçalo Coelho, the other by Christovão Jaques.[1] Coelho's fleet consisted of six ships, one of which was commanded by Vespucius. From Hindustan had come reports of the great wealth and commanding situation of the city of Malacca, a most important gateway and warehouse for the Gangetic sea, and much farther east and south than Calcutta. The purpose of Coelho and Jaques was to investigate the relations of the Brazilian coast to this rich gateway of the East. Of Jaques's voyage we know little except that he seems to have skirted the coast of Patagonia as far as 52° S., and may have caught a glimpse of the opening which Magellan afterward (by sailing through it) proved to be a strait. Why he should have turned and gone home, without verifying this point, is a question which will naturally occur to the reader who allows himself for a moment to forget the terrible hardships that were apt to beset these mariners and frustrate their plans. We shall have no difficulty in understanding it when we come to see how the crews of Magellan felt about entering this strait.

[1] The date 1503 for the Jaques voyage has been doubted (Varnhagen, *Primeiras negociaões diplomáticas respectivas ao Brazil,* Rio Janeiro, 1843). I here follow the more generally received opinion. For the French voyage of Gonneville in 1504 on the Brazilian coast as far as 26° S., see Avezac, "Campagne du navire l'Espoir de Honfleur," in *Annales des voyages,* juin et juillet, 1869; Gaffarel, *Histoire du Brésil Français au seizième siècle,* Paris, 1878.

As for Coelho's expedition, starting from Lisbon June 10, 1503, its first stop was at the Cape Verde islands, for a fresh supply of water and other provisions. From this point Vespucius wished to take a direct course for Brazil, but Coelho insisted upon keeping on southerly to Sierra Leone, for no earthly reason, says Americus rather tartly, "un-

Fourth voyage of Vespucius, — with Coelho, 1503.

Ships of the time of Vespucius.[1]

less to exhibit himself as the captain of six ships;"[2] but I suspect that while the scientific Italian would have steered boldly across the trackless waste

[1] From the original edition of the letter to Soderini, Florence, 1505–06, photographed from Varnhagen's facsimile reproduction.

[2] "Et come elnostro capitano maggiore fusse huomo p⟨͜⟩ sumptuoso & molto cauezuto [i. e. Portuguese *cabeçudo*, " headstrong "], uolle andare a riconoscere la Serra liona, . . . senza tenere necessitá alcuna, se no' p⟨͜⟩ farsi uedere, ch' era capitano di sei naui," etc.   *Lettera*, etc., fol. c. iii. verso.

straight at his goal, the Portuguese commander preferred the old-fashioned and more timid course of following two sides of a triangle and was not going to take advice from any of your confounded foreigners. But as several of the captains and pilots sustained Americus, the course actually followed, without much rhyme or reason, looks like the resultant of a conflict of opinions. Early in August, after much rough weather, they discovered a small uninhabited island near the Brazilian coast in latitude 3° S., since known as the island of Fernando Noronha; and there one of the ships, a carrack of 300 tons burthen, in which were most of the stores, staved in her bows against a rock and "nothing was saved but the crew." By the chief captain's orders Americus with his own ship sought a harbour on this island and found an excellent one about four leagues distant. His boat had been retained for general service by Coelho, who promised to send it after him with further instructions. We are not informed as to the weather, but it was probably bad, for after waiting a week in the harbour, Americus descried one of the ships on her way to him. She brought news that Coelho's ship had gone with him to the bottom and the other two had disappeared. So now the two ships of Vespucius and his consort, with one boat between them, were left alone at this little island. "It had plenty of fresh water," says Americus, "and a dense growth of trees filled with innumerable birds, which were so simple that they allowed us to catch them with our hands. We took so many that we loaded the boat with them." [1] After thus providing against famine, they sailed to the Bay of All Saints, which had been designated as a rendezvous in case of accidents, and there they faithfully waited two months in the vain hope of being overtaken by their comrades. Then giving up this hope, they weighed anchor again and followed the coast southward to Cape Frio, just under the tropic of Capricorn. Finding there a great quantity of brazilwood, they decided to establish a colony there, and what follows we may let Vespucius tell in his own words: — "In this port we staid five months, building a block-house and loading our ships with dyewood. We could go no farther, for want of men and equipments. So after finishing this work we decided to return to Portugal, leaving

Conclusion of the letter to Soderini.

twenty-four men in the fortress, with twelve pieces of cannon, a good outfit of small arms, and provisions for six months.[2] We made peace with all the natives in the neighbourhood, whom I have not mentioned in this voyage, but not because we did not see and have dealings with great numbers of them. As many as thirty of us went forty leagues inland, where we saw so

[1] This is another of the little observations which keep impressing us with the accuracy and fidelity of Vespucius in his descriptions. Modern naturalists are familiar with the fact that on desolate islands, where they have lived for many generations unmolested, birds become so tame that they can be caught by hand, and even the catching of a multitude of them will not frighten the others. For many instances of this, and the explanation, see Darwin's *Voyage of the Beagle*, new ed., London, 1870, p. 398; Spencer's *Essays*, 2d series, London, 1864, p. 134.

[2] This little colony or factory at Cape Frio was still kept up in 1511 and after. See Varnhagen, *Histoire générale du Brésil*, tom. i. p. 427.

many things that I omit to relate them, reserving them for my book, the *Four Journeys*. . . . The bearer of this letter, Benvenuto di Domenico Benvenuti, will tell your Magnificence of . . . such things as have been omitted to avoid prolixity. . . . *I have made the letter as short as possible, and refrained from mentioning many things very natural to be told, through fear of seeming tedious.*"

This passage, and especially the last sentence which I have italicized, affords abundant explanation of that reticence of Vespucius about many things which we should like to know; a reticence which the bats and moles of historical criticism, with these plain words staring them in the face, profess to regard as unaccountable!

When Americus arrived at Lisbon, June 18, 1504, the missing ships had not yet arrived, and were given up for lost, but after some time they returned, having extended their explorations perhaps as far as the mouth of the river La Plata.[1]

[1] This is the opinion of Varnhagen, who believes that Juan de Solis was then in the Portuguese service and in this fleet, and on this occasion made his first acquaintance with the river La Plata, which would almost surely be mistaken for a strait. If this opinion as to Solis be sustained, one can see a common feature in the shifting of two such captains as Vespucius and Solis from Spain to Portugal and back, coupled with the subsequent transfer of Magellan from the Portuguese service. The discovery of Brazil seemed to open an avenue for Portuguese enterprise in western waters, and so began to draw over navigators from Spain; but by 1504 it began to appear that the limit of achievement under the Portuguese flag in that direction had been reached, and so the tide of interest set back toward Spain. If Solis saw La Plata in 1504 and believed it to be a strait, he must have known that it was on the Spanish side of the line of demarcation. Its meridian is more than 20° west of Cape San Roque.

For some reason unknown Vespucius left the service of Portugal by the end of that year 1504, or somewhat earlier. This step may have been connected with his marriage, which seems to have occurred early in 1505; it may have been because he had become sufficiently impressed with the southwesterly trend of the Brazilian coast-line to realize that further discoveries in that direction would best be conducted under the Spanish flag; or it may have been simply because King Ferdinand outbid King Emanuel, whose policy was too often pennywise. At any rate, Americus made his way back to Spain. In February, 1505, just before starting from Seville on his journey to court, he called on his sick and harassed friend Columbus, to see what kind service he could render him. The letter which Vespucius carried from Columbus to his son Diego is very interesting.[1] The Admiral speaks of Vespucius in terms of high respect, as a thoroughly good and honourable man, to whom Fortune had not rendered such rewards as his labours deserved; a staunch friend who had always done his best to serve him and was now going to court with the determination to set his affairs right if possible. There is something very pleasant in the relations thus disclosed between the persecuted Discoverer, then almost on his death-bed, and the younger navigator, to whom yet grosser injustice was to be done by a stupid and heedless world.[2]

Americus returns to Spain,

and visits Columbus.

[1] The original is preserved in the family archives of the Duke of Veràguas, and a copy is printed in Navarrete, tom. i. p. 351.

[2] " If not among the greatest of the world's great men, he is

The transactions of Vespucius at court, and the nature of the maritime enterprises that were set on foot or carried to completion during the next few years, are to be gathered chiefly from old account-books, contracts, and other business documents unearthed by the indefatigable Navarrete, and printed in his great collection. The four chief personages in the Spanish marine at that time, the experts to whom all difficult questions were referred and all arduous enterprises entrusted, were Vespucius and La Cosa, Pinzon and Solis. Unfortunately account-books and legal documents, having been written for other purposes than the gratification of the historian, are — like the "geological record" — imperfect. Too many links are missing to enable us to determine with certainty just how the work was shared among these mariners, or just how many voyages were undertaken. But it is clear that the first enterprise contemplated was a voyage by Pinzon, in company with either Solis or Vespucius or both, in the direction of the river La Plata, for the purpose of finding an end to the continent or a passage into the Indian ocean. What Vespucius had failed to do in his last voyage for Portugal, he now proposed to do in a voyage for Spain. It was this expedition, planned for 1506, but never carried out, that Herrera a century later mistook for that voyage of Pinzon and Solis to Honduras and

The Pinzon expedition to La Plata; planned for 1506, but not carried out.

among the happiest of those on whom good fortune has bestowed renown." S. H. Gay, apud Winsor, *Narr. and Crit. Hist.*, ii. 152. Is it, then, such a happy fortune to be unjustly stigmatized as a liar by ten generations of men ?

the gulf of Mexico which the contemporary Oviedo (supported by Martyr and confirmed by Gomara) positively declares to have been made before 1499. As I have already shown, Pinzon did not leave Spain for any long voyage in 1506.[1] The remonstrances of Portugal put a stop to the enterprise, and the ships were used for other purposes.

Meanwhile the search for a passage west of the Pearl Coast was conducted by La Cosa and Vespucius. In this voyage, from May to December, 1505, they visited the gulf of Darien and ascended the Atrato river for some 200 miles. Of late years it has been proposed to make an interoceanic canal by connecting this river with the San Juan, which flows into the Pacific. To Vespucius and La Cosa it turned out not to be the strait of which at first its general aspect had given promise, but in its shallow upper stretches they found its sandy bottom gleaming and glistening with particles of gold. For three months they explored the neighbouring country, and found plenty of gold in the wild mountain streams. On the way home they seemed to have stopped on the Pearl Coast and gathered a goodly store of pearls. The immediate profit of the voyage was so great that it was repeated two years later. During the year 1506 Vespucius was busy in Spain preparing the armament for Pinzon, and when, in March, 1507, that expedition was abandoned, Vespucius and La Cosa started at once for the gulf of Darien, and returned in November, heavily freighted with gold. This, of course, was

Fifth and sixth voyages of Vespucius, — with La Cosa.

[1] See above, p. 68.

purely a commercial voyage. But during the summer the way for further discovery had been prepared, and in some way or other the Portuguese
difficulty had been surmounted, for soon after New
Year's, 1508, Americus told the Venetian ambassador at the court of Spain that a way to the lands
of spice was to be sought, and that the ships would
start in March without fail.[1]

They did not start, however, until June 29. In
the interval La Cosa was appointed *alguazil mayor*,
or high constable of the province about to be organized at the gulf of Darien, and afterwards called
Golden Castile (*Castilla del Oro*), so that, as we
shall by and by see, these two voyages which he
made with Vespucius were the first links in the

---

[1] My brief mention of the doings of Vespucius, Pinzon, Solis,
and La Cosa, between 1504 and 1509, is based upon the original
documents relating to these four navigators scattered through the
third volume of Navarrete's *Coleccion*, as illuminated by two
precious bits of information sent to the Venetian senate by its
diplomatic agents in Spain. The letter of Girolamo Vianello
from Burgos, December 23, 1505 (dated 1506, according to an old
Spanish usage which began the New Year at Christmas and sometimes even as early as the first of December), establishes the fact
of the fifth voyage of Vespucius in 1505. This letter was found
in Venice by the great historian Ranke, and a few lines of it
copied by him for Humboldt, who published the scrap in his
Examen critique, tom. v. p. 157, but was puzzled by the date, because Americus was indisputably in Spain through 1506 (and
Humboldt supposed through 1505 also, but a more attentive
scrutiny of the documents shows him to have been mistaken).
Varnhagen, delving in the Biblioteca di San Marco at Venice,
again found the letter, and a copy of the whole is printed, with
valuable notes, in his *Nouvelles recherches*, pp. 12–17. In 1867
Mr. Rawdon Brown discovered in Venice the two brief letters of
the ambassador Francesco Cornaro, which have established the
sixth voyage of Vespucius, in 1507. They are printed in Harrisse,
Bibl. Amer. Vetust., Additions, Paris, 1872, p. xxvii.

chain of events that ended in the conquest of Peru. In March Vespucius received his appointment as pilot major, which kept him in Spain, and his place in the voyage with Pinzon was taken by Solis, who had probably visited the mouth of La Plata with Coelho in 1504.

Voyage of Pinzon and Solis, 1508–09.

Pinzon and Solis sailed June 29, followed the Brazilian coast, passed the wide mouth of that river without finding it, and kept on, according to Herrera, as far as the river Colorado, in latitude 40° S. There was disagreement between the two captains, and they returned home, probably somewhat peevish with disappointment, in October, 1509. Nothing more was done in this direction for six years. After the death of Vespucius in 1513, he was succeeded by Solis as pilot major of Spain. Pinzon here disappears from our narrative, except as a witness in the *Probanzas.* He seems to have gone on no more voyages. He was ennobled in 1519.[1] Solis started on another search for the river La Plata in October, 1515. He entered that "fresh-water sea" (*mar dulce*) the following January, and while he was exploring its coast in a boat with eight companions the Indians suddenly swarmed upon the scene. Solis and his men were instantly captured, and their horrified comrades on shipboard, unable to save them, could only look on while they were deliberately roasted and devoured by the screaming and dancing demons.[2]

Last voyage and death of Solis, 1515–16.

[1] See the document in Navarrete, tom. iii. p. 145.

[2] The words of Peter Martyr in a different connection might well be applied here : — " they came runninge owte of the wooddes

During these years events were gradually preparing the way for the emergence of the idea of a
separate New World, a *western hemisphere* forming no part of the ancient Œcumene. Emergence of
the idea of a
western hemi-
sphere; Stob-
nicza's map,
1512.
There is nothing to indicate that any
such idea was ever conceived by Vespucius. Its emergence was so gradual
and so indefinite that it is not easy to trace it in
literary documents or in maps. A hypothetical
indication of an ocean corresponding in position to
what we know as the Pacific may be seen upon the
rude map of the Polish geographer Jan Stobnicza,
published at Cracow in 1512, in an Introduction
to Ptolemy. Like the *Tabula Terre Nove*, it is
derived from a common original with the Cantino
map. At the north is shown the land discovered
by the Cabots. The name Isabella is transferred
from Cuba to Florida, and the legend above seems
to refer to the "C. de bonauentura" of the *Tabula
Terre Nove*. Cape San Roque in Brazil is called
"Caput S. Crucis." The rude indication of the
gulf of Mexico is repeated from the *Tabula Terre
Nove* or its prototype. But the new and striking
feature in this Stobnicza map is the combination of
the northern and southern continents with an ocean
behind them open all the way from north to south.
As the existence of the Pacific was still unknown
in 1512, this ocean was purely hypothetical, and
so was the western coast-line of America, if it is

with a terrible crye and most horrible aspect, much lyke vnto the
people cauled *Picti Agathyrsi* of whom the poete virgile speak-
eth. . . . A man wold thinke them to bee deuylles incarnate
newly broke owte of hell, they are soo lyke vnto helhoundes."
Eden's translation, 1553, dec. i. bk. vii.

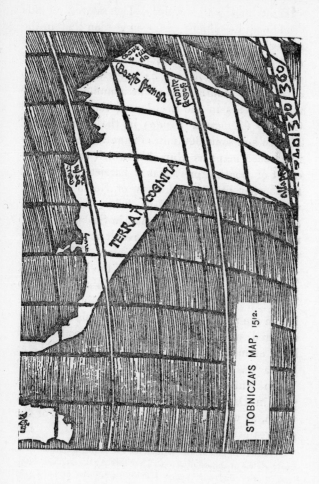

STOBNICZA'S MAP, 15¹².

proper to call coast-line this mere cut-off drawn in
straight lines with a ruler. The interest of this
crude map lies chiefly in its suggestion that in the
maker's mind *the whole transatlantic coast already
visited* (except the Cabot portion) *was conceived
not as part of Asia, but as a barrier in the way
of reaching Asia.* The vague adumbration of the
truth appears in the position of the great island
Cipango (*Zypangu insula*) in the ocean behind
Mexico and some 600 miles distant. Before Stobnicza such maps as Ruysch's, which took full account of South America as a barrier, detached it
from what little was known of North America,
which was still reckoned as Asia. The peculiar
combinations of land and water in Stobnicza's map
make it dimly prefigure the result attained nearly
thirty years afterward by Mercator. The sugges-

First sight of
the Pacific by
Balboa, 1513.

tion was in advance of the knowledge of
the time, and the map does not seem to
have exerted any commanding influence;
but in the next year after it was published an event
occurred which, if correctly understood, would
have seemed to justify it. In 1513 the Terra
Firma was crossed at its narrowest place, and
Vasco Nuñez de Balboa, from the summit of a
peak in Darien, gazed upon an expanse of waters,
which, as we have since learned, made part of the
greatest ocean upon the globe.[1]

[1] Colonel Higginson will pardon me for calling attention to an
inadvertence of the kind which I have already so often characterized as projecting our modern knowledge into the past : — "Columbus discovered what he thought was India [i. e. Asia], but
Balboa proved that half the width of the globe still separated
him from India." *Larger History of the United States*, p. 70. **If**

It was not so much, however, the brief glimpse of Balboa as the steady eastward progress of the Portuguese that began to reveal to prac- Eastward progress of the Portuguese to China and the Moluccas, 1504–17. tical navigators the character and extent of the waters west of Mundus Novus. The arrival of Portuguese traders in the Indian ocean was the signal for a tremendous struggle for commercial supremacy. In every seaport they found Arabs, or, as they called them, "Moors," their hereditary enemies. Arabs held nearly all the points of entrance and exit in that ocean, and the Portuguese at once perceived the necessity of seizing these points. Blows were exchanged from the start, and the ensuing warfare forms one of the most romantic chapters in history. It would not

Balboa could prove this by standing on a mountain in Darien and looking at the water before him, he must have had a truly marvellous pair of eyes! Surely he had no positive means of knowing that this water stretched away for more than a hundred miles. Mere vision scarcely carried his discovery out into the open ocean beyond the gulf of Panama, though, in accordance with information received from the Indians, he rightly interpreted it as a "South Sea" upon which one might hug the coast to the "Golden Kingdom," soon to be known as Peru. The first discoverer who proved the width of the Pacific was Magellan, who sailed across it. — Such little slips as the one here criticised are easy to make, and one cannot feel sure that one does not unwittingly do it oneself. The old poets were flagrant sinners in this respect. Lope de Vega, in a famous drama, makes Columbus know of "the New World" even before 1492. Why is it, asks Christopher in a talk with his brother Bartholomew, why is it that I, a poor pilot, a man with broken fortunes, yearn to add to this world another, and such a remote one? —

> Un hombre pobre, y aun roto,
> Que ansí lo puedo decir,
> Y que vive de piloto,
> Quiere á este mundo añadir
> Otro mundo tan remoto!
>
> *El Nuevo Mundo Descubierto*, Jorn. i.

be easy to point out two commanders more swift in intelligence, more fertile in resource, more unconquerable in action, than Francisco de Almeida and Alfonso de Albuquerque. The result of their work was the downfall of Arab power in the Indies, and the founding of that great commercial empire which remained in the hands of the Portuguese until it was taken from them by the Dutch.[1] On the African coast, from Sofala to the strait of Bab-el-Mandeb, the Portuguese held all the important trading stations. They seized the island of Socotra, established themselves in force along the coasts of Oman and Makran, and capturing the wealthy Hormuz they gained secure control of the outlet to the valley of the Euphrates. They held the whole western coast of Hindustan from above Bombay down to Cape Comorin, while on the Coromandel coast they had stations at Mylapur and Negapatam. In 1506 Almeida first visited Ceylon, which was afterward annexed to the Portuguese empire. In 1508 Sequeira advanced as far as Sumatra, and in 1511 the famous Malacca, the Gateway of the East, was conquered by Albuquerque. The way to the "lands where the spices grow" was thus at last laid open, and Albuquerque

[1] The story of the Portuguese empire in the East Indies is told by Barros, *Decadas da Asia*, Lisbon, 1778–88, with the continuation by Couto, in all 24 vols. ; Bras Affonso de Albuquerque, *Commentarios do grande Afonso Dalboquerque*, Lisbon, 1774, in 4 vols. I give the dates of my own copies, which are, I think, the best editions. The great work of Barros began to be published in 1552 ; that of Albuquerque, son of the conqueror, was published in 1557. See also Faria y Sousa, *Asia Portuguesa*, Lisbon, 1666, in 3 vols.

had no sooner riveted his clutch upon Malacca than he sent Antonio d'Abreu and Francisco Serrano, with three galleons, to make a friendly visit to the Spice Islands *par excellence*, the Moluccas. Sailing down by Java, and between Celebes and Flores, this little fleet visited Amboina and Banda, and brought away as heavy a load of nutmegs and cloves as it was safe to carry.[1] Six years afterward, in 1517, Fernam de Andrade conducted the first European ship that ever sailed to China. He reached Canton and entered into friendly commercial relations with that city.

Thus data were beginning to accumulate in evidence that the continent of Asia did not extend nearly so far to the east as Toscanelli and Columbus had supposed. A comparison of longitudes, moreover, between the Moluccas and the Brazilian coast could hardly fail to bring out the fact of a great distance between them. Still theory did not advance so surely and definitely as it might seem to us with the modern map in our minds. The multitude of unfamiliar facts was bewildering, and the breadth of the Pacific ocean was too much for the mind to take in except by actual experience. We have now, in concluding this long chapter, to consider the heroic career of the man who finished what Columbus had begun, and furnished proof — though even this was not immediately understood — that the regions discovered by the Admiral belonged to a separate world from Asia.

Dim rudimentary conception of a separate ocean between Mundus Novus and Asia.

[1] For some account of the Spice Islands and their further history, see Argensola, *Conquista de las islas Molucas*, Madrid, 1609, folio.

Ferdinand Magellan, as we call him in English,[1] was a Portuguese nobleman of the fourth grade, but of family as old and blood as blue as any in the peninsula. He was born at Sabrosa, near Chaves,[2] in one of the wildest and gloomiest nooks of Tras-os-Montes, in or about the year 1480. The people of that province have always been distinguished for a rugged fidelity, combined with unconquerable toughness of fibre, that reminds one of the Scotch; and from those lonely mountains there never came forth a sturdier character than Ferdinand Magellan. Difficulty and danger fit to baffle the keenest mind and daunt the strongest heart only incited this man to efforts wellnigh superhuman. In his portrait, as given in Navarrete,[3] with the great arching brows, the fiery

Ferdinand Magellan.

[1] The Portuguese name is Fernão da Magalhães; in Spanish it becomes Fernando de Magallanes, pronounced *Mah-gah-lyáh-nays*. In English one often, perhaps commonly, hears it as *Ma-jel'-lan*. One does not like to be pedantic in such trifles, and I don't mind slaughtering a consonant or two when necessary, but to shift the accent of a word seems to destroy its identity, so that *Ma-jel-lan'*, which we sometimes hear, seems preferable.

The documentary sources of the life of Magellan are chiefly to be found in the fourth volume of Navarrete's *Coleccion de viages*. The early accounts of his voyage have been collected and translated by the late Lord Stanley of Alderley, *The First Voyage Round the World*, London, 1874 (Hakluyt Society). A good biography, almost the first in any language, has lately appeared in English : Guillemard, *The Life of Ferdinand Magellan and the First Circumnavigation of the Globe*, London, 1890.

[2] Various writers have given Lisbon, or Oporto, or some village in Estremadura as his birthplace ; but Sabrosa seems clearly established. See the reference to his first will, in Guillemard, p. 23.

[3] *Coleccion de viages*, tom. iv. p. xxiv. ; it is reproduced in Lord Stanley's volume ; in Winsor, *Narr. and Crit. Hist.*, ii. 593 ; and elsewhere ; but one gets the effect most completely in Navarrete.

black eyes, the firm-set lips, and mastiff jaw, covered but not concealed by the shaggy beard, the strength is almost appalling. Yet in all this power there was nothing cruel. Magellan was kind-hearted and unselfish, and on more than one occasion we see him risking his life in behalf of others with generosity worthy of a paladin.

Nothing is known of his childhood and youth except that at an early age he went to Lisbon and was brought up in the royal household. In 1505 he embarked as a volunteer in the armada which the brilliant and high-souled Almeida, first Portuguese viceroy of India, was taking to the East. There followed seven years of service under this commander and his successor Albuquerque. Seven years of anxious sailing over strange waters, checkered with wild fights against Arabs and Malays, trained Magellan for the supreme work that was to come. He was in Sequeira's expedition to Malacca, in 1508–09, the first time that European ships had ventured east of Ceylon. While they were preparing to take in a cargo of pepper and ginger, the astute Malay king was plotting their destruction. His friendly overtures deceived the frank and somewhat too unsuspicious Sequeira. Malay sailors and traders were allowed to come on board the four ships, and all but one of the boats were sent to the beach, under command of Francisco Serrano, to hasten the bringing of the cargo. Upon the quarter-deck of his flagship Sequeira sat absorbed in a game of chess, with half-a-dozen dark faces intently watching him, their deadly purpose veiled with polite

Sequeira's expedition and the Malay plot, 1509.

words and smiles. Ashore the houses rose terrace-like upon the hillside, while in the foreground the tall tower of the citadel — square with pyramidal apex, like an Italian bell-tower — glistened in the September sunshine. The parties of Malays on the ships, and down on the bustling beach, cast furtive glances at this summit, from which a puff of smoke was presently to announce the fatal moment. The captains and principal officers on shipboard were at once to be stabbed and their vessels seized, while the white men ashore were to be massacred. But a Persian woman in love

Sequeira and Serrano saved by Magellan.

with one of the officers had given tardy warning, so that just before the firing of the signal the Portuguese sailors began chasing the squads of Malays from their decks, while Magellan, in the only boat, rowed for the flagship, and his stentorian shout of "Treason!" came just in time to save Sequeira. Then in wild confusion, as wreaths of white smoke curled about the fatal tower, Serrano and a few of his party sprang upon their boats and pushed out to sea. Most of their comrades, less fortunate, were surrounded and slaughtered cn the beach. Nimble Malay skiffs pursued and engaged Serrano, and while he was struggling against overwhelming odds, Magellan rowed up and joined battle with such desperate fury that Serrano was saved. No sooner were all the surviving Portuguese brought together on shipboard than the Malays attacked in full force, but European guns were too much for them, and after several of their craft had been sent to the bottom they withdrew.

This affair was the beginning of a devoted friendship between Magellan and Serrano, sealed by many touching and romantic incidents, like the friendship between Gerard and Denys in "The Cloister and the Hearth;" and it was out of this friendship that in great measure grew the most wonderful voyage recorded in history. After Albuquerque had taken Malacca in 1511, Serrano commanded one of the ships that made the first voyage to the Moluccas. On its return course his vessel, loaded with spices, was wrecked upon a lonely island which had long served as a lair for pirates. Fragments of wreckage strewn upon the beach lured ashore a passing gang of such ruffians, and while they were intent upon delving and searching, Serrano's men, who had hidden among the rocks, crept forth and seized the pirate ship. The nearest place of retreat was the island of Amboina, and this accident led Serrano back to the Moluccas, where he established himself as an ally or quasi-protector of the king of Ternate, and remained for the rest of his short life. Letters from Serrano aroused in Magellan a strong desire to follow his friend to that "new world" in the Indian waves, the goal so long dreamed of, so eagerly sought, by Columbus and many another, but now for the first time actually reached and grasped. But circumstances came in to modify most curiously this aim of Magellan's. He had come to learn something about the great ocean intervening between the Malay seas and Mundus Novus, but failed to form

Serrano's shipwreck, and his stay at the Moluccas.

The antipodal line of demarcation between Spanish and Portuguese waters.

any conception of its width at all approaching the reality. It therefore seemed to him that the line of demarcation antipodal to Borgia's meridian must fall to the west of the Moluccas, and that his friend Serrano had ventured into a region which must ultimately be resigned to Spain. In this opinion he was wrong, for the meridian which cuts through the site of Adelaide in Australia would have come near the line that on that side of the globe marked the end of the Portuguese half and the beginning of the Spanish half; but the mistake was easy to make and hard to correct.

About this time some cause unknown took Magellan back to Lisbon, where we find him in the midsummer of 1512. His hope of a speedy return to India was disappointed. Whether on account of a slight disagreement he had once had with Albuquerque, or for some other reason, he found himself out of favour with the king. A year or more of service in Morocco followed, in the course of which a Moorish lance wounded Magellan in the knee and lamed him for life. After his return to Portugal in 1514, it became evident that King Emanuel had no further employment for him. He became absorbed in the study of navigation and cosmography, in which he had always felt an interest. It would have been strange if an inquiring mind, trained in the court of Lisbon in those days, had not been stirred by the fascination of such studies. How early in life Magellan had begun to breathe in the art of seamanship with the salt breezes from the Atlantic we do not know; but

Magellan's return to Portugal ; his scheme for sailing westward to the Moluccas.

at some time the results of scientific study were combined with his long experience in East Indian waters to make him a consummate master. He conceived the vast scheme of circumnavigating the globe. Somewhere upon that long coast of Mundus Novus, explored by Vespucius and Coelho, Jaques and Solis, there was doubtless a passage through which he could sail westward and greet his friend Serrano in the Moluccas!

Upon both of Schöner's globes, of 1515 and 1520, such a strait is depicted, connecting the southern Atlantic with an ocean to the west of Mundus Novus. This has raised the question whether any one had ever discovered it before Magellan.[1] That there was in many minds a belief in the existence of such a passage seems certain; whether because the wish was father to the thought, or because the mouth of La Plata had been reported as the mouth of a strait, or because Jaques had perhaps looked into the strait of Magellan, is by no means clear. But without threading that blind and tortuous labyrinth, as Magellan did, for more than 300 geographical miles, successfully avoiding its treacherous bays and channels with no outlet, no one could prove that there was a practicable passage there; and there is no good reason for supposing that any one had accomplished such a feat of navigation before Magellan.

The strait on Schöner's globes.

[1] See the discussion in Wieser, *Magalhães-Strasse und Austral-Continent auf den Globen des Johannes Schöner*, Innsbruck, 1881; Kohl, *Geschichte der Entdeckungsreisen und Schiff-fahrten zur Magellans-Strasse*, Berlin, 1877; Winsor, *Narr. and Crit. Hist.*, viii. 375–387; Guillemard's *Magellan*, pp. 188–198.

The scheme of thus reaching the Moluccas by the westward voyage was first submitted to King Emanuel. To him was offered the first opportunity for ascertaining whether these islands lay within his half of the heathen world or not. He did not smile upon the scheme, though he may have laughed at it. The papal bulls and the treaty of Tordesillas prohibited the Spaniards from sailing to the Indies by way of the Cape of Good Hope; and unless they could get through the barrier of Mundus Novus there was no danger of their coming by a westerly route. Why not let well enough alone? Apparently Emanuel did not put much faith in the strait. We are told by Gaspar Correa that Magellan then asked the royal permission to go and offer his services to some other master. "The King said he might do what he pleased. Upon this Magellan desired to kiss his hand at parting, but the King would not offer it."[1]

Magellan's proposals are rejected by the king of Portugal;

The alternative was thus offered to Magellan of abandoning his scheme of discovery or entering the service of Spain, and he chose the latter course. For this he has been roundly abused, not only by Portuguese writers from that day to this, but by others who seem to forget that a man has as clear a right to change his country and his allegiance as to move his home from one town to another. In the relations between state and individual the duty is not all on one side. As Faria y Sousa, more sensible than many of his countrymen, observes, the

and accordingly he enters the service of Spain.

---

[1] Guillemard, p. 82.

great navigator did all that honour demanded
when by a special clause in his agreement with
Spain he pledged himself to do nothing prejudicial
to the interests of Portugal.[1]

It was in October, 1517, that Magellan arrived in
Seville and became the guest of Diego Barbosa,
alcaide of the arsenal there, a Portuguese gentleman who had for several years been in the Spanish
service.   Before Christmas of that year   Magellan's
he was married to his host's daughter   marriage.
Beatriz de Barbosa, who accompanied him to the
court.   Magellan found favour in the eyes of the
boy king, Charles V., and even obtained active
support from Bishop Fonseca, in spite of that prelate's ingrained hostility to noble schemes and honourable men.   It was decided to fit out an expedition to pursue the search in which Solis had
lately lost his life.   More than a year was consumed in the needful preparations, and it was not
until September 20, 1519, that the little fleet
cleared the mouth of the Guadalquivir and stood
out to sea.

There were five small ships, commanded as follows: —

1. Trinidad, 110 tons, captain-general Ferdinand Magellan, pilot, Estevan Gomez;

2. San Antonio, 120 tons, captain Juan de
Cartagena;

3. Concepcion, 90 tons, captain Gaspar Quesada;

---

[1] Faria y Sousa, *Comentarios á la Lusiada de Camões*, x. 140;
Guillemard, p. 85.   Cf. Lord Stanley of Alderley, *First Voyage
Round the World*, pp. ii.–xv.

4. Victoria, 85 tons, captain Luis de Mendoza;

5. Santiago, 75 tons, captain Juan Serrano.

It is a striking illustration of the shiftlessness
with which things were apt to be done by the government, and the difficulties under which great nav-

Ships and
men of the
great expedi-
tion.

igators accomplished their arduous work,
that these five ships were all old and decidedly the worse for wear. All seem to
have been decked, with castles at the stern and fore.
About 280 men were on board, a motley crew of
Spaniards and Portuguese, Genoese and Sicilians,
Flemings and French, Germans and Greeks, with
one Englishman from Bristol, and a few negroes
and Malays. Of Portuguese there were at least
seven-and-thirty, for the most part men attached
to Magellan and who had left their country with
him. It was fortunate that he had so many such,
for the wiles of King Emanuel had pursued him
into Spain and out upon the ocean. When that
sovereign learned that the voyage was really to be
made, he determined that it must not be allowed
to succeed. Hired ruffians lurked about street
corners in Seville, waiting for a chance that never
came for rushing forth and stabbing the wary navigator; orders were sent to captains in the East
Indies — among them the gallant Sequeira whom
Magellan had saved — to intercept and arrest the
fleet if it should ever reach those waters; and,
worst of all, the seeds of mutiny were busily and
but too successfully sown in Magellan's own ships.

Traitors in
the fleet.

Of the four subordinate captains only
one was faithful. Upon Juan Serrano,
the brother of his dearest friend, Magellan could

absolutely rely. The others, Cartagena, Mendoza, and Quesada, sailed out from port with treason in their hearts. A few days after their start a small caravel overtook the Trinidad, with an anxious message to Magellan from his wife's father, Barbosa, begging him to be watchful, "since it had come to his knowledge that his captains had told their friends and relations that if they had any trouble with him they would kill him." For reply the commander counselled Barbosa to be of good cheer, for be they true men or false he feared them not, and would do his appointed work all the same.[1] For Beatriz, left with her little son, Rodrigo, six months old, the outlook must have been anxious enough.

Our chief source of information for the events of the voyage is the journal kept by a gentleman from Vicenza, the Chevalier Antonio Pigafetta, who obtained permission to accompany the expedition, "for to see the marvels of the ocean."[2] Pigafetta's journal. After leaving the Canaries on the 3d of October the armada ran down toward Sierra Leone and was becalmed, making only three leagues in three weeks. Then "the upper air burst into life" and the frail ships were driven along under bare poles, now and then dipping their yard-arms. During a month of Crossing the this dreadful weather, the food and Atlantic. water grew scarce, and the rations were dimin-

[1] Correa, *Lendas da India*, tom. ii. p. 627 ; Guillemard, p. 149.

[2] Pigafetta's journal is contained, with other documents, in the book of Lord Stanley of Alderley, already cited. There is also a French edition by Amoretti, *Premier Voyage autour du Monde,* Paris, 1800.

ished. The spirit of mutiny began to show itself. The Spanish captains whispered among the crews that this man from Portugal had not their interests at heart and was not loyal to the Emperor. Toward the captain - general their demeanour grew more and more insubordinate, and Cartagena one day, having come on board the flagship, faced him with threats and insults. To his astonishment Magellan promptly collared him, and sent him, a prisoner in irons, on board the Victoria (whose captain was unfortunately also one of the traitors), while the command of the San Antonio was given to another officer. This example made things quiet for the moment.

On the 29th of November they reached the Brazilian coast near Pernambuco, and on the 11th of January they arrived at the mouth of La Plata, which they investigated sufficiently to convince them that it was a river's mouth and not a strait. Three weeks were consumed in this work. Their course through February and March along the coast of Patagonia was marked by incessant and violent storms, and the cold became so intense that, finding a sheltered harbour, with plenty of fish, at Port St. Julian, they chose it for winter quarters and anchored there on the last day of March. On the next day, which was Easter Sunday, the mutiny that so long had smouldered broke out in all its fury.

Winter quarters at Port St. Julian.

The hardships of the voyage had thus far been what staunch seamen called unusually severe, and it was felt that they had done enough. No one except Vespucius and Jaques had ever approached so near to the south pole, and if they had not yet found a strait, it was doubtless because there was none to find. The rations of bread and wine were becoming very short, and common pru- Reasons for returning home; Magellan's refusal. dence demanded that they should re- turn to Spain. If their voyage was practically a failure it was not their fault; there was ample excuse in the frightful storms they had suffered and the dangerous strains that had been put upon their worn-out ships. Such was the general feeling, but when expressed to Magellan it fell upon deaf ears. No excuses, nothing but performance, would serve his turn; for him hardships were made only to be despised and dangers to be laughed at; and, in short, go on they must, until a strait was found or the end of that continent reached. Then they would doubt- less find an open way to the Moluccas, and while he held out hopes of rich rewards for all, he ap- pealed to their pride as Castilians. For the in- flexible determination of this man was not em- bittered by harshness, and he could wield as well as any one the language that soothes and persuades.

So long as all were busy in the fight against wind and wave, the captain-general's arguments were of avail. But the deliberate halt to face the hardships of an antarctic winter, with no prospect of stirring until toward September, was too much. Patience under enforced inactivity was a virtue higher than these sailors had yet been called upon to exhibit. The treacherous captains had found their opportunity and sowed distrust broadcast by hinting that a Portuguese commander could not

better serve his king than by leading a Spanish armada to destruction.   They had evidently secured
their men and prepared their blow before the fleet came to anchor.   The ringleaders of the mutiny were the captains
Quesada, of the Concepcion, and Mendoza, of the
Victoria, with Juan de Cartagena, the deposed
captain of the San Antonio, which was now commanded by Magellan's cousin, Alvaro de Mesquita.
On the night of Easter Sunday, Cartagena and
Quesada, with thirty men, boarded the San Antonio, seized Mesquita and put him in irons; in the
brief affray the mate of the San Antonio was mor-
tally wounded.   One of the mutineers, Sebastian
Elcano, was put in command of the ship, such of
the surprised and bewildered crew as were likely to
be loyal were disarmed, and food and wine were
handed about in token of the more generous policy
now to be adopted.   All was done so quickly and
quietly that no suspicion of it reached the captain-
general or anybody on board the Trinidad.

On Monday morning the traitor captains felt
themselves masters of the situation.   Three of the
five ships were in their hands, and if they chose to
go back to Spain, who could stop them?   If they
should decide to capture the flagship and murder
their commander, they had a fair chance of success, for the faithful Serrano in his little ship
Santiago was no match for any one of the three.
Defiance seemed quite safe, and in the
forenoon, when a boat from the flagship
happened to approach the San Antonio
she was insolently told to keep away, since Ma-

The mutiny
at Port St.
Julian, April
1, 1520.

Desperate
situation of
Magellan.

gellan no longer had command over that ship.
When this challenge was carried to Magellan he
sent the boat from ship to ship as a test, and soon
learned that only the Santiago remained loyal.
Presently Quesada sent a message to the Trinidad
requesting a conference between the chief commander and the revolted captains. Very well, said
Magellan, only the conference must of course be
held on board the Trinidad; but for Quesada and
his accomplices thus to venture in the lion's jaws
was out of the question, and they impudently insisted that the captain - general should come on
board the San Antonio.

Little did they realize with what a man they
were dealing. Magellan knew how to make them
come to him. He had reason to be- His bold
lieve that the crew of the Victoria was stroke.
less disloyal than the others and selected that ship
for the scene of his first *coup de main*. While he
kept a boat in readiness, with a score of trusty men
armed to the teeth and led by his wife's brother,
Barbosa, he sent another boat ahead to the Victoria, with his alguazil, or constable, Espinosa, and
five other men. Luis de Mendoza, captain of the
Victoria, suffered this small party to come on
board. Espinosa then served on Mendoza a formal summons to come to the flagship, and upon his
refusal quick as lightning sprang upon him and
plunged a dagger into his throat. As the corpse
of the rebellious captain dropped upon the deck,
Barbosa's party rushed over the ship's side with
drawn cutlasses, the dazed crew at once surrendered, and Barbosa took command.

The tables were now turned, and with three ships in loyal hands Magellan blockaded the other two in the harbour. At night he opened fire upon the San Antonio, and strong parties from the

The mutiny suppressed.

Trinidad and the Victoria boarding her on both sides at once, Quesada and his accomplices were captured. The Concepcion thereupon, overawed and crestfallen, lost no time in surrendering; and so the formidable mutiny was completely quelled in less than four-and-twenty hours. Quesada was beheaded, Cartagena and a guilty priest, Pero Sanchez, were kept in irons until the fleet sailed, when they were set ashore and left to their fate; all the rest were pardoned, and open defiance of the captain-general was no more dreamed of. In the course of the winter the Santiago was wrecked while on a reconnoissance, but her men were rescued after dreadful sufferings, and Serrano was placed in command of the Concepcion.

At length on the 24th of August, with the earliest symptoms of spring weather, the ships, which

Discovery of the strait.

had been carefully overhauled and repaired, proceeded on their way.[1] Violent storms harassed them, and it was not until the

---

[1] While they were staying at Port St. Julian the explorers made the acquaintance of many Patagonians, — giants, as they called them. "Their height appears greater than it really is, from their large guanaco mantles, their long flowing hair, and general figure : on an average their height is about six feet, with some men taller and only a few shorter ; and the women are also tall." Darwin, *Voyage of the Beagle*, London, 1870, p. 232. These Patagonians invoked a deity of theirs (or as Pigafetta puts it, " the chief of their devils ") by the name of Setebos. Shakespeare makes Caliban use this name twice in the *Tempest*, act i.

21st of October (St. Ursula's day) that they
reached the headland still known as Cape Virgins.
Passing beyond Dungeness they entered a large
open bay, which some hailed as the long-sought
strait, while others averred that no passage would
be found there.   It was, says Pigafetta, in Eden's
version, "the straight now cauled the straight of
Magellanus, beinge in sum place. C. x. leaques in
length: and in breadth sumwhere very large and
in other places lyttle more than halfe a leaque in
bredth.   On both the sydes of this strayght are
great and hygh mountaynes couered with snowe,
beyonde the whiche is the enteraunce into the sea
of Sur. . . . Here one of the shyppes stole away
priuilie and returned into Spayne."   More than
five weeks were consumed in passing through the
strait, and among its labyrinthine twists and half-
hidden bays there was ample opportunity for desertion.   As advanced reconnoissances kept reporting
the water as deep and salt, the conviction grew
that the strait was found, and then the question
once more arose whether it would not be best to go
back to Spain, satisfied with this dis- Desertion of
covery, since with all these wretched de- Gomez, with
lays the provisions were again running tonio.
short.   Magellan's answer, uttered in measured
and quiet tones, was simply that he would go on
and do his work "if he had to eat the leather off
the ship's yards."   Upon the San Antonio there

scene 2, and act v. scene 1; in all probability he had been reading Eden's translation of Pigafetta, published in London in 1555.
Robert Browning has elaborately developed Shakespeare's suggestions in his *Caliban on Setebos.*

had always been a large proportion of the malcontents, and the chief pilot, Estevan Gomez, having been detailed for duty on that ship, lent himself to their purposes. The captain Mesquita was again seized and put in irons, a new captain was chosen by the mutineers, and Gomez piloted the ship back to Spain, where they arrived after a voyage of six months, and screened themselves for a while by lying about Magellan.

As for that commander, in Richard Eden's words, "when the capitayne Magalianes was past the strayght and sawe the way open to the other mayne sea, he was so gladde therof that for ioy the teares fell from his eyes, and named the poynt of the lande from whense he fyrst sawe that sea *Capo Desiderato.* Supposing that the shyp which stole away had byn loste, they erected a crosse uppon the top of a hyghe hyll to direct their course in the straight yf it were theyr chaunce to coome that way." The broad expanse of waters before him seemed so pleasant to Magellan, after the heavy storms through which he had passed, that he called it by the name it still bears, Pacific. But the worst hardships were still before him. Once more a Sea of Darkness must be crossed by brave hearts sickening with hope deferred. If the mid-Atlantic waters had been strange to Columbus and his men, here before Magellan's people all was thrice unknown.

Entering the Pacific.

> "They were the first that ever burst
> Into that silent sea;"

and as they sailed month after month over the waste of waters, the huge size of our planet began

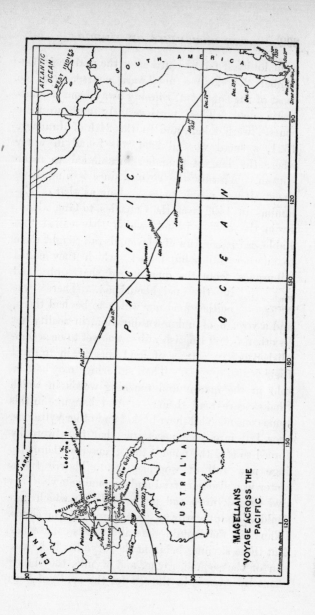

MAGELLAN'S VOYAGE ACROSS THE PACIFIC

LIBRARY OF
MUSKINGUM COLLEGE

to make itself felt.   Until after the middle of December they kept a northward course, near the coast of the continent, running away from the antarctic cold.   Then northwesterly and westerly courses were taken, and on the 24th of January, 1521, a small wooded islet was found in water where the longest plummet-lines failed to reach bottom.   Already the voyage since issuing from the strait was nearly twice as long as that of Columbus in 1492 from the Canaries to Guanahani. From the useless island, which they called San Pablo, a further run of eleven days brought them to another uninhabited rock, which they called Tiburones, from the quantity of sharks observed in the neighbourhood.   There was
Famine and scurvy.   neither food nor water to be had there, and a voyage of unknown duration, in reality not less than 5,000 English miles, was yet to be accomplished before a trace of land was again to greet their yearning gaze.   Their sufferings may best be told in the quaint and touching words in which Shakespeare read them: — "And hauynge in this tyme consumed all theyr bysket and other vyttayles, they fell into such necessitie that they were inforced to eate the pouder that remayned therof beinge now full of woormes. . . . Theyre freshe water was also putrifyed and become yelow.   They dyd eate skynnes and pieces of lether which were foulded abowt certeyne great ropes of the shyps. [Thus did the captain-general's words come true.] But these skynnes being made verye harde by reason of the soonne, rayne, and wynde, they hunge them by a corde in the sea for the space of foure

or fiue dayse to mollifie them, and sodde them, and eate them. By reason of this famen and vnclene feedynge, summe of theyr gummes grewe so ouer theyr teethe [a symptom of scurvy], that they dyed miserably for hunger. And by this occasion dyed. xix. men, and . . besyde these that dyed, xxv. or. xxx. were so sicke that they were not able to doo any seruice with theyr handes or arms for fee-blenesse: So that was in maner none without sum disease. In three monethes and. xx. dayes, they sayled foure thousande leaques in one goulfe by the sayde sea cauled Pacificum (that is) peaceable, whiche may well bee so cauled forasmuch as in all this tyme hauyng no syght of any lande, they had no misfortune of wynde or any other tempest. . . . So that in fine, if god of his mercy had not gyuen them good wether, it was necessary that in this soo greate a sea they shuld all haue dyed for hunger. Whiche neuertheless they escaped soo hardely, that it may bee doubted whether euer the like viage may be attempted with so goode successe." [1]

One would gladly know — albeit Pigafetta's journal and the still more laconic pilot's log-book leave us in the dark on this point — how the igno-rant and suffering crews interpreted this everlast-ing stretch of sea, vaster, said Maximil- Vastness be-ian Transylvanus, "than the human yond concep-tion. mind could conceive." To them it may well have seemed that the theory of a round and limited earth was wrong after all, and that their infatuated commander was leading them out into the fathomless abysses of space, with no welcom-

[1] *The First Three English Books on America*, p. 253.

ing shore beyond. But that heart of triple bronze,[1] we may be sure, did not flinch. The situation had got beyond the point where mutiny could be suggested as a remedy. The very desperateness of it was all in Magellan's favour; for so far away had they come from the known world that retreat meant certain death. The only chance of escape lay in pressing forward. At last, on the 6th of March, they came upon islands

The Ladrone islands. inhabited by savages ignorant of the bow and arrow, but expert in handling their peculiar light boats. Here the dreadful sufferings were ended, for they found plenty of fruit and fresh vegetables, besides meat. The people were such eager and pertinacious thieves that their islands received the name by which they are still known, the Islas de Ladrones, or isles of robbers.

On the 16th of March the three ships arrived at the islands which some years afterward were named Philippines, after Philip II. of Spain. Though these were islands unvisited by Euro-

The Philippines. peans, yet Asiatic traders from Siam and Sumatra, as well as from China, were to be met there, and it was thus not long before Magellan became aware of the greatness of his triumph. He had passed the meridian of the Moluccas, and knew that these islands lay to the southward within an easy sail. He had accomplished the circumnavigation of the earth through its unknown portion, and the remainder of his

[1] Illi robur et æs triplex
Circa pectus erat, etc.
Horat., *Carm.*, i. 3 ; cf. Æschylus, *Prometh.*, 242.

route lay through seas already traversed. An erroneous calculation of longitudes confirmed him in the belief that the Moluccas, as well as the Philippines, properly belonged to Spain. Meanwhile in these Philippines of themselves he had discovered a region of no small commercial importance. But his brief tarry in these interesting islands had fatal results, and in the very hour of victory the conqueror perished, slain in a fight with the natives, the reason of which we can understand only by considering the close complication of commercial and political interests with religious notions so common in that age.

As the typical Spaniard or Portuguese was then a persecutor of heresy at home, so he was always more or less of a missionary abroad, and the missionary spirit was in his case intimately allied with the crusading spirit. If the heathen resisted the gospel, it was quite right to slay and despoil them. Magellan's nature was devoutly religious, and exhibited itself in the points of strength and weakness most characteristic of his age. After he had made a treaty of alliance with the king of the island of Sebu, in which, among other things, the exclusive privilege of trading there was reserved to the Spaniards, Magellan made the unexpected discovery that the king and his people were ready and even eager to embrace Christianity! They had conceived an exalted idea of the powers and accomplishments of these white strangers, and apparently wished to imitate them in all things. So in less than a week's time a

The mediæval spirit.

Conversion of the people of Sebu.

huge bonfire had been made of the idols, a cross
was set up in the market, and all the people on
the island were baptized! Now the king of Sebu
claimed allegiance from chieftains on neighbouring islands who were slow to render it; and having adopted the white man's "medicine" he naturally wished to test its efficacy. What was
Christianity good for if not to help you to humble
your vassals? So the Christian king of Sebu demanded homage from the pagan king of Matan,
and when the latter potentate scornfully refused,
there was a clear case for a crusade! The steadfast commander, the ally and protector of his new
convert, the peerless navigator, the knight without
fear and without reproach, now turned crusader
as quickly as he had turned missionary. Indeed
there was no turning. These various aspects of
life's work were all one to him; he would have
summed up the whole thing as "serving God and
doing his duty." So Magellan crossed over to
the island of Matan, on the 27th of April, 1521,
and was encountered by the natives in overwhelming force. After a desperate fight the Spaniards
were obliged to retreat to their boats, and their
commander, who years before had been the last
man to leave a sinking ship, now lingered on the
Death of Ma-   brink of danger, screening his men, till
gellan.   his helmet was knocked off and his
right arm disabled by a spear thrust. A sudden blow brought him to the ground, and then,
says the Chevalier Pigafetta, "the Indians threw
themselves upon him with iron-pointed bamboo
spears and scimitars, and every weapon they had,

the ranks, with foretopmast gone by the board and foreyard badly sprung, cleared the Return of the Victoria. Cape of Good Hope, and thence was borne on the strong and friendly current up to the equator, which she crossed on the 8th of June. Only fifty years since Santarem and Escobar, first of Europeans, had crept down that coast and crossed it! Into that glorious half-century what a world of suffering and achievement had been crowded! Dire necessity compelled the Victoria to stop at the Cape Verde islands. Her people sought safety in deceiving the Portuguese with the story that they were returning from a voyage in Atlantic waters only, and thus they succeeded in buying food. But while this was going on, as a boat-load of thirteen men had been sent ashore for rice, some silly tongue, loosened by wine in the head of a sailor who had cloves to sell, babbled the perilous secret of Magellan and the Moluccas. The thirteen were at once arrested and a boat called upon the Victoria, with direful threats, to surrender; but she quickly stretched every inch of her canvas and got away. This was on the 13th of July, and eight weeks of ocean remained. At last, on the 6th of September [1] — the thirtieth anniver-

---

[1] They were surprised to hear their friends at home calling it the 7th: — "And amonge other notable thynges . . . wrytten as touchynge that vyage, this is one, that the Spanyardes hauinge sayled abowt three yeares and one moneth, and the most of them notynge the dayes, day by day (as is the maner of all them that sayle by the ocean), they founde when they were returned to Spayne that they had loste one daye. So that at theyr arryuall at the porte of Siuile, beinge the seuenth daye of September, was by theyr accompt but the sixth day. And where as Don Peter Martyr declared the strange effecte of this thynge to a certeyne

sary of the day when Columbus weighed anchor
for Cipango — the Victoria sailed into the Guadalquivir, with eighteen gaunt and haggard survivors to tell the proud story of the first circumnavigation of the earth.[1]

The voyage thus ended was doubtless the greatest feat of navigation that has ever been performed, and nothing can be imagined that would
surpass it except a journey to some other planet.
An unpar- It has not the unique historic position
alleled voyage. of the first voyage of Columbus, which
brought together two streams of human life that
had been disjoined since the Glacial Period. But
as an achievement in ocean navigation that voyage
of Columbus sinks into insignificance by the side
of it, and when the earth was a second time encompassed by the greatest English sailor of his
age, the advance in knowledge, as well as the different route chosen, had much reduced the difficulty of the performance. When we consider
the frailness of the ships, the immeasurable extent
of the unknown, the mutinies that were prevented
or quelled, and the hardships that were endured,
we can have no hesitation in speaking of Magellan
as the prince of navigators. Nor can we ever fail
to admire the simplicity and purity of that devoted

excellente man, who, for his singular lernynge, was greately ad-
uanced to honoure in his common welthe and made Themperour's
ambassadoure, this worthy gentelman, who was also a greate
Philosopher and Astronomer, answered that it coulde not other-
wyse chaunce unto them, hauynge sayled three yeares contin-
ually, euer folowynge the soonne towarde the West." *The First
Three English Books on America*, p. 246.

[1] Their names are given below in Appendix D.

life in which there is nothing that seeks to be
hidden or explained away.

It would have been fitting that the proudest
crest ever granted by a sovereign — a
terrestrial globe belted with the legend Elcano's crest.
Primus circumdedisti me (Thou first encompassed
me) — should have been bestowed upon the son
and representative of the hero ; but when the Victoria returned there was none to receive such
recognition. In September, 1521, Magellan's son,
the little Rodrigo, died, and by March, 1522, the
gentle mother Beatriz had heard, by way of the
Portuguese Indies, of the fate of her husband and
her brother.[1] In that same month — " grievously
sorrowing," as we are told — she died. The coat-
of-arms with the crest just mentioned, along with
a pension of 500 ducats, was granted to Elcano, a
weak man who had ill deserved such honour. Espinosa was also, with more justice, pensioned and
ennobled.

One might at first suppose that the revelation
of such an immensity of water west of Mundus
Novus would soon have resulted in the evolution
of the conception of a distinct western How slowly
hemisphere. This effect was, however, the result was
compre-
very slowly wrought in men's minds. hended.
The fact was too great and too strange to be easily
taken in and assimilated with the mass of mingled
fact and theory already existing. It was not until
1577–80 that the Pacific was crossed, for the second
time, by Sir Francis Drake. How imperfectly its
dimensions were comprehended may be seen from

[1] Guillemard, p. 90.

the globe of Orontius Finæus, 1531, of which a sketch has already been given. In his *Opusculum Geographicum*, published in 1533, Schöner placed Newfoundland and Florida in Asia and identified the city of Mexico with Marco Polo's Quinsay. To bring out the correct outline and huge continental mass of North America, and to indicate with entire precision its relations to Asia, was the Work of Two Centuries, a brief sketch of which will be given hereafter. But before we can properly come to that final chapter in the history of the Discovery of America, there are other points which demand attention. Something must be said concerning the earliest contact between the civilization of Europe just emerging from the Middle Ages and the semi-civilizations of the archaic world of America, similar in many respects to those that had flourished in the eastern hemisphere before the times of Abraham and Agamemnon. No scenes in history are more remarkable than those which attended this earliest contact. It would be hard to point to a year more fraught with thrilling interest than 1519, when in the month of November, at the very time that Magellan was breasting the storms of the southern Atlantic, on the way to his long-sought strait, Hernando Cortes was anxiously inspecting the terraced roofs and picturesque drawbridges of the strange city to which Montezuma had just admitted him. We have now to deal briefly with that episode in the Discovery of America known as the Conquest of Mexico.

The work of two centuries.

What next concerns us.

CHAPTER VIII.

THE CONQUEST OF MEXICO.

IF we were engaged upon a philosophical history of the human mind, the career of maritime discovery in the fifteenth and sixteenth centuries would have great interest for us, with regard to its influence upon men's habits of thought. In the long run, the effect of increased knowledge of the earth is to dispel mythological mystery and the kind of romance that goes with it, and to strengthen men's belief in the constancy of nature. As long as nothing was known of the lands beyond the equator, it was easy enough to people them with gnomes and griffins. There was no intrinsic improbability in the existence of a "land east of the sun and west of the moon," or any of the other regions subject to the Queen of the Fairies, — any more than in the existence of Cipango or Cathay, or any other real country which was indefinitely remote and had but rarely been visited. As long as men's fancy had free sweep, beyond the narrow limits of "the world as known to the ancients," there was plenty of room for fairyland. But in these prosaic days our knowledge of the earth's surface has become so nearly complete as to crowd out all thought of enchanted ground. Beyond

Effects of increased knowledge of geography upon the romantic spirit.

the dark and perilous sea we no longer look for El Dorado, since maps and gazetteers have taught us to expect nothing better than the beautiful but cruel, the romantic but humdrum, world with which daily experience has already made us so well acquainted. In this respect the present age, compared with the sixteenth century, is like mature manhood compared with youth. The bright visions have fled, but the sober realities of life remain. The most ardent adventurer of our time has probably never indulged in such wild fancies as must have flitted through the mind of young Louis de Hennepin when he used to hide behind tavern doors while the sailors were telling of their voyages. "The tobacco smoke," he says, " used to make me very sick; but, notwithstanding, I listened attentively to all that was said about their adventures at sea and their travels in distant countries. I could have passed whole days and nights in this way without eating." [1]

The first effect of the voyages of Columbus and his successors was to arouse this spirit of romantic curiosity to fever heat. Before the newly-found lands had been explored, there was no telling what they might not contain. Upon one point, however, most of the early adventurers were thoroughly agreed. The newly-found coasts must be near Cipango and Cathay, or at any rate somewhere within the territories of the "Grand Khan;" and the reports of Marco Polo, doubtless bravely embellished in passing

Romantic dreams of the Spanish explorers.

---

[1] Hennepin, *Voyage Curieux* (1704), 12, cited in Parkman's *La Salle*, p. 120.

from mouth to mouth, whetted the greed for gold
and inflamed the crusading zeal of the sturdy men
who had just driven the Moor from Granada and
were impatiently longing for " fresh woods and
pastures new." It was taken for granted that the
countries beyond the Sea of Darkness abounded in
rich treasure which might be won without labour
more prosaic than fighting ; for as heathen treasure
it was of course the legitimate prey of these soldiers of the Cross. Their minds were in a state
like that of the heroes of the Arabian Nights who,
if they only wander far enough through the dark
forest or across the burning desert, are sure at
length to come upon some enchanted palace whereof
they may fairly hope, with the aid of some gracious
Jinni, to become masters. But with all their unchecked freedom of fancy, it is not likely that
the Spaniards who first set foot upon the soil of
Mexico had ever imagined anything stranger than
the sights they saw there ; nor did ever a slave of
the lamp prepare for man a triumph so astounding
as that of which the elements were in readiness
awaiting the masterful touch of Hernando Cortes
in the year 1519.

I have already described, in its most general
outlines, the structure of society in ancient Mexico.[1] A glance at its history is now necessary,
if we would understand the circumstances of its
sudden overthrow. A very brief sketch is all that
is here practicable, and it is all that my purpose
requires.

[1] See above, vol. i. pp. 100–131.

The earliest date which we can regard as clearly established in the history of Mexico is 1325 A. D., the year in which the great Aztec pueblo was founded. For whatever happened before that time we have to grope our way in the uncertain light of vague or conflicting traditions and tempting but treacherous philological speculations. It is somewhat as in the history of Greece before the first Olympiad. Sundry movements of peoples and a few striking incidents loom up through the fog of oblivion, and there is room for surmises that things may have happened in this way or in that way, but whether we succeed in putting events into their true order, or get them within a century or so of their real dates, remains very doubtful. According to Mr. Hubert Bancroft, the cool Mexican table-land, since often known as Anáhuac,[1] or "lake country," was occupied during the sixth and seventh centuries of the Christian era by tribes of various degrees of barbarism belonging to the group ever since known as Nahuas. In the fertile valleys horticulture became developed, population increased, arts of construction throve, and in course of time a kind of supremacy over the whole region east and south of the lakes is said to have been secured by certain confederated tribes called Toltecs, a name which has been explained as meaning "artificers" or "builders." It has

Prehistoric Mexico.

The "Toltecs."

---

[1] There was no such thing as an "empire of Anáhuac," nor was the name peculiar to the Mexican table-land; it was given to any country near a large body of water, whether lake or sea. See Brasseur de Bourbourg, *Ruines de Palenqué*, p. 32.

been supposed that the name may have been loosely applied to pueblo-builders by other people who did not erect such structures. Among the principal seats of Toltec supremacy we hear much of the city or pueblo of Tollan, on the site of the modern village of Tula, some forty miles to the northwest of the city of Mexico. It is well to beware, however, about meddling much with these Toltecs. In some respects they remind one of the Pelasgi. Whatever seemed strange or inexplicable in the early history of Greece, the old historians used to dispose of by calling in that mysterious people, the Pelasgi. Greek history had its Pelasgic dark cupboard into which it used to throw its nondescript rubbish of speculation; and I suspect that the Toltecs have furnished a similar dark cupboard to the historians of Mexico. There was doubtless, as we shall presently see, a tribe of Toltecs which dwelt for a time at Tollan, and it was the misfortune of this people to have its name become the vehicle of divers solar myths associated with the fair god Quetzalcoatl. The name Tollan, which means " place of the sun," occurs in other parts of Mexico; it was quite commonly applied to Cholula, the pueblo especially sacred to Quetzalcoatl.[1] Wherever legends came to be located in which the Fair God figured, his followers the Toltecs naturally figured likewise. " All arts and sciences, all knowledge and culture, were ascribed to this wonderful mythical people ; and wherever the natives were asked concerning the origin of ancient and unknown structures,

[1] Bandelier, *Archæological Tour in Mexico*, p. 194.

they would reply: ' The Toltecs built them.' " [1]
In this way seems to have been generated that
notion of a " Toltec empire " which has bewildered
and misled so many writers.

In opposition to the Toltecs we find frequent
The "Chichi-   mention of the Chichimecs, whose name
mecs."   is said to mean " barbarians." Such
an epithet would indicate that their enemies held
them in scorn, but does not otherwise give us
much information. At the time of the Discovery
it was applied in two very different senses; 1. in
general, to the roaming savage tribes far to the
north of Anáhuac, and 2. in particular, to the
" line of kings " (i. e. clan out of which the head
war-chiefs were chosen) at Tezcuco.[2] This may
indicate that at some time the great pueblo-town
of Tezcuco was seized and appropriated by a people somewhat inferior in culture ; or that neighbouring pueblos applied to the Tezcucans an op-
probrious epithet which stuck ; or, perhaps, that
at some time the Tezcucans may have repelled an
invasion of lower peoples, so that their chiefs

[1] See Brinton, " The Toltecs and their Fabulous Empire," in
his *Essays of an Americanist*, pp. 83–100, an admirable treatment
of the subject. The notion of the Toltec empire pervades M. de
Charnay's *Ancient Cities of the New World*, and detracts from
the value of that able book. M. de Charnay's archæological
work is very good, but his historical speculations will bear considerable revision and excision.

[2] Their history has been written by their descendant Fernando
de Ixtlilxochitl (born in 1570), *Histoire des Chichimèques, et des
anciens rois de Tezcuco*, Paris, 1840, 2 vols. This work contains
many valuable facts, but its authority is gravely impaired by the
fact that Ixtlilxochitl " wrote for an interested object, and with
the view of sustaining tribal claims in the eyes of the Spanish
government." See Bandelier, *Archæological Tour*, p. 192.

were called Chichimecs by way of compliment, as
Roman warriors were called Germanicus or Afri-
canus. Ingenuity may amuse itself with surmises,
but the true explanation is often something that
nobody would have thought of. It is not even
certain that the name means barbarian, or anything of the sort.[1] The Chichimecs are no more
than the Toltecs a safe subject for speculation.[2]

It may have been anywhere from the ninth to the
eleventh century that a number of Nahua tribes,
coming from some undetermined north-   The Nahua
erly region which they called Aztlan,[3] in-   tribes.
vaded the territory of Anáhuac, and planted them-

[1] Mr. Bandelier, improving upon a hint of the learned Veytia
(*Historia antigua del Méjico*, cap. xii. p. 143), suggests that the
word Chichimecs may mean "kin of red men." *Peabody Museum
Reports*, ii. 393.

[2] The learned Rèmi Siméon, in his introduction to the *Annales
de Chimalpahin Quauhtlehuanitzin*, Paris, 1889, has not quite succeeded in avoiding the pitfalls which surround this subject; e. g.
"Ces trois grands peuples, les Toltèques, les Mexicains, et les
Chichimèques, avaient donc chacun leur caractère particulier.
Les Toltèques étaient artisans, les Mexicains guerriers et com-
merçants, les Chichimèques agriculteurs," etc., p. xxxvi. This
sort of generalization does not help us much.

[3] The situation of Aztlan, and the meaning of the name, have
furnished themes for much speculation. Mr. Morgan, following
Acosta and Clavigero, interpreted Aztlan as "place of cranes,"
and inferred that it must have been in New Mexico, where
cranes abound (*Houses and House-Life*, p. 195). Duran translated it "place of whiteness" (*Historia de Nueva España*, i. 19);
but, as Dr. Brinton observes, it may mean "place by salt water"
(*Essays of an Americanist*, p. 88). Father Duran thought that
Aztlan was situated within the region of our Gulf States; cf.
Brasseur, *Hist. des nations civilisées de l'Amerique centrale*, ii. 292.
Some writers have supposed it was the home of the "mound-
builders" in the Mississippi, and in recent times a group of
earthworks in Wisconsin has been named Aztlan or Aztalan.

selves at various commanding points. It is probable that there was a series of waves of invasion
by peoples essentially the same in blood and speech.
As Dr. Brinton has ably pointed out, the story of
Tollan and its people as we find it in three of the
most unimpeachable authorities — Father Duran,
Tezozomoc, and the Codex Ramirez — virtually
identifies Toltecs with Aztecs. The situation of

Tollan and the Serpent Hill. that Tollan which is now called Tula
was on one of the principal ancient
trails from the north into the elevated Valley of
Mexico. It was a natural pass or gateway, and
had the importance which belongs to such places.
The ruins of the ancient town are upon a small
hill, known as Coatepetl, or Serpent Hill, which
figures largely in the legends about the Toltecs.
The town consisted of large edifices built of rub-
ble-stone mingled with adobe-brick, with flat and
terraced roofs, somewhat after the fashion, perhaps, of the pueblos in New Mexico. Mural paint-
ing and figure-carving were practised by its inhabitants. According to the authorities just cited,
there was a division among the Nahua tribes
migrating from Aztlan. Some passed on into the
Valley of Mexico, while others fortified themselves on the Serpent Hill and built a temple to
the war-god Huitzilopochtli. The city of Tollan
thus founded lasted for some generations, until its
people, hard pressed by hostile neighbours, re-

Much more probable are the views of Mendieta (*Historia Eccle-
siastica*, p. 144), who places it in the province of Xalisco ; or of
Orozco y Berra (*Historia antigua de Mexico*, tom. iii. cap. 4), who
places it in Michoacan. Albert Gallatin expressed a similar view
in *Trans. Amer. Ethnolog. Soc.*, ii. 202.

treated into the Valley of Mexico, and afterward built the city which has become famous under that name.[1]

In this story the founders of Mexico are virtually identified with those of Tollan. Following this hint, we may suppose the "Toltec period" in Mexican tradition to have been simply the period when the pueblo-town of Tollan was flourishing, and domineered most likely over neighbouring pueblos. One might thus speak of it as one would speak of the "Theban period" in Greek history. After the "Toltec period," with perhaps an intervening "Chichimec period" of confusion, came the "Aztec period;" or in other words, some time after Tollan lost its importance, the city of Mexico came to the front. Such, I suspect, is the slender historical residuum underlying the legend of a "Toltec empire." [2]

The fabulous "Toltec empire."

The Codex Ramirez assigns the year 1168 as the date of the abandonment of the Serpent Hill by the people of Tollan. We begin to leave this twilight of legend when we meet the Aztecs already encamped in the Valley of Mexico. Finding the most obviously eligible sites preoccupied, they were sagacious enough to detect the advantages of a certain marshy spot through which the outlets of lakes Chalco and Xochimilco, besides sundry rivulets, flowed northward and eastward into Lake Tezcuco. Here in

The Aztecs, and the founding of the city of Mexico.

---

[1] Duran, *Historia de las Indias de Nueva España*, cap. iii.; Tezozomoc, *Crónica Mexicana*, cap. ii.; *Codex Ramirez*, p. 24.

[2] See Brinton, *op. cit.* p. 89.

the year 1325 they began to build their pueblo, which they called Tenochtitlan, — a name whereby hangs a tale. When the Aztecs, hard pressed by foes, took refuge among these marshes, they came upon a sacrificial stone which they recognized as one upon which some years before one of their priests had immolated a captive chief. From a crevice in this stone, where a little earth was imbedded, there grew a cactus, upon which sat an eagle holding in its beak a serpent. A priest ingeniously interpreted this symbolism as a prophecy of signal and long-continued victory, and forthwith diving into the lake he had an interview with Tlaloc, the god of waters, who told him that upon that very spot the people were to build their town. The place was therefore called Tenochtitlan, or " p'ace of the cactus-rock," but the name under which it afterward came to be best known was taken from Mexitl, one of the names of the war-god Huitzilopochtli. The device of the rock and cactus, with the eagle and serpent, formed a tribal totem for the Aztecs, and has been adopted as the coat-of-arms of the present Republic of Mexico. The pueblo of Tenochtitlan was surrounded by salt marshes, which by dint of dikes and causeways the Aztecs gradually converted into a large artificial lake, and thus made their pueblo by far the most defensible stronghold in Anáhuac, — impregnable, indeed, so far as Indian modes of attack were concerned.[1]

[1] According to Mr. Bandelier the only Indian position comparable with it for strength was that of Atitlan, in Guatemala. *Peabody Museum Reports*, vol. ii. p. 97.

The advantages of this commanding position were slowly but surely realized. A dangerous neighbour upon the western shore of the lake was the tribe of Tecpanecas, whose principal pueblo was Azcaputzalco. The Aztecs succeeded in making an alliance with these Tecpanecas, but it was upon unfavourable terms and involved the payment of tribute to Azcaputzalco. It gave the Aztecs, however, some time to develop their strength. Their military organization was gradually perfected, and in 1375 they elected their first *tlacate-cuhtli*, or " chief-of-men," whom European writers, in the loose phraseology formerly current, called " founder of the Mexican empire." The name of this official was Acamapichtli, or " Handful-of-Reeds." During the eight-and-twenty years of his chieftaincy the pueblo houses in Tenoch- titlan began to be built very solidly of stone, and the irregular water-courses

The first four Aztec " chiefs-of-men."

flowing between them were improved into canals. Some months after his death in 1403 his son Hui- tzilihuitl, or " Humming-bird," was chosen to succeed him. This Huitzilihuitl was succeeded in 1414 by his brother Chimalpopoca, or " Smoking Shield," under whom temporary calamity visited the Aztec town. The alliance with Azcaputzalco was broken, and that pueblo joined its forces to those of Tezcuco on the eastern shore of the lake. United they attacked the Aztecs, defeated them, and captured their chief-of-men, who died a prisoner in 1427. He was succeeded by Izcoatzin, or " Obsidian Snake," an aged chieftain who died in 1436.

During these nine years a complete change came over the scene. Quarrels arose between Azcaputzalco and Tezcuco; the latter pueblo entered into alliance with Tenochtitlan, and together they over- whelmed and destroyed Azcaputzalco, and butchered most of its people. What was left of the conquered pueblo was made a slave mart for the Aztecs, and the remnant of the people were removed to the neighbouring pueblo of Tlacopan, which was made tributary to Mexico. By this great victory the Aztecs also acquired secure control of the springs upon Chepultepec, or " Grasshopper Hill," which furnished a steady supply of fresh water to their island pueblo.

Destruction of Azcaputzalco.

The next step was the formation of a partner- ship between the three pueblo towns, Tenochtitlan, Tezcuco, and Tlacopan, for the organized and sys- tematic plunder of other pueblos. All the tribute or spoils extorted was to be divided into five parts, of which two parts each were for Tezcuco and Te- nochtitlan, and one part for Tlacopan. The Aztec chief-of-men became military commander of the confederacy, which now began to extend operations to a distance. The next four chiefs-of-men were Montezuma, or " Angry Chief," the First, from 1436 to 1464; Axayacatl, or " Face- in - the - Water," from 1464 to 1477 ; Tizoc, or " Wounded Leg," from 1477 to 1486; and Ahui- zotl, or " Water-Rat," from 1486 to 1502. Un- der these chiefs the great temple of Mexico was completed, and the aqueduct from Chepultepec was increased in capacity until it not only supplied

The Mexican Confederacy.

TABLE OF THE SUCCESSION (ELECTIVE) AND OF THE RELATIONSHIPS OF THE ELEVEN MEXICAN *TLACATECUHTLI*, OR "CHIEFS-OF-MEN."

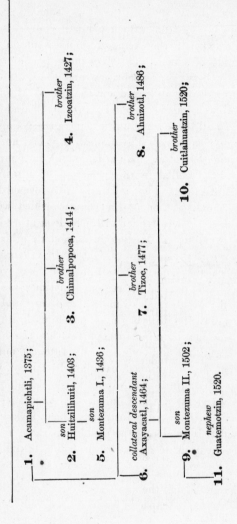

1. Acamapichtli, 1375;

2. *son* Huitzilihuitl, 1403;

3. *brother* Chimalpopoca, 1414;

4. *brother* Izcoatzin, 1427;

5. *son* Montezuma I., 1436;

6. *collateral descendant* Axayacatl, 1464;

7. *brother* Tizoc, 1477;

8. *brother* Ahuizotl, 1486;

9. *son* Montezuma II., 1502;

10. *brother* Cuitlahuatzin, 1520;

11. *nephew* Guatemotzin, 1520.

water for ordinary uses, but could also be made to maintain the level of the canals and the lake. In the driest seasons, therefore, Tenochtitlan remained safe from attack. Forth from this well-protected lair the Aztec warriors went on their errands of blood. Thirty or more pueblo towns, mostly between Tenochtitlan and the Gulf coast, scattered over an area about the size of Massachusetts, were made tributary to the Confederacy; and as all these communities spoke the Nahua language, this process of conquest, if it had not been cut short by the Spaniards, might in course of time have ended in the formation of a primitive kind of state. This tributary area formed but a very small portion of the country which we call Mexico. If the reader will just look at a map of the Republic of Mexico in a modern atlas, and observe that the states of Queretaro, Guanaxuato, Michoacan, Guerrero, and a good part of La Puebla, lie outside the region sometimes absurdly styled " Montezuma's Empire," and surround three sides of it, he will begin to put himself into the proper state of mind for appreciating the history of Cortes and his companions. Into the outlying region just mentioned, occupied by tribes for the most part akin to the Nahuas in blood and speech, the warriors of the Confederacy sometimes ventured, with varying fortunes. They levied occasional tribute among the pueblos in these regions, but hardly made any of them regularly tributary. The longest range of their arms seems to have been to the eastward, where they sent their tax-gatherers along the coast into the isthmus of Te-

huantepec, and came into conflict with the warlike
Mayas and Quiches. On the other hand, as already
observed, the Confederacy did not effect any true
military occupation of the country near at hand,
and within twenty or thirty leagues of Tenochtitlan such pueblo towns as Cholula and Tlascala,
with populations of about 30,000 persons, retained
their independence. The Tlascalans, The hostile
indeed, were a perpetual thorn in the Tlascalans.
side of the Confederacy. Occupying a strong defensive position, they beat back repeatedly the
forces of the chief-of-men and aided and abetted
recalcitrant pueblos in refusing tribute. The state
of feeling between Tlascalans and Aztecs was like
that between Romans and Carthaginians, or Turks
and Montenegrins.

Such was, in general outline, what we may call
the political situation in the time of the son of
Axayacatl, the second Montezuma, who was elected
chief-of-men in 1502, being then thirty- The second
four years of age. One of the first Montezuma.
expeditions led by this Montezuma, in 1503, was
directed against the Tlascalans for the purpose of
obtaining captives for sacrifice; it met with disastrous defeat, and furnished victims for the Tlascalan altars. A raid of Montezuma's into Michoacan was also repulsed, but upon the eastern coast
he was more successful in wringing tribute from
the pueblo towns, and in arousing in their inhabitants a desperate rage, ready to welcome any
chance of delivery from the oppressor. Many
towns refused tribute and were savagely punished;
and as always happens upon the eve of a crisis in

history, we hear wild rumours of supernatural por-
tents.   There was the usual tale of comet and
eclipse, and the volcanic craters in the Cordillera
were thought to be unwontedly active.[1]   At length,
in the course of the year 1518, came the handwriting on the wall.   A certain Indian named
Pinotl was Montezuma's tax-gatherer (*calpixca*)
and spy at the pueblo of Cuetlachtlan, some thirty
miles inland from the Gulf coast and about as far to
the southward from San Juan de Ulloa.   To this
officer there came one day an Indian from the neigh-

An amazing
story.

bouring pueblo of Mictlan-Quauhtla on
the coast, with a story the like of which
no man in all that country had ever heard.   He
had seen a great tower, with wings, moving hither
and thither upon the sea.   Other Indians, sent to
verify the rumour, saw two such towers, and from
one of them a canoe was let down and darted
about on the water, and in it were a kind of men
with white faces and heavy beards, and they were
clad in a strange and shining raiment.[2]   At this
news the tax-gatherer Pinotl, with a body of attendants, hastened down to the shore and met the
Spanish squadron of Juan de Grijalva.   Pinotl

Pinotl visits
the mysteri-
ous strangers.

went on board one of these marvellous
winged towers, and exchanged gifts with
its commander, who was pleased to hear
about the wealth and power of Pinotl's master,

[1] Bancroft, *History of Mexico*, i. 113.

[2] Tezozomoc, ii. 232; Duran, ii. 359–377; Bancroft, *loc. cit.*
Tezozomoc says that this Indian's ears, thumbs, and big toes were
mutilated; concerning the purport of which a query will presently be made.

and promised some day before long to come and
pay him a visit in his great city among the mountains. When the dread strangers had gone on
their way, the tax-gatherer's party took the short-
est trail to Tenochtitlan, and hurrying to the tecpan, or council-house, informed Montezuma that
they had seen and talked with gods. On strips of
maguey paper they had made sketches of the
Spaniards and their ships and arms, along with
abundant hieroglyphic comments; and when all
this was presently laid before the tribal council for
consideration, we may dimly imagine the wild and
agitated argument that must have ensued.

No doubt the drift of the argument would be
quite undecipherable for us were it not for the
clue that is furnished by the ancient Mexican
beliefs concerning the sky-god and culture-hero,
Quetzalcoatl. This personage was an ob-
ject of reverence and a theme of myth- Quetzalcoatl.
ical tales among all the Nahua and Maya peoples.[1]
Like Zeus and Woden he has been supposed to
have been at some time a terrestrial hero who became deified after his death, but it is not likely
that he ever had a real existence, any more than
Zeus or Woden. In his attributes Quetzalcoatl resembled both the Greek and the Scandinavian deity.
He was cloud gatherer, wielder of the thunderbolt,
and ruler of the winds. As lord of the clouds he
was represented as a bird; as lord of the lightning
he was represented as a serpent;[2] and his name

[1] The Mayas called him Cukulcan.

[2] I have fully explained this symbolism in *Myths and Myth-
Makers*, chap. ii., "The Descent of Fire."

Quetzal-Coatl means "Bird-Serpent." [1] In this
character of elemental deity he was commonly associated with Tlaloc, the god of rain, of waters, and of
spring verdure.[2] This association is depicted upon
the two famous slabs discovered by Mr. Stephens
in 1840 in the course of his researches at Palenque.
The slabs were formerly inlaid in the pillars that
supported the altar in the building known as the
"Temple of the Cross, No. 1." They are about
six feet in length by three in width. On the left-
hand slab Tlaloc appears as a "young man magni-
ficently arrayed; he wears a richly embroidered
cape, a collar and medallion around his neck,
a beautiful girdle to his waist; the ends of the
maxtli[3] are hanging down front and back, co-

---

[1] Or "Feathered Serpent." Mr. Bandelier (*Archæol. Tour*, p.
170) suggests that the word *quetzalli* "only applies to feathers in
the sense of indicating their bright hues," and that the name
therefore means "Shining Serpent." But in the Mexican picture-writing the rebus for Quetzalcoatl is commonly a feather
or some other part of a bird in connection with a snake; and
the so-called "tablet of the cross" at Palenque represents the
cross, or symbol of the four winds, "surmounted by a bird and
supported by the head of a serpent" (Brinton, *Myths of the New
World*, p. 118). Here the symbolism is complete and unmistakable. The cross is the symbol of Tlaloc, the rain-god, who
is usually associated with Quetzalcoatl.

Two very learned and brilliant accounts of Quetzalcoatl are
those of Bandelier (*Archæol. Tour*, pp. 168–216), and Brinton
(*American Hero-Myths*, pp. 63–142). It seems to me that the
former suffers somewhat from its Euhemerism, and that Dr.
Brinton, treating the subject from the standpoint of comparative
mythology, gives a truer picture. Mr. Bandelier's account, however, contains much that is invaluable.

[2] Sahagun, *Hist. de las cosas de la Nueva España*, lib. ii. cap. 1.

[3] "Maxtlatl, bragas, o cosa semejante," Molina, *Vocabolario,*
s. v.

thurni cover his feet and legs up to the knee. On the upper end of his head-dress is the head of a stork, having a fish in his bill, whilst other fishes are ranged below it." [1] The right-hand slab represents Quetzalcoatl as an old man, clad in the skin of an ocelot, or Mexican "tiger," and blowing puffs of air through a tube. The bird's brilliant feathers and sharp beak are seen in his head-dress, and about his waist is the serpent twisting and curling before and behind.

Quetzalcoatl and Tlaloc.

The building at Palenque in which these sculptured slabs once adorned the altar appears to have been a temple consecrated to Quetzalcoatl and Tlaloc. The connection between the two deities was so close that their festivals "were celebrated together on the same day, which was the first of the first month of the Aztec calendar, in February." [2] There was nothing like equality between the two, however. Tlaloc remained specialized as the god of rains and giver of harvests; he was attached as a subordinate appendage to the mighty Blower of Winds and Wielder of Lightning, and his symbolism served to commemorate the elemental character of the latter. On the other hand Quetzalcoatl, without losing his attributes as an elemental deity, acquired many other attributes. As has frequently happened to sky-gods and solar heroes, he became generalized until almost all kinds of activities and interests were ascribed to him. As god of the seasons, he was

Specialization of Tlaloc as elemental deity.

Generalization of Quetzalcoatl as culture-hero.

---

[1] Charnay, *Ancient Cities of the New World*, p. 216.
[2] Brinton, *American Hero-Myths*, p. 125.

said to have invented the Aztec calendar. He taught men how to cut and polish stones; he was patron of traders, and to him in many a pueblo ingenious thieves prayed for success, as Greek thieves prayed to Hermes. It was he that promoted fertility among men, as well as in the vegetable world; sterile wives addressed to him their vows. Yet at the same time Quetzalcoatl held celibacy in honour, and in many pueblos houses of nuns were consecrated to him. Other features of asceticism occurred in his service; his priests were accustomed to mutilate their tongues, ears, and other parts of the body by piercing them with cactus thorns.

As Zeus had his local habitation upon Mount Olympus and was closely associated with the island of Crete, so Quetzalcoatl had his favourite spots. Cholula was one of them; another was Tollan, but, as already observed, this place was something more than the town which commanded the trail from Mexico into the north country. Like Cadmus and Apollo, this New World culture-deity had his home in the far east; there was his Tollan, or "place of the sun." And here we come to the most interesting part of the story, the conflict between Light and Darkness, which in all aboriginal American folk-lore appears in such transparent and unmistakable garb.[1] One of the most

---

[1] In this aspect of the power of light contending against the power of darkness, Quetzalcoatl is the counterpart of the Algonquin Michabo, the Iroquois Ioskeha, and the Peruvian Viracocha, to whom we shall by and by have occasion to refer. See Brinton, *Myths of the New World*, chap. vi.

important figures in the Mexican pantheon was
Tezcatlipoca, the dread lord of night *The dark Tez-*
and darkness, the jealous power that *catlipoca.*
visited mankind with famine and pestilence, the
ravenous demon whose food was human hearts.
No deity was more sedulously worshipped than
Tezcatlipoca, doubtless on the theory, common
among barbarous people, that it is by all means
desirable to keep on good terms with the evil
powers. Between Quetzalcoatl and Tezcatlipoca
there was everlasting hostility. The latter deity
had once been the sun, but Quetzalcoatl had
knocked him out of the sky with a big club, and
jumping into his place had become the sun instead
of him. Tezcatlipoca, after tumbling into the sea,
rose again in the night sky as the Great Bear;
and so things went on for awhile, until suddenly
the Evil One transformed himself into a tiger, and
with a blow of his paw struck Quetzalcoatl from
the sky. Amid endless droll and uncouth incidents the struggle continued, and the combatants
changed their shapes as often as in the Norse tale
of Farmer Weathersky.[1] The contest formed the
theme of a whole cycle of Mexican legends, some
grave, some humorous, many of them quite pretty.[2]
In some of these legends the adversaries figured,
not as elementary giants, but as astute and potent
men. The general burden of the tale, the conclu-

[1] See also the delicious story of the Gruagach of Tricks, in
Curtin's *Myths and Folk-Lore of Ireland*, pp. 139–156.
[2] Quite a number were taken down by Father Sahagun (about
1540) from the lips of the natives, in the original Nahuatl, and
are given in his *Hist. de las cosas de Nueva España*, lib. iii., and
in Brinton's *American Hero-Myths*, pp. 106–116.

sion most firmly riveted in the Mexican mind, was that Quetzalcoatl had been at last outwitted by his dark enemy and obliged to forsake the land.[1]

Exile of Que-
tzalcoatl.

Accompanied by a few youthful worshippers he fared forth from Cholula, and when he had reached the eastern shore, somewhere in the Coatzacualco country, between Cuetlachtlan and Tabasco, he bade farewell to his young companions, saying that he must go farther, but at some future time he should return from the east with men as fair-skinned as himself and take possession of the country. As to whither he had gone, there was a difference of opinion. Some held that he had floated out to sea on a raft of serpent skins ; others believed that his body had been consumed with fire on the beach, and that his soul had been taken up into the morning star. But in whatever way he had gone, all were agreed that in the fulness of time Quetzalcoatl would return from the eastern ocean, with white-faced companions, and renew his beneficent rule over the Mexican people.[2]

His return, it would seem, must needs involve the dethronement of the black Tezcatlipoca. According to one group of legends the fair culture-

---

[1] What a pathos there is in these quaint stories ! These poor Indians dimly saw what we see, that the Evil One is hard to kill and often seems triumphant. When things seem to have arrived at such a pass, the untutored human mind comforts itself with Messianic hopes, often destined to be rudely shocked, but based no doubt upon a sound and wholesome instinct, and one that the future career of mankind will justify. It is interesting to watch the rudimental glimmerings of such a hope in such a people as the ancient Mexicans.

[2] Brinton, *op. cit.* pp. 117, 133.

hero condemned the sacrifice of human beings, and held that the perfume of flowers and in- Expectation of his return. cense was sufficient without the shedding of blood; in similar wise he was said to look with disapproval upon wars and violence of whatever sort. If the theory which found expression in these legends should prove correct, the advent of Quetzalcoatl would overturn the worship of Tezcatlipoca, who demanded human victims, and likewise that of his grewsome ally Huitzilopochtli, the war-god who presided over the direful contests in which such victims were obtained. In short, it would revolutionize the whole system upon which the political and social life of the Nahua peoples had from time immemorial been conducted. One is naturally curious to know how far such a theory could have expressed a popular wish and not merely a vague speculative notion, but upon this point our information is lamentably meagre. It does not appear that there was any general longing for the reign of Quetzalcoatl, like that of the Jews for their Messianic Kingdom. But the notion that such a kingdom was to come was certainly a common one in ancient Mexico, and even in that fierce society there may well have been persons to whom the prevalence of wholesale slaughter did not commend itself, and who were ready to welcome the hope of a change.

When the Spanish ships arrived upon the Mexican coast in 1518, the existence of this general belief was certainly a capital fact, and probably the supreme fact, in the political and military situation. It effectually paralyzed the opposition to their entrance into the country. Surely such **a**

Fulfilment of prophecy; extraordinary coincidences.

grouping of fortunate coincidences was never known save in fairy tales. As the Spanish ships came sailing past Tabasco, they were just reversing the route by which Quetzalcoatl had gone out into the ocean; as he had gone, so they were coming in strict fulfilment of prophecy! Mictlan-Quauhtla was evidently a point from which the returning deity was likely to be seen ; and when we read that the Indian who ran with the news to Cuetlachtlan had his ears, thumbs, and toes mutilated, how can we help remembering that this particular kind of self-torture was deemed a fit method of ingratiating oneself into the favour of Quetzalcoatl? When Pinotl went on board ship he found the mysterious visitors answering in outward aspect to the requirements of the legend. In most mythologies the solar heroes are depicted with abundant hair. Quetzalcoatl was sometimes, though not always, represented with a beard longer and thicker than one would have been likely to see in ancient America. The bearded Spaniards were, therefore, at once recognized as his companions. There were sure to be some blonde Visigoth complexions among them,[1] and their general hue was somewhat fairer than that of the red men. Nothing more was needed to convince the startled Aztecs that the fulfilment of the prophecy was at hand. Mon.

[1] Indeed, we know of at least one such blonde on this fleet, Pedro de Alvarado, whom the Mexicans called *Tonatiuh*, "sun-faced," on account of his shaggy yellow hair and ruddy complexion.

tezuma could hardly fail thus to understand the
case, and it filled him with misgivings. We may
be sure that to the anxious council in the tecpan
every shooting-star, every puff from the crater of
Popocatepetl, and whatever omen of good or evil
could be gathered from any quarter, came up for
fresh interpretation in the light of this strange intelligence. Let us leave them pondering the situation, while we turn our attention to the Spaniards,
and observe by what stages they had approached
the Mexican coast.

From the island of Hispaniola as a centre, the
work of discovery spread in all directions, and not slowly, when one considers the difficulties involved in it.
With the arrival of Diego Columbus,
as admiral and governor of the Indies, in 1509,
there was increased activity. In 1511 he sent
Velasquez to conquer Cuba, and two years later
Juan Ponce de Leon, governor of Porto Rico,
landed upon the coast of Florida. In the autumn
of 1509 the ill-fated expeditions of Ojeda and Nicuesa began their work upon the coast of Darien ;
and in 1513 Balboa crossed that isthmus and discovered the Pacific ocean. Rumours of the distant
kingdom of the Incas reached his ears, and in 1517
he was about starting on a voyage to the south,
when he was arrested on a charge of premeditating
treason and desertion, and was put to death by Pedrarias, governor of Darien. This melancholy
story will claim our attention in a future chapter.
It is merely mentioned here, in its chronological

Diffusion of the work of discovery from Hispaniola.

order, as having a kind of suggestiveness in connection with the conduct of Cortes.

After the fall of Balboa the Spaniards for some time made little or no progress to the southward, but their attention was mainly directed to the westward. In 1516 food was scarce in Darien, and to relieve the situation about a hundred of the colonists were sent over to Cuba; among them was Córdova's expedition, 1517. the soldier of fortune, Bernal Diaz de Castillo, afterward one of the most famous of chroniclers. These men had plenty of Indian gold, with which they fitted up a couple of ships to go slave-catching in the bay of Honduras. The governor, Velasquez, added a ship of his own to the expedition, and the chief command was given to Francisco Hernandez de Córdova, a man "very prudent and courageous, and strongly disposed to kill and kidnap Indians."[1] The chief pilot was Antonio de Alaminos, who had been with Columbus on his fourth voyage, and there were in all more than a hundred soldiers. From Santiago they sailed, in February, 1517, through the Windward Passage around to Puerto Principe to take in sundry supplies. While they were waiting there the pilot, recalling to mind some things that Columbus had told him, was seized with the idea that a rich country might be discovered within a short distance by sailing to the west. Córdova was persuaded by his arguments, and loyally sent

[1] Las Casas, *Historia de las Indias*, tom. iv. p. 369. This sort of expedition was illegal, and so it was publicly announced that the expedition was fitted out for purposes of discovery. See Bancroft's *Mexico*, vol. i. p. 6.

word to Velasquez, asking if he might be allowed
to act as governor's lieutenant in any new lands he
might discover.[1]   Assent having been given, the
little fleet finally sailed from the lately-founded town
of Havana, and presently reached the northeastern
corner of the peninsula of Yucatan.   Here the
Spaniards for the first time saw signs of that Oriental civilization for which they had so long been
looking in vain.   Strange-looking towers or pyramids, ascended by stone steps, greeted their eyes,
and the people, who came out in canoes to watch
the ships, were clad in quilted cotton doublets, and
wore cloaks and brilliant plumes.   These Mayas
were bitterly hostile.   Apparently they
had heard of the Spaniards.   It would   Hostile de-
                                            meanour of
have been strange indeed if, in the six   the Mayas.
years since Velasquez had invaded Cuba, not a
whisper of all the slaughter and enslavement in

[1] This is graphically told by Las Casas : — "Y estando allé,
dijo el piloto Alaminos al capitan Francisco Hernandez que le
parecia que por aquella mar del Poniente, abajo de la dicha isla
de Cuba, le daba el corazon que habia de haber tierra muy rica,
porque cuando andaba con el Almirante viejo, siendo él muchacho,
via que el Almirante se inclinaba mucho à navegar hacia aquella
parte, con esperanza grande que tenia que habia de hallar tierra
muy poblada y muy más rica que hasta allí, ó que así lo afirmaba,
y porque le faltaron los navíos no prosiguió aquel camino, y tornó,
desde el cabo que puso nombre de Gracias á Dios, atras á la
provincia de Veragua.   Dicho ésto, el Francisco Hernandez, que
era de buena esperanza y buen ánimo, asentándosele aquestas
palabras, determinó de enviar por licencia á Diego Velasquez,"
etc.   *Op. cit.* p. 350.   Alaminos had evidently confused in his
memory the fourth voyage of Columbus with the second.   It was
in the second that Columbus felt obliged to turn back, and it is
clear that in the fourth he had no intention of going west of Cape
Honduras.

that island had found its way across the one hundred miles of salt water between Cape San Antonio and Cape Catoche. At several places along the shore the natives are said to have shouted " Castilians! Castilians! " At Catoche their demeanour was at first friendly, but after the Spaniards had come ashore they drew them into an ambush and attacked them, killing two and wounding several. The Spaniards then reëmbarked, taking with them a couple of young captives whom they trained as interpreters. After a fortnight's sail along the coast they arrived at Campeche. Here the Maya natives invited them into the town, and showed them their huge pueblo fortresses and their stone temples, on the walls of which were sculptured enormous serpents, while the altars dripped fresh blood. " We were amazed," says Bernal Diaz, " at the sight of things so strange, as we watched numbers of natives, men and women, come in to get a sight of us with smiling and careless countenances." [1]   Presently, however, priests approaching with fragrant censers requested the visitors to quit the country ; and they deemed it prudent to comply, and retired to their ships. Proceeding as far as Champoton, the Spaniards were obliged to go ashore for water to drink. Then the Indians set upon them in overwhelming numbers and wofully defeated them, slaying more than half their number, and wounding nearly all the rest. The wretched survivors lost no time in getting back to Cuba, where Córdova soon died of his wounds. Worse

Defeat of the Spaniards at Champoton.

---

[1] Diaz, *Historia verdadera*, cap. iii.

luck they could hardly have had, but they brought back a little gold and some carved images stolen from a temple, and their story incited Velasquez to prepare a new expedition.

Four caravels were accordingly made ready and manned with 250 stout soldiers. The chief command was given to the governor's nephew, Juan de Grijalva, and the captains of two of the ships were Pedro de Alvarado and Francisco de Montejo. Sailing from Santiago early in April, 1518, they landed first at the island of Cozumel, and then followed the Yucatan coast till they reached Champoton, where they came to blows with the natives, and being fully prepared for such an emergency defeated them. In June they came to a country which they called Tabasco, after the name of a chief [1] with whom they had some friendly interviews and exchanged gifts. It was a few days later, at the little bay near the shore of which stood the pueblo of Mictlan-Quauhtla, that they were boarded by the tax-gatherer Pinotl who carried such startling intelligence of them to Montezuma. The demeanour of the Nahua people in this neighbourhood was quite friendly; but the Spaniards were more and more struck with horror at the ghastly sights they saw of human heads raised aloft on poles, human bodies disembowelled, and grinning idols dripping blood from their jaws. On St. John's day they stopped at an island, the name of which they understood

Grijalva's expedition, 1518.

---

[1] The Spaniards often mistook the name of some chief for a territorial name, as for example Quarequa, Pocorosa, Birú, etc., of which more anon.

to be Ulua,[1] and so they gave it the name now commonly written San Juan de Ulloa. Here Alvarado was sent back to Cuba with fifty or more sick men, to report what had been done and get reinforcements with which to found a colony. Grijalva kept on with the other three ships, as far, perhaps, as the river Pánuco, beyond the region of pueblos tributary to the Aztecs. By this time their ships were getting the worse for wear, and they began once more to encounter fierce and hostile Indians. Accordingly they turned back, and retracing their course arrived in Cuba early in November.

The effect of this expedition was very stimulating. A quarter of a century had elapsed since Columbus's first voyage, and the Spaniards had been

Excitement of
the Spaniards.

active enough in many directions, but until lately they had seen no indications of that Oriental civilization and magnificence which they had expected to find. They had been tossed on weather-beaten coasts, and had wandered mile after mile half-starved through tropical forests, for the most part without finding anything but rude and squalid villages inhabited by half-naked barbarians. Still hope had not deserted them; they were as confident as ever that, inasmuch as they were in Asia, it could not be so very far to the dominions of the Great Khan. Now Grijalva's tidings seemed to justify their lingering hope. Pinotl and other Indians had told him that far up in that country dwelt their mighty king who ruled over many cities and had no end of gold. Of

---

[1] An imperfect hearing of Culhua, a name common in Mexico

course this must be the Great Khan, and the goal
which Columbus had hoped to attain must now be
within reach! The youthful Grijalva was flushed
with anticipations of coming glory.

No sooner had he arrived in Cuba, however, than
he was taught the lesson that there is many a slip
betwixt the cup and the lip. He had found occasion to censure Alvarado, and that captain, nurs-
ing his spite and getting home some time before
his young commander, had contrived to poison the
mind of his uncle the governor. So Grijalva
was set aside, all his fine hopes turned sick with
chagrin. The prize was not for him, but for another young man, a native of Estremadura, who
in 1504 had come over to the Indies. The name
of this knight-errant, now in his thirty-fourth year,
bold and devout, fertile in devices and unscrupulous, yet perhaps no more so than many a soldier
whose name is respected, an Achilles for bravery,
an Odysseus for craft and endurance, Hernando
was Hernando Cortes. In 1511 he had Cortes.
served with distinction under Velasquez in the
expedition which conquered Cuba, and he was at
this time *alcalde* (chief judge) of the newly founded
town of Santiago on that island. He now persuaded Velasquez to appoint him to command the
important expedition fitted out in the autumn of
1518 for operations on the Mexican mainland.

Before Cortes started, Velasquez began to worry
lest he might prove too independent a spirit, and
he twice sent messengers after him to recall him
and put another in his place. Cortes politely disregarded the messages, thus verifying the govern-

or's fears. Early in March, 1519, he landed at Tabasco, found the natives unfriendly, defeated

Expedition of Cortes, 1519. them in a sharp skirmish, seized a fresh stock of provisions, and proceeded to San Juan de Ulloa, whence he sent messengers to Montezuma with gifts and messages as from his sovereign Charles V. Presently he ascertained that the yoke of the Aztec confederacy was borne unwillingly by many tributary towns and districts, and this was one of the main facts that enabled him to conquer the country. At first Cortes contrived to play a double game, encouraging the tributary towns to arrest Montezuma's tax-gatherers, and then currying favour with these officials by quietly releasing them and sending them with soft words to Montezuma.

It was now desirable to make a quick, bold stroke and enlist all his followers irrevocably in the enterprise. Cortes laid the foundations of the town of Vera Cruz (a little to the north of its

The scuttling of the ships. present site), and a municipal government was then and there framed. Cortes then resigned his commission from Velasquez, and was at once reëlected captain-general by his municipality. He was doing pretty much the same thing that Balboa had been wrongly accused of doing, and he knew well that the alternative before him was victory or the headsman's block. He sent his flagship to Spain, with Montejo and a few other influential and devoted friends, to gain the ear of the grave young king who, while these things were going on, had been elected to the imperial throne of Charlemagne and the Othos.

Then, with a strange mixture of persuasion and stealth, he had his ships one after another scuttled and sunk.[1] Nothing was left but to march on Mexico-Tenochtitlan.

[1] It is often carelessly said that Cortes burned his ships. Three or four were at first secretly scuttled, and there was more or less discussion as to whether the sinking was done by worms. Then the mariners who were in the secret reported other ships unseaworthy. Cortes's first argument was that it would not be worth while to waste time in trying to repair such extensive damages; then he advanced to the position that perhaps it would be wise to sink all that were left, so as to be able to take the sailors along on the march into the country. All were then scuttled but one. Presently some of the malcontents in the camp discovered how the scuttling had been done, and loudly upbraided Cortes. He then boldly faced them, and asked for whom but cowards were means of retreat necessary! There was one ship left; if there were any craven-hearted enough to wish to abandon the enterprise, in God's name let them go at once and in that ship. Cortes well knew what chord to touch in a soldier's heart. As the complaints were drowned in cheers, he went on and suggested that inasmuch as that last ship was of no use it might as well be sunk likewise; which was forthwith done. See Bernal Diaz, *Historia verdadera*, cap. xxx.–xl.

It was the Sicilian general Agathokles who *burned* his ships when he invaded the territory of Carthage in 310 B. C., and it is interesting to compare the graphic description of Diodorus Siculus (lib. xx. cap. 7) with that of Bernal Diaz. The characteristics of the two commanders and the two different ages are worth noting. After crossing the Mediterranean, despite some real danger from Carthaginian cruisers of superior strength and much fancied danger from a total eclipse of the sun, Agathokles determined to destroy his ships, since guarding them would detain a part of his force, while in the event of his defeat they would not avail to save him from the Carthaginian fleet. So he gathered his army together and performed the customary sacrifices to the patron goddesses, Demeter and Persephone. The auspices turned out to be favourable. Then he told the soldiers that in an anxious moment upon the water he had vowed, if these goddesses should conduct him safely to the African shore, to make a burnt-offer-

A wonderful march! At one point (Iztacmix-titlan) they came upon a valley where "for four successive leagues there was a continuous line of houses, and the Lord of the valley," we are told, "lived in a fortress such as was not to be found in the half of Spain, surrounded by walls and bar-bicans and moats." What was the force with which our knight-errant ventured into such a country? It consisted of 450 Spaniards, many of them clad in mail, half-a-dozen small cannon, and fifteen horses. It was not enough that the Spanish soldier of that day was a bull-dog for strength and courage, or that his armour was proof against stone arrows and lances, or that he wielded a Toledo blade that could cut through silken cushions, or that his arquebus and cannon were not only death-dealing weapons but objects of superstitious awe. More potent than all else together were those frightful monsters, the horses. Before these animals men, women, and children fled like sheep, or skulked and peeped from behind their walls in an ecstasy of terror. It was that paralyzing, blood-curdling fear of the supernatural, against which no amount of physical bravery, nothing in the world but modern know-ledge, is of the slightest avail. Perhaps Sir Arthur Helps is right in saying that it was the horse that overthrew the kingdoms of the Aztecs and the

The Spanish force.

ing of his fleet in honour of them. The peremptory obligation was at once recognized by the army. Agathokles with a torch set fire to his flagship, and at the same moment all the other ships were set blazing by their own captains, amid the murmured prayers of the soldiers and the solemn notes of the trumpet. The event, on the whole, justified the daring policy of Agathokles.

Incas.[1] But besides all this, there was the legend of the bright Quetzalcoatl coming to win back his ancient kingdom from the dark Tezcatlipoca. And strongly coöperating with all other circumstances was the readiness of the hounded and crestfallen tributary pueblos to welcome any chance that might humble the Triple Tyrant of the Lake! Surely, if ever the stars in their courses fought for mortal man, that man was Hernando Cortes. This luck, however, should not lessen our estimate of his genius, for never was man more swift and sure in seizing opportunities. To offer chances to a dull-witted man is like casting pearls before swine.

As the little army advanced, its progress was heralded by awe-struck couriers who made pictures of the bearded strangers and their hoofed monsters, and sent them, with queer hieroglyphic notes and comments, to the Great Pueblo on the lake. Cortes soon divined the situation, albeit imperfectly, and displayed an audacity the like of which was perhaps never seen before in the world. At the town of Cempoala *Audacity of Cortes at Cempoala.* he had already set free the victims held for sacrifice, and hurled the misshapen idols from the temple. But his boldness was wedded to prudence, and while he did this he seized the persons of the principal chiefs. It had been observed in Cuba and other islands that if the cacique were taken prisoner the Indians seemed unable to fight. " Under Indian customs the prisoner was put to death,

[1] See the striking passage in his *Spanish Conquest*, vol. iii. p. 547.

and, if a principal chief, the office reverted to the tribe and was at once filled." But when the Spaniards took the principal chief and held him captive, he " remained alive and in possession of his office, so that it could not be filled. The action of the people was paralyzed by novel circumstances." [1] Cortes put the Cempoalans in this position, and learned a lesson from which he was soon to profit on a tremendous scale. The Cempoalans were overawed, and looked on in silence while their temples were purified and crosses set up. By one of the many strange coincidences in this meeting of two grades of culture so widely sundered, the cross was not only a Christian but also a Mexican symbol. It was one of the emblems of Quetzalcoatl, as lord of the four cardinal points and the four winds that blow therefrom. Doubtless, therefore, many of the Cempoalans must have reasoned that the overthrow of the idols was no more than Tezcatlipoca had a right to expect from his great adversary. Others doubtless fumed with rage, but when it came to venting their wrath in some kind of united action they knew not how to act without their chiefs.

It was on the 16th of August, 1519, that Cortes started from Cempoala on his march toward the city of Mexico. His route lay past Xicochimalco and Teoxihuacan to Texotla, and thence to Xocotlan,[2] a town described as having thirteen pyramid-temples, whence we may perhaps infer that the people were grouped in thirteen clans. The Span-

[1] Morgan, *Ancient Society*, p. 211, note.

[2] The route is well described in Bancroft's *Mexico*, chap. xii.

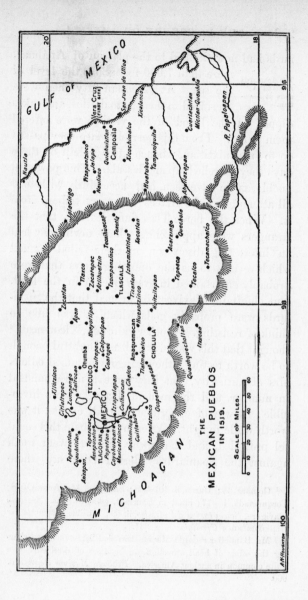

THE
MEXICAN PUEBLOS
IN 1519.

SCALE OF MILES.
0 10 20 30 40 50 60

iards had now climbed to the plateau of Anáhuac,

The Spaniards received as gods at Xocotlan. more than 7,000 feet above the level of the sea. At Xocotlan fifty men were sacrificed to them as to deities, and cakes dipped in the blood of the victims were offered them to eat.[1] From this horrible place they passed on to Iztacmixtitlan, whence after a halt of three days they marched upon Tlascala. This powerful pueblo, as we have seen, had successfully withstood all attempts of the Aztecs to extort tribute from it. When the fierce Tlascalans learned that the strangers were approaching their town, they had an interesting discussion in their tribal council which reveals to us the opposing views that were probably entertained in every pueblo in the land. One chieftain, Maxixcatzin, argued that the Spaniards were probably gods whom it was idle to think of resisting. Another chieftain, Xicotencatl,[2] thought that this view was at least doubtful enough to be worth testing; the strangers assumed odious airs of authority, but they were a mere handful in number, and the men of Tlascala were invincible; by way of experiment, at all events, it was worth while to fight. After much debate this counsel prevailed, and the tawny warriors went forth against the Spaniards. Bernal Diaz says there

---

[1] Gomara, 68; Duran, ii. 401–408; Sahagun, 14; Acosta, 518; Torquemada, i. 417; cited in Bancroft, *op. cit.* i. 196. See also Clavigero, *Storia antica del Messico,* ii. 69; Müller, *Geschichte der Amerikanischen Urreligionen,* p. 631.

[2] Mr. Bandelier regards Maxixcatzin and Xicotencatl as sharing the office of head war-chief, an instance of dual executive quite common in ancient America. *Peabody Museum Reports,* ii. 660.

were 50,000 of them in the field, and later writers
have swelled the number to 150,000. In studying the conquest of Mexico one soon gets used to
this sort of thing. Too many of its historians be-
long to a school of which Falstaff, with his men in buckram, was the founder. Bernal Diaz was an eye-witness; he took part in the battle, and, if we strike off about one cipher from his figure and make it 5,000, we shall get somewhere within the bounds of credibility, and the odds will remain sufficiently great to attest the valour of the Spaniards. The Tlascalan army was apparently marshalled in phratries, one of them from the allied pueblo of Huexotzinco. They were distinguished by the colours of their war-paint. They wore quilted cotton doublets, and carried leather shields stretched upon a framework of bamboo and decorated with feathers. Upon their heads they wore helmets of stout leather fashioned and trimmed with feather-work so as to look like heads of snakes or jaguars, and the chiefs were distinguished by gorgeous plumes. Their weapons were long bows, arrows tipped with obsidian, copper-pointed lances, slings, javelins, and heavy wooden swords with sharp blades of obsidian inserted in both edges.[1] With this bar-baric host the Spaniards had two days of desultory fighting. By the end of that time a great many Tlascalans had been killed; a few Spaniards had been wounded, and one or two had been killed,[2] but

*Battle be-
tween Span-
iards and
Tlascalans.*

[1] Bancroft, *Native Races of the Pacific States*, vol. ii. pp. 406–410.

[2] The ingrained Mexican custom of trying to capture their

they were so carefully buried by their comrades that the enemy did not learn the fact, and it was sagely concluded that the white men must be more than mortal.

The sturdy Xicotencatl, however, was not willing to give up the case without one more trial. He took counsel with soothsayers, and the opinion was suggested that the strangers, as solar deities, were very probably dependent for their strength, and perhaps for their invulnerability, upon direct contact with the solar radiance. Possibly in the night-time they might turn out to be mortal. At all events it was worth trying, and Xicotencatl made up his mind to act on his own account that very night. In making his preparations for an attack he sent a small party of spies to the Spanish camp with presents and soft words. They were to watch things keenly, and bring back such information as might prove useful. Some were to stay in the camp and at an appointed signal set fire to it. Cortes received these Indians graciously, but presently their behaviour excited suspicion, and to their utter terror and confusion they suddenly found themselves arrested and charged with treachery! There was no use in lying to superhuman beings who clearly possessed the godlike power of

Scheme of the Tlascalan soothsayers.

---

enemies for sacrifice, instead of slaying them on the field, is cited by Bandelier as a reason why more Spaniards did not get killed in these straggling fights. "Thus, for the sake of capturing a single horseman, they recklessly sacrificed numbers of their own, when they thought to be able to surround him, and cut him off from his corps or detachment. The custom was general among the Nahuatlac tribes." *Peabody Museum Reports,* ii. 128.

reading the secret thoughts of men; so the spies, or some of them, made confession. Thus informed of the situation, Cortes waited till nightfall, and then cut off the thumbs of the spies and sent them to tell Xicotencatl that he would find the white man as invincible by night as by day.[1]

Cortes followed the messengers at no great distance with a party of horsemen; and while the Tlascalan warriors were limp with amazement at this penetration of their design, the party charged in among them at full gallop, scattering them in wildest panic and cutting them down by the score.[2]

Complete triumph of Cortes.

It was clear that nothing was to be gained by opposing these children of the sun. The unfortunate soothsayers who had advised the night attack were disembowelled, stewed with chile pepper, and served in a ragout; and the Tlascalan tribal council, taught wisdom by adversity, decided to improve the situation by making an alliance with the wielders of thunder and lightning, and enlisting, if possible, their resistless strength in the work of humbling Tlascala's ancient enemy. Upon the people of the Aztec Confederacy these events made a most profound impression. They freely acknowledged that beings who could so easily defeat the Tlascalans must be more than human. But when it was

Alliance between Tlascalans and Spaniards.

[1] "Y los embió para que dixessen a Xicotěcatl su capitan-general, que lo mismo haria de quantas espias pudiesse auer, y que fuesse cõ su exercito, porque siempre conoceria que los Castellanos eran inuencibles de dia y de noche." Herrera, decad. ii. lib. vi. cap. 8.

[2] Diaz, *Historia verdadera*, cap. xlvii.-l.

learned that these dreaded strangers had entered into friendly alliance with the "republic" of Tlascala,[1] and were now leading an army of its warriors toward Tenochtitlan, we can well imagine the consternation that must have pervaded the streets of that great pueblo.

From this time the community of interests kept the Tlascalans faithful to the white men even after the illusion as to their supernatural qualities had died away. If we would form a true conception of the conquest of Mexico by a handful of Spaniards, we must remember that Tlascala, with its few allied pueblos, had shown itself nearly a match for the Aztec Confederacy; and the advantage of this alliance was now added to the peculiar combination of circumstances that made the Spaniards so formidable.

Affairs having duly been arranged at Tlascala, the little army, now followed by a formidable body of dusky allies, approached Cholula, a strong pueblo allied with the Confederacy and especially identified with the worship of Quetzalcoatl.[2] The town was not only one of the principal markets in Mexico, but it was held in much reverence for its religious associa-

Treachery at Cholula, discovered by Doña Marina.

---

[1] It is curious to see Tlascala commonly mentioned as a "republic" and the Aztec Confederacy as an "empire," ruled by an absolute monarch, when in reality the supreme power in both was vested in the tribal councils. This indicates that the Aztec *tlacatecuhtli* had acquired higher dignity than that merely of head war-chief. He had joined to this the dignity of chief priest, as we shall see.

[2] There is an excellent account of Cholula in Bandelier's *Archæological Tour*, pp. 79–262.

tions. With the aid and approval of emissaries from Tenochtitlan, the chiefs of Cholula prepared an ambuscade for the Spaniards, who were politely and cordially admitted into the town with the intention of entrapping them. But with Cortes there was a handsome young Indian woman from Tabasco, who had fallen in love with him there and remained his faithful companion through all the trials of the conquest. Her aid was invaluable, since to a thorough familiarity with the Nahuatl and Maya languages she soon added a knowledge of Spanish, and for quick wit and fertility of resource she was like Morgiana in the story of the Forty Thieves. The name given to this young woman on the occasion of her conversion and baptism was Marina, which in Nahuatl mouths became Malina, and oddly enough the most common epithet applied to Cortes, by Montezuma and others, was Malintzin or Malinche, "lord of Marina." It was through her keenness that the plot of the Cholultec chiefs was discovered and frustrated. Having ascertained the full extent of their plans, Cortes summoned the principal chiefs of Cholula to a conference, announced his intention of starting on the morrow for Tenochtitlan, and with an air of innocent trust in them, he asked them to furnish him with an additional supply of food and with an auxiliary force of Cholulans. In childish glee at this presumed simplicity, and confident that for once the white stranger was not omniscient, the chiefs readily promised the men and provisions. Several three-year-old babes had been sacrificed that day, and

The gods too confident.

the auspices were favourable. So the chiefs spent
the night in arranging their *coup de main* for the
next morning, while Cortes saw that his cannon
were placed in suitable positions for raking the
streets. In the morning a throng of Cholultec
warriors crowded into the square where the Spaniards were quartered, and the chiefs felt so sure of
their game that to the number of thirty or more
they accepted an invitation to meet "Malinche"
in private and receive his parting blessing. When
they were assembled, and with them the Aztec
emissaries, whom Cortes took care to have at
hand, they heard such words as froze them with
terror. It seems that, here as well as at Tlascala,
there were two parties, one counselling submission,
the other resistance, only here the resistance had
assumed the form of treachery. Having been
primed by Marina with full and accurate information, Cortes conveyed to the astounded chiefs the
secret history of their little scheme, and informed
them that they were his prisoners, but he knew
how to separate sheep from goats and only the
guilty should be punished. As for Montezuma,
though it was said that he was privy to the Cho-
lulan plot, Cortes declared himself unwilling to
Massacre at   believe such a slander against one whom
Cholula.   he had always understood to be a worthy
prince. It was his policy for the moment to soothe
the emissaries from Tenochtitlan while he exhibited
his fiend-like power. We can dimly imagine the
paralyzing amazement and terror as the chiefs who
had counselled submission were picked out and
taken aside. At this moment the thunder of ar-

tillery, never heard before in Cholula, burst upon
the ear. Bloody lanes were ploughed through the
mass of dusky warriors in the square, hippocen-
taurs clad in shining brass charged in among them,
and the Tlascaltec warriors, who had been encamped outside, now rushed into the town and
began a general massacre. Several hundred, perhaps some thousands, were slain, including the
head war-chief. Of the captured chiefs a few were
burned at the stake, doubtless as a warning example for Montezuma. Cortes then released all the
caged victims fattening for sacrifice, and resumed
his march.

From Cholula the little army proceeded to Hue-
xotzinco and thence to Amaquemecan, where they
were met by chiefs from Tlalmanalco, inveighing
against the tyranny of the Aztecs and begging for
deliverance. Passing Tlalmanalco and Iztapala-
tzinco, the Spaniards went on to Cuitlahuac, situated upon the causeway leading across the lake of
Chalco. This was one of the many towns in the
lately-found Indies which reminded the Spaniards
of Venice; i. e. it was built over the water, with
canals for streets. Its floating gardens and its
houses glistening in their stucco of white gypsum
delighted the eyes of the Spaniards. Crossing the
causeway they marched on to Iztapalapan, where
they arrived on the 7th of November, First sight of
1519, and saw before them the Queen Tenochtitlan.
of Pueblos. "And when we beheld," says Bernal
Diaz, "so many cities and towns rising up from
the water, and other populous places situated on
the terra firma, and that causeway, straight as a

level, which went into Mexico, we remained astonished, and said to one another that it appeared
like the enchanted castles which they tell of in the
book of Amadis, by reason of the great towers,
temples, and edifices which there were in the

THE
VALLEY OF MEXICO
IN 1519.
Spanish Leagues

water, and all of them work of masonry. Some
of our soldiers asked if this that they saw was not
a thing in a dream."[1]

It may well be called the most romantic moment
in all history, this moment when European eyes

[1] Diaz, *Historia verdadera*, cap. lxxxvii.

first rested upon that city of wonders, the chief
ornament of a stage of social evolution
two full ethnical periods behind their A most ro-
own. To say that it was like stepping ment.
back across the centuries to visit the Nineveh of
Sennacherib or hundred-gated Thebes is but in-
adequately to depict the situation, for it was a
longer step than that. Such chances do not come
twice to mankind, for when two grades of culture
so widely severed are brought into contact, the
stronger is apt to blight and crush the weaker
where it does not amend and transform it. In
spite of its foul abominations, one sometimes feels
that one would like to recall that extinct state
of society in order to study it. The devoted lover
of history, who ransacks all sciences for aid toward understanding the course of human events,
who knows in what unexpected ways one stage of
progress often illustrates other stages, will sometimes wish it were possible to resuscitate, even
for one brief year, the vanished City of the Cactus Rock. Could such a work of enchantment
be performed, however, our first feeling would
doubtless be one of ineffable horror and disgust,
like that of the knight in the old English bal-
lad, who folding in his arms a damsel of radiant
beauty finds himself in the embrace of a loathsome
fiend.

But inasmuch as the days of magic are long
since past, and the ointment of the wise dervise,
that enabled one to see so many rich and buried
secrets, has forever lost its virtues, the task for
the modern student is simply the prosaic one of

setting down such few details as can be gathered
from the Spanish narratives [1] and sifted in view of
what little we know about such points as the Spaniards were liable to misinterpret.   A few such
details will help us to understand the way in which
this archaic phase of human development was so
abruptly cut short.

The city of Mexico stood in a salt lake, and was
approached by three causeways of solid masonry,
each, as the Spanish soldiers said, two lances in
breadth, which might mean from twenty to thirty
feet.   Being from four to five miles in length, and
assailable on both sides by the canoes of the city's
defenders, they were very dangerous avenues for
an enemy, whether advancing or retreating.   Near
the city these causeways were interrupted by wooden drawbridges.   Then
they were continued into the city as main thorough-
fares, and met in the great square where the temple stood.   The city was also connected with the

The cause-
ways.

---

[1] My authorities for the description of Tenochtitlan are Cortes,
Cartas y relaciones al emperador Carlos V., Paris, 1866; Bernal
Diaz, *Historia verdadera*, Madrid, 1632; Icazbalceta, *Coleccion de
documentos*, etc., Mexico, 1858–66; *Relatione fatta per un gentil'
huomo del Signor Fernando Cortese*, apud Ramusio, *Navigationi et
Viaggi*, Venice, 1556; Tezozomoc, *Histoire de Mexique*, Paris,
1853; Ixtlilxochitl, *Relaciones*, apud Kingsborough's *Mexican
Antiquities*, London, 1831–48, vol. ix.; Sahagun, *Historia general
de las cosas de Nueva España*, Mexico, 1829; Torquemada,
Monarquía indiana, Madrid, 1723; Clavigero, *Storia antica del
Messico*, Cesena, 1780; Oviedo, *Historia general y natural de las
Indias*, Madrid, 1851–55; Gomara, *Historia de Mexico*, Antwerp,
1554; Herrera, *Historia general de los hechos de los Castellanos*
etc., Madrid, 1601; Veytia, *Historia antigua de Mejico*, Mexico
1836; Vetancurt, *Teatro mexicano*, Mexico, 1870.

mainland by an aqueduct in solid masonry leading down from Chepultepec. The streets might have reminded one of Venice, in so far as some were canals alive with canoes, while others were dry footpaths paved with hard cement, and the footways often crossed the canals on bridges. These paths and canals ran between immense houses of red stone, many of them coated with a hard white stucco. The houses enclosed great court-

The houses.

yards, and vast as were the spaces covered by them there was seldom a third story. The low flat roofs, often covered with flower-gardens, were protected by stone parapets with small towers at intervals, so that every house was a fortress. The effect must have been extremely picturesque. Military precautions were everywhere visible. The bridges across the canals could be drawn up at a moment's notice. The windows were mere loop-holes, and they as well as the doorways were open. The entrance to the house could be barricaded, but doors had not been invented. Sometimes a kind of bamboo screen was hung in the doorway and secured by a cross-bar; sometimes, especially in interior doorways, there were hangings of cotton or feather-work.[1]

---

[1] The portière is much more ancient than the door, and goes back at least as far as the lower period of barbarism; as e. g. the Mandan buffalo robe above mentioned, vol. i. p. 81. The Greeks in the upper period of barbarism had true doors with hinges and latches. One of the cosiest pictures in the delicious Odyssey is that of the old nurse Eurykleia showing Telemachus to his chamber, when leaving him tucked under the woollen rug she goes out, and closes the door with its silver ring and fastens the latch with a thong : —

ὤϊξεν δὲ θύρας θαλάμου πύκα ποιητοῖο,
ἕζετο δ᾽ ἐν λέκτρῳ, μαλακὸν δ᾽ ἔκδυνε χιτῶνα·

The number of the houses and of their occu-
pants has been the subject of curious misappre-
hensions.   The Licentiate Zuazo, a scholarly and
careful man whom Cortes left in charge of the
city in 1524; and who ought to be good authority,
said that there were 60,000 *vecinos*.[1]   As I have
before observed,[2] this Spanish word may mean
either " inhabitants " or " householders."   The latter interpretation was given to it by Gomara and
Peter Martyr,[3] and has been generally adopted;
but as nobody has given the circumference of the
city as more than four leagues, and as it was in
all probability less than that,[4] there would not have
begun to be room enough for 60,000 of these

The popula-
tion.

huge houses, along with the space occupied by canals and open squares, temples with their pyramids, and gardens between
the houses.[5]   The book of one of Cortes's com-

καὶ τὸν μὲν γραίης πυκιμηδέος ἔμβαλε χερσίν.
ἡ μὲν τὸν πτύξασα καὶ ἀσκήσασα χιτῶνα,
πασσάλῳ ἀγκρεμάσασα παρὰ τρητοῖς λεχέεσσιν,
βῆ ῥ' ἴμεν ἐκ θαλάμοιο, θύρην δ' ἐπέρυσσε κορώνῃ
ἀργυρέῃ, ἐπὶ δὲ κληῒδ' ἐτάνυσσεν ἱμάντι.
ἔνθ' ὅγε παννύχιος, κεκαλυμμένος οἰὸς ἀώτῳ,
βούλευε φρεσὶν ᾗσιν ὁδὸν τὴν πέφραδ' Ἀθήνη.

Odyssey, i. 436.

M. Charnay, in his investigations at Uxmal, found " four rings or
stone hooks inside the doorways near the top, from which it is
easy to conjecture that a wooden board was placed inside against
the opening, and kept in place by two transversal bars entering
the stone hooks."   *Ancient Cities of the New World*, p. 398.

[1] *Carta de Licenciado Zuazo*, MS., apud Prescott, *Conquest of
Mexico*, bk. iv. chap. i.

[2] See above, vol. i. p. 95.

[3] Gomara, *Crónica de la Nueva España*, Saragossa, 1554, cap.
lxxviii. ; Martyr, *De Orbe Novo*, dec. v. cap. iii.

[4] Bandelier, *Archæological Tour*, p. 50.

[5] " Nearly all the old authors describe the public buildings as

panions, known as the Anonymous Conqueror,
survives only in an Italian translation, and this
has 60,000 *habitatori*, which can mean nothing

surrounded by pleasure-grounds or ornamental gardens. It is
very striking that, the pueblo having been founded in 1325, and
nearly a century having been spent in adding sufficient artificial
sod to the originally small solid expanse settled, the Mexicans
could have been ready so soon to establish purely decorative
parks within an area, every inch of which was valuable to them
for subsistence alone! " Bandelier, in *Peabody Museum Reports*,
vol. ii. p. 422. That the corn-growers of Tenochtitlan were
cramped for room is plain from the fact that they constructed
"floating gardens," or rafts covered with black loam which were
moored at various points in the shallow lake. These artificial
gardens (*chinampas*) were usually rectangular in shape and from
thirty to fifty yards in length; maize, beans, tomatoes, and other
vegetables were raised in them. See Torquemada, *Monarquía
indiana*, tom. ii. p. 483; Acosta, *Historia de las Indias*, p. 472;
Clavigero, *Storia di Messico*, tom. ii. p. 152. This practice indicates that there was no superfluous space in the city. Nevertheless the testimony of "nearly all the old authors," that extensive flower gardens were to be seen, is not to be lightly
rejected. Flowers were used in many of the religious festivals,
and there is abundant evidence, moreover, that the Mexicans
were very fond of them. This is illustrated in the perpetual
reference to flowers in old Mexican poems: — "They led me
within a valley to a fertile spot, a flowery spot, where the dew
spread out in glittering splendour, where I saw various lovely
fragrant flowers, lovely odorous flowers, clothed with the dew,
scattered around in rainbow glory; there they said to me,' Pluck
the flowers, whichever thou wishest, mayest thou the singer be
glad, and give them to thy friends, to the chiefs, that they may
rejoice on the earth.' So I gathered in the folds of my garment
the various fragrant flowers, delicate scented, delicious," etc.
Brinton, *Ancient Nahuatl Poetry*, p. 57. Of the twenty-seven
ancient Mexican songs in this interesting collection, there is
scarcely one that does not abound with ecstatic allusions to flowers: — "The delicious breath of the dewy flowers is in our homes
in Chiapas;" "my soul was drunken with the flowers;" "let
me gather the intoxicating flowers, many coloured, varied in
hue," etc.

but inhabitants.[1] Taking 60,000 as the population, which seems a reasonable figure, the number of communal houses can hardly have exceeded 300, as the number of persons in a house can hardly have averaged less than 200. We have already, in the first chapter of this work, seen how the organization of the Aztec tribe in four

The four wards. phratries divided the city into four quarters, each with its curial temple and peculiar ceremonies. It reminds one of the threefold division of Rome by tribes at the time when the Ramnes occupied the Palatine hill, while the Tities lived on the Quirinal, and the Luceres on the Esquiline.[2] The communal houses, as Richard Eden has it, were "palaices of maruelous bygnes, and curiously buylded with many pleasaunt diuises." Upon the front of each was sculptured the totem or beast-symbol of the clan to which it belonged, that upon the one in which Montezuma received the strangers being an eagle with a wildcat (*ocelotl*) grasped in its beak. It was customary to carve upon the jambs, on either side of the doorway, enormous serpents with gaping mouths.

The dress of the people was of cotton, the men

[1] *Relatione fatta per un gentil' huomo del Signor Fernando Cortese*, apud Ramusio, *Navigationi et Viaggi*, Venice, 1556, tom. iii. fol. 309. Mr. Morgan (*Ancient Society*, p. 195) thinks the number of inhabitants could not have exceeded 30,000, but I see no reason for doubting the statements of Zuazo and the Anonymous Conqueror.

[2] Tlatelulco constituted a fifth quarter, for the Tlatelulcans, who had been conquered in 1473, deprived of tribal rights, and partially re-adopted; an interesting case, for which see Bandelier, *Peabody Museum Reports*, ii. 593.

wearing loose cloaks and ample fringed sashes, and the women long robes reaching to the ground. These cotton garments were Dress. often elaborately embroidered and dyed with the rich scarlet of the cochineal. Capes of fur or doublets of feather-work were worn in cold weather. The feet were protected by a kind of sandal, and the head by a white cotton hood. The hair was ordinarily worn long, and a deep violet hair-dye was used by the women. Faces were sometimes smeared with red or yellow ointment, and the teeth stained with cochineal. Gold and silver bracelets and anklets and rings for fingers, ears, and nose were worn by men and women.

In the interior of the houses cedar and other fine woods were used for partitions and ceilings. The chief decorations were Interiors. the mural tapestries woven of the gorgeous plumage of parrots, pheasants, cardinals, and humming-birds, and one purpose of the many aviaries was to furnish such feathers. Except a few small tables and stools, there was not much furniture. Palm-leaf mats piled on the hard cemented floor served as beds, and sometimes there were coverlets of cotton or feather-work. Resinous torches were used for lights. The principal meal of the day was served on low tables, the people sitting on mats or cushions in long rows around the sides of the room, with their backs against the wall. A lighted brazier stood in the middle, and before tasting the food each person threw a morsel into the brazier as an offering Dinner. to the fire-god. The commonest meat was the turkey, a bird as characteristic of Mexico as its cactuses. The name of this fowl preserves a curious illustration of the mixture of truth and error which had led to the discovery of America. When it was first introduced into European barn-yards in 1530, people named it on the theory that it was an Asiatic fowl. The Germans for a while called it *Calecutische hahn* or Calicut cock; the French still call it *dinde*, which at first was *poulet d'Inde* or India fowl; and the English called it the Turkey fowl; but the Oriental country which it came from was really Mexico, many thousand miles east of Asia.

Cookery had made some progress among the Aztecs. Indian meal beaten up with eggs was baked in loaves, and there were cakes resembling the modern *tortilla*. Then there was the *tamale*, a kind of pie of meat and vegetables with a covering of Indian meal. Fresh fish were abundant. There were various ragouts intensely hot with tabasco and chile sauce. Bernal Diaz counted thirty such dishes upon Montezuma's table. One favourite mess was frog spawn and stewed ants peppered with chile; another was human flesh cooked in like manner. To the cannibalism almost universal among American aborigines the people of Mexico and Central America added this epicure's touch.[1]

Dishes.

[1] The first dish mentioned by Bernal Diaz seemed to Mr. Prescott both startling and apocryphal, and even the old soldier himself, in spite of the cannibalism he had witnessed, was slow to admit the truth of what he was told. It was a fricassee of very young children: — " E como por passatiempo oi dezir, que le solian guisar carnes de muchachos de poca edad," etc. (*Historia verdadera*, cap. xci.) When we bear in mind, however, that in

These viands were kept hot by means of chafing dishes and were served on earthenware bowls or

times of public excitement and peril it was customary to obtain the auspices by sacrificing young children, and that the flesh of the human victim seems invariably to have been eaten, there is nothing at all improbable in what was told to Diaz.

Sir Henry Yule, in one of his learned notes to Marco Polo, mentions instances which show the connection between cannibalism and sundry folk-lore notions; e. g. " after an execution at Peking certain large pith balls are steeped in the blood, and under the name of *blood-bread* are sold as a medicine for consumption. It is only to the blood of decapitated criminals that any such healing power is attributed." There is evidence that this remnant of cannibalism is not yet extinct in China. Among civilized peoples in modern times instances of cannibalism have been for the most part confined to shipwrecked crews in the last stages of famine. Among savages and barbarians of low type, famine and folk-lore probably combine to support the custom. When the life of the Jesuit priest Brébeuf had gone out amid diabolical torments, during which he had uttered neither cry nor groan, an Iroquois chief tore out his heart and devoured it for the very practical purpose of acquiring all that courage ; on the other hand, when one of Mr. Darwin's party asked some Fuegians why they did not eat their dogs instead of their grandmothers, they replied, probably in some amusement at his ignorance of sound economical principles, "Doggies catch otters ; old women no ! " In mediæval Europe instances of cannibalism can be traced to scarcity of food, and among the Turks there seem to have been cases quite sufficient to explain the fabulous picture of King Richard, in the presence of Saladin's ambassadors, dining on a curried Saracen's head

> " soden full hastily
> With powder and with spysory,
> And with saffron of good colour."

In the interior of northern Sumatra dwell a people called Battas, civilized enough to use a phonetic alphabet. Their ancient cannibalism is now restricted by law. Three classes of persons are condemned to be eaten ; 1. a commoner guilty of adultery with a Rajah's wife ; 2. enemies taken in battle outside their own village ; 3. traitors and spies, in default of a ransom equivalent to 60 dollars a head. See Yule's *Marco Polo*, vol. i. pp. 275–277 ; vol. ii. p. 231 ; Parkman, *Jesuits in North America*, p. 389 ; Darwin, *Voyage of the Beagle*, London, 1870, p. 214.

plates, for the making of which Cholula was especially noted. Chocolate, flavoured with
Drinks.
vanilla, was the ordinary beverage.
Food was handled with the fingers, but bowls of
water and towels were brought in at the end of the
meal, and the next thing in order was to smoke
tobacco and get drunk with *pulque*, the fermented
juice of the century plant.[1]

The trade implied by this sort of life was not
done in shops. There were no shops in this Aztec
pueblo, but two spacious market-places, with fairs
every fifth day. There were displayed
Markets.
foods, cloths, and ornaments; tools,
weapons, and building materials; mats and stools,
dye-stuffs and pottery. Traffic was chiefly barter,
but there were such rudimentary attempts at currency as quills packed with gold-dust, bags of
cocoa seed, and queer little bits of copper and tin
shaped like the letter T. There were no coins or
scales, and selling by weight was unknown. In
most of the pueblos traders came in from the country, or from other towns, with their wares borne
on litters, the only kind of wagon or carriage in
use; but in Mexico such conveyance was done
chiefly by canoes. In the market-place there were
booths where criminals were tried and sentenced.

---

[1] The maguey, or *Agave americana*, sometimes called American aloe. One of these plants in a green tub stood on either side
of the steps leading up to the front door of George Nupkins, Esq.,
magistrate, in Ipswich (*Pickwick Papers*, chap. xxv.). For a good
account of the many and great uses of the century-plant, see
Bandelier, *Archæological Tour*, p. 217; Garcilasso, *Comentarios
reales*, pt. i. lib. viii. cap. 13. From the pulque, a kind of strong
brandy, called *mescal*, is distilled.

Crime was frequent, and punishment swift and cruel.[1] Another feature of the market-place would seem in itself to epitomize all the incongruousness of this strange Aztec world. A barber's shop seems to suggest civilization as vividly as a stone knife suggests barbarism. In the Mexican market there were booths where the scanty beards of the dusky warriors were shaved with razors of obsidian![2]

Close by the principal market and in the centre of the pueblo was the great enclosure of the temple, surrounded by stone walls eight feet in height, and entered by four gateways, _{The temple.} one from each of the wards or quarters above described. Within were not less than twenty *teocallis*, or truncated pyramids, the tallest of which was the one dedicated to the war-god. It was ascended by stone stairs on the outside, and as the Spaniards counted 114 stairs it was probably not far from 100 feet in height. This height was divided into five stages, in such wise that a man, after ascending the first flight of stairs, would walk on a flat terrace or ledge around to the opposite side of the pyramid, and there mount the second flight. Thus the religious processions on their way to the summit would wind four times about the pyramid, greatly enhancing the spectacular effect. This may or may not have been the purpose of the arrangement; it was at any rate one of its

[1] The subject of crimes and punishments in ancient Mexico is well summarized by Bandelier, *Peabody Museum Reports*, vol. ii. pp. 623–633.

[2] Prescott, *Conquest of Mexico*, bk. iv. chap. ii.; on American beards, cf. Brinton, *The American Race*, p. 40.

results.   On the summit was a dreadful block of
jasper, convex at the top, so that when the human
Human sacri-
fices. victim was laid upon his back and held
down, the breast was pushed upward,
ready for the priest to make one deep slashing cut
and snatch out the heart.   Near the sacrificial
block were the altars and sanctuaries of the gods
Tezcatlipoca, Huitzilopochtli, and others, with
idols as hideous as their names.[1]   On these altars
smoked fresh human hearts, of which the gods
were fond, while other parts of the bodies were
made ready for the kitchens of the communal
houses below.   The gods were voracious as wolves,
and the victims were numerous.[2]   In some cases

[1] See the photograph of an idol, probably of Huitzilopochtli,
dug up in 1790 near the cathedral, which stands on the site of
the heathen temple, in Bandelier, *Archæological Tour*, p. 59.

[2] A native Mexican author, born in 1579, says that at the
dedication of the new temple to Huitzilopochtli, in 1487, the
number of victims was 80,600 (Chimalpahin Quauhtlehuanitzin,
Sixième et Septième Relations, ed. Siméon, Paris, 1889, p. 158).   I
rather think that, even for such a grand occasion, we must at
least cut off a cipher.   There can be little doubt, however, that
within this whole snake-worshipping world of Mexico and Central America there were many thousand victims yearly, — men,
women, and children.   A very complete view, with many of the
hideous details, is given in Bancroft's *Native Races of the Pacific
States,* vol. ii. pp. 302–341, 687–714 ; see also Fergusson, *Tree and
Serpent Worship,* p. 40 ; Stephens, *Central America,* vol. ii. p. 185.
For a human sacrifice among the Pawnees, somewhat similar to
the Mexican custom, see Brinton, *The American Race,* p. 97.   For
some references to human sacrifices among the ancient Germans
and Huns, see Gibbon, chap. xxx., xxxiv. ; Leo, *Vorlesungen über
die Geschichte des Deutschen Volkes,* Halle, 1854, bd. i. p. 96 ;
Mone, *Geschichte des Heidenthums,* Leipsic, 1822, ii. 20, 136 ; Milman, *Latin Christianity,* vol. i. p. 244 ; among the Saxons, Sido-
nius Apollinaris, lib. viii. epist. 6 ; among the Carthaginians,
Grote, *History of Greece,* vol. xii. p. 565.

the heart was thrust into the mouth of the idol with a golden spoon, in others its lips were simply daubed with blood. In the temple a great quantity of rattlesnakes, kept as sacred objects, were fed with the entrails of the victims. Other parts of the body were given to the menagerie beasts, which were probably also kept for purposes of religious symbolism. Blood was also rubbed in the mouths of the carved serpents upon the jambs and lintels of the houses. The walls and floor of the great temple were clotted with blood and shreds of human flesh, and the smell was like that of a slaughter-house. Just outside the temple, in front of the broad street that led across the causeway to Tlacopan, stood the *tzompantli*, which was " an oblong sloping parallelogram of earth and masonry, one hundred and fifty-four feet [long] at the base, ascended by thirty steps, on each of which were skulls. Round the summit were upwards of seventy raised poles about four feet apart, connected by numerous rows of cross-poles passed through holes in the masts, on each of which five skulls were filed, the sticks being passed through the temples. In the centre stood two towers, or columns, made of skulls and lime, the face of each skull being turned outwards, and giving a horrible appearance to the whole. This effect was heightened by leaving the heads of distinguished captives in their natural state, with hair and skin on. As the skulls decayed, or fell from the towers or poles, they were replaced by others, so that no vacant place was left." [1] If Lucretius could have visited such a

The place of skulls.

[1] Bancroft, *Native Races*, etc., vol. ii. p. 586.

tzompantli he would have found a fit text for his sermon on the evils of religion.

It was into this strange city that on the 8th of November, 1519, Montezuma, making the best of bitter necessity, welcomed his long-bearded visitors with timorous politeness, and assigned them a great house near the temple for their lodgings. This house is supposed to have been a *tecpan* or tribal council-house built in the time of Axayacatl, but for some reason superseded in general use by another tecpan since built in the same neighbourhood. It was large enough to afford ample accommodation for the 450 Spaniards with their 1,000 or more Tlascalan allies, and Cortes forthwith proceeded quietly to station his sentinels along the parapet and to place his cannon where they could do the most good. After a few days spent in accepting the hospitalities proffered by Montezuma and in studying the city and its people, the Spanish commander went to work with that keen and deadly sagacity which never failed him. Safety required that some step should be taken. From what had occurred at Tlascala and Cholula, it is fair to suppose that in Tenochtitlan also there were two parties, the one inclined to submit to the strangers as representatives of Quetzalcoatl, the other disposed to resist them as interlopers. With time the latter counsels were almost certain to prevail. Familiarity with the sight of the strangers about the streets would deaden the vague terror which their presence at first inspired. Ceasing to be dreaded as gods they

Entry of the Spaniards into Tenochtitlan.

would not cease to be regarded as foreigners, and to the warrior of Tenochtitlan a foreigner was interesting chiefly as meat, — for his idols, his rattlesnakes, and himself. Whether as strangers or as emissaries of Quetzalcoatl, the Spaniards had already incurred the deadly hatred of those obscene carrion-birds, the priests of the black Tezcatlipoca and his ally Huitzilopochtli. And then had they not brought into the city a host of its eternal enemies the Tlascalans? How would the Romans of Hannibal's time have felt and acted toward anybody who should insolently have brought into Rome a force of Carthaginians? It was clear enough to Cortes and his men that their situation A dangerous situation. was excessively dangerous. Sooner or later an outbreak was to be expected, and when it should come the danger was immeasurably greater than before Tlascala or in Cholula; for if the people should simply decide to blockade and starve the Spaniards, there would be no escape save by a desperate fight through the streets and along those interminable causeways. Truly no hero of fairyland astray in an ogre's castle was ever in worse predicament than Cortes and his little army cooped in this stronghold of cannibals! There was no ground for surprise if they should one and all get dragged to the top of the great pyramid on their way to the kettles of the communal kitchens.

It was therefore necessary to act decisively and at once, while all the glamour of strangeness still enveloped them. Cortes acted upon the principle that the boldest course was the safest. A blow

must be struck so promptly and decisively as to
forestall and fatally cripple resistance,
and here Cortes was aided by his experience at Cempoala. One can hardly
fail to see that on that occasion, as at present, his
own extraordinary sagacity must have derived no
little aid from such facts about the ideas and habits of the people as his keenly observant and devoted Marina could tell him. We have seen that
at Cempoala the capture of a few chiefs quite paralyzed the people, so that even if the party opposed
to the Spaniards had prevailed in the council it
would probably have been for a time incapacitated
for action. It seems to me that this incapacity
arose from the paramount necessity of performing
sacrifices and taking the auspices before fighting,
and that nobody but the head war-chief — or, in
the case of a dual executive, perhaps one of the two
head war-chiefs — was properly qualified to perform these ceremonies. Early Greek and Roman
history afford abundant illustrations of a stage of
culture in which people did not dare to precipitate
hostilities without the needful preliminary rites ;
since to do so would simply enrage the tutelar deities and invite destruction. If we would understand the conduct of ancient men we must not
forget how completely their minds were steeped in
folk-lore.

Now we have already had occasion to observe
that the people of the Aztec Confederacy had
joined the priestly to the military function in their
tlacatecuhtli, or " chief-of-men," thus taking a
step toward developing the office to the point at-

Effect of seizing the head war-chief.

tained by the Greek *basileus*, or king, of the Homeric period.[1] We learn from Sahagun that in ancient Mexico there were two high-priests, and the first of these *Montezuma was a priest-commander.* was called Quetzalcoatl and surnamed *Totec*, " our Lord."[2] Now one of Montezuma's titles, as shown by his picture in the Codex Vaticanus, was *Quetzalcoatl Totec tlamazqui* (i. e. Quetzalcoatl our Lord Priest) of Huitzilopochtli. As supreme military commander, Montezuma's title was *Tlacochtecuhtli* or *Tlacochcalcatl*. For the generalissimo to become chief priest of the war-god is a development so natural and so practical that we find it repeated in every society where we have data for tracing back the kingship to its origins. In Mexican mythology the primitive Totec was a comrade of the fair god Quetzalcoatl ; this cheerful creature used to go about clad in a garment of human skins, and Torquemada tells us of a certain great festival at which Montezuma performed a religious dance clothed in such a garment. Torquemada adds that to the best of his knowledge and belief this was not a freak of Montezuma's, but an ancestral custom.[3] Clearly it was a symbolic identification of Montezuma with Totec. At the ceremony of investiture with the office of *tlacatecuhtli*, Montezuma was solemnly invested with the garments of the war-god, a blue breechcloth and blue sandals, a cloak of blue network, and a necklace and diadem of turquoises. His fan-shaped head-dress was

---

[1] See above, vol. i. p. 114.
[2] Sahagun, *Historia*, lib. iii. cap. ix.
[3] Torquemada, *Monarquía indiana*, lib. vii. cap. xx.

made chiefly of the brilliant golden-green feathers of the *quetzal*, or paradise-trogon, relieved with a bit of bright red from the *tlauquechol*, or roseate spoonbill. Attached to this head-dress, over the forehead, was a clasp of burnished gold in the likeness of a humming-bird's beak; and this emblem denoted that Montezuma was the living representative of Huitzilopochtli.[1] None but him could without sacrilege assume this emblem. This group of facts seems to prove that Montezuma had acquired the functions of supreme pontiff in addition to those of supreme war-chief. Indeed in his blue raiment, with the gold beak over his forehead, he was attired in the paraphernalia of a " god-king," and to that dignity and authority his office would probably in course of time have developed if things had been allowed to take their natural course.[2] Montezuma was not the first " chief-of-men " at Tenochtitlan in whom the functions of high priest and head war-chief were combined. That stage of development had already been reached in his immediate predecessors Ahuizotl, Tizoc, and Axayacatl, if not earlier.

Just how far Cortes understood the natural effect of capturing such a personage and holding him in durance, one can hardly say. Incredibly

---

[1] For the facts mentioned in this paragraph I am indebted to the learned monograph of Mrs. Zelia Nuttall, " Standard or Head-dress ? an Historical Essay on a Relic of Ancient Mexico," in Peabody Museum, *Archæological and Ethnological Papers*, vol. i. No. 1, Cambridge, 1888. This essay shows that Mrs. Nuttall has made notable progress in the difficult work of deciphering the ancient Mexican hieroglyphic writing.

[2] See below, p. 347.

audacious as the plan must have seemed, it was probably the only thing that could have saved the Spaniards, and Cortes (as he wrote to Charles V.) had been in the city only six days when his decision was made. Events had lately come to his knowledge which furnished a pretext. The affair of Quauhpopoca. A small band of Spaniards had been left at Vera Cruz, and Quauhpopoca — an Aztec chief, probably one of Montezuma's tax-gatherers sent to collect tribute from the pueblo of Nautla — had picked a quarrel with these Spaniards, and there had been a fight in which the white men were victorious, but not without losing half-a-dozen of their number. The fact was thus revealed that the strangers were mortal. Cortes decided to make this affair the occasion for taking possession of Montezuma's person. After a night spent with his captains and priests in earnest prayer,[1] he visited the "chief-of-men," in company with the big blonde "sun-faced" Alvarado and other mail-clad warriors, and taking, as usual, his trusty Marina as interpreter. Cortes told Montezuma that charges had been brought against him of having instigated the conduct of Quauhpopoca; not that Cortes believed these charges, O dear, no! he had too much respect for the noble *tlacatecuhtli* to believe them, but still it was his duty to investigate the facts of the case. Montezuma promptly despatched a messenger to bring home the unlucky

[1] "E como teniemos acordado el dia antes de prender al Monteçuma, toda la noche estuuimos en oracion con el Padre de la Merced, rogando á Dios, que fuesse de tal modo, que redundasse para su santo servicio." Diaz, *Historia verdadera*, cap. xcv. fol. 74 verso.

Quauhpopoca. Very good, pursued Cortes with much suavity, but until the inquiry should be brought to some satisfactory termination, of course his august friend could not entertain the slightest objection to coming and making his quarters in the tecpan occupied by the white men. It appeared, however, that Montezuma did entertain most decided objections to any such surrender of himself. But his arguments and entreaties were of no avail against the mixture of soft persuasion with ominous threats in which Cortes knew so well how to deal. So when the Spanish captains returned to their fortress they took Montezuma with them, paying him every outward mark of respect. It was a very subtle scheme. The *tlacatecuhtli* was simply transferred from one tecpan to another; the tribal council could meet and public business be transacted in the one place as well as in the other. That the fact of Montezuma's virtual imprisonment might not become too glaring, Cortes sometimes let him go to the temple, but on such occasions not less than a hundred Spaniards, armed to the teeth, served as an escort. Cortes was now acting governor of Tenochtitlan and of the Confederacy, with Montezuma as his mouthpiece and the *tlatocan*, or tribal council, holding its meetings under his own roof!

When Quauhpopoca arrived, a couple of weeks after the seizure of Montezuma, Cortes had him tried for treason, and condemned him, with several of his friends, to be burned alive in the square in front of his tecpan; and with a refinement of

Seizure of Montezuma.

prudence and of audacity at which one cannot sufficiently marvel, he sent his men around to the dart-houses and collected a vast quan- Burning of tity of arrows and javelins which he Quauhpopoca. caused to be piled up about the stakes to which the victims were chained, so that weapons and warriors were consumed in the same blaze. A conspiracy for the release of Montezuma, in which his brother Cuitlahuatzin and the tribal chiefs of Tezcuco and Tlacopan were implicated, was duly discovered, and it was not long before Cortes had these three dignitaries safely confined in his tec-pan and in irons, while he contrived, through Montezuma, to dictate to the tribal councils at Tezcuco and Tlacopan the summary deposition of the old chiefs and the election of such new ones as he deemed likely to be interested on their own account in his safety. He does not seem to have realized the full importance of his capture of Cuitlahuatzin, who stood next to Montezuma in the customary line of succession. In Tenochtitlan Cortes began an image-breaking crusade. The cruel custom of human sacrifices greatly shocked him, as men are wont to be shocked by any kind of wickedness with which they are unfamiliar; and devil-worship was something that his notions of Christian duty required him to suppress. His action in this direction might have been over rash but for the sagacious counsel of his spiritual adviser, Father Olmedo, who warned him Cleansing of not to go too fast. So at first he con- one of the tented himself with taking possession of pyramids. one of the pyramids, where he threw down the

idols, cleansed the reeking altar and sprinkled it
with holy water, set up the crucifix and an image
of the Virgin, and had the mass performed there,
while the heathen multitude in the square below
looked on and saw it all. If we did not understand the possible interpretation of these acts as
sanctioned by Quetzalcoatl, and also the superstitious incapacity of the people to act without
their priest-commander, it would be utterly in-
comprehensible that the fires of Aztec wrath should
have smouldered so long. The long winter passed
Arrival of   in sullen quiet, and April flowers were
Narvaez.   blooming, when picture-writing, sent up
from the coast, was fraught with sudden intelligence alarming to Cortes. Pánfilo de Narvaez,
with 18 ships and not less than 1,200 soldiers, had
anchored at San Juan de Ulloa, sent from Cuba
by Velasquez, with orders to pursue the diso-
bedient knight-errant and arrest him.

Cortes was not the man to waste precious moments in wondering what he had better do. He
left Pedro de Alvarado, with about 150 men, to
take charge of Montezuma and Mexico. With the
Defeat of   remaining 300 he hastened to the coast,
Narvaez.   came down upon Narvaez unawares like
a thief in the night, defeated and captured him,
entranced his troops with tales of the great Mexican pueblo, whetted their greed with hopes of
plunder, kindled the missionary zeal of the priests,
and ended by enlisting every man of them under
his own banner. Thus with more than quadrupled
force he marched back to Mexico. There evil
news awaited him. Alvarado's cast of mind was

of far lower grade than that of Cortes. He had
in him less of Reynard and more of Isegrim. Not
fathoming the reasons of the Aztecs for forbear-
ance, he made the grave mistake of despising them
as spiritless cowards. There were some grounds
for a suspicion that the chiefs of the clans were
meditating an attack upon the Spaniards in the
city, and Alvarado, in this imminent peril, with
nerves intensely strained, made up his mind to be
beforehand. There was in the Aztec city a great
spring festival, the gladdest of the year, the May
day of rejoicing over the return of verdure and
flowers. Every year at this season a young man,
especially chosen for manly beauty and prowess,
was presented with four brides and feasted sump-
tuously during a honeymoon of twenty
days. On the twenty-first day all mili- Festival of
tary deeds and plans were held in abeyance, and
the city was given up to festivities, while a solemn
procession of youths and maidens, clad in dainty
white cotton and crowned with garlands of roasted
maize, escorted the chosen young man to the summit of the great pyramid. There they knelt and
adored him as an incarnation of the god Tezcatlipoca. Then he was sacrificed in the usual manner, and morsels of his flesh were sent about to
the clan chiefs to be stewed and eaten with devout
hymns and dances.[1]

---

[1] The sacrifice of a she-goat by some of the barbarians in the
army of Alboin, King of the Lombards, afforded Gibbon an opportunity for one of his ingenious little thrusts at the current
theology of his time. " Gregory the Roman (*Dialog.*, iii. 27) supposes that they likewise adored this she-goat. I know of but one
religion in which the god and the victim are the same " (!) *De-*

It was this day of barbaric festivity in the year 1520 that the imprudent Alvarado selected for delivering his blow. In the midst of the ceremonies the little band of Spaniards fell upon the

Alvarado's massacre.

people and massacred about 600, including many chiefs of clans. Thus Alvarado brought on the sudden calamity which he had hoped to avert. The Aztecs were no cowards, and had not the Spaniards still possessed the priest-commander Montezuma it would have gone hard with them. As it was they soon deemed it best to retreat to their fortress, where they were surrounded and besieged by a host of Indians who began trying in places to undermine the walls. By threats Alvarado compelled Montezuma to go out upon the roof and quiet the outbreak. Things went on for some weeks without active fighting, but the Indians burned the brigantines on the lake which Cortes had built during the winter as a means of retreat in case of disaster. The Spaniards by good luck found a spring in their courtyard and their store of corn was ample, so that thirst and hunger did not yet assail them.

When Cortes entered the city on the 24th of June, he found the streets deserted, the markets closed, and many of the drawbridges raised. A

cline and Fall, chap. xlv., note 14. Ancient Mexico would have furnished the learned historian with another example, and a more extensive study of barbarous races would have shown him that the case of Christianity is by no means exceptional. Indeed the whole doctrine of vicarious sacrifice, by which Christianity was for a time helped, but has now long been encumbered, is a survival from the gross theories characteristic of the middle period of barbarism.

few Indians from their doorways scowled at the passing troops. When Cortes met Alvarado he told him that he had behaved like a madman, but it was now the turn of Cortes himself to make a mistake. He could not be ex- *Return of Cortes.* pected to know that in that community there was an ulterior power behind the throne. That ulterior power was the *tlatocan*, or tribal council, which elected the priest-commander from the members of a particular family, in accordance with certain customary rules of succession. In a great emergency the council which thus elected the ruler could depose him and elect another. Now Cortes had in his fortress Montezuma's brother Cuitlahuatzin, who stood next in the regular line of succession, and he evidently did not understand the danger in letting him out. The increase of numbers was fast telling upon the stock of food, and Cortes sent out Cuitlahuatzin with orders to have the markets opened. This at once brought matters to a terrible crisis. Cuitlahuatzin convened the *tlatocan*, which instantly deposed Montezuma and elected him in his place. *Deposition of Montezuma.* Early next morning came the outbreak. A hoarse sound arose, like the murmur of distant waters, and soon the imprisoned Spaniards from their parapet saw pyramids, streets, and house-tops black with raging warriors. They attacked with arrows, slings, and javelins, and many Spaniards were killed or wounded. The Spanish cannon swept the streets with terrible effect and the canals near by ran red with blood, but the Indians pressed on, and shot burning arrows through the embrasures until the interior woodwork began to take fire.

At Cortes's direction Montezuma presented himself on the terraced roof and sought to assuage the wrath of the people, but now he found that his authority was ended. Another now wore the golden beak of the war-god. He was no longer general, no longer priest, and his person had lost its sacred character. Stones and darts were hurled at him; he was struck down by a heavy stone, and died a few days afterward, whether from the wound, or from chagrin, or both. Before his death the Spaniards made a sortie, and after terrific hand to hand fighting stormed the great temple which overlooked and commanded their own quarters and had sadly annoyed them. They flung down the idols among the people and burned the accursed shrines. It was on the last day of June that Montezuma died, and on the evening of the next day, fearing lest his army should be blockaded and starved, Cortes evacuated the city. The troops marched through quiet and deserted streets till they reached the great causeway leading to Tlacopan. Its three drawbridges had all been destroyed. The Spaniards carried a pontoon, but while they were passing over the first bridgeway the Indians fell upon them in vast numbers, their light canoes swarming on both sides of the narrow road. The terrible night that ensued has ever since been known in history as *la noche triste*. Cortes started in the evening with 1,250 Spaniards, 6,000 Tlascalans, and 80 horses. Next morning, after reaching

His death.

The Melancholy Night.

terra firma he had 500 Spaniards, 2,000 Tlascalans, and 20 horses. All his cannon were sunk in the lake; and 40 Spaniards were in Aztec clutches to be offered up to the war-god. Then Cortes sat down upon a rock, and buried his face in his hands and wept.

Not for one moment, however, did he flinch in his purpose of taking Mexico. In a few days the Indians from that and other neighbouring pueblos attacked him in overwhelming force in the valley of Otumba, hoping to complete his destruction, but he won such a decisive and murderous victory as to reëstablish his shaken prestige. It was well, for Mexico had sent an embassy to Tlascala, and in that pueblo the council of clan chiefs were having an earnest debate much like those that one reads in Thucydides or Xenophon. There were speakers who

Victory at Otumba and its effects.

feared that success for the Spaniards would ultimately mean servitude for Tlascala, and the Aztec envoys played upon this fear. Nothing could have happened at this time so likely to ensure the destruction of Cortes as the defection of the Tlascalans. But his victory at Otumba determined them to keep up their alliance with him. During the autumn Cortes occupied himself with operations, military and diplomatic, among the smaller pueblos, defeating any that ventured to resist him and making alliances with such as were eager to wreak their vengeance upon the hated Tenochtitlan. It is enough to say that all this work was done with characteristic skill. Cortes now found ships useful. Taking some of those that had come with Narvaez, he sent them to Hispaniola for horses, cannon, and soldiers ; and by Christmas Eve he found himself at the head of a thoroughly equipped army of 700 infantry armed with pikes and cross-bows, 118 arquebusiers, 86 cavalry, a dozen can-non, and several thousand Indian allies. Though the belief that white men could not be killed had been quite overthrown, yet the prestige of Cortes as a resistless warrior was now restored, and the prospect of humbling the Aztecs kindled a fierce enthusiasm in the men of Quauquechollan, Hue-xotzinco, Chalco, and other pueblos now ranked among his allies.

Starting at Christmas on his final march against the mighty pueblo, Cortes first proceeded to Tez-cuco. In that community there was disaffection toward its partner on the lake, resulting from re-cent quarrels between the chiefs, and now Ixtlil-xochitl, the new war-chief of the Tezcucans, gave

Gaining of Tezcuco.

in his adherence to Cortes, admitted him into the town, and entertained him hospitably in the tecpan. This move broke up the Aztec Confederacy, placed all the warriors of Tezcuco at the disposal of Cortes, and enabled him without opposition to launch a new flotilla of brig-antines on the lake and support them with swarms of agile Tezcucan canoes. Thus the toils were closing in upon doomed Tenochtitlan. Meanwhile small-pox had carried off Cuitlahuatzin, and his nephew Guatemotzin was now " chief-of-men," — a brave warrior whom Mexicans to this day regard with affectionate admiration for his gallant defence of their city. For ferocious courage the Aztecs were not surpassed by any other Indians on the continent, and when Cortes at length began the siege of Mexico, April 28, 1521,[1] the fighting that ensued was incessant and terrible. The fresh water supply was soon cut off, and then slowly but surely the besiegers upon the three causeways and in the brigantines closed in upon their prey. Points of advantage were sometimes lost by the Aztecs through their excessive anxiety to capture Spaniards alive. Occasionally they succeeded, and then from the top of the great pyramid would resound the awful tones of the sacrificial drum made of serpent skins, a sound that could be heard in every quarter of this horrible city; and the souls of the soldiers sickened as they saw their wretched comrades dragged up the long staircase, to be offered as sacrifices to Satan. Every inch of ground was contested by the Aztecs with a fury that reminds one of the resistance of Jerusalem to the soldiers of Titus. At last, on the 13th of August, the resistance came to an end. Canals and footways were choked with corpses, and a great part of the city lay in ruins. The first work of the conquerors was to cleanse and rebuild. The ancient religion soon passed away, the ancient society was gradually metamorphosed, and Mexico assumed the aspect of a Spanish town. On the site of the heathen temple a Gothic church was erected, which in 1573 was replaced by the cathedral that still stands there.

The capture of Tenochtitlan was by no means

Siege of Mexico.

[1] The death of Magellan, at Matan, occurred the day before, April 27.

equivalent to the conquest of the vast territory
that now goes under the name of Mexico. Much
work was yet to be done in all directions, but it is
not necessary for the purposes of this book that I
should give an account of it. I am concerned
here with the Conquest of Mexico only in so far
as it is an episode in the Discovery of America,
only in so far as it illustrates a phase of the earliest contact between the two hemispheres, each
hitherto ignorant of the other, each so curiously
affected by its first experience of the other ; and
for my purpose the story here given will suffice.
Nor is it necessary to recount the vicissitudes of
the later years of Cortes, who had to contend
against the enmity of Bishop Fonseca and a series
of untoward circumstances connected therewith.
His discovery of the peninsula of California will
be mentioned in a future chapter. He returned
finally to Spain in 1540, and served with great
merit in the expedition against Algiers
in the following year ; but he was
neglected by the emperor, and passed the rest of
his life in seclusion at Seville. He died at a
small village near that city on the 2d of December, 1547.

Death of
Cortes.

A great deal of sentimental ink has been shed
over the wickedness of the Spaniards
in crossing the ocean and attacking
people who had never done them any
harm, overturning and obliterating a " splendid
civilization," and more to the same effect. It is
undeniable that unprovoked aggression is an ex-

How the Span-
ish conquest
should be re-
garded.

tremely hateful thing, and many of the circumstances attendant upon the Spanish conquest in
America were not only heinous in their atrocity,
but were emphatically condemned, as we shall
presently see, by the best moral standards of the
sixteenth century. Yet if we are to be guided
by strict logic, it would be difficult to condemn
the Spaniards for the mere act of conquering
Mexico without involving in the same condemnation
our own forefathers who crossed the ocean and
overran the territory of the United States with
small regard for the proprietary rights of Algon-
quins, or Iroquois, or red men of any sort. Our forefathers, if called upon to justify themselves, would
have replied that they were founding Christian
states and diffusing the blessings of a higher civilization ; and such, in spite of much alloy in the
motives and imperfection in the performance, was
certainly the case. Now if we would not lose or
distort the historical perspective, we must bear in
mind that the Spanish conquerors would have returned exactly the same answer. If Cortes were
to return to this world and pick up some history
book in which he is described as a mere picturesque adventurer, he would feel himself very
unjustly treated. He would say that he had
higher aims than those of a mere fighter and gold-
hunter ; and so doubtless he had. In the complex tangle of motives that actuated the mediæval
Spaniard — and in his peninsula we may apply
the term mediæval to later dates than would be
proper in France or Italy — the desire of extending the dominion of the Church was a very real and

powerful incentive to action. The strength of the missionary and crusading spirit in Cortes is seen in the fact that where it was concerned, and there only, was he liable to let zeal overcome prudence.

There can be no doubt that, after making all allowances, the Spaniards did introduce a better state of society into Mexico than they found there. It was high time that an end should be put to those hecatombs of human victims, slashed, torn open, and devoured on all the little oc-

It was a good thing for Mexico.

casions of life. It sounds quite pithy to say that the Inquisition, as conducted in Mexico, was as great an evil as the human sacrifices and the cannibalism; but it is not true.[1] Compared with the ferocious barbarism of ancient Mexico the contemporary Spanish modes of life were mild, and this, I think, helps further to explain the ease with which the country was conquered. In a certain sense the prophecy of Quetzalcoatl was fulfilled, and the coming of the Spaniards did mean the final dethronement of the ravening Tezcatlipoca. The work of the noble Franciscan and Dominican monks who followed closely upon Cortes, and devoted their lives to the spiritual welfare of the Mexicans, is a more attractive subject than any picture of military conquest. To this point I shall return hereafter, when we come to consider the sublime career of Las Casas. For the present we may conclude in the spirit of one of the noblest of Spanish historians, Pedro de

---

[1] As Llorente, the historian of the Inquisition who has fully set forth its enormities, once wittily observed, "Il ne faut pas calomnier même l'Inquisition."

Cieza de Leon, and praise God that the idols are
cast down.[1]

The conquest of Mexico was followed at intervals by the reduction of Guatemala, Honduras,
and Yucatan; and while this work was going on,
captains from Darien overran Nicaragua, so that
what we may call the northern and southern
streams of Spanish conquest — the stream which
started from Hispaniola by way of Cuba, and that
which started from Hispaniola by way of Darien
— at length came together again. The southern
stream of Spanish conquest, thus stopped in one
direction at Nicaragua, kept on its course southward along the Pacific coast of South America
until it encountered a kind of semi-civilization
different from anything else that was to be seen
in the western hemisphere. We are now prepared for the sketch, hitherto postponed, of Ancient Peru.

[1] *Crónica del Peru,* pt. i. cap. lviii.

CHAPTER IX.

ANCIENT PERU.

FROM the elevated table-lands of New Mexico and Arizona to the southward as far as the mountain fastnesses of Bolivia, the region of the Cordilleras was the seat of culture in various degrees more advanced than that of any other parts of the New World. Starting from Central America, we find in the tombs of the little province of Chiriqui, between Costa Rica and Veragua, a wealth of artistic remains that serve in some respects to connect the culture of Central America with that of the semi-civilized peoples beyond the isthmus of Darien.[1] Of these peoples the first were the Muyscas, or Chibchas, whose principal towns were near the site of Bogotá. There were many tribes of Chibchas, speaking as many distinct dialects of a common stock language. They had no writing except rude pictographs and no means of recording events. Their family was in a rudimentary state of development, and kinship was traced only through the female line. There was a priesthood, and the head war-chief, whose office was elec-

Chiriqui.

The Chibchas.

[1] See Holmes, "Ancient Art of the Province of Chiriqui," *Reports of the Bureau of Ethnology*, vol. vi. pp. 13–187; Bollaert, *Antiquarian Researches in New Granada*, London, 1860.

tive, had begun to exercise the highest priestly functions. They were idolaters, with human sacrifices, but seem to have abandoned cannibalism. Their funeral customs deserve mention. We have observed that the Mexicans practised cremation. In some parts of Central America the dead were buried, in others burnt. But in coming down to the isthmus of Darien we begin to find mummies. Among the people of the Andes in the middle status of barbarism, it was customary to embalm the bodies of chiefs and other important personages, and to wrap them closely in fine mantles adorned with emeralds. The mummy was then buried, and food, weapons, and living concubines were buried with it. Such was the practice among the Chibchas.

The houses of these people were very large, and shaped either like the frustum of a cone or like that of a pyramid. The walls were built of stout timbers fastened with wedges and cemented with adobe clay. Maize and cotton were cultivated, and cotton cloth of various coloured designs was made. The rafts and rope bridges resembled those of the Peruvians hereafter to be mentioned. Chiefs and priests were carried on wooden litters. In every town there were fairs at stated intervals. Goods were sold by measure, but not by weight. Round tiles of gold, without stamp or marking of any sort, served as a currency, and when there was not enough of it salt was used as a medium of exchange. Trade, however, was chiefly barter. The Chibchas had some slight intercourse with the people of Quito and some knowledge of the Inca kingdom beyond.[1]

This Chibcha culture, in many respects lower, but in some respects higher, than that of the Mexicans, was probably typical of the whole Andes region for unknown centuries before its various peoples were brought under the comparatively civilizing sway of the Incas. On the eastern slopes of the giant mountains this semi-civilization maintained itself precariously against the surging waves of lower barbarism and savagery. The ethnology of South America has been much less thoroughly studied than that of North America, and our subject does not require us to attempt to enumerate or characterize these lower peoples. They have been arranged provisionally in four groups, although it is pretty clear that instances of non-related tribes occur in some if not in all the groups. At the time of the Discovery the ferocious Caribs inhabited the forests of Venezuela and Guiana, and had established themselves upon many of the West India islands.

The Caribs.

---

[1] The principal sources of information about the Chibchas are Piedrahita, *Historia del Nuevo Reyno de Granada*, Antwerp, 1688 ; Simon, *Tercera (y cuarta) noticia de la segunda parte de las Noticias Historiales de las Conquistas de Tierra Firme en el Nuevo Reyno de Granada*, 1624 (in Kingsborough's *Mexican Antiquities*, vol. viii.) ; Herrera, *Historia General de los hechos de los Castellanos*, etc., Madrid, 1601 (especially the fifth book) ; Joaquin Acosta, *Compendio Historico del Descubrimiento y Colonizacion de la Nueva Granada*, Paris, 1848 ; Cassani, *Historia de la Compagnia de Jesus del Nuevo Reino de Granada*, Madrid, 1741 ; Uricoechea, *Memoria sobre las Antiguedades Neo-Granadinas*, Berlin, 1854. The subject is well tabulated in Spencer's *Descriptive Sociology*, No. ii.

Their name, first written in Latin form "Cari-
bales" by Columbus in 1498, was presently cor-
rupted into "Canibales," and has thus furnished
European languages with an epithet since applied
to all eaters of human flesh. Adjacent to the
Caribs, but distinct from them, were the Maypures, whose tribes ranged from the headwaters of
the Orinoco southward into Bolivia. The Caribs
and Maypures make up what is geographically
rather than ethnologically known as the Orinoco
group of Indians. A second group, called Ama-
zonians, includes a great number of tribes, mostly in the upper status of Various savage groups.
savagery, ranging along the banks of the Amazon
and its tributaries; about their ethnology very little is known. Much better defined is the third or
Tupi-Guarani group, extending over the vast country southward from the Amazon to La Plata. This
family of tribes, speaking a common stock language,
is more widely diffused than any other in South
America; and it is certain that within the area
which it occupies there are other tribes not related
to it and not yet classified. The fourth group is
merely geographical, and includes families so different as the Pampas Indians of the Argentine
Republic, the inhabitants of Patagonia and Tierra
del Fuego, and the brave Araucanians of Chili.[1]

All the peoples here mentioned were, when discovered, either in the upper status of savagery or
the lower status of barbarism, and to many of

[1] See Keane's essay on the "Ethnography and Philology of
America," appended to Bates's *Central and South America*, 2d ed.
London, 1882, pp. 443-561.

them the same description would still be applicable. Lowest of all were the Fuegians and some of the tribes on the Amazon; highest of all were the Araucanians, with their habitat on the western slope of the Andes.

The whole of this Pacific slope, from the country of the Araucanians northward to that of our friends the Chibchas, was occupied by the family of Quichua-Aymara tribes, since commonly known as Peruvians. These tribes were probably the first in all America to emerge from the lower status of barbarism, and at the time of the Discovery they had approached much nearer to the formation of a true nationality than any others. In some important respects they were much more civilized than the people of Mexico and Central America, but they had not attained to the beginnings of true civilization, inasmuch as they had neither an alphabet nor any system of hieroglyphic writing. In preserving traditions the Peruvian *amautas*, or "wise men," were aided by a queer system of mnemonics worked out by tying complicated knots in cords of divers colours.[1]

Quichua-Aymara tribes.

---

[1] Mr. Tylor's description of the *quipus* is so good that I cannot do better than insert it here in full: — "When a farmer's daughter ties a knot in her handkerchief to remember a commission at market by, she makes a rudimentary *quipu*. Darius made one when he took a thong and tied sixty knots in it, and gave it to the chiefs of the Ionians, that they might untie a knot each day, till, if the knots were all undone and he had not returned, they might go back to their own land. (Herodotus, iv. 98.) . . . This is so simple a device that it may have been invented again and again. . . . It has been found in Asia (Erman's *Siberia*, i. 492), in Africa (Klemm's *Culturgeschichte*, i. 3), in

These knotted cords, or *quipus*, were also used in keeping accounts, and in some ways they were curi-

Mexico, among the North American Indians (Charlevoix, vi. 151); but its greatest development was in South America." The Peruvian *quipu* consists "of a thick main cord, with thinner cords tied on to it at certain distances, in which the knots are tied. . . . The cords are often of various colours, each with its own proper meaning; red for soldiers, yellow for gold, white for silver, green for corn, and so on. This knot-writing was especially suited for reckonings and statistical tables; a single knot meant ten, a double one a hundred, a triple one a thousand, two singles side by side twenty, two doubles two hundred. The distances of the knots from the main cord were of great importance, as was the sequence of the branches, for the principal objects were placed on the first branches and near the trunk, and so in decreasing order. This art of reckoning is still in use among the herdsmen of the Puna (the high mountain plateau of Peru)," and they explained it to the Swiss naturalist Tschudi "so that with a little trouble he could read any of their *quipus*. On the first branch they usually register the bulls, on the second the cows, these again they divide into milch cows and those that are dry; the next branches contain the calves, according to age and sex, then the sheep in several subdivisions, the number of foxes killed, the quantity of salt used, and lastly the particulars of the cattle that have died. On other *quipus* is set down the produce of the herd in milk, cheese, wool, etc. Each heading is indicated by a special colour or a differently twined knot. It was in the same way that in old times the army registers were kept; on one cord the slingers were set down, on another the spearmen, on a third those with clubs, etc., with their officers; and thus also the accounts of battles were drawn up. In each town were special functionaries whose duty was to tie and interpret the *quipus;* they were called *quipucamayocuna*, or 'knot-officers.' . . . They were seldom able to read a *quipu* without the aid of an oral commentary; when one came from a distant province, it was necessary to give notice with it whether it referred to census, tribute, war, etc. . . . They carefully kept the *quipus* in their proper departments, so as not, for instance, to mistake a tribute-cord for one relating to the census. . . . In modern times all the attempts made to read the ancient *quipus* have been in vain. The difficulty in deciphering them is very great, since every knot indi-

ously analogous on the one hand to Indian wampum belts and on the other hand to the tally-sticks used in old times by officers of the exchequer in France and England. Learned Spaniards were astonished at seeing how many things the Peruvians could record with their *quipus.* Nevertheless, as compared with hieroglyphics even as rude as those of Mexico, these knotted cords were very inefficient instruments for recording knowledge. For this reason the historic period of the Peruvian people goes but a short distance back of the Discovery. All lists of the Incas agree in beginning with Manco Capac; [1] and there is practical

cates an idea, and a number of intermediate notions are left out. But the principal impediment is the want of the oral information as to their subject-matter, which was needful even to the most learned decipherers." As to the ancient use of the *quipu* in Mexico, "Boturini placed the fact beyond doubt by not only finding some specimens in Tlascala, but also recording their Mexican name, *nepohualtzitzin,* a word derived from the verb *tlapohua,* ' to count.' (Boturini, *Idea de una nueva Historia,* etc., Madrid, 1746, p. 85). . . . *Quipus* are found in the Eastern Archipelago and in Polynesia proper, and they were in use in Hawaii forty years ago, in a form seemingly not inferior to the most elaborate Peruvian examples. . . . The fate of the *quipu* has been everywhere to be superseded, more or less entirely, by the art of writing. . . . When, therefore, the Chinese tell us (Goguet, *Origine des Lois,* etc., tom. iii. p. 322 ; Mailla, *Hist. générale de la Chine,* Paris, 1777, tom. i. p. 4) that they once upon a time used this contrivance, and that the art of writing superseded it, the analogy of what has taken place in other countries makes it extremely probable that the tradition is a true one." Tylor, *Researches into the Early History of Mankind,* London, 1865, pp. 154–158. See also Garcilasso, *Comentarios reales,* lib. ii. cap. 13 ; lib. vi. cap. 8, 9.

[1] The pronunciation of this name is more correctly indicated by writing it *Ccapac.* The first *c* is " a guttural far back in the throat ; the second on the roof of the mouth." Markham's *Quichua Grammar,* p. 17. The result must be a kind of guttural click.

unanimity as to the names and order of succession of the Incas. But when we come to dates
for the earlier names, all is indefinite.

Manco has been variously placed from $\quad$ Lists of Incas.
the eleventh to the thirteenth century, the later
date being far more probable than the earlier if
we have regard for the ordinary rules of human
longevity. The first Inca whose career may be
considered strictly historical is Viracocha, whose
reign probably began somewhere about A. D. 1380,
or a century and a half before the arrival of the
Spaniards in Peru.[1] Moreover throughout the
fifteenth century, while the general succession of

---

[1] The following list of the Incas will be useful for reference : —

1. Manco Capac	. . . .	cir. 1250 ?
2. Sinchi Rocca	. . . .	
3. Lloque Yupanqui	. . .	
4. Mayta Capac	. . . .	
5. Capac Yupanqui	. . .	
6. Inca Rocca	. . . .	
7. Yahuar-huaccac	. . .	
8. Viracocha	. . .	cir. 1380.
9. Inca Urco	. . .	cir. 1400.
10. Pachacutec Inca Yupanqui	.	cir. 1400.
11. Tupac Yupanqui	. . .	cir. 1439.
12. Huayna Capac	. . .	cir. 1475.
13. Huascar	. . .	1523.
14. Atahualpa (*usurper*)	. .	1532.
15. Manco Capac Yupanqui	.	1533.
16. Sayri Tupac	. . .	1544.
17. Cusi Titu Yupanqui	. .	1560.
18. Tupac Amaru	. . .	1571.

The last Inca reigned only a few months and was beheaded in
1571. This list in the main follows that of Mr. Markham (Winsor, *Narr. and Crit. Hist.*, i. 232), but on the weighty authority
of Cieza de Leon and others less weighty I insert the name of
the Inca Urco, whose evil fortune, presently to be mentioned,
furnishes no valid reason for omitting his name from the roll.

LIBRARY OF
MUSKINGUM COLLEGE
New Concord, Ohio.

events is quite clear, the dates are much less precise than in Mexico, where hieroglyphic records were kept.

But although the historic period for Peru dates no farther back than for Mexico, there are some reasons for supposing that if the whole story of the semi-civilization of the Incas were accessible, it would carry us much farther into the past than anything to be found in Mexico, even if we were to accept a good deal of what has been imagined about the Toltecs and their deeds, and other prehistoric circumstances in the land of the Nahuas.

The country about Lake Titicaca, the Lake Titicaca. traditional cradle of Peruvian culture, is in some respects the most remarkable spot in the New World. In that elevated region, of which the general altitude nearly answers to that of such Alpine summits as the peak of the Jungfrau, but which is still a valley, dominated by those stupendous mountains, Sorata and Illimani, inferior only to the highest of the Himalayas, there are to be seen remnants of cyclopean architecture at which all beholders, from the days of the first Spanish visitors down to our own, have marvelled. These works, to judge from the rude carvings upon them, are purely American, and afford no ground for the notion that they might have been constructed by others than the aboriginal inhabitants of the New World; but they certainly imply a greater command of labour than is to be inferred from an inspection of any other buildings in America. These cyclopean structures, containing monoliths which, in the absence of beasts of burden, must have required large companies of men to move, are found at Tiahuanacu, hard by Lake Titicaca; and it would appear that to this Thibet of the New World we must assign the first development of the kind of semi-civilization that the Spaniards found in Peru. According to one of the foremost authorities, Mr. Clements Markham, an extensive and more or less consolidated empire was at one time governed from Tiahuanacu. Peruvian tradition handed over to the Spanish historians the names of sixty-five kings belonging to a dynasty known as the Piruas. Allowing an av- The alleged erage of twenty years for a reign, which Pirua dynasty. is a fair estimate, these sixty-five kings would cover just thirteen centuries.[1] As there was a further tradition of a period of disintegration and confusion intervening between the end of the Pirua dynasty and the time of Manco Capac, Mr. Markham allows for this interval about four centuries. Then the series of sixty-five Pirua kings, ending about the ninth century of our era, would have begun in the fifth century before Christ.

In such calculations, however, where we are dealing with mere lists of personal names, unchecked by constant or frequent reference to historic events connected with the persons, the chances

[1] The 50 English sovereigns, from Egbert to William IV. inclusive (omitting the Cromwells as covering part of the same time as Charles II., and counting William and Mary as one) reigned 1,009 years; almost exactly an average of 20 years. The 44 Frankish and French kings, from Pepin to Louis XVI. inclusive (omitting Eudes as covering time otherwise covered) reigned 1,042 years; an average of nearly 24 years, raised by the two exceptionally long reigns of Louis XIV. and Louis XV., which covered 131 years.

of error are so numerous as to leave little room
for confidence in the conclusion.   One is much inclined to doubt whether anything can properly be
said to be known about the so-called Pirua dynasty
or its works.   It is customary to ascribe the so-
called fortress on the Sacsahuaman hill

Ruins on the
Sacsahuaman
hill.

overlooking Cuzco to the same people
and the same period as the ruins of
Tiahuanacu; but according to Cieza de Leon, the
most careful and critical of the early Spanish
writers on Peru,[1] this great building was begun in

---

[1] "The work of Pedro de Cieza de Leon," says Mr. Markham,
"is, in many respects, one of the most remarkable literary pro-
ductions of the age of Spanish conquest in America.   Written by
a man who had passed his life in the camp from early boyhood,
it is conceived on a plan which would have done credit to the
most thoughtful scholar, and is executed with care, judgment,
and fidelity."

Cieza de Leon was probably born in Seville about 1519, and
died about 1560.   At the age of fourteen he came to the New
World, and remained until 1550, and in the course of these seventeen years of very active service he visited almost every historic
point in western South America from Darien to Potosi.   In 1541
he began keeping a journal, which formed the basis of his
"Chronicle," of which the first part was published at Seville in
1553, and dedicated to the prince afterwards Philip II.   In the
dedication Cieza says, "The attempt savours of temerity in so un-
learned a man, but others of more learning are too much occupied in the wars to write.   Oftentimes, when the other soldiers
were reposing, I was tiring myself by writing.   Neither fatigue
nor the ruggedness of the country, nor the mountains and rivers,
nor intolerable hunger and suffering, have ever been sufficient to
obstruct my two duties, namely, writing and following my flag
and my captain without fault. . . . Much that I have written I
saw with my own eyes, and I travelled over many countries in
order to learn more concerning them.   Those things which I did
not see, I took great pains to inform myself of, from persons of
good repute, both Christians and Indians."   There can be no
doubt that he took great pains.   For minuteness of observation

the time of Pachacutec, and continued under his successors,. Tupac, Huayna, and Huascar, so that

and accuracy of statement his book is extraordinary. Wherever he went he was careful to describe the topography of the country, its roads and ruined buildings, the climate, vegetation, animals tame and wild, the manners and occupations of the people, and their beliefs and traditions. Along with the instincts of a modern naturalist he had the critical faculty and sifted his authorities in a way that was unusual in his time. He had also an eye for the glorious beauty of the landscape. He was eminently honourable and humane, and strongly condemned the atrocities so often committed by the Spaniards. While his book is thus in many respects modern in spirit and method, it is full of the oldtime quaintness. Where a modern writer, for example, in order to explain similarities in the myths and heathen customs of different parts of the world, would have recourse in some cases to the hypothesis of a community of tradition and in other cases to the general similarity of the workings of the human mind under similar conditions, Cieza, on the other hand, is at once ready with an unimpeachable explanation; the similarity simply shows that "the Devil manages to deceive one set of people in the same way as he does another." At one time Cieza served in New Granada under a certain Robledo, who was shockingly cruel to the natives and caused many to be torn in pieces by bloodhounds; afterwards, in visiting the scene of some of his worst actions, Robledo was arrested for insubordinate conduct, and hanged, and his body was cooked and eaten by the natives. Wherefore, says Cieza, after telling of his evil deeds, " God permitted that he should be sentenced to death in the same place, and have for his tomb the bellies of Indians."

The plan of Cieza's great work, as announced in his prologue, was a noble one : —

" PART I. The divisions and description of the provinces of Peru.

PART II. The government, great deeds, origin, policy, buildings, and roads of the Incas.

PART III. Discovery and conquest of Peru by Pizarro, and rebellion of the Indians.

PART IV. *Book* i. War between Pizarro and Almagro.

Book ii. War of the young Almagro.

Book iii. The civil war of Quito.

Book iv. War of Huarina.

Book v. War of Xaquixaguana.

the work was apparently still going on when the Spaniards arrived. Precisely the same account of the matter is given by Garcilasso de la Vega, who must be regarded as an authority scarcely less important than Cieza de Leon. Garcilasso says that

Commentary I. Events from the founding of the Audience to the departure of the President.

Commentary II. Events to the arrival of the Viceroy Mendoza." The first of these parts, as already observed, was published at Seville in 1553; it has been reprinted several times and translated into other languages. Part II. remained in manuscript until 1873; it was dedicated to Dr. Juan Sarmiento, who was for a short time President of the Council of the Indies, but was never in America. At the beginning of his manuscript Cieza says it is for (*para*) Dr. Sarmiento. By one of those curious slips which the wisest are liable to make, Mr. Prescott, who used this manuscript, translated *para* as if it were *por* (by), and assumed that Sarmiento was the writer. Mr. Prescott hardly knew which author most to admire, Sarmiento or Cieza! but we now know that his praise, bestowed upon both, belongs wholly to the latter. Part III. and the first two books of Part IV. are not yet to be obtained. We are assured by Don Ximenez de Espada that he knows where the manuscript is, though he has not seen it. The manuscript of the third book of Part IV. is in the Royal Library at Madrid; a copy of it found its way in 1849 into the hands of the late Mr. James Lenox, of New York, who paid $3,000 for it. It was at length edited by Espada, and published at Madrid in 1877. The fourth and fifth books of Part IV. and the two commentaries were completed by Cieza de Leon before his death, but whether they are in existence or not is not known. Perhaps we may yet be so fortunate as to recover the whole of this magnificent work, which ranks indisputably foremost among the sources of information concerning ancient Peru. The first two parts have been translated into English, and edited, with learned notes and introductions, by Mr. Clements Markham, to whom I am indebted for this sketch of the strange vicissitudes of the book. See Markham, *The Travels of Cieza de Leon, contained in the First Part of his Chronicle of Peru*, London, 1864; *The Second Part of the Chronicle of Peru*, London, 1883 (both published by the Hakluyt Society).

the fortress was fifty years in building and was not finished until the reign of Huayna Ca-pac, if indeed it could properly be said to have been finished at all. "These works," says Garcilasso, "with many others throughout the empire, were cut short by the civil wars which broke out soon afterwards between the two brothers Huascar Inca and Atahualpa, in whose time the Spaniards arrived and destroyed everything; and so all the unfinished works remain unfinished to this day." [1]   It has become fashionable

Testimony of Cieza and Garcilasso.

[1] Compare Garcilasso, *Royal Commentaries*, ed. Markham, vol. ii. p. 318, with Markham's Cieza de Leon, vol. ii. p. 163. The father of the historian Garcilasso Inca de la Vega belonged to one of the most distinguished families of Spain. In 1531, being then twenty-five years old, he went to Guatemala and served under Pedro de Alvarado as a captain of infantry. When Alvarado invaded Peru in 1534, but consented to retire and left a great part of his force behind him (see below, p. 408), the captain Garcilasso was one of those that were left. For eminent military services he received from Pizarro a fine house in Cuzco and other spoils. In 1538 he was married to Chimpa Ocllo, baptized as Doña Isabel, a granddaughter of the great Inca Tupac Yupanqui. Mr. Markham informs us that "a contemporary picture of this princess still exists at Cuzco — a delicate looking girl with large gentle eyes and slightly aquiline nose, long black tresses hanging over her shoulders, and a richly ornamented woollen mantle secured in front by a large gold pin." The Inca Garcilasso de la Vega, son of this marriage, was born in Cuzco in 1540. He was carefully educated by an excellent Spanish priest, and became a good scholar. His father, one of the most honourable and high-minded of the Spanish cavaliers, was made governor of Cuzco, and his home was a place where Spaniards and Incas were hospitably entertained. From infancy the young Garcilasso spoke both Spanish and Quichua, and while he was learning Latin and studying European history, his mother and her friends were steeping him in Peruvian traditions. At about the age of twelve he lost this gentle mother, and in 1560 his gallant father also died. Garcilasso then went to Spain and served

in recent times to discredit this testimony of Garcilasso and Cieza, on the ground of their want of
extensive archæological knowledge; but it seems
to me that in this case scepticism is carried rather
too far. Garcilasso was great-great-grandson of
the Inca Pachacutec under whom the work at
Sacsahuaman is said to have begun, and his statements as to the progress of that work which went
on until it was stopped by the civil war between
his mother's cousins Huascar and Atahualpa are
too nearly contemporaneous to be lightly set aside,
especially when independently confirmed by so

for some years in the army. After retiring from the service,
somewhere from 1570 to 1575, he settled in Cordova and devoted
himself to literary pursuits until his death in 1616. His tomb is
in the cathedral at Cordova. Besides other books Garcilasso Inca
wrote *The Royal Commentaries of the Incas*, in two parts, the
first of which, treating of the history and antiquities of Peru
before the arrival of the Spaniards, was published at Lisbon in
1609; the second part, treating of the conquest of Peru and the
civil wars of the conquerors, was published at Cordova in 1616.
There have been several editions and translations in various
languages. An English translation of the first part, by Mr.
Clements Markham, has been published by the Hakluyt Society,
London, 1869, 2 vols. Garcilasso's unrivalled opportunities for
gathering information, and his excellent use of them, give to his
book an authority superior to all others except that of Cieza de
Leon, and Garcilasso was better able than the latter to understand
the Peruvian view of the situation. He often quotes from Cieza,
and always with high respect. His book is at once learned and
charming; its tone is kindly and courteous, like the talk of a
thoroughbred gentleman. One cannot read it without a strong
feeling of affection for the writer.

Throughout this chapter — except in a few cases, where it
seems desirable to give the Spanish — I cite from Mr. Markham's version of Garcilasso and Cieza; but, as I cite by book and
chapter, instead of volume and page, the references are equally
convenient for any edition or version.

careful an inquirer as Cieza. This testimony is
positive that the cyclopean architecture at Sacsahuaman was the work of recent Incas. With Tiahuanacu the case may be quite different. Garcilasso, indeed, in giving the names of the four
chief architects who were successively employed
at Sacsahuaman, lets drop the remarkable statement, " The third was Acahuana Inca, to whom
is also attributed a great part of the edifices at
Tiahuanacu." [1] But in another place Garcilasso
quotes without dissent the statement of Cieza that
contemporary Peruvians believed the buildings at
Tiahuanacu to be much older than the Sacsahuaman fortress, and indeed that the recent Incas
built the latter work in emulation of the former.[2]
So, perhaps, in his remark about the architect
Acahuana having superintended the works at Tiahuanacu, Garcilasso's memory, usually so strong
and precise,[3] may for once have tripped. It might
fail to serve him about works at distant Lake Titicaca, but such a slip, if it be one, should not discredit his testimony as to the great edifice near
Cuzco, about the stones of which he had often
played with his Spanish and Peruvian schoolfel-
lows, regarding them as the work of his mother's
immediate ancestors.

Assuming as correct the statement in which
Garcilasso and Cieza agree, that the Incas of the

---

[1] Garcilasso, lib. vii. cap. xxix.

[2] Cieza, pt. i. cap. cv. ; Garcilasso, lib. iii. cap. i.

[3] He often observes, with winning modesty, that it is so long
since he left Peru that his memory may deceive him ; but in
such cases, whenever we can bring other evidence to bear, the
dear old fellow turns out almost invariably to be correct.

fifteenth century built the Sacsahuaman fortress
in emulation of the ancient structures at Tiahuanacu, in order to show that they could equal or
surpass the mighty works of by-gone ages, it must
be acknowledged that they were successful. Sacsahuaman is, according to Mr. Markham, " without comparison the grandest monument of an
ancient civilization in the New World. Like the
Pyramids and the Coliseum, it is imperishable." [1]

If this colossal building could have been erected
under the later Incas, it is clearly unnecessary to
suppose for the works at Tiahuanacu any intru-
sive agency from the Old World, or any condition
of society essentially different from that into which
the mother of the historian Garcilasso Inca was
born. This style of building will presently furnish
us with an instructive clue to the state of Peruvian
society in the century preceding the arrival of the
Spaniards. Meanwhile there is no occasion for
supposing any serious break in the continuity of
events in prehistoric Peru. It is not necessary to
suppose that the semi-civilization of the Incas was
preceded by some other semi-civilization distinct
from it in character. As for the Pirua dynasty of
sixty-five kings, covering a period of thirteen centuries, it does not seem likely that the " wise men "
of Cieza's time, with their knotted strings, could

---

[1] Winsor, *Narr. and Crit. Hist.*, vol. i. p. 221. Cf. Squier's remarks, in his *Peru: Incidents of Travel and Exploration in the
Land of the Incas*, New York, 1877, p. 470: — " The heaviest
works of the fortress . . . remain substantially perfect, and will
remain so . . . as long as the Pyramids shall last, or Stonehenge
and the Colosseum shall endure, for it is only with those works
that the Fortress of the Sacsahuaman can be properly compared."

have preserved any trustworthy testimony as to such a period.

Without assuming, however, any historical know-ledge of the times that preceded the rule of the Incas, we have other grounds for believing that the Peruvian culture was much older than that of the Mexicans and Mayas. In other words, the Peruvians had probably attained to the middle status of barbarism at a much earlier date than the Mexicans and Mayas, and had in many striking features approached nearer to civilization than the latter. First, we may note that the Peruvians were the only American aborigines that ever domesticated any other animal than the dog. The *llama*, developed from the same stock with the wild *huanacu*, is a very useful beast of burden, yielding also a coarse wool; and the *alpaca*, developed from the ancestral stock of the wild *vicuña*, is of great value for its fine soft fleece.[1] While the huanacu and vicuña are to-day as wild as chamois, the llama is as thoroughly domesticated as cows or sheep, while the alpaca has actually become unable to live without the care of man; and Mr. Markham argues, with much force, that such great variation in these animals implies the lapse of many centuries since men first began to tame them. A similar inference is drawn from the facts that while the ancient Peruvians produced several highly cultivated varieties of maize, that cereal in a wild state is un-

Domesticated animals.

---

[1] Darwin, *Variation of Animals and Plants under Domestication*, London, 1868, vol. ii. p. 208. These four species belong to the genus *auchenia* of the family *camelidæ*.

known in their country ; " the Peruvian species of the cotton plant also is known only under cultiva-

The potato.   tion. The potato is found wild in Chili, and probably in Peru, as a very insignif-icant tuber. But the Peruvians, after cultivating it for centuries, increased its size and produced a great number of edible varieties." [1] Now the wild potato seems to be a refractory vegetable. There is a variety in Mexico, no bigger than a nut, and sedulous efforts, kept up during many years, to in-crease its size and improve its quality, have proved futile ; from which Mr. Markham reasonably infers that the high state of perfection to which the Pe-ruvians brought the potato indicates a very con-siderable lapse of time since they began to work upon its wild ancestral form.[2]

[1] Markham, " The Inca Civilization in Peru," in Winsor, *Narr. and Crit. Hist.*, i. 213. As for maize, Mr. Darwin found ears of it, along with sundry species of recent sea-shells, on the coast of Peru, "embedded in a beach which had been upraised at least eighty-five feet above the level of the sea." Darwin, *Geological Observations on South America*, London, 1846, p. 49.

[2] Cieza de Leon (pt. i. cap. xl.) describes the potato as " a kind of earth nut, which, after it has been boiled, is as tender as a cooked chestnut, but it has no more skin than a truffle, and it grows under the earth in the same way. This root produces a plant like a poppy." Humboldt says, " La pomme de terre n'est pas indigène au Pérou " (*Essai sur la Nouvelle Espagne*, Paris, 1811, 8vo, tom. iii. p. 113) ; but Cuvier declares, " il est impos-sible de douter qu'elle ne soit originaire de Pérou" (*Histoire des sciences naturelles*, Paris, 1831, p. 185). Further research seems to sustain Cuvier's view. The legitimate conclusion from Hum-boldt's facts, however, does not carry the original home of the potato very far from Peru, but points to the Chilian or Bolivian Andes, whence its cultivation seems to have spread northward, until at the time of the Discovery it was found among the people of Quito and among the Chibchas. The potato was not cultivated

In cultivating such vegetables the Peruvians
practised irrigation on an extensive scale, and had

anywhere north of the isthmus of Darien. The ships of Raleigh's
expedition, returning from Albemarle sound in 1586, carried the
first potatoes to Ireland (Beckmann, *Grundsätze der teutschen
Landwirthschaft*, 1806, p. 289), and in Gerarde's *Herball*, published in 1597, these vegetables were called " Virginia potatoes ; "
whence it is sometimes said that Raleigh's people " found potatoes in Virginia." But that is highly improbable. As Humboldt says, potatoes were common all over the West Indies before
1580, and had even found their way into the gardens of Spain and
Italy. In 1586 Lane's party of Raleigh's people, a hundred or
more in number, had been staying for a year upon Roanoke
island, where they had hoped to found a colony. They were
terribly short of food, when all at once Sir Francis Drake arrived
from the West Indies and brought them a supply of provisions,
with which they prudently decided to go home to England. Evidently their potatoes, which were planted on an estate of Raleigh's
in Ireland, did not come from " Virginia," but from the West
Indies. The potato was very slow in coming into general use in
Europe. It was not raised on an extensive scale in Lancashire
until about 1684 ; it was first introduced into Saxony in 1717, into
Scotland in 1728, into Prussia in 1738 (cf. Humboldt, *op. cit.* tom.
iii. p. 120). It has been said that potatoes were first made known
in France about 1600 by the celebrated botanist Charles de Lé-
cluse (Legrand d'Aussy, *Hist. de la vie privée des Français*,
tom. i. p. 143) ; but they certainly did not begin to come into
general use among the people till just before the Revolution. A
very graphic account of their introduction into Alsace from Han-
over is given in that charming story of Erckmann-Chatrian, *Histoire d'un paysan*, tom. i. pp. 54–83. They were at first received
with cries of " à bas les racines du Hanovre ! " and a report was
spread that persons had been seized with leprosy after eating
them ; so for a while people kept aloof from them until it was
learned that the king had them on his table ; " alors tout le
monde voulut en avoir." This account of the matter is strictly
correct. See the works of Parmentier, *Examen chimique des
pommes de terre*, Paris, 1773 ; *Recherches sur les végétaux nourris-
sants*, Paris, 1781 ; *Traité sur la culture des pommes de terre*, Paris,
1789. Parmentier was largely instrumental in introducing the
potato. Accurate statistics are given in Arthur Young's *Travels*

from time immemorial been accustomed to use
guano as manure.[1] By right of such careful and
methodical agriculture, as well as by right of having domesticated animals for other purposes than
hunting, the ancient Peruvians had entered upon
the middle period of barbarism, and evidently at a
much earlier date than any other known people
of aboriginal America. At the time of the Discovery an unknown number of centuries had
elapsed since the general condition of these people
had begun to be that which characterized the
middle period of barbarism in North America.
The interval was no doubt long enough for very
remarkable social changes to have taken place,
and in point of fact such changes had taken place.
Yet, as already observed, true civilization, in the
sense in which we have agreed with Mr. Morgan
to understand it, had not been attained by people
who could record events only by *quipus*. Nor
had Peruvian society acquired the characteristic
features which in the Old World marked the upper
period of barbarism, the stage reached by the Hebrew patriarchs and the conquerors of Troy.
Though iron mines were at hand, the Peruvians
did not know how to work the ore.[2] Their axes,

in France, 2d ed., Bury St. Edmunds, 1794, 2 vols. 4to, vol. i.
p. 77.

For further mention of the Peruvian potato, see Ulloa, *Voyage
to South America*, London, 1772, vol. i. p. 287; Tschudi, *Travels
in Peru*, London, 1847, pp. 178, 368, 386. The importance of the
study of cultivated plants in connection with the early history of
mankind receives some illustration in Humboldt's *Essai sur la
géographie des plantes*, Paris, 1805.

[1] Cieza, pt. i. cap. lxxv.; Garcilasso, lib. v. cap. iii.

[2] Garcilasso, lib. ii. cap. xxviii.

gimlets, chisels, and knives were of bronze; [1] they
had no tongs or bellows, and no nails,
in lieu of which they fastened pieces of   Tools.
wood together with thongs.[2] Their ploughs were
made of a hard wood, and were commonly pulled
through the ground by men, though now and then
llamas may have been employed.[3]

In another respect the Peruvians lacked the
advantages which in the Old World gave to
the upper period of barbarism some of its most
profoundly important characteristics. We have
seen that in the eastern hemisphere the middle
period was the time when horses were tamed to
men's uses and great herds of kine were kept.
This was not only a vast enlargement of men's
means of subsistence, affording a steady diet of
meat and milk; it not only added greatly to men's
control of mechanical forces by enlisting the giant
muscular strength of horses and oxen Influence of
in their service; but its political and cattle upon
 the evolution
social consequences were far-reaching. of society.
In the absence of a pastoral life, the only possible
advance out of a hunting stage, with incipient
horticulture, into any higher stage, was along the
line of village communities like those of Iroquois
or Mandans into pueblo-houses and pueblo-towns
like those of Zuñis and Aztecs. The clan must
remain the permanent unit of organization, because
the inchoate family could not acquire strength
enough to maintain a partial independence. It

---

[1] Markham's *Cieza,* p. xxviii.

[2] Garcilasso, lib. vi. cap. iv.

[3] Garcilasso, lib. v. cap. ii. ; see also above, vol. i. p. 62.

could not release itself from the compact communal organization without perishing from lack of the means of subsistence and defence. But in a pastoral society the needs of pasturage extended the peaceful occupations of the clan over a considerable territory; and the inchoate family, with its male chief, his underling warrior herdsmen and his horses and cattle, could maintain itself in a partial isolation which would have been impossible in a society of mere hunters, or of hunters and primitive corn-growers, with no helping animal but the dog. Life came to be more successfully conducted in scattered tents than in the communal household. Thus there grew up a tendency to relax or break down the compact communal organization; the primeval clan, based upon the tie of a common maternal descent, declined in authority, and the family of patriarchal type became the most important unit of society. In course of time a metamorphosis was wrought in the structure of the clan; it came to be a group of closely-related patriarchal families, and such is the sort of clan we find in Old World history, for the most part, from the days of Esau to those of Rob Roy.

One phase of the growing independence of cow-keeping patriarchal families, and of the loosening of the primitive communal clan organizations,[1] was the rapid and masterful development of the notion of private property. The earliest instance of property

[1] As a general rule social progress has been achieved through successive tightenings and loosenings of sundry forms of social or political organization, the proper condition of development being neither anarchy nor despotic rigidity, but plastic mobility. See my *Cosmic Philosophy*, part II. chap. xx.

on a large scale, which was not the common pos-
session of a clan, but the private posses- _{Private prop-}
sion of a family represented by its patri- _{erty (pecu-}
archal head, was property in cattle. Of _{lium).}
very little save his blanket and feathers, his toma-
hawk and his string of scalps, could the proudest
Indian sachem say " it is mine ; " of nothing that
was part of the permanent stock of food could he
say as much, for it all belonged to the clan ; and
his own official importance was simply that of a
member of the clan council. But the Arab sheikh,
as head of a patriarchal group, could say " this
family is mine, and these are my cattle." This
early preëminence of the cow as private property
has been commemorated in the numerous Aryan
words for money and wealth derived from the
name of that animal.[1]

---

[1] For example, in Latin, *pecus* is "herd," *pecunia* is "money,"
peculium is "private property," whence we have *peculiarity*, or
"that which especially pertains to an individual." Sir Henry
Maine sees no reason for doubting the story "that the earliest
coined money known at Rome was stamped with the figure of an
ox" (*Early History of Institutions*, London, 1875, p. 49). Gothic
faihu = Old English *feoh* = modern German *Vieh* is "cow ; " in
modern English the same word *fee* is "pecuniary reward." In
Gaelic, *bosluag* is "herd of cows," and *bosluaiged* is "riches."
When you go to a tavern to dine you pay your *shot* or *scot* before
leaving ; or perhaps you get into a ticklish situation, but escape
scot-free. In King Alfred's English *sceat* was "money," and the
Icelandic *skattr* and Gothic *skatts* had the same meaning ; while the
same word in Gaelic, *skath*, means "herd," and in Old Bulgarian,
as *skotu*, it means "cow." So in Sanskrit, *rupa* is "cow," and
rupya is "money," whence we have the modern *rupee* of Bengal.
The great importance of the cow in early Aryan thought is shown
not only by the multitude of synonyms for the creature, but still
more strikingly by the frequency of similes, metaphors, and
myths in the Vedas in which the cow plays a leading part.

Now in ancient Peru the llama and alpaca played an important part,[1] but in no wise comparable to that taken by cattle in the eastern hemisphere. Camels and sheep, the nearest Old World equivalents to the llama and alpaca, would be far from adequate to the functions that have been performed by horses and cows. The contrast, moreover, was not merely in the animals, but in the geographical conditions. The valleys and platforms of the Andes did not favour the development of true pastoral life like the vast steppes of Scythia or the plains of lower Asia. The domestication of animals in ancient Peru was a powerful help to the development of a stable agricultural community, but no really pastoral stage of society was reached there. The

No true pastoral life in ancient Peru.

---

[1] According to Garcilasso the llamas gave no more milk than was required for their own young, and were therefore not available for dairy purposes (lib. viii. cap. xvi.). Garcilasso has many amusing reminiscences connected with the introduction of European animals and plants into Peru, — how he came upon a litter of pigs in the square at Cuzco, how his father bought the first donkey in Cuzco in 1557, how he was sent around to his father's neighbours with dishes of the first grapes that came to Cuzco and helped himself on the way, how he saw his father regaling his friends with asparagus and carrots but got none himself (lib. ix. caps. xviii., xix., xxv., xxx.), and how he played truant to see the first bullocks at work, yoked to an iron plough: — " A whole army of Indians took me to see them, who came from all parts, astonished at a sight so wonderful and novel for them and for me. They said that the Spaniards were too idle to work, and that they forced those great animals to do their work for them. I remember all this very well, because my holiday with the bullocks cost me a flogging consisting of two dozen stripes: one dozen administered by my father, because I was not at school; and the other dozen by the schoolmaster, because I had only had one dozen " (lib. ix. cap. xvii.).

llamas were kept in large flocks on pastures maintained by sedulous irrigation, just as the maize
and potato crops were made to thrive.[1] It was an
agricultural scene. There was nothing in it like
the old patriarchal life on the plain of Mamre or
by the waters of the Punjab. Here we get a clue
to a feature of Peruvian society unlike anything
else in the world. That society may be said to
have constituted a nation. It was, indeed, a nation of very rudimentary type, but still in a certain sense a nation. It was the only
instance in ancient America in which a   Attainment
                                         of nationality
people attained to nationality in any   without the
                                         notion of pri-
sense; and so far as history knows, it   vate property.
was the only instance in the world in which the
formation of nationality, with the evolution of a
distinct governing class, took place before there
had been any considerable development of the idea
of private property. The result, as we shall see
toward the close of this chapter, was a state organized upon the principle of communistic despotism.

Let us first, however, observe some of the steps
by which this rudimentary nationality   The four
was formed. The four tribes in which   tribes.
we can first catch sight of the process were the
Quichuas, situated about the headwaters of the
river Apurimac, the Incas of the upper Yucay val-

[1] It must be borne in mind that the vapour-laden trade winds
from the Atlantic ocean are robbed of their moisture by the cold
peaks of the Andes, so that, while Brazil has a rainfall and consequent luxuriance of vegetation quite unequalled, on the other
hand Peru is dry, in many places parched, and requires much
irrigation. In this respect the conditions were not unlike those
in our Rocky mountain region.

ley, and the Canas and Cauchis of the mountains between the site of Cuzco and Lake Titicaca. The first of these tribes gave the name Quichua to the common language of the Peruvian empire, the second gave the name Incas to the conquering race or upper caste in Peruvian society, while the names of the other two tribes lapsed into obscurity. These four tribes formed the nucleus of the Peruvian nationality. They were a race of mountaineers, short in stature, but strongly and lithely built, with features aquiline and refined, very soft skin, cinnamon complexion, fine black hair, and little or no beard. In the time of Manco Capac these tribes appear to have been made up of clans called *ayllus* or " lineages." His tribe, the Incas, established themselves in the elevated valley of Cuzco, and from that point began to subdue the neighbouring kindred tribes. They did not confine themselves, like the Aztecs, to extorting tribute from the conquered people, but they effected a military occupation of the country, a thing which the Aztecs never did. Manco's three successors confined their attention chiefly to building Cuzco (cir. 1280–1300) and taking measures to consolidate their government. We may perhaps refer to this period the beginnings of that very remarkable military organization of society presently to be described. By this time the Canas and Cauchis had been brought entirely under Inca rule, and the fifth king, Capac Yupanqui, completed the subjugation of the Quichuas. The two following reigns seem to have been spent in work of internal organization; and then under the eighth Inca,

Viracocha, the work of imperial expansion fairly began. It is now that, as already observed, we come out into the daylight of history.

This eighth Inca had a somewhat notable name. The title of Inca, applied alike to all the sovereigns, was simply the old tribal name, and continued to be applied to the descendants of the original tribe, who came to form a kind of patrician caste. The king was simply The Inca *par excellence*, very much as the chief of an Irish tribe was called The O'Neil. Of the epithets attached to this title, some, such as Manco and Rocca, may perhaps be true proper names, with the meaning lost, such as we do not find among any other people in ancient America;[1] others, such as Lloque, "left-handed," are nicknames of a sort familiar in European history; the most common ones are laudatory epithets, as Tupac, " splendid," Yupanqui, "illustrious," Capac, " rich." The eighth Inca alone has a name identifying him with deity. Viracocha was the name of the sun-god or sky-god. It was very much as if the Romans, instead of calling their emperor Divus Augustus, had called him Jupiter outright.

The Inca Viracocha conquered and annexed the extensive country about Lake Titicaca, inhabited by a kindred people usually called Aymaras, whose forefathers, perhaps, had built the cyclopean walls at Tiahuanacu. Vira-

Names of the Incas.

Conquest of the Aymaras;

---

[1] Markham, in Winsor's *Narr. and Crit. Hist.*, i. 231. It may be, however, that they are simply archaic words to which *we* have lost the clue, — which is a very different thing. It is quite doubtful, therefore, whether this should be cited as a slight exception to my former statement, vol. i. p. 69.

cocha's son and successor, Urco, met with misfortunes. North of the Quichua country were two powerful groups of kindred tribes, the Chancas and Huancas, extending nearly to the equator, and beyond them were the Quitus, whose country reached to the confines of the Chibchas. While Viracocha was engaged in his conquests at the south, the Chancas overran the Quichua country, and shortly after Urco's accession they marched to the very gates of Cuzco; but in a decisive battle, fought just outside the town, the invaders were totally defeated by Urco's brother, Yupanqui.

Then Urco was deposed and his brother and of the was elected to succeed him. Presently
Chancas and
Huancas. the Quichua country was won back, with the aid of its own people, who preferred the Inca rule to that of the Chancas. After a while this masterful Inca Yupanqui had conquered the whole Chanca country and that of the Huancas to boot. Next he turned his arms against the Chimus, a people of alien blood and speech, who occupied the Pacific coast from near the site of Lima northward to that of Tumbez.

These Chimus, whose name Humboldt thinks may have survived in that of the giant mountain Chimborazo,[1] were an interesting people, with a semi-civilization of their own, apparently quite different from that of the Incas. From Mr. Squier's archæological investigations[2] I am inclined to sus-

[1] Humboldt, *Ansichten der Natur*, ii. 48.

[2] See Squier's *Peru: Incidents of Travel and Exploration in the Land of the Incas*, New York, 1877, pp. 135–192; see also Markham's valuable note in Winsor, *Narr. and Crit. Hist.*, i. 275–278; not often do we find more food for the historian packed into three pages.

pect that it may have been a semi-civilization of the Pueblo type, with huge communal Conquest of the Chimus. houses. However this may have been, the Inca Yupanqui conquered the Chimus. At his death the Inca sway extended from the basin of Lake Titicaca to the equator, and from the Andes to the coast; and when we compare the end of his reign with its beginning, it is clear that he fairly earned the epithet by which he was distinguished among the members of the Inca dynasty. He was the great hero of Peruvian history; and the name given him was Pachacutec, or "he who changes the world." The historian Garcilasso de la Vega was his grandson's grandson.

Under Tupac Yupanqui, son and successor of Pachacutec, the career of conquest was Conquest of the Quitus; further extended. It was first necessary to suppress a rebellion of the Aymaras. Then Tupac completed the conquest of the Quitus. So great a stretch of territory had been brought into subjection that it now seemed necessary to have a second imperial city from which to govern its northern portions. Accordingly Tupac founded the city of Quito, saying: "Cuzco must be the capital of one part of my empire and Quito of the other."[1] Then, returning southward, he brought all the coast valleys under his sway, including the valley of Pachacamac, "where was the very ancient and sacred temple of the Yuncas, which he wished very much to see. . . . Many Indians say that the Inca himself spoke with the Devil who was in the idol of Pachacamac, and that he

[1] Cieza, pt. ii. cap. lvi.

heard how the idol was the creator of the world, and other nonsense, which I do not put down, because it is not worth while." [1] The Inca, says Cieza, did not molest this temple, but built a house of the Sun in the neighbourhood. After returning to Cuzco, he subjected some more barbarous tribes in the Charcas country southeast from Lake Titicaca, and then invaded Chili and penetrated as far as the river Maule, in almost 34° south latitude.

and of Chili.

The conquest of Chili as far as this point was completed by Tupac's son, Huayna Capac, who was then called to the northward by a rebellion of the tribes about Quito. The absorption of Inca strength in conquest at one end of this long territory was apt to offer opportunities for insurrection at the other end. In an obstinate battle near Quito the rebels were defeated with great slaughter. Many hundreds of prisoners were taken. " Very few were able to hide themselves. Near the banks of a lake the Inca ordered them all to be beheaded in his presence, and their bodies to be thrown into the water. The blood of those who were killed was in such quantity that the water lost its colour, and nothing could be seen but a thick mass of blood. Having perpetrated this cruelty, . . . Huayna Capac ordered the sons of the dead men to be brought before him, and, looking at them, he said, *Campa manan pucula tucuy huambracuna*, which means, ' You will not make war upon me, for you are all boys now.' From that time the conquered people

Rebellion at Quito suppressed.

[1] Cieza, pt. ii. cap. lviii.

were called 'Huambracuna' to this day, and they were very valiant. The lake received the name it still bears, which is *Yahuarcocha*, or 'the lake of blood.'"[1] The last years of Huayna's long reign were spent in Quito. Upon his death in 1523 his eldest legitimate son, Huascar, succeeded him, and presently there broke out the civil war between Huascar and his bastard brother, the usurper Atahualpa, which lasted until the Spaniards arrived upon the scene.

The territory subject to Huayna Capac in 1523 extended from near Popayan, north of the equator, to the river Maule in Chili, a distance of nearly 2,700 miles. If the Spaniards had not interfered, the next enemies would have been the Chibchas on the north and the invincible Araucanians on the south. The average breadth of this Peruvian empire was from 300 to 350 miles, so that the area was more than 800,000 square miles, about equal to the united areas of Austria-Hungary, the German Empire, France, and Spain, or to the area of that part of the United States comprised between the Atlantic ocean and the Mississippi river. If we contrast with this vast territory the extent of Montezuma's so-called empire, about equivalent to the state of Massachusetts or the kingdom of Wurtemberg, we cannot but be struck with the difference. The contrast is enhanced when we remember that the

Dimensions of the empire.

[1] Cieza, pt. ii. cap. lxvii. One is reminded of Bajazet's wholesale massacre of French prisoners after the battle of Nicopolis in 1396, of which there is a graphic description in Barante, *Histoire des ducs de Bourgogne de la maison de Valois*, 7e éd., Paris, 1854, tom. ii. p. 198.

Aztec confederacy did not effect a military occupation of the country over which its operations extended, nor did it undertake to administer the government of conquered pueblo towns; it simply extorted tribute. Now the conquests of the Incas went much farther than this; they undertook, and to some extent effected, a military occupation and a centralized administration of the whole country. In this work their success was naturally most complete among the four original tribes about Cuzco; probably less complete among the Aymaras, still less among the Chimus and other coast tribes, and least at the two extremities in Quito and Chili.

"The grand aim and glory of the Incas," says

The Incas sought to assimilate conquered peoples.

Garcilasso, "was to reduce new tribes and to teach them the laws and customs of the children of the Sun." [1] The Incas imposed their language upon each conquered tribe,[2] until it came to be spoken in all parts of their territory, often side by side with the local tongues, somewhat as Hindustani is spoken throughout the greater part of British India, side by side with Bengali, Guzerati, Punjabi, etc. The Incas, moreover, to the best of their ability abolished cannibalism and other savage customs wherever they found them, and introduced their own religious ceremonies and festivals.[3] They appointed governors (*curacas*) for all places.[4] They established garrisons at various

[1] Garcilasso, lib. vii. cap. xviii.

[2] Id., lib. vii. cap. i.; Cieza, pt. ii. cap. xxiv.

[3] Garcilasso, lib. vi. cap. xvii.; lib. viii. caps. iii., vii.; and *passim*.

[4] Id., lib. v. cap. xiii.

points in order to secure their conquests;[1] and
they built military roads, with storehouses at suitable intervals where provisions and arms could
be kept.[2] In connection with these stations were
barracks where the troops could find shelter.
These roads, which radiated from Cuzco to many
parts of the Inca's dominions, were about twenty-
five feet in width, and almost as level as railroads,
which in that rugged country involved much cutting through rocks and much filling of gorges.
The central highway from Quito to The military
Cuzco, which was finished by Huayna roads.
Capac, and was connected with a similar road extending from Cuzco southward, is described with
enthusiasm by Cieza de Leon, whose accuracy
cannot lightly be questioned. "The great road
from Quito to Cuzco, which is a greater distance
than from Seville to Rome, was as much used as
the road from Seville to Triana, and I cannot say
more.[3] . . . I believe that since the history of
man has been recorded, there has been no account
of such grandeur as is to be seen in this road,
which passes over deep valleys and lofty mountains, by snowy heights, over falls of water, through
live rocks, and along the edges of furious torrents.
In all these places it is level and paved, along
mountain slopes well excavated, by the mountains
well terraced, through the living rock cut, along
the river banks supported by walls, in the snowy
heights with steps and resting places, in all parts

[1] Garcilasso, lib. vi. cap. xvi.; Cieza, pt. ii. caps. ix., xxii.
[2] Garcilasso, lib. v. cap. viii.; Cieza, pt. i. cap. lx.
[3] Cieza, pt. ii. cap. lvii.

clean swept, clear of stones, with post- and store-houses and temples of the Sun at intervals. Oh! what greater things can be said of Alexander, or of any of the powerful kings who have ruled in the world, than that they had made such a road as this, and conceived the works which were required for it! The roads constructed by the Romans in Spain . . . are not to be compared with it." [1] These roads facilitated the transmission of political and military intelligence. At intervals of a league and a half, says Polo de Ondegardo, there stood small relay houses, each

The couriers.   "adapted to hold two Indians, who served as postmen, and were relieved once a month, and they were there night and day. Their duty was to pass on the messages of the Inca from Cuzco to any other point, and to bring back those of the governors, so that all the transactions and events of the empire were known. When the Inca wished to send anything to a governor, he said it to the first *chasqui* [courier], who ran at full speed for a league and a half, and passed the message to the next as soon as he was within hearing, so that when he reached the post the other man had already started." [2] The Spaniards made use of this system of couriers, and were

---

[1] Cieza, pt. ii. cap. lxiii.

[2] "Report by Polo de Ondegardo," in Markham's *Narratives of the Rites and Laws of the Yncas*, London, 1873, p. 169 (Hakluyt Society). The original MS. is in the National Library at Madrid, and has, I believe, not yet been published. Ondegardo was a learned lawyer who came to Peru in 1547 with Gasca, and was afterwards "corregidor" or chief magistrate of Cuzco. His brief document is of much value.

thus able to convey letters from Cuzco to Lima,
a distance of nearly four hundred miles, in three
days.[1] Such a system for written despatches
would of course do very well; but one is inclined
to wonder how a verbal message, transmitted
through a dozen or fifty mouths, should have retained enough of its original shape to be recog-
nizable. For all except the very simplest messages the *quipus* must have been indispensable.

Remarkable as were these roads, and the ar-
rangements connected with them, the limitations
under which the Peruvians worked might be seen
as soon as there was a river or a broad and deep
ravine to be crossed. Here the difference between
civilization and middle-barbarism comes out forcibly. The Incas could command enough human
brawn and muscle to build cyclopean masonry;
but as they did not understand the principle of
the arch,[2] they could not build stone bridges, nor
had they sufficient knowledge of carpentry and en-

[1] Ondegardo adds that these couriers were used to bring up
fresh fish from the sea to Cuzco. A similar but ruder system
of couriers was used in Mexico (Bandelier, in *Peabody Museum
Reports*, vol. ii. p. 696). Something similar existed in ancient
Persia (Herodotus, viii. 98), only there they used horses, as well
as swift dromedaries (Strabo, xv. p. 724; Diodorus, xvii. 80;
Quintus Curtius, vii. 2, 11–18). Marco Polo (lib. ii. cap. 26) describes the relays of mounted couriers in China in the thirteenth
century. The carrying of dainties for the table from the coast
to Cuzco was nothing to what was done for the Fatimite caliph
Aziz, in the tenth century, according to Makrizi, iv. 118, quoted
by Colonel Yule. As the caliph craved a dish of Baalbec cher-
ries, his vizier "caused 600 pigeons to be despatched from Baalbec to Cairo, each of which carried attached to either leg a small
silk bag containing a cherry!" Yule's *Marco Polo*, vol. i. p. 392.

[2] Garcilasso, lib. v. cap. xxii.; lib. vii. cap. xxix.

gineering to make bridges of wood.   Their ingenu-

Rope bridges.
ity was therefore driven to assert itself by stretching huge osier ropes across from side to side of the river or chasm, and laying upon the ropes a flooring of transverse planks. The sides of these swaying bridges were protected by a slight rope railing.   Llamas with their burdens could be driven across such bridges, as mules can be driven across them to-day ; but they are not comfortable places for people with unsteady nerves, and in a high wind they are unsafe.[1]

This extensive system of roads would of itself indicate a military empire that had passed beyond the mere stage of tribal confederation.   A similar indication is furnished by the remarkable system of military colonies (*mitimaes*) established by the great Inca Pachacutec,[2] or perhaps by his father

Military colonies.
Viracocha Inca.   It was a custom peculiarly incident to the imperfect rudimentary development of nationality, and reminds

[1] The picture of the rope bridge over the Apurimac river, still in use, which may be seen in Squier's *Peru*, p. 545, is enough to give one a turn of vertigo.   For a description of this and other bridges in the Inca period, see Garcilasso, lib. iii. cap. vii.

[2] " Although some Indians say that the *mitimaes* were planted from the time of Viracocha Inca, those may believe it who please to do so.   For my part I took such pains to ascertain the facts, that I do not hesitate to affirm the colonizing system to have been instituted by [Pachacutec] Inca Yupanqui." Cieza de Leon, ed. Markham, pt. ii. cap. xxii.   The system is more likely to have grown up gradually than to have been invented all at once.   Mr. Bandelier suggests that possibly there may have been a rude germ of it in Mexico, in the occasional repeopling of an abandoned pueblo by colonists of Nahuatl race, as in the case of Alahuitzlan, related by Father Duran (cap. xlv.) and Tezozomoc (cap. lxxiv.). — *Peabody Museum Reports*, vol. ii. p. 140.

one strongly of what was formerly to be seen in
Assyria. The ancient kings of Babylon and Nineveh used to transfer a considerable part of a conquered population from their old homes to a new
habitat in some distant part of the empire, in order to break up local patriotism and diminish the
tendency to revolts. Sometimes such a population
was transferred in block, and some other population put in its place; but more often it was broken
into small bodies and scattered. It was thus that
Tiglath-Pileser and Sargon of Nineveh carried off
the ten tribes of Israel,[1] and that a part of the
people of Judah were kept in exile by the waters
of Babylon until the great Cyrus released them.[2]
Now this same system of deportation was extensively practised by the Incas, and for the same
reason. For example, Tupac Yupanqui removed
from the islands of Lake Titicaca their entire
population, and scattered it in different places;
he replaced it on the islands by people taken from
forty-two tribes in various parts of his dominions.[3] When the same Inca founded the city of
Quito he peopled it with *mitimaes*, largely from
the regions near Cuzco and likely to be loyal.
Huayna Capac did the same sort of thing in Chili.
In many cases chiefs and other important men
among these transported populations received especial marks of favour from the Inca and were

[1] Rawlinson's *Ancient Monarchies*, 2d ed., London, 1871, vol. ii.
p. 152; 2 Kings xviii. 9–11. Similar things were now and then
done by the Romans; see Dio Cassius, liv. 11; Florus, iv. 12.

[2] Ewald's *History of Israel,* vol. iv. pp. 263, 274; Rawlinson,
op. cit. vol. iii. p. 385.

[3] Garcilasso, lib. viii. cap. vi.

taught to regard their fortunes as dependent upon him. Strangers from all quarters, moreover, were brought to Cuzco and assigned their several quarters there, so that the city was a kind of epitome of the Inca's dominions.[1]

Now the features of Peruvian polity thus far enumerated — the imposing of a new language and religion upon conquered tribes, the appointment of governors (usually if not always of the Inca blood), the maintenance of garrisons, the system of military roads, and the wholesale deportation of peoples — are all features attendant upon the incipient development of nationality through conquest and fusion of tribes and the breaking down of primitive tribal institutions. There were points of genuine analogy between this development in Peru and in Assyria. This kind of incipient nationality is of very low type. It is held together not by a national spirit of patriotism, but by the systematic coercion exercised by the ruling tribe, which has been developed into what is practically a ruling caste. Oriental history affords plenty of examples of the ease with which countries under such conditions are sometimes conquered. It is only necessary for the invader to strike down the sovereign and get control of the machinery of government, and the thing is done; the subject tribes simply exchange one master for another, or if here and there a tribe rebels, it is rather to regain its original independence than to restore the state of

Incipient nationality.

[1] Instructive notices of the *mitimaes* may be found in Cieza, pt. i. cap. xciii. ; pt. ii. caps. xiii., xxii., lii., lvi., lxii.

things immediately preceding the catastrophe. Sometimes it succeeds in its attempt, but often the new master, wielding the same resources as the old one, or even greater, reduces it again to submission.

In this rudimentary form of nationality, where anything like the application of representative government to nation-making is utterly above and beyond the range of men's thought, the only shape which government can assume is military despotism, exercised either by a royal family or by a caste. The despotic government of ancient Peru seems to have partaken of both these characters; it was exercised by a caste in which a particular family was preëminently sovereign. The Incas, as already observed, were originally a conquering tribe; and they remained superimposed upon the conquered peoples as an upper caste. Garcilasso tells us that "the Incas were free from the temptations which usually lead to crime, such as passion for women, envy and covetousness, or the thirst for vengeance; because if they desired beautiful women, it was lawful for them to have as many as they liked; and any pretty girl they might take a fancy to, not only was never denied to them, but was given up by her father with expressions of extreme thankfulness that an Inca should have condescended to take her as his servant. The same thing might be said of their property; for as they never could feel the want of anything, they had no reason to covet the goods of others; while as governors they had command over all the property of the Sun

and of the Inca; and those who were in charge
were bound to give them all that they required,
as children of the Sun, and brethren of the Inca.
They likewise had no temptation to kill or wound
any one either for revenge or in passion; for no
one ever offended them. On the contrary, they
received adoration only second to that offered to
the royal person; and if any one, how high soever his rank, had enraged any Inca, it would
have been looked upon as sacrilege and very
severely punished." Of course some allowances
must be made in accepting these statements; such
sweeping generalizations always require more or
less qualification; and it is not likely that there
ever existed a society of which this description of
Garcilasso's would have been literally accurate.
But after making due allowances, it remains quite
clear that his Incas constituted a distinct caste,
and were regarded by the mass of people as beings
of a superior order. They were not only an upper
caste, but they were a ruling caste, and furnished
for every part of the empire governors allied to
one another by a keen sense of kinship.

The chief of this Inca caste, called *par excellence* The Inca, was no doubt the descendant and
representative of the ancient chiefs of the Inca
tribe. Just how far the different attributes of
royalty were united in his person and
office, it is not easy to say. With regard to the highest legislative and judi-
ciary powers, our authorities do not make it perfectly clear how far they were exercised by the

The Inca sov-
ereign and
council.

[1] Garcilasso, li'). ii. cap. xv.

Inca solely, or by the Inca in connection with a council. That there was a council is unquestionable, and that it was a development from the council of the primitive Inca tribe is in a high degree probable; but we are insufficiently informed as to the extent of its powers. From sundry statements, however, it may be inferred that these powers were considerable, and that the Inca was perhaps not quite so full-blown a despot as some of Mr. Prescott's authorities declared him to be. The statement that, if he had taken it into his head to put to death a hundred thousand Indians, his decree would have been executed without a murmur, has a strong smack of hyperbole.[1] On the other hand, we are told that before deciding upon any measure of importance, the council was always consulted; upon this point, says Cieza de Leon, all his informants were agreed.[2] As to the crucial question, however, how far the Inca's authority was effectively limited by the council, Cieza leaves us in the dark. Garcilasso refers to "Tupac Yupanqui and all his council" ordaining that two of the royal concubines should be legitimized and regarded as true queens, in order to provide against a possible failure in the succession, because the heir apparent, Huayna Capac, had no children by his first and legitimate queen.[3] Here the consent

---

[1] "Su palabra era ley, i nadie osaba ir contra su palabra ni voluntad : aunque obiese de matar cient mill Indios, no havia ninguno en su reino que le osase decir que no lo hiciese." *Conquista i poblacion del Peru*, MS., apud Prescott, *Conq. of Peru*, book i. chap. i.

[2] Cieza, pt. ii. cap. xxvi.

[3] Garcilasso, lib. viii. cap. viii.

of the council, in a measure of prime importance, is evidently assumed to be essential. Still more significant is the brief mention made by Cieza of the deposition of the Inca Urco.[1] This ruler's military conduct had been disastrous. The invading Chancas had, in spite of him, arrived within sight of Cuzco, when they were defeated with prodigious slaughter by his brother, afterward famous as Pachacutec Yupanqui. After the victory there was earnest discussion within the city. Cieza does not mention the council by name, but except the council there was no authoritative body in which such a discussion could take place. Cieza's description throughout implies that the proceedings were regular, and that the decision was at once accepted as final. It was decided that the unworthy Urco should not be allowed to enter the city, and that the fringed and feathered crimson cap, or *borla*, which served as the Inca diadem, should be taken from him and bestowed upon his victorious brother. In spite of Urco's protests this was done. It is further said that Urco's lawful queen, who had borne him no children, forthwith abandoned him, and, coming into Cuzco, became the lawful queen of Pachacutec.[2] All these proceedings seem to me consistent

The deposition of Urco.

---

[1] Cieza, pt. ii. cap. xlvi.

[2] Cieza does not tell us what became of the deposed and forsaken king. "I say no more concerning Inca Urco, because the Indians only refer to his history as a thing to laugh at."

Garcilasso tells a different story. He places the invasion of the Chancas two generations earlier, in the reign of Urco's grandfather, Yahuar-huaccac. That Inca, says Garcilasso, fled from Cuzco, and his son Viracocha Inca defeated the invaders, where-

and probable, and they clearly indicate that the power of deposing and degrading the king, and filling his place by the prince next in the customary order of succession, was retained by the Inca council at Cuzco, as it was retained by the *tlatocan* at the city of Mexico, and could be exerted in cases of emergency.

On the whole, I am inclined to the opinion that the reigning Inca had practically acquired control of judicial, administrative, and legislative affairs through his paramount influence in the council; and that this is one reason why such meagre information about the council has come down to us. The Inca was, in all probability, much more a king than Agamemnon, — more like Rameses the Great.

One is the more inclined to this opinion because of the excessive development of sacerdotal supremacy in the Inca. As already observed, in the order of historic evolution the king is primarily the military chief; next he becomes chief priest, and in virtue of this combination of exalted functions, he acquires so much influence as to appropriate to himself by degrees the other functions of government, judicial, administrative, and legisla-

upon the son dethroned the father, but allowed him to live in a comfortable palace in the pleasant Yucay valley (lib. v. cap. xviii.–xx.). But in this story also, the act which dethrones the father and enthrones the son is the act of " the court, which was the head of the kingdom, to avoid scandals and civil wars, and above all because there was no use in resisting, so that all that the prince desired was agreed to." Nothing could be more significant. The victorious prince is all-powerful in the council, but still the action, to be lawful, must be the action of the council. This preserves the reminiscence of despotism in the making, at a time when despotism was practically completed.

tive.[1] Now the Inca, originally the head war-chief of the Inca tribe, came naturally to be military head of the Inca empire. As to his sacerdotal functions he came to be something more than chief priest ; his position was that of vice-deity, analogous to what Herbert Spencer calls a god-king. To illustrate this properly a few words must be devoted to an account of the Inca religion.

The Inca was a "god-king."

This religion was a comparatively high form of polytheism, in which ancestor-worship coexisted with worship of the Sun ; and now and then some idea crudely suggestive of monotheism found expression, as in the remark attributed by Father Blas Valera to the Inca Tupac Yupanqui, that the Sun, who goes on his unvarying round like a tethered beast, must be obeying the mandates of an unseen power.[2] In the mind of the Inca this unseen power was probably Pachacamac, whose name means "Creator of the World." "All the theology of the Incas," says Garcilasso, "was included in the word *Pachacamac.*" They believed that things must have been made somehow by somebody, but beyond that point they did not carry their speculations, for they had little science and still less theology, and "knew not how to raise their minds to invisible things."[3] In all Peru there was but one temple consecrated to Pachacamac. It was on the coast, some distance south

Pachacamac.

---

[1] See above, vol. i. p. 112.

[2] The same remark was attributed by Father Acosta to Tupac's son, Huayna Capac. See Garcilasso, lib. viii. cap. viii. ; lib. ix. cap. x. Cf. *Myths and Mythmakers*, pp. 169–171.

[3] Garcilasso, lib. ii. cap. xxv.

of the site of Lima. It was a very old temple, standing on the top of a small hill and built of adobe brick. The interior walls were covered with figures of wild beasts. Within was an idol endowed with oracular powers, and its priests, when consulted, went off into paroxysms like the Cumæan Sibyl.[1] To the valley of Pachacamac came pilgrims with their offerings from all quarters to consult the oracle. It seems to have been a relic of the old idolatrous religion of the coast people, which the sagacious Tupac Yupanqui, instead of destroying it, converted to the uses of a more spiritual religion, somewhat as early Roman missionaries cleansed pagan temples and turned them into Christian churches.[2] The general policy of the Incas, however, was to suppress idolatry among the peoples annexed to their dominicns.[3] Garci-

[1] At Phœbi nondum patiens, immanis in antro
Bacchatur vates, magnum si pectore possit
Excussisse Deum. Tanto magis ille fatigat
Os rabidum, fera corda domans, fingitque premendo.
Ostia jamque domus patuere ingentia centum
Sponte sua, vatisque ferunt responsa per auras.

Virg., *Æn.*, vi. 77.

[2] Cieza's remarks are entertaining. He says that " the devil Pachacamac " was much pleased with the arrangement, and " showed great satisfaction in his replies, seeing that his ends were served both by the one party and the other, while the souls of the unfortunate simpletons remained in his power. Some Indians say that this accursed demon Pachacamac still talks with the aged people. As he sees that his authority and credit are gone, and that many of those who once served him have now formed a contrary opinion, he declares that he and the God of whom the Christians preach are one, and thus with other false and deceitful words induces some to refuse the water of baptism " (pt. i. cap. lxxii.). There was nothing of the comparative mythologist about Cieza!

[3] Garcilasso, lib. vi. cap. x. ; lib. viii. cap. iii.

lasso declares most positively that the Inca people "worshipped no other gods but the Sun, although there are not wanting persons who state the contrary." [1]   The reverence for tutelar domestic deities, the spirits of deceased ancestors, Garcilasso would probably not have regarded as a real exception to his general statement, any more than, as a Catholic, he would have recognized the reverence for patron saints as an evanescent phase of polytheism.   The public worship was Sun-worship.

Sun-worship.

Some reverence was paid to the moon, the three brightest planets, and the Pleiades, but this was but accessory to the adoration of the orb of day.   This worship was celebrated chiefly at four great festivals at the solstices and equinoxes of each year.[2]   At these festivals there were sacrifices of "sheep," i. e. llamas or alpacas, and their lambs; of rabbits and birds used for food; of maize and other vegetables, of the strength-sustaining herb *coca*,[3] of the exhilarating *chicha*, or maize beer,[4] and of fine cloths.   "They burnt

[1] Garcilasso, lib. iii. cap. xx.

[2] For the method in which the Peruvians measured the year and determined the solstices and equinoxes by means of the shadows cast by towers, see Garcilasso, lib. ii. cap. xxii.   They used the solar year, and intercalated a period at the end of the lunar year to bring it up to the solar.   This period they called "finished moon."   See Markham's note, to Garcilasso, vol. i. p. 179.

[3] The dietetic and medicinal uses of this valuable narcotic, especially useful to mountaineers, are described in Garcilasso, lib. viii. cap. xv.; and Cieza, pt. i. cap. xcvi.; cf. Johnston, *Chemistry of Common Life*, vol. ii. pp. 116–135; Bibra, *Die Narkotischen Genussmittel und der Mensch*, pp. 151–174.

[4] The maize beer is described in Garcilasso, lib. viii. cap. ix. The Peruvians were sturdy tipplers; the quantity of beer they

these things as a thank-offering to the Sun for having created them for the support of man." [1] As for human sacrifices, Garcilasso assures us, and with evident knowledge of the subject, that there was nothing of the sort under the Incas. In the times before the Inca supremacy, and among many of the peoples whom the Incas conquered, there were human sacrifices accompanied by cannibalism; [2] but both these practices were sternly suppressed by the Incas. Their abolition he would date as far back as the time of Manco Capac,[3] which was equivalent to " a time whereof the memory of man runneth not to the contrary." If some Spanish writers assert that there were human sacrifices in Peru, it shows that they do not exercise proper discrimination. Within the vast limits of the Inca dominion there were included a number of peoples with whom such sacrifices had long been customary, and it might well be that the Incas had not completely succeeded everywhere in stamping out the abomination. Garcilasso mentions a writer who described human sacrifices " in Peru ; " but it was in a place more than twelve hundred miles north of Cuzco, i. e. in a region recently conquered and imperfectly

No human sacrifices.

consumed, says our author (lib. vi. cap. iii.), " is a thing almost incredible." After the Spaniards introduced barley, the natives made beer from it (Cieza, pt. i. cap. xl.) ; but the *chicha* is still in common use. See Squier's *Peru*, p. 126 *et passim*.

[1] Garcilasso, lib. ii. cap. viii.

[2] Compare Dr. Haug's remarks on the prevalence of human sacrifices in Vedic times and their abandonment by the Brahmans, in Muir's *Sanskrit Texts*, vol. i. p. 11.

[3] Garcilasso, lib. i. cap. xx.

reorganized. "I am a witness," says the good Garcilasso, "to having heard my father and his contemporaries frequently compare the states of Mexico and Peru; and in speaking of these sacrifices of men, and of the practice of eating human flesh, they praised the Incas of Peru because they neither practised nor permitted such acts, while they execrated the Mexicans for doing both the one and the other in the city in so diabolical a fashion." [1] Little if any doubt is now left that Garcilasso was quite right, and that among the burnt-offerings to the Sun on his great festal days there were no human creatures.

The duties and ceremonies of this Sun-worship were in charge of quite a hierarchy of ministering priests and confessors, sacrificers, hermits, and soothsayers, at the head of all the Villac Umu, "chief soothsayer" or high priest, and above him the Inca.[2] The soothsayers, like the Roman augurs, divined by the flight of birds or by inspecting the entrails of animals sacrificed. The ministering priests received confessions and

The priest-hood.

---

[1] Garcilasso, lib. ii. cap. viii. Mr. Prescott (*Conquest of Peru*, book i. chap. iii.) was inclined to admit that human sacrifices were performed, though very rarely, under the Incas, and quoted five contemporary authorities (including Cieza) against Garcilasso. But Mr. Markham has shown that Cieza and others were misled by supposing that the words *yuyac* and *huahua* signified "men" and "children," whereas, as applied to the victims of sacrifice, these words signified "adult beasts" and "lambs." Mr. Markham also quotes seven other important contemporary authorities (not mentioned by Mr. Prescott) in support of Garcilasso; so that the question appears to be settled in his favour. See Winsor, *Narr. and Crit. Hist.*, i. 237, 238.

[2] The priesthood is described by Mr. Markham, in Winsor, *Narr. and Crit. Hist.*, i. 240.

served as the mouthpieces of oracles. The hermits dwelt in solitary places, and were, in some instances if not always, organized into a kind of celibate monastic brotherhood with a chief hermit at the head. To these remarkable coincidences with various customs in the Old World may be added the special coincidence with ancient Egypt in mortuary customs. In Peru as in Egypt the bodies of the dead, swathed and wrapped in complicated fashion, were preserved as mummies, and sundry treasures and utensils were buried with them.[1]

Not the least interesting of these coincidences was the keeping of the sacred fire. Each year at the autumnal equinox a " new fire was kindled by collecting the sun's rays on a burnished mirror, and this fire was kept alive through the year by consecrated maidens (*acllacuna*) analogous to the Roman vestal nuns. These

The vestal nuns.

[1] Compare Cieza de Leon, pt. i. cap. lxiii. with Maspero's *Egyptian Archæology*, chap. iii. "Many of these ceremonies," says Cieza, " are now given up, because these people are learning that it suffices to inter the bodies in common graves, as Christians are interred, without taking anything with them other than good works. In truth, all other things but serve to please the Devil, and to send the soul down to hell the more heavily weighted." In several passages Cieza speaks of the custom of burying widows alive with their husband's mummy as if it were a common custom in Peru. It was undoubtedly common among many of the peoples conquered by the Incas, but it was not an Inca custom, and they did what they could to suppress it. A very high contemporary authority, known as " the anonymous Jesuit," declares that "in none of the burial-places opened by the Spaniards in search of treasure were any human bones found, except those of the buried lord himself." Markham, in Winsor, *Narr. and Crit. Hist.*, i. 237. Specimens of the mummies may be seen at the Peabody Museum in Cambridge.

vestals lived in convents presided over by matrons (*mama-cuna*). If the fire happened to go out it was an evil omen. If a nun broke her vow of chastity she was buried alive,[1] just as in Rome. But as compared with the Peruvian system of vestals, the Roman system seems either like a dwindled survival of something similar, or perhaps a parallel case of development arrested at an earlier stage. It was a much more extensive affair in Peru than in Rome, and its meaning is in many respects more obvious. In Rome there were six priestesses of Vesta, who were treated with most signal deference.[2] In Peru an *aclla-cuna* was treated with much deference, as a kind of superior being, but the number of them was very large. There were about 1,500 of these vestals in the *aclla-huasi*, or " nuns'-house " at Cuzco, and in all parts of the kingdom a temple of the Sun generally had such a convent attached to it. Their vow of perpetual celibacy meant that they were the Sun's wives; whence it was quite natural that the punishment for infidelity should be burial in the dark grave out of the offended husband's sight. As wives of the Sun, they had certain household duties. They baked cakes and brewed beer for the great sacrificial festivals of the winter solstice and the vernal equinox.

[1] Garcilasso, lib. iv. cap. iii. According to Zarate (*Conquista del Peru*, ii. 7), the woman's paramour was burned alive.

[2] " They were emancipated from the *patria potestas* and became *sui juris;* . . . a lictor cleared the way before them; a seat of honour was reserved for them at the public shows; the fasces of a prætor or consul were lowered to them; and if they met a criminal on his way to execution he was reprieved." Ramsay, *Roman Antiquities*, p. 163.

They also wove cloth of fine cotton and vicuña wool, and made clothes for their husband the Sun; but as the celestial spouse, so abundantly cared for, could not come down from the sky to take these clothes, the Inca took and wore them. We are thus prepared for the information that the Inca, as representative of the Sun, was husband of all these consecrated women. They were concubines for the Inca. The convents were not equivalent to Eastern harems, for the Inca did not visit them. But he sent and took from them as many concubines as he wished; those who were not thus taken remained virgins.[1] It was absolutely required that the nuns at Cuzco should be of pure Inca blood; and as every reigning Inca had two or three hundred enumerated children,[2] the race seemed to be in no danger of dying out.

The theory of the Inca's person, upon which these customs were based, regarded him as the human representative or incarnation of the solar deity. He was the Sun, made flesh and dwelling among men. Such dignity was greater than that of mediæval Pope or Emperor; it was even greater than that of the Caliph, who was a Mussulman pope and emperor combined; and this is in har-

[1] Many interesting details concerning these vestals are given in Garcilasso, lib. iv. caps. i.–vii.

[2] How many more he may have had cannot be reckoned. Apparently any woman in the Inca's dominions might at any time be summoned to be his concubine, and felt honoured and exalted by the summons. According to Garcilasso, his great-grandfather Tupac Yupanqui had 200 children in his family (lib. viii. cap. viii.); and his great-uncle Huayna Capac had from 200 to 300 (lib. ix. cap. xv.).

mony with the view that the Inca's rule was practically absolute. As for instances of monarchs
with power strictly unlimited, like the king in a
fairy-tale, they are not easy to find anywhere in
history.

Great pains were taken to keep the lineage of
this august person as narrowly definite as possible.
The Inca's legitimate wife. The Inca could have but one legitimate
wife, and it was imperatively required
that she should be his full sister, — the child of
the same father by the same mother.[1] The children of the Inca by this incestuous marriage were
thus as completely and narrowly royal in blood as
possible, and the eldest son was the legitimate heir
to the kingdom.[2] If the Inca had no children by
his eldest sister, he married the second, and the
third, and so on, until a legitimate heir was born
to him. Only such an heir could be legitimate.
The Inca's two or three hundred children by the
vestals, of pure Inca blood, were counted as legitimate, but could not inherit the kingship. His
children by ordinary women were mere bastards,
and counted for nothing, although they were respected as nobler than common people.

Such notions of caste, of distinction between
noble and ignoble blood, such extreme deification
of the military head of the community, would
have been inconceivable in any part of aboriginal

[1] This one legitimate wife was called *Coya*, equivalent to
queen. See Garcilasso, lib. iv. cap. ix.; Cieza, pt. ii. cap. lxix.

[2] In its origin this rule was probably a device for keeping the
"royal succession in the male line, where otherwise succession
through females prevailed." See Spencer, *Principles of Sociology*, vol. ii. p. 346.

America except Peru. In purely tribal society
there is no such thing as caste, no such
thing as monarchy. Caste and monarchy are results of the partial fusion
of tribal societies through ·conquest.
The conquering tribe becomes the ruling caste, its head war-chief becomes the semi-
divine monarch. Nowhere except in Peru had
there been enough conquest and fusion to produce
any such results. The Mexican *tlacatecuhtli* afforded an instance of primitive kingship developed
almost as far as was possible in a purely tribal
society; he was a priest-commander, almost but
not quite equivalent to the early Greek *basileus*,
or priest - judge - commander. If the conquering
career of the Aztec confederacy had gone on unchecked until the present time, it would probably
have effected a military occupation of the whole
Mexican territory, with garrisons in the principal
pueblo-towns; the *calpixqui*, or tax - gatherers,
would probably have developed into permanent
satraps or governors, like the Peruvian *curacas ;*
the Aztec tribe might very likely have developed
into a ruling caste, supported entirely by the
labour of the subjected peoples; and the Aztec
" chief-of-men " might well have become exalted
into a despot like Xerxes or Tupac Yupanqui; while
the Aztec tribal council would have come to be an
evanescent affair seldom mentioned by historians,
like the council at Cuzco.

Thus the governmental development in ancient
Peru was such as to indicate that society must, at
least in some respects, have passed beyond the

Society had
undergone
further devel-
opment in
Peru than
elsewhere in
America.

tribal stage as exemplified elsewhere throughout aboriginal America. We have other indications of a similar kind. There are reasons for believing that the primitive clan system was to a very considerable extent broken up.

Breaking up of the clan system.

Upon such points, indeed, our information is meagre and unsatisfactory. The ethnologist and the archæologist have not done so much for us in Peru as they have done in North America. There is much need in this field for work like that of Morgan, Cushing, and Bandelier. It would be interesting to know, for example, how far the great communal house or fortress, of the pueblo type, may have been common in Peru. One would gladly see the remarkable ruins at Caxarmarquilla [1] and at Chimu,[2] near Truxillo, explored with especial reference to this question. If it should turn out, however, that these and other structures in the coast region are the remains of ancient pueblos, it would still be unsafe to infer too hastily that the state of society implied by them was like that which prevailed nearer to Cuzco. It is probable that before the Inca conquests the entire coast region, from the isthmus of Darien to Chili, was the seat of a semi-civilization in many respects like that of Mexico and Central America, in some respects cruder. These coast peoples were skilful irrigators and built huge structures of adobe brick; they were cannibals, they sacrificed human beings to dog-headed idols, and they buried widows alive with their dead husbands. All such heathenish practices the conquer-

[1] Squier's *Peru*, p. 93.   [2] *Id.*, pp. 143–164.

ing Incas, to the best of their ability, suppressed. If we were to infer, from the cannibalism practised by these peoples, that the Incas were likewise cannibals, we should make a grave mistake. It would clearly, therefore, be unsafe to infer, from any vestiges of communal living in this region, that the same sort of communal living formed any part of the Inca phase of society.

In this connection a certain passage in Garcilasso de la Vega is very suggestive. Eastward of the Andes, in a part of what is now Bolivia, lived a fierce race of barbarians called Chiri- The Chirihuanas, — such cannibals that " if they huanas. come upon shepherds watching sheep [alpacas], they prefer one shepherd to a whole flock of sheep." In 1572 (i. e. in Garcilasso's own time, when he was thirty-two years old), the viceroy Don Francisco de Toledo undertook to invade the country of the Chirihuanas and chastise them into good behaviour. But their country, situated on the rainy side of the giant mountains, was a frightful maze of swampy forests, and Don Francisco was baffled, as in earlier days the great Inca Pachacutec had been baffled in the same enterprise. " The viceroy came back as a fugitive, having left behind all he had taken with him, that the Indians might be satisfied with their captures and leave him to escape. He came out by so bad a road that, as the beasts were unable to drag the litter in which he travelled, the Spaniards and Indians had to carry him on their shoulders. The Chirihuanas followed behind, with derisive shouts, and cried out to the bearers to throw that old woman [his highness, the viceroy!] out of the basket, that they might eat her alive."

Now of these Chirihuanas Garcilasso goes on to say that they learned from the Incas how to make dwellings, in which they lived in common.   There is a possible ambiguity about this sentence if it is carelessly read.   From the context I understand it to mean, not that the Incas taught them their communal style of living, in which they resembled savages and low barbarians generally; but that they copied from neighbouring peoples under Inca sway certain building arts which they applied to their own purposes.   Perhaps Garcilasso is mistaken in supposing that they learned their art of building from the Incas; for on that point he speaks as an antiquary.   In the next sentence he speaks as a contemporary.   A Chirihuana dwelling, he says, is a very large house, divided into as many apartments as there are families; these apartments, though small, are quite sufficient for people without much encumbrance in the shape of clothes or household furniture; and each great house may be called a village (*pueblo*). Upon such a state of things Garcilasso looks with some disgust.   "This is enough to say about the brutal condition and manner of life of the Chirihuanas, and it will be a great marvel if we are able to draw them out of it." [1]

Their communal houses.

1 "Tambien aprendieron los Chirihuanas de los Incas à hazer casas para su morada, no particulares, sino en comun: porque hazen un galpon grandissimo, y dentro tantos apartadijos quantos son los vezinos, y tan pequeños que no caben mas de las personas y les basta porque no tienen axuar ni ropa de vestir, que andan en cueros.   Y desta manera se podra llamar pueblo cada galpon

This is not the way in which the Inca historian
would have mentioned pueblo-houses if he had
been familiar with them from boyhood. He tells
us, moreover, that the Peruvians of whom he had
personal knowledge, in Cuzco and other cities, did
not join their houses together, but each one stood
by itself; on one side was usually a large living
room, on the other were small chambers and
closets.[1] The inference, that the normal Peruvian
household was a family and not a clan, is supported
by the fact that in the remarkably symmetrical
and artificial organization of society, about to be
described, the unit of composition was not the
clan, but the family averaging five or six persons.

It is quite in harmony with such a stage of family
development that marriage was ordinarily indissol-
uble;[2] that most men had but one wife,
though in certain cases polygamy was   Monogamy.
permissible;[3] and that prostitutes were treated

de aquellos. Esto es lo que ay que dezir acerca de la bruta con-
dicion y vida de los Chirihuanas, que sera gran marauilla poderlos
sacar della." Garcilasso, lib. vii. cap. xvii. (Lisbon, 1609). In
his translation of this passage Mr. Markham is evidently wrong
as to the meaning of that tricksome word *vezinos;* here it clearly
means families, not individuals. Garcilasso surely did not mean
to describe the house as " divided into as many partitions as there
are inhabitants."

[1] " Advertimos que los Indios del Peru . . . no trauauan vnas
pieças con otras, sino que todas las hazian sueltas cada vna de
porsi: quando mucho de vna muy gran sala o quadra sacauan a
vn lado, y a otro sendos aposentos pequeños que seruian de re-
camaras," lib. vi. cap. iv.

[2] Report by Cristoval de Molina, in Markham's *Rites and Laws
of the Yncas*, London, 1873 (Hakluyt Soc.), p. 54.

[3] " When any man had received a woman as his legitimate wife
or *mamanchu*, he could not take another except through the favour

as outside the pale of society. They were obliged
to live in huts in the fields, outside of the towns,
and were called *pampayruna*, or "women of the
fields." They were treated by men "with extreme
contempt. Women could not speak to them, on
pain of receiving the same name, being shorn in
public, declared as infamous, and repudiated by
their husbands if married." [1]

Such a development of the family indicates a
The industrial great advance from the primitive type
army. of clan organization. But the extent to
which the clan system had been broken up and
superseded by a very peculiar and artificial system is illustrated in the industrial organization of
the Peruvian people in their village communities.
There everything was arranged as symmetrically
as in the administration of departments, arrondisse-
ments, cantons, and communes in modern France;
and such symmetry of arrangement is explicable
only as the result of the action of a more or less

of the Inca, which was shown for various reasons, either to one
who had special skill in any art, or to one who had shown valour
in war, or had pleased the Inca in any other way." Report by
Polo de Ondegardo, in Markham, *op. cit.* p. 166.

[1] Garcilasso, lib. iv. cap. xiv. There is a *double entendre* in the
word *pampayruna;* inasmuch as *pampa* means not only a field,
but is also sometimes used to designate a public square, open to
all comers, so *pampayruna* conveys the meaning of a public
woman or strumpet. They were never called by their names,
says Garcilasso, but only by this scornful epithet; i. e. they lost
personality and were no longer entitled to personal names, but
only to a common noun. The Incas preserved the tradition of a
former state of comparative promiscuity, and with this former
state, as well as with the loose sexual relations among neighbouring peoples, they contrasted the higher development of the family
among themselves. *Id.*, lib. i. caps. xiv., xv.

thoroughly centralized government. This industrial organization in ancient Peru was really a
military organization applied to industrial purposes; it was a system of army government
extended through the whole framework of society.
Families and villages were organized upon a decimal system, like companies and regiments. The
average monogamous family of five persons was the
unit. Ten such families made a *chunca*, ten *chun-
cas* made one *pachaca*, ten *pachacas* one *huaranca*,
and ten *huarancas* one *hunu*, so that a *hunu* was
a district with a population of about 50,000 persons.[1] Each of these decimal subdivisions had its
presiding officer, who was responsible directly to
his immediate superior and ultimately to the Inca.
"The decurion was obliged to perform two duties
in relation to the men composing his division.
One was to act as their caterer, to assist them
with his diligence and care on all occasions when
they required help, reporting their necessities to
the governor or other officer, whose duty it was to
supply seeds when they were required for sowing;
or cloth for making clothes; or to help to rebuild
a house if it fell or was burnt down; or whatever
other need they had, great or small. The other
duty was to act as a crown officer, reporting every
offence, how slight soever it might be, committed
by his people, to his superior, who either pronounced the punishment or referred it to another
officer of still higher rank." [2]

[1] Ondegardo, in Markham, *op. cit.* p. 155; Garcilasso, lib. ii.
cap. xi.
[2] Garcilasso, lib. ii. cap. xii.

The land was divided into little areas called *tupus*, one *tupu* being enough to support a man and his wife. As fast as children were born, "another *tupu* was granted for each boy, and half a *tupu* for each girl."[1] This land did not belong to the family or its head, but to the *chunca* or village community; and as the *chunca* was originally reckoned the equivalent of an *ayllu*, or "lineage," we have here a connecting link between this elaborate system and the earlier system of clan ownership which preceded it.[2] The *ayllu*, or fragment of an overgrown and disintegrated clan, was trimmed into a definite size, and thus survived as the *chunca* in the new decimal system. The *chunca* owned the land in the sense of occupying it, and at intervals of time there was a redistribution of it, in order to maintain equality, as among the ancient Germans and the modern Russians.[3] The produce of the land was divided into three shares, one for the Inca, one for the priesthood, one for the people. Every man who had been present at the sowing had his equal share of the people's third; if he had not been present at the sowing, it was because he was absent in the Inca's service (as, for example, on a campaign), and thus he had his share in the Inca's

Allotment of lands and produce.

[1] Garcilasso, lib. v. cap. iii.

[2] See Bandelier's remarks on Peruvian land-tenure, in *Peabody Museum Reports*, vol. ii. p. 423.

[3] Maine, *Village Communities*, London, 1871; Nasse, *The Agricultural Community in the Middle Ages*, London, 1872; Phear, *The Aryan Village in India and Ceylon*, London, 1880; Mackenzie Wallace's *Russia*, London, 1877; Laveleye, *Primitive Property* London, 1878.

third ; or else he had been employed in work about
the temples, and accordingly took his share from
the priesthood's third. There was no room for
idlers or for millionaires. There were special census
officers, statistics were strictly kept on the *quipus*,
and allotments made accordingly. Irrigation and
tillage were directed by the decurion, or village
overseer. If a village suffered from war, or pestilence, or earthquake, assessments were made upon
more fortunate villages for repairing the damage.
On the whole it was the most complete illustration
of government socialism that the historian can discover by looking backward.

One is quite prepared to learn that in such a
society as this there was very little division of labour. "They had no special
tradesmen, as we have, such as tailors,
shoemakers, or weavers; but each man learnt all,
so that he could himself make all that he required.
All men knew how to weave and make clothes; so
that when the Inca gave them wool, it was as good
as giving them clothes. All could till and manure
the land without hiring labourers. All knew how
to build houses. And the women knew all these
arts also, practising them with great diligence and
helping their husbands." [1] A society in which
division of labour had been considerably developed
would not have lent itself so readily to such a mo-
notonous and spiritless regimentation as that of the
Incas. As already observed, this system, which
seems to have been fully developed by the time
that the extensive conquests began under Vira-

[marginal note: Little or no division of labour.]

[1] Garcilasso, lib. v. cap. ix.

cocha Inca, and which was imposed successively upon one conquered people after another, was really an application of military organization to industrial purposes, and was incompatible with advanced progress in industrial art. As Herbert Spencer observes, in considering what constitutes a true industrial society, we are concerned, "not with the quantity of labour but with the mode of organization of the labourers. A regiment of soldiers can be set to construct earthworks; another to cut down wood; another to bring in water; but they are not thereby reduced for the time being to an industrial society. The united individuals do these things under command; and, having no private claims to the products, are, though industrially occupied, not industrially organized." [1]

We are here brought back to the statement, made some time since,[2] that in Peru the formation of nationality, with the evolution of a distinct governing class, took place before there had been any considerable development of the idea of private property; so that the result was a state organized upon the principle of communistic despotism. It was a kind of industrial army.

If we recur now to the tripartite division of the produce of the land, we observe that it was an army in which the lion's share of this produce was consumed in the support of the administration. One third of the crop was evenly divided among the cultivators; two thirds really went to the gov-

---

[1] Spencer, *Principles of Sociology*, vol. ii. p. 694, where the case of Peru is cited in point.

[2] See above, p. 319.

ernment in the shape of taxes. Members of the Inca nobility and the priesthood, as non-producers, contributed nothing to these taxes, but were supported out of that portion of them which remained after military and other administrative outlays had been made. The taxes were paid in crops, woollen or cotton cloth, shoes, weapons, coca, or in cables for moving great stones.[1]

With this military organization of labour it becomes possible to understand how such buildings as the Sacsahuaman fortress could have been reared by people but slightly acquainted with the art of engineering. The marvellous and impressive feature in this cyclopean architecture is Cyclopean simply its massiveness. We do not works. admire it as an expression of intellectual qualities, as we praise a Greek temple for its beauty, or a Gothic church for its sublimity. Not even as fine mason-work, in the modern sense of the term, does it appeal to us. It simply amazes us with its herculean exhibition of brute force. The Sacsahuaman fortress was built of unhewn stones, often quite irregular in shape and very unequal in size, so chosen as to fit together without mortar. The marvel of it is simply how the huge stones could have been dragged to the spot and hoisted into place. A certain Spanish priest asked Garcilasso " whether it was possible to put them in their positions without the aid of the Devil " [2] But the

---

[1] Garcilasso, lib. v. cap. vi. ; Cieza de Leon, pt. ii. cap. xviii.

[2] Garcilasso, lib. vii. cap. xxviii. Mr. Markham, from his own measurements, gives some of the sizes of stones in the outer wall as fourteen feet by eight, fourteen by twelve, sixteen feet six inches by six feet one inch, etc.

amautas doubtless told the truth when they said
it was all done by an enormous expenditure of human brawn and sinew. Of one huge monolith,
famous as the "tired stone" because "it became
tired and could not reach its place," the *amautas*
said that more than 20,000 Indians were employed
in dragging it with stout cables. The conditions
of the case were not so very unlike those under
which the pyramids of Egypt were erected, though
the architecture and mason-work of the latter are
of far higher type and show much more range of
thought than any ancient structures in the New

Communistic despotism. World.[1] So far as mere command of
human labour went, the communistic
despotism of Peru could do things similar in kind,
though lesser in degree, to the despotism of the
Pharaohs.

This industrial army succeeded, as we have seen,
in carrying agriculture to a considerable degree of
perfection. The extent to which every available
spot of ground was utilized indicates a somewhat
dense population, though it must be remembered
that much of the area included within the Inca's

Agriculture. dominions was wild land unsuitable for
cultivation. Gardens were carried up
the mountain-sides on terraces, as in modern Italy.

[1] See Rawlinson's *History of Egypt*, vol. i. pp. 182–211. According to Herodotus (ii. 124, 125) the Great Pyramid consumed
the labour of 100,000 men for thirty years. Such numbers must
be understood with much latitude. The Egyptians had oxen, and,
according to Herodotus, made use of inclined planes in working
upon the pyramids. Possibly the Peruvians may have been able
here and there to utilize the principle of the inclined plane. For
some remarks on early Phœnician building, see Brown's *Poseidon*,
pp. 21, 27.

Mr. Markham says that the finest Sea Island cotton of our day is not superior to the best crops raised under the Incas. The potato and maize crops were also very fine. If Thorfinn Karlsefni and his men had seen Peruvian maize-fields, they would not have fancied that such corn grew wild. As for the Peruvian wools, we are beginning to learn that in comparison with the vicuña all other material for clothing seems both cumbrous and coarse.[1]

The vicuña and the huanacu were the wild animals hunted by the Peruvians, but a very tame affair was this hunting as compared with galloping after the hounds in England. There was no chance for sport; everything in this industrial army must be done to order. Nobody was allowed to kill one of these animals, except at the periodical government hunts, in which whole **Government hunts.** villages, led by their overseers, took part. The people surrounded their game and closed in on it, and then it was methodically disposed of, — some of the beasts released till next time, some shorn and then released, some killed for the table. A strict record of all this was kept on the *quipus* by the census officer, — a thing, says Polo de Ondegardo, "which it would be difficult for me to believe if I had not seen it."[2] The huanacu wool

[1] The Spaniards were not long in learning the merits of the vicuña's fleece. Blankets made of it were sent to Spain for the bed of Philip II.; see Garcilasso, lib. vi. cap. i.

[2] Markham's *Rites and Laws of the Yncas*, p. 165. Mr. Darwin has pointed out how the selection of certain of these animals for slaughter and others for release and further breeding was so managed as to improve the race. *Variation of Animals and Plants under Domestication*, vol. ii. p. 208.

was divided among the people, but the vicuña wool was reserved for those of Inca blood.

Of these wools, as well as of the cottons, fine cloth was woven and dyed of various hues,[1] and ornamental tapestries were wrought and embroi-

Arts.

dered. Gold was obtained with ease and in great quantity by washing the sands of the rivers in the province of Caravaya. Blast furnaces were used for smelting silver. Gold and silver were valued for their beauty, and reserved for the Inca or for use in the temples, and dishes, vases, and trinkets innumerable were made of them. But there was no currency or money of any kind.[2] All trade was simple barter, but in using scales and estimating certain goods by weight, the Peruvians were more advanced than the people of Mexico. In their implements of war and husbandry, which were fashioned in bronze, they were far superior to the Aztecs. In the pottery, which was made in great abundance, the superiority was perhaps less marked. In certain arts and inventions they had not advanced so far as the people of Mexico; their *balsas*, or rafts,[3] for example, were rude contrivances compared to the nimble Mexican canoes.

If we compare the culture of ancient Peru, as a whole, with that of the Mexicans and Mayas, we cannot fail to be struck with the contrast. In some points it was further removed from savagery

[1] For the excellent fast vegetable dyes, see Garcilasso, vol. i. p. 319, Markham's note.

[2] Garcilasso, lib. v. cap. vii. ; lib. vi. caps. i., ii.

[3] Garcilasso, lib. iii. cap. xvi.

by nearly the full length of an ethnical period. The cardinal points of superiority were the further development of the monogamous family, the advance from tribal confederation to- General summary. ward rudimentary nationality, the progress into a more spiritual form of polytheism with the abandoning of human sacrifices and cannibalism, the domestication of animals and further development of agriculture, the improvement in roads, and the prevailing use of bronze for weapons and tools. This further progress from savagery was, however, attended with some disadvantages. In becoming nationalized, the Inca government had stiffened into despotism,[1] as was sure to be the case with all nations formed before the comparatively modern development of the ideas of legal contract and political representation; and, as we have seen, the peculiar form of this despotism was communistic because it grew up among a people whose ideas of private property were still very imperfectly developed.

In point of humaneness and refinement the people of Peru were unquestionably superior to the Mayas and Mexicans. Their criminal code

[1] As contrasted with the Peruvians, the tribes of Mexico and Central America thus possessed an advantage somewhat analogous to that of the Germans whom Tacitus knew over the Romans of his own time with whom he so suggestively compared them. They retained plasticity, whereas the society governed by the Incas had become rigid. The greatest of all the inherited advantages which English-speaking people to-day enjoy is the fact that our ancestral Teutonic society retained its tribal mobility and plasticity of organization to so late a period in history that it was able to profit to the fullest extent by Roman civilization without being swamped by Roman imperialism.

was severe, and now and then we read of whole
sale beheadings for treason, or of pris

Humaneness.   oners being burned alive; [1] but in civilized Europe one need go back scarcely a century
to find the guillotine busy in Paris, and scarcely
more than a century to witness an *auto de fe* in
Spain, — not of criminals, but of useful and meritorious free-thinkers. . On the whole, for a society
in most respects within the middle period of barbarism, for a society less advanced intellectually
than the Egyptians of the Old Empire, it would
appear that the Inca society was remarkable for
mildness and humanity. It was not cursed, like
Mexico, with the daily spectacle of men and women torn open and cut into pieces. It looked upon
such people as the Chibchas as ferocious barbarians, and it would have justly entertained a similar opinion of the people of Uxmal and Tezcuco if
it had known anything about them. The pages of
Cieza de Leon bear frequent testimony to the clemency and moderation of the Incas in many of their
dealings with vanquished peoples; and one point,
upon which he speaks emphatically, is quite startling in its unlikeness to what was common in ancient society. Soldiers were forbidden to pillage,
under penalty of death, and this rule was enforced.[2]

With regard to intellectual culture, as exhibited
in literary production, the Peruvians were at a
disadvantage compared to the peoples north of the
isthmus of Darien. The data for a comparison
are meagre indeed. There was some written lit-

[1] Garcilasso, lib. iii. cap. iv.   [2] Cieza, pt. ii. cap. xxiii.

erature, as we have seen, among the Mexican and
Maya-Quiché peoples, but very little of Intellectual
it remains in a decipherable state. Such culture.
of it as is still accessible to the modern reader is,
of course, rude and primitive in thought and sen-
timent. The Nahuatl hymns collected by Dr.
Brinton, in his " Rig-Veda Americanus," are quite
childlike as compared to the hymns of the great
Rig-Veda of the Aryans. Of Peruvian thought,
as expressed in poetry, we know even less than of
Mexican. The Incas had bardic recitals and theatrical exhibitions ; and one ancient Inca drama,
entitled " Ollanta," has come down to us.[1] It is
a love story, with the scene laid in the time of the
great Inca Pachacutec ; it would make a pleasant
scene upon the stage, and is undeniably a pretty
poem. We have already mentioned the special
class of *amautas*, or " wise men," differentiated
from the priesthood, whose business it was to preserve historic traditions and literary compositions.
But unfortunately the Peruvian method of recording admitted of no considerable development in
such sort of work. It led nowhere. Now and
then we see animals, such as starfishes, which have
started on a path of development that can lead
only a very little way. In that queer spiny radiated structure there are nothing like the possibilities of further evolution that there are in the soft,
loosely-segmented, and mobile worm ; and so the
starfish stays where he is, but from the worm come

[1] *Ollanta : an Ancient Ynca Drama.* Translated from the
original Quichua by Clements R. Markham, London, 1871 ; later
editions are those of Zegarra (Paris, 1878) and Middendorf
(Leipsic, 1890) ; the last is the most accurate.

insects and vertebrates. So with their knotted and twisted cords the Peruvians could keep rude records for a time, but in such a method there were no future possibilities. One might sooner expect to see systems of higher arithmetic and algebra developed with Roman instead of Arabic numerals, than to see a true literature developed with *quipus* instead of hieroglyphs. Until the Incas had either devised some better method or learned it from other people, their literary period would have had to wait. But the Mexicans, and still more the Mayas, with their hieroglyphics, had started on the road that leads by natural stages to that grand achievement of the human mind, supreme in its endless possibilities, the achievement which more than any other marks the boundary-line between barbarism and civilization, between the twilight of archæology and the daylight of history, — the phonetic alphabet, the A B C.

Here we may bring to a close this brief sketch of the Inca society, one of the most curious and instructive subjects to which the student of history can direct his attention. In the next chapter we shall see the elements of weakness in that primitive form of nationality, characterized by conquest with imperfect fusion, well illustrated by the ease with which a handful of Spaniards seized and kept control over the dominions of the Incas.

CHAPTER X.

THE CONQUEST OF PERU.

THE chain of circumstances that led to the discovery and conquest of Peru, like the chain that
led to the conquest of Mexico, had its origin in
the island of Hispaniola, and was closely connected with the calamitous work of colonizing the
isthmus of Darien. In July, 1509, Diego Columbus, bringing with him his vice-queen Maria de
Toledo, came out to San Domingo, to
enter upon the government and colonization of such countries as had been
discovered by his father, as well as of
such as might be discovered by himself or his
appointed captains. Such at least was his own
theory of the situation, but the crown took a different view of it. As we have seen, Diego had
already set on foot a law-suit against the crown
to determine the extent of his rights and privileges, and matters were to come to such a pass
that in four years an attempt was to be made to
invalidate his father's claim to the discovery of
the Pearl Coast. We have already made some
mention of that attempt and its failure, in the
great judicial inquiry usually known in this connection as the *Probanzas*. The result of that
inquiry was entirely favourable to Columbus, but

Relations of the Admiral Diego Colum-bus to the crown.

anything like practical control over the affairs of
Terra Firma had already been virtually taken
out of Diego's hands. We have seen that the
immediate result of the third voyage of Columbus,
in which the rich Pearl Coast was discovered,
was the sending of an expedition by his enemy
Fonseca to the same region. This was the expedition of 1499, commanded by Alonso de Ojeda,
and from that time forth Ojeda was closely associated with this coast, made further explorations
there, and was appointed governor of the small
island of Coquibacoa. La Cosa and Vespucius,
also, who had been Ojeda's pilots in 1499, did
further work in this neighbourhood. We have
seen these two great navigators, in 1505 and 1507,
exploring the gulf of Darien and the Atrato river,
where they had hoped to find a passage to the
Moluccas. Instead of such a passage they found
gold in the river-beds. After their return we
have seen Vespucius made pilot major of Spain,
and La Cosa made "alguazil mayor," or high constable, of a colony about to be founded at Darien.
Now if King Ferdinand had been well disposed
toward Diego Columbus and his claims he would
naturally have entrusted this important enterprise
to his uncle Don Bartholomew, about
whose ability and integrity there could
be no question. But the relations of
the crown to the Columbus claims made
any such appointment impossible, and the governorship was given to the brave but incompetent
Ojeda. About the same time Diego de Nicuesa,
another court favourite like Ojeda, but better

*Provinces of
Terra Firma
granted to
Ojeda and Ni-
cuesa.*

educated and of finer mould, applied for the same position, and King Ferdinand arranged the matter by creating two provinces, one for each favourite. The country between the gulfs of Urabá (Darien) and Maracaibo was to be the province for Ojeda, while the Veragua and Honduras coasts, from the gulf of Urabá to Cape Gracias á Dios, were assigned to Nicuesa. The former province did not trench upon any territory discovered by Columbus, but the latter was chiefly made up of coasts first visited by him, and the appointment of Nicuesa was hardly less than an affront to the Admiral Diego.

Thus when the joint expedition was getting ready to start from Hispaniola, in the autumn of 1509, everything had been arranged as ingeniously as possible to hinder cordial coöperation. To the rivalry between the two governors was added the dislike felt for both by Diego Columbus. First, the two governors wrangled over the boundary-line between their provinces, until La Cosa persuaded them to agree upon the Atrato Starting of the expeditions. river. Then came the more important question of supplies. To ensure a steady supply of food, the island of Jamaica was to be placed at the disposal of Ojeda and Nicuesa; but as that was an invasion of the rights of Diego Columbus, he would not consent to it. So they started without any established base of supply, trusting themselves to luck. A sudden arrest for debt detained Nicuesa, so that Ojeda got off about a week before him. Before reaching the gulf of Urabá, at a place near the site of Cartagena, the rash Ojeda made up his mind to go ashore and catch a few slaves to be sent over to Hispaniola in payment for food. Against the advice of the veteran La Cosa he insisted upon going, with about seventy men, and La Cosa went with him to screen him from the effects of such hardihood, for he had found out that the Indians in that region used poisoned arrows. A few drops of poison sometimes quite neutralized the advantages of armour and cross-bows and gunpowder. La Cosa and all the other Spaniards save two were slain ; one of these two was Ojeda, who was picked up four or five days later and carried aboard ship just in time to save him from death by starvation. Nicuesa now arrived upon the scene with his ships, and, forgetting past quarrels, treated his unfortunate rival with much kindness and courtesy. After he had passed by, Ojeda stopped at the entrance to the gulf of Urabá and began to build a rude town there which he called San Sebastian. The proceedings were soon checked by famine, and as a piratical fellow named Talavera happened to come along in a ship which he had stolen, Ojeda concluded to embark with him and hurry over to Hispaniola in quest of supplies and reinforcements. His party kept their ships, and it was agreed that if Ojeda should not return within fifty days they might break up the expedition and go wherever they liked. So Ojeda departed, leaving in temporary command an Estremaduran named Francisco Pizarro, of whom we shall have more to say.

Death of La Cosa.

Famine.

The unfortunate commander never returned. After a voyage anything but agreeable in company with Talavera's ruffians, the stolen ship was wrecked on the coast of Cuba. In course of time Ojeda, sadly the worse for wear, got Death of back to San Domingo, but long before Ojeda. that time his party had been scattered, and he had

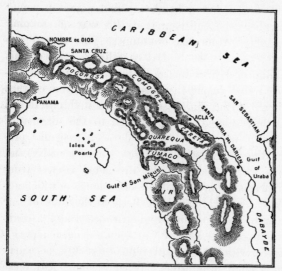

no means of making a fresh start. He died at San Domingo in abject misery, in 1515.

While the shipwrecked Ojeda was starving on the coast of Cuba, a couple of ships, with horses, food, and ammunition, started from San Domingo to go to the relief of San Sebastian. The commander was a lawyer, the Bachelor Expedition of Martin Fernandez de Enciso, after- Enciso. wards distinguished as a historian and geographer.[1] He was a kind of partner in Ojeda's enterprise, having invested some money in it. He was in many respects an estimable person, but hardly fitted for the work to which he had put his hand, for he was made of red tape, without a particle of tact about him. Among the barrels in Enciso's ship was one that contained neither bread nor gunpowder, but a handsome and penniless young cavalier who had contrived this way of escaping

Appearance of Balboa.

from his creditors. This was Vasco Nuñez de Balboa, who in spite of this undignified introduction is by far the most attractive figure among the Spanish adventurers of that time. After the vessel had got well out to sea Balboa showed himself, much to the disgust of Enciso, who could not abide such irregular proceedings. He scolded Vasco Nuñez roundly, and was with some difficulty dissuaded from setting him ashore on a small desert island, — which apparently would not have been in the eyes of our man of red tape an irregular proceeding! Arriving upon the site of Cartagena, Enciso met Pizarro, with the haggard remnant of Ojeda's party in a small brigantine. What business had these men here? thought this rigid and rigorous Enciso; they must be deserters and had better be seized at once and put in irons. With much ado they convinced him of the truth of their story. As the fifty days had expired without news of Ojeda, they had abandoned the enterprise. But now they

---

[1] His valuable work *Suma de Geografía, que trata de todas las partidas y provincias del mundo, en especial de las Indias*, was published at Seville in 1519. There were later editions in 1530 and 1546. It is now excessively rare.

were ready to follow Enciso, and all thus proceeded amicably together to the gulf of Urabá. After some mishaps Balboa, who had formerly been on that coast with Bastidas and La Cosa, advised the party to choose the western shore of the gulf for their settlement, inasmuch as the Indians on that side did not use poisoned arrows. This sound advice was adopted, and the building of the town of Santa Maria del Darien was begun. Enciso's overbearing temper soon proved too much for his followers and they resolved to depose him, but could not agree upon a successor. By crossing the gulf they had entered Nicuesa's province, and some thought that he ought therefore to become their commander, while some favoured Balboa, and a few remained loyal to Enciso. It was at length decided to elect Nicuesa, and until he should come Balboa remained the leading spirit of the little colony.

Enciso deposed by his men.

It was now December, 1510. Nicuesa's story had been an appalling record of famine and mutiny. Out of more than 700 men who had left Hispaniola with him thirteen months before, not more than 70 remained alive at the little blockhouse which they had built and called Nombre de Dios. The Spanish adventurers in America need all the allowances that charity can make for them, and in rehearsing their deeds one is sometimes led to reflect that their prolonged sufferings in the wilderness must have tended to make them as savage as wolves.[1] One

Awful sufferings of Nicuesa and his party.

---

[1] "The more experience and insight I obtain into human na-

sees this illustrated in the melancholy fate of poor Nicuesa. That kind-hearted gentleman had become maddened by hardship until his harshness began to alarm his men. His friend Colmenares, bringing food from Hispaniola and a message of invitation from the men at Darien, found him, " of all lyuynge men most infortunate, in maner dryed vppe with extreeme hunger, fylthye and horrible to beholde, with onely three score men . . . lefte alyve of seven hundreth. They al seemed to hym soo miserable, that he noo less lamented theyr case than yf he had founde them deade." [1] As soon as they had recovered strength enough to

Cruel treatment of Nicuesa by the men of Darien. move about, they started in two caravels for Darien. Nicuesa's unwonted harshness continued, and he was heard to utter a threat of confiscating the gold which the men of Darien had found within his territory. This foolish speech sealed his fate. The other caravel, reaching Darien before his own, warned the party there against him, and when he arrived they would not let him come ashore. With seventeen comrades left who would not desert him, the unfortunate Nicuesa put out to sea and was never heard of again.

This affair left Vasco Nuñez in undisputed com-

ture, the more convinced do I become that the greater portion of a man is purely animal. Fully and regularly fed, he is a being capable of being coaxed or coerced to exertion of any kind, love and fear sway him easily, he is not averse to labour however severe ; but when starved it is well to keep in mind the motto ' Cave Canem,' for a starving lion over a raw morsel of beef is not so ferocious or so ready to take offence." Stanley, *In Darkest Africa*, vol. i. p. 270.

[1] *Decades of the Newe Worlde*, dec. ii. lib. iii.

mand at Darien, and as he was thus the most conspicuous gainer from it, there was an opportunity for his enemies to cast upon him the blame for the cruel treatment of Nicuesa. On this grave charge, however, he was afterward tried and acquitted by an un-

Balboa left in undisputed command.

friendly tribunal, and it seems clear that without opposing the decision not to receive Nicuesa as commander he tried his best to save him from harm. But his conduct toward the Bachelor Enciso was the very height of folly. Doubtless he found that martinet unendurable, but what could be more unwise than first to imprison him and then to set him free on condition of leaving the colony in the first available ship? The angry Enciso went home to Spain and complained at court. Vasco Nuñez indeed tried to provide against such an adverse influence by sending his friend Zamudio to talk with King Ferdinand; but the trained advocate Enciso proved a better talker than Zamudio.

Balboa forthwith proceeded to explore the isthmus. He made an alliance with the chief Careta, who gave him his daughter in marriage. Then he added to the alliance a powerful chief named Comogre, whose town he visited with some of his men. This, it will be observed, was in 1512, before any rumour of the existence of Mexico had reached the ears of the Spaniards, and they were agreeably surprised at the sight of the house in which Comogre received them, which was much finer than any that they had hitherto beheld, and seemed to indicate that at length they were approaching the confines of Asiatic civilization. It was 150 paces in length by 80 feet in breadth, with finely wrought floors and ceiling, and, besides granaries, cellars, and living rooms, contained a kind of chapel where the bodies of deceased members of the clan were preserved as mummies.[1] The chief gave the Spaniards a large quantity of gold and seventy slaves. These Indians knew nothing of gold as a purchasing medium, but made it into trinkets, and they were sorely mystified at seeing the Spaniards melt it into bars or ingots, which they weighed with scales. A dispute, or, as Eden calls it, a "brabbling," arose among the Spaniards as they were weighing and dividing this gold. Then a son of Comogre got up and told the visitors that if they set so much value on this yellow stuff as to quarrel about it they had better go to a country where they could get more than enough for all. Over across the sierras there was a great sea, and far to the southward on the shore of this sea there was a land where gold was so plentiful that people used it instead of pottery for their bowls and cups. This was the first distinct and undoubted mention of the country of the Incas. Vasco Nuñez sent news of this speech to the Spanish court, accompanied by the king's share of the gold, one fifth of the amount; but unfortunately the vessel was wrecked in the Caribbean sea, and neither message nor gold found its way to King Ferdinand. It was not until the next spring that messengers reached the Spanish court, and then it was learned that Enciso had the

Speech of Comogre's son.

---

[1] Peter Martyr, *De Orbe Novo*, Alcalá, 1516, dec. ii. lib. iii.

king's ear, and legal proceedings against Vasco
Nuñez were about to be begun.

Soon afterward, our adventurer received from
the government in Hispaniola the appointment of
captain - general over Darien. His satisfaction,
however, was sadly clouded by the news from
Spain, and he determined at once to cross the
sierra, in the hope of finding the great sea and
thus establishing a claim to favourable treatment.
There was no use in waiting for reinforcements,
for the same ship that brought fresh troops might
bring an order for his dismissal and arrest. Early
in September, 1513, accordingly, Balboa started
across the isthmus with about 200 men and a small
pack of bloodhounds. From Careta's territory he
entered that of a cacique named Quarequa, who
undertook to oppose his advance through that difficult country. But no sooner did it come to fighting than the Indians fled in wild terror from
enemies who wielded thunder and lightning. Capturing some of these Indians and winning their
confidence by kind treatment, Balboa used them
as guides through the mountains. On
the 25th of September, from one of the
boldest summits in Quarequa's country,
Balboa looked down upon the waste of waters
which was afterwards shown to be the greatest
ocean upon the globe.[1]

Discovery of
the Pacific
ocean.

Four more days of arduous toil brought the
Spaniards down from the mountains to the shore
of the gulf which, because they reached it on

[1] Keats in his beautiful poem inadvertently puts Cortes in
place of Balboa.

Michaelmas, they named San Miguel. After launching out upon this rough sea in a small flo-

Further news of the golden kingdom.

tilla of canoes, and navigating a portion of it at the imminent risk of perishing in an equinoctial gale, Vasco Nuñez effected a landing upon its northern shore in the country of the chieftain Tumaco, whom he first defeated and then by kind treatment won his friendship. Tumaco confirmed the story of a rich empire far to the south, and produced a clay figure of a llama in illustration of some of his statements.

It was now high time to return to Darien with the tidings of what had been accomplished. Vasco Nuñez arrived there early in January, 1514, but too late for his achievement to effect such a result as he had hoped for. He might not unreasonably have expected to be confirmed in his governorship of the isthmus. But stories of the golden kingdom

Affairs in Spain.

mentioned by Comogre's son had already wrought their effect in Spain. The victories of the French in Italy under the brilliant Gaston de Foix had alarmed King Ferdinand ; an army for Italy had been collected and the command given to Gonsalvo de Córdova. But before this expedition started news came of the retreat of the French, and the king ordered Gonsalvo to disband his men.[1] Many of the gay cavaliers who had enlisted with fiery enthusiasm under the Great Captain were thus thrown out of occupation, to their intense disgust ; when all at once there came

[1] *Chronica del Gran Capitan.* lib. iii. cap. 7 ; Mariana, *Historia de España*, lib. xxx. cap. 14.

to Spain the report of an unknown sea beyond the Terra Firma, and of a kingdom abounding in wealth. There ensued one of the bursts of excitement so common in that age of marvels, and which the reading of Don Quixote enables one to appreciate. On the word of an unknown Indian youth, before it had been even partially confirmed by Balboa's discovery of the sea, these cavaliers were at once ready to cross the Atlantic. If they were not to go to Italy they would seek adventures in the Indies. A fleet was accordingly fitted out, with accommodations for 1,200 men, but at least 1,500 contrived to embark. The admiral of the fleet and new governor of Terra Firma Pedrarias was a man over seventy years of age, Dávila. named Pedrarias Dávila, one of those two-legged tigers of whom Spain had so many at that time. He was a favourite at court, and his wife was a niece of that Marchioness of Moya who had been the friend of Queen Isabella and of Columbus. For the next sixteen years Pedrarias was a leading figure in the Indies, and when he died the historian Oviedo, in a passage of surpassing quaintness, tried to compute how many souls of his murdered victims he would be called upon to confront at the Day of Judgment.[1] Oviedo was inclined to put the figure at 2,000,000. If we were to strike off a couple of ciphers, we should have a figure quite within the limits of credibility, and

[1] Oviedo, *Historia de las Indias*, xxix. 34. This historian cherished a personal grudge against Pedrarias; but all the other best authorities — Peter Martyr, Las Casas, Andagoya, Benzoni, Remesal — are in substantial agreement as to his atrocious character.

sufficiently terrible. It is hardly necessary to add that this green-eyed, pitiless, perfidious old wretch was an especial pet of Bishop Fonseca.

The arrival of this large force in Darien was the beginning of a self-sustaining colony. The collection of rude cabins called Santa Maria del Darien was made a " cathedral city," and Juan de Quevedo was appointed bishop. Gonsalvo Hernandez de Oviedo, afterwards famous as a historian, came out as inspector-general of the new colony. Gaspar de Espinosa was chief judge, and Enciso returned to the scene as chief constable. His first business was to arrest Vasco Nuñez, who was tried on various charges before Espinosa, but was presently acquitted and set free. The news of his discovery and the arguments of admiring friends had begun to win favour for him at the Spanish court. For more than two years Vasco

Jealousy between Pedrarias and Balboa. Nuñez contrived to avoid a serious quarrel with the governor, whose jealousy of him was intense, and made all the more so by the comparisons which men could not help drawing between the two. The policy of Pedrarias toward the Indian tribes was the ordinary one of murder and plunder ; in a few instances he chose incompetent lieutenants who were badly defeated by the Indians ; once he was defeated in person ; and such results could not but be contrasted with those which had attended the more humane, honest, and sagacious management of Balboa. In October, 1515, the latter wrote to the king, complaining of the governor's cruel conduct and its effect in needlessly alienating the Indians ; and it is

impossible to read that letter to-day [1] and not feel
that Vasco Nuñez, with all his faults, was a wise
and true-hearted man, with ample warrant for
every word that he said. But the king could not
very well read such a letter without some echoes
of it finding their way back to the New World.
Matters grew so stormy that Juan de Quevedo,
the Bishop of Darien, who was friendly to Balboa,
thought it necessary to negotiate a kind of treaty
between him and the governor. Balboa was to
be sent, with a proper force, to visit the golden
kingdom at the South, and the bishop proposed to
cement the alliance by a betrothal between Balboa
and the daughter of Pedrarias. Doubtless the
worthy clergyman, like most white men of his
time, thought that an Indian wife counted for nothing. Vasco Nuñez did not think so. He was
devotedly fond of the Indian girl and she of him,
but as the other young lady was in Spain and her
father in no great haste about the matter, Vasco
Nuñez assented to this article in the
treaty. Then he went off to Acla, a newly *An expedition prepared to go in search of*
founded port on the Atlantic side of the *the golden kingdom.*
isthmus, to engage in the herculean task
of taking his ships piecemeal across the sierra to
the point where they were to be put together and
launched on the Pacific.[2] After many months of

---

[1] Balboa, *Carta dirigida al Rey*, 16 Octubre, 1515, in Navarrete,
Coleccion de viages, iii. 375.

[2] Bishop Quevedo afterward reported to the Emperor Charles
V. that " more than 500 Indians " perished under the hardships
of this terrible undertaking ; but Quevedo's secretary told Las
Casas that the real number of deaths was not less than 2,000, a
figure which the bishop refrained from stating, through fear of

toil four ships, the first European keels to plough the great " Sea of the South," were ready to weigh anchor, and 300 men were ready to embark. Nothing was wanted but a little iron and pitch, and the delay thus caused was to bring swift ruin upon Vasco Nuñez.

A rumour had just arrived that the king had superseded old Pedrarias and appointed a new governor for the Terra Firma. The rumour was not so much false as premature, for the complaints against Pedrarias had wrought some effect at court, and the appointment of Lope de Sosa was made in the course of the next year. This premature rumour had serious consequences. Now that things had advanced so far, Balboa was more disturbed than pleased, for being used to the frying pan he preferred it to the fire ; a new governor might interfere and prevent his departure, and if it were not for that iron and pitch it would be prudent to sail at once. But since these articles were much wanted, let the small party sent back for them to Acla use some discretion and begin by ascertaining how much or how little truth there might be in the rumours. If the new governor should have arrived, perhaps it might be best to return as quietly and quickly as possible ; but if Pedrarias should still be in power, then it were best to go in boldly and ask for the iron and pitch.

being accused of exaggeration. See Las Casas, *Historia de las Indias*, iv. 233. At the same time, says Las Casas, Balboa was no mere slave-driver. Whenever the hardest work was to be done he was foremost, taking hold with his own hands and every·where aiding and cheering.

Thus Balboa talked with two friends one summer evening on the rude veranda of a cabin which he had used for headquarters while the ar- duous shipbuilding had been going on. A fatal conversation.
So far as Pedrarias was concerned, there does not seem to have been a word of treason in the conversation, but while they were talking in an undertone it began to rain, and a sentinel, pacing near headquarters, came up under the eaves for shelter, and listened. From the fragments which reached his ears he concluded that Balboa was intending to throw off his allegiance to Pedrarias and set up a new government for himself; and so, translating his crude inferences into facts, this fellow contrived to send information to La Puente, the treasurer at Acla, a man with whom Vasco Nuñez had once had a little dispute about some money.

Now it happened that a man named Andres Garavito,[1] having become enamoured of Balboa's Indian wife, had made overtures which were indignantly repulsed by the woman, and called forth stern words of warning from Vasco Nuñez. The wretched Garavito thereupon set out to compass Balboa's death. Having been sent on some business to Acla, he told Pedrarias that Balboa never meant to marry his daughter, inasmuch as he cared for no one but the Indian woman; moreover he was now about to go off in his ships to the

---

[1] The name is often written *Garabito*. The habitual confusion of these two labials in the Spanish language long ago called forth from Julius Scaliger the epigram: —

Haud temere antiquas Vasconia voces
Cui nihil est aliud vivere quam bibere.

De Causis Linguæ Latinæ, i. 14.

golden kingdom and gain wealth in his own behoof

with which to withstand and ruin Pedrarias. While the old man was cursing and raving over this story, the party coming for iron and pitch halted on the edge of the forest, and sent one of their number into the town after nightfall to make inquiries. It was this man's luck to be arrested as a spy, but he sent word to his comrades, and they, coming into town, protested their innocence so strongly and stated the true object of their visit so clearly that the angry governor was more than half convinced, when all at once the treasurer La Puente came to see him and told what he had heard from the sentinel. This sealed the fate of Vasco Nuñez. The governor sent him a crafty letter, couched in terms of friendship, and asking him to return to Acla before sailing, as there were business matters in which he needed advice. The unsuspecting Balboa set forth at once to recross the sierra. We are told that his horoscope had once been taken by a Venetian astrologer, who said that if he were ever to behold a certain planet in a certain quarter of the heavens it would mean that he was in sore peril, but if he should escape that danger he would become the greatest lord in all the Indies. And there is a legend that the star now appeared one evening to Vasco Nuñez, whereupon he told his attendants about the prophecy and mocked at it. But as he drew near to Acla there came out a company of soldiers to arrest him, and the captain of this company was Francisco Pizarro, one of his old comrades who had served under him ever since the time when the lawyer Enciso was deposed from command. "How is this, Francisco Pizarro?" said Balboa, "it is not thus that thou wert wont to come forth to meet me." But he offered no resistance, and when put upon his trial he simply asked why, if he had really been meditating treason and desertion, he should have come back so promptly when called. A guilty man would have staid away. But it was no use talking.[1] The governor had made up his mind, and before the sun went down Vasco Nuñez and four of his friends had been tried, condemned, and beheaded.[2]

Balboa put to death by Pedrarias.

Thus perished in the forty-second year of his age the man who but for that trifle of iron and pitch would probably have been the conqueror of Peru. It was a pity that such work should not

[1] "Valboa con giuramento negò, dicendo, che inquanto toccaua alla informatione che contra lui s'era fatta di solleuargli la gente che l'era à torto, e falsamente accusato, e che considerasse bene quello che faceua, e se lui havesse tal cosa tentata, non saria venuto alla presentia sua, e similmente del resto, si difese il meglio che puote ; ma dove regnano le forze, poco gioua defendersi con la ragione." Benzoni, *Historia del Mondo Nuovo*, i. 51, Venice, 1572.

[2] In the accounts of the Garavito treachery as given by Oviedo and Herrera, there is some confusion. Oviedo represents Garavito as having been arrested by Pedrarias and telling his base story in order to turn the governor's wrath away from himself. But as Sir Arthur Helps (*Spanish Conquest*, vol. i. p. 432) has pointed out, the discrepancy seems to have arisen from confounding Andres Garavito with his brother Francisco, who was one of the company sent for the iron and pitch and was faithful to Vasco Nuñez. The man who was arrested as a spy seems to have been Luis Botello, one of the four friends who were executed with Vasco Nuñez. See Pascual de Andagoya, *Relacion*, in Navarrete, *Coleccion de viages y descubrimientos*, iii. 405.

have fallen into his hands, for when at length it was done, it was by men far inferior to him in character and calibre. One cannot but wish that he might have gone on his way like Cortes, and worked out the rest of his contemplated career in accordance with the genius that was in him. That bright attractive figure and its sad fate can never fail to arrest the attention and detain the steps of the historian as he passes by. Quite possibly the romantic character of the story may have thrown something of a glamour about the person of the victim, so that unconsciously we tend to emphasize his merits while we touch lightly upon his faults. But after all, this effect is no more than that which his personality wrought upon the minds of contemporary witnesses, who were unanimous in their expressions of esteem for Balboa and of condemnation for the manner of his taking off.

Seven years passed before the work of discovering the golden kingdom was again seriously taken up. It was work of almost insuperable difficulty in the absence of a base of operations upon the Pacific coast of the isthmus; and, as we shall see, men's attention was distracted by the question as to the Molucca islands. During this

An interval.

interval of seven years the conquest of Mexico was begun and completed, so far as the towns once tributary to the Aztec Confederacy were concerned. By 1524 the time had arrived when the laurels of Cortes would not allow other knights-errant to sleep, and then Balboa's enterprise was taken up by his old comrade Francisco Pizarro.

This man, like Cortes and Balboa, was a native of the province of Estremadura. He was an illegitimate son of Gonzalo Pizarro, an officer of good family, who had served in Italy under the Great Captain. As the mother of Cortes was a Pizarro, it has been supposed that there was relationship between the two families. Francisco Pizarro, whose mother was a young woman of humble station, was born somewhere between Francisco Pizarro. 1470 and 1478. Unlike Cortes, who had some scant allowance of university education, Pizarro had no schooling at all, and never learned to write his own name. His occupation in youth seems to have been that of a swineherd, though he may, according to one doubtful tradition, have accompanied his father in one or more Italian campaigns. His first distinct appearance in history was in Ojeda's expedition in 1509, when he was left in command of the starving party at San Sebastian, to await the arrival of the succours brought by Enciso. He served under Balboa for several years, was with that commander when he first saw the great South Sea, and happened — as we have seen — to be the officer sent out by Pedrarias to arrest him.

In 1515, two years before Balboa's fall, Pizarro took part in an expedition under Gaspar de Morales, sent by Pedrarias to explore the coasts of the gulf of San Miguel. The expedition, as usual, was characterized by wonderful endurance of hardship on the part of the Spaniards and by fiendish cruelty toward the Indians. They invaded the territory of a warlike chief named Birú,

on the southern shore of the gulf, and met with
such a hot reception that, although victorious, they
did not care to risk a second fight, but retreated
to the isthmus. It was some years before the
Spaniards got so far south again, and when they
Origin of the name " Peru." had occasion to refer to the unvisited
territory beyond the gulf of San Miguel
they fell into a habit of speaking of it as the *Birú*
or *Perú* country. The golden kingdom, about
which there had been so much talk, was said to
be somewhere upon that coast, and in such wise
it seems to have received its modern name.[1] Not
long after Balboa's death Pedrarias learned that
Lope de Sosa had at length been appointed governor in his place. It was unwelcome news. The
old man had good reason to fear the result of an
examination into his conduct. It might be held
Lope de Sosa appointed to supersede Pedrarias. that in executing Balboa without allowing an appeal to the crown he had ex-
ceeded his powers, and the Spanish court
sometimes showed itself quite jealous of such en-
croachments upon its royal prerogative of revision
and pardon. There were, moreover, numerous instances of judicial robbery and murder that could
easily be brought home to their perpetrator. Accordingly Pedrarias thought it wise to put the
mountains between himself and the Atlantic coast,
so that in case of necessity he might do just what
he had beheaded Vasco Nuñez for doing, — quit
the dangerous neighbourhood and set up somewhere for himself.

[1] See Andagoya's *Narrative*, translated by Markham, London,
1865, p. 42 ; also Winsor, *Narr. and Crit. Hist.*, ii. 505.

This prudent resolve led to the founding of Panama by Pedrarias in August, 1519. Later in the same year the opposite port of Nombre de Dios was founded, and a rude road through the wilderness, connecting these two places, was begun. When Lope de Sosa arrived at Darien in May, 1520, with 300 men, Pedrarias happened to be on the spot, but was favoured with one of those inscrutable providences that are so apt to come to the rescue of such creatures. Before setting foot on shore the new governor was suddenly taken sick and died in his cabin. This left Pedrarias in office. The newly-arrived *alcalde*, before whom his examination was to take place, published notices and summons in due form for thirty days; but no man was hardy enough to enter complaint against him so long as he still remained invested with the insignia of power. The crafty old governor could thus look on smiling while a certificate that no one accused him was despatched on its way to Spain. Then he retired to Panama, which forthwith became the base for operations along the Pacific coast.

Sudden death of Lope de Sosa.

This stroke of fortune gave Pedrarias a new lease of undisputed power for nearly seven years. Meanwhile, as the judge Espinosa was involved along with him in the risk attendant upon the case of Balboa, he had sent that pearl of magistrates to take command of Balboa's little fleet and therein seek safety in a fresh voyage of discovery. As Magellan's voyage had not yet been made and the existence of a broad ocean south and west of the

Espinosa's voyage in Balboa's ships.

isthmus of Darien was still unknown,[1] the Spaniards upon the isthmus still supposed themselves to be either in eastern Asia or at no great distance from that continent ; and accordingly Espinosa, instead of sailing southward in search of the golden kingdom, turned his prows westward, apparently in the hope of settling the vexed question as to the Spice Islands. This would have required a voyage of nearly 11,000 English miles. After accomplishing some 500 miles, as far as Cape Blanco, in what is now the state of Costa Rica, Espinosa returned to the isthmus late in 1519.

Just at that time the controversy over the Moluccas was occupying a foremost place in the public attention. It was on the 10th of August, 1519, that Magellan started on his epoch-making voyage. Gil Gonzalez Dávila. Earlier in that year one of Balboa's pilots, Andres Niño, was at the Spanish court, urging that the ships of his late commander might be sent to find the Spice Islands. On the 18th of June a royal order was issued, authorizing such an expedition and entrusting the command of it to Gil Gonzalez Dávila, a man of high reputation for ability and integrity.

How fortunate it was for Magellan that his theory of the situation led him far away to the southward, subject indeed to trials as hard as ever man encountered, but safe from the wretched intrigues and savage conflicts of authority that were raging in Central America ! Had he chosen the route of Gil Gonzalez he would have begun

[1] It must be remembered that Balboa could not see across the ocean.

by encountering obstacles more vexatious, if not more insuperable, than those of the lonely and barren sea. When Gil Gonzalez arrived at Acla in the spring of 1520 and demanded the ships that had been Balboa's, Pedrarias refused to give them up. The death of Lope de Sosa confirmed the old man in this contumacy; so that nothing was left for Gil Gonzalez but to build and equip ships for himself. A flotilla, constructed with incredible toil, was destroyed by worms and weather. The dauntless Gil Gonzalez built a second, consisting of four small vessels, and early in 1522 he set sail for the coveted Moluccas. After eighteen months he returned to Panama, loaded with gold, after having discovered the coast of Nicaragua as far as the bay of Fonseca. As he crossed the isthmus, Pedrarias, in a frenzy of greed, sent officers to arrest him, but he eluded them and got safely to Hispaniola. Troubles of Gil Gonzalez. There he was authorized to return and take possession of Nicaragua. This time he approached it from the north by way of the Honduras coast, in order to avoid the isthmus and its dangerous governor. But among the vices of Pedrarias listlessness and sloth were not included. He laid claim to Nicaragua by reason of the prior voyage of Espinosa, and had already despatched Francisco Hernandez de Córdova,[1] with a considerable force, to occupy that country. Córdova's second in com-

---

[1] He must not be confounded with his namesake Francisco Hernandez de Córdova, the discoverer of Yucatan, mentioned above, p. 240. The latter, it will be remembered, died of his wounds on returning from his ill-starred voyage in 1517.

mand was Fernando de Soto, a young man whom
we shall meet again more than once in the course
of our story. Gil Gonzalez, marching down from
the north, encountered Soto and defeated him, but
was afterwards obliged to retire before Córdova's
superior force. Retreating into Honduras, Gil
Gonzalez was captured by Cristóval de Olid, whom
Cortes had sent from Mexico to occupy that country. A wild scramble ensued, — every man for
himself and the devil take the hindmost. Córdova threw off his allegiance to Pedrarias, but in
an incredibly short time that alert octogenarian
had come to Nicaragua and the severed head of
the insubordinate lieutenant, thrust aloft upon a
pole, was baking in the sun. Olid threw off his
allegiance to Cortes, and was presently assassi-
nated, probably with the complicity of Gil Gonzalez, who forthwith tried to come to an understanding with the conqueror of Mexico as to the
boundary between their respective prov-

His death.

inces. At this juncture Gil Gonzalez
was seized by some of Olid's friends and sent to
Spain to be tried for murder. Arriving at Seville
in 1526, the strength of this much-enduring man
suddenly gave way, and he died of hardship and
grief.

The voyage of Magellan, revealing the breadth
of the ocean between America and Asia, destroyed
the illusion as to the nearness of the Moluccas ; and
the discovery of Nicaragua convinced

Attention
again turned
to the golden
kingdom.

the Spaniards on the isthmus of Darien
that there was no use in sending expeditions to the westward, inasmuch as the way was

closed and the ground preoccupied by the conquerors of Mexico. Their attention was thus
turned decisively to the southward, whence fresh
rumours of the wealth of the Incas had lately
reached their ears. In 1522 Pascual de Andagoya crossed the gulf of San Miguel and gathered
much information concerning the golden kingdom.
A voyage of discovery to the southward was projected, and as Andagoya was completely disabled
by an attack of acute rheumatism, Pizarro formed
a partnership with a couple of his friends, Almagro and Luque, and Pedrarias entrusted to them
the enterprise. Diego Almagro, a man of unknown parentage, was probably not less than fifty
years old. Of fiery but generous disposition, he
had the gift of attaching men to his fortunes, but
there is little to be said in praise of his intelligence or his character. As compared with Cortes
and Balboa, or with the humane and virtuous
Andagoya, both Pizarro and Almagro were men
of low type. The third partner, Fernando de
Luque, a clergyman, at Panama, was associated in
the enterprise as a kind of financial agent, con-
tributing funds on his own account and also on
that of the judge Espinosa.

The distance to the land of the Incas was much
greater than had been supposed, and the first expedition, which started in 1524, returned in a very
dilapidated state, having proceeded as
far as the mouth of the river San Juan, *Pizarro and Almagro start in search of the golden kingdom.*
scarcely one third of the way to Tum-
bez. On the second expedition, in 1526,
Pizarro landed most of his men at the San Juan,

while he sent his pilot Bartholomew Ruiz forward
in one of the two ships, and Almagro in the other
went back to Panama for reinforcements and provisions. Ruiz, after crossing the equator [1] and
coming within sight of the snow-clad summit of
Chimborazo, returned to Pizarro with some native Peruvians whom he had captured on a sailing-
raft. The story of the grandeur of the Inca kingdom was confirmed afresh by these men.

These things were going on while Pedrarias
was wielding his headsman's axe in Nicaragua.

Death of Pedrarias. About this time he was really deposed
from his government at Panama, but
by dint of skilful chicanery he succeeded in keeping possession of Nicaragua for four years more,
committing cruelties worthy of Nero, until his
baleful career was ended by a natural death in
1530.

Having obtained from the new governor, Pedro
de los Rios, fresh men and supplies, Almagro
returned to the San Juan, where he found his
comrades nearly dead with hunger. Explorers
and military men will all agree that it is not easy
to carry on operations at a distance of a thousand miles from one's base. In those dreary expeditions each step in advance necessitated a step
backward, and the discouragement must have
been hard to endure. On the third start the adventurers coasted nearly down to the equator and

[1] In Mr. Markham's chapter on the Conquest of Peru in Winsor's *Narrative and Critical History*, vol. ii. p. 507, Ruiz is said to
have been "the first European to cross the equator on the Pacific
Ocean." Magellan had crossed it five years before from south to
north. *Aliquando dormitat bonus Homerus.*

were finding more frequent symptoms of civilization upon the shores they passed, when at length
it became necessary to send back again to Panama.
Again Pizarro halted, this time upon the little
island of Gallo, until his partner should return.
After many weeks of misery spent under the
drenching tropical rain, the starving men descried
a white sail in the offing ; but it was not Almagro.
The governor, disgusted at such a prolonged wild-
goose chase, had detained that commander, and
sent a ship with strict orders to bring back Pizarro and all his men. For the most part the
weary creatures had lost heart for their The scene at
work, and were eager to go. But the Gallo.
dogged Pizarro, whose resolution had kept stiffen-
ing with each breath of adversity, refused to budge.
Drawing an east-and-west line upon the sandy
beach with the point of his long sword, he briefly
observed that to the south of that line lay danger
and glory, to the north of it ease and safety ; and,
calling upon his men to choose each for himself,
he stepped across. Sixteen staunch men followed
their commander ;[1] the rest embarked and went

[1] The names of the sixteen have been preserved, and may be
found, with brief biographical notices, in Winsor, *op. cit.* ii. 510.
Among them, fortunately, was the daring and skilful pilot Ruiz.
A second was the Cretan artillery officer, Pedro de Candia, whose
son was afterwards, at Cuzco, a schoolmate of Garcilasso de la
Vega, the historian. Garcilasso relates the incident with much
precision of detail, Sir Arthur Helps is inclined to dismiss it as
theatrical and improbable. Perhaps he would regard Pedro de
Candia's testimony as worthless anyway, in view of the old adage
Κρῆτες ἀεὶ ψεῦσται. Seriously, however, the evidence (including
that of Pizarro's secretary Xeres) seems to be very good indeed,
and as for the melodramatic character of the story, it must be

on their way. After they had gone Pizarro and
his comrades made a raft and paddled to the island of Gorgona, where they lived on such shell-
fish as they could find upon the shore, and now
and then shot a passing bird.

When the ship arrived at Panama without them,
Los Rios declared that he would leave such fool-
hardy creatures to their fate ; but he was presently
persuaded to send another ship, which found Pizarro
Discovery of   and his party after they had staid seven
Peru.   months upon Gorgona. The skill of the
pilot Ruiz now came into play, and in this little
ship the party made a voyage of discovery, landed
at Tumbez, and admired the arts and wealth of one
of the most important of the Inca's cities. Thence
they continued coasting beyond the site of Tru-
jillo, more than 600 miles south of the equator,
when, having seen enough to convince them that
they had actually found the golden kingdom, they
returned to Panama, carrying with them live
llamas, fine garments of vicuña wool, curiously
wrought vases of gold and silver, and two or three
young Peruvians to be taught to speak Spanish
and serve as interpreters.

Enough had now been ascertained to make it
desirable for Pizarro to go to Spain and put the

borne in mind that the sixteenth century was a theatrical age,
i. e. the sober realities of that time are theatrical material for
our own. It is interesting and curious to see how differently Mr.
Prescott regards Pizarro's act : — "He announced his own purpose in a laconic but decided manner, characteristic of a man
more accustomed to act than to talk, and well calculated to make
an impression on his rough followers." — *Conquest of Peru*,
Book II. chap. iv.

enterprise upon a more independent footing. On his arrival at Seville in the summer of 1528, it was his luck to encounter the lawyer Enciso, who straightway clapped him into jail for a small debt which dated from the founding of Darien some eighteen years before. But the discoverer of Peru was now in high favour at court; so the man of red tape was snubbed, and Pizarro went on to Toledo to pay his respects to the emperor. The story of his romantic adventures made him the hero of the hour. He was ennobled by letters patent, and so were the comrades who had crossed the line with him at Gallo. He was appointed captain-general and *adelantado* of Peru, titles which he was to make good by conquering that country for thrifty Charles V.; and so in 1530 he returned to Panama, taking with him his four brothers and a small party of enthusiastic followers.

Pizarro's visit to Spain.

Of all the brothers Fernando was the eldest and the only legitimate son of his father. His character has perhaps suffered somewhat at the hands of historians through the sympathy that has been generally felt for the misfortunes of his enemy, the "under dog," Almagro. Fernando Pizarro was surely the ablest and most intelligent of the family. He had received a good education. To say that he was not more harsh or unscrupulous than his brethren is faint commendation; but there were times when he showed signal clemency. Gonzalo and Juan Pizarro were full brothers of Francisco, but much younger; Martinez de Alcántara was son of the same frail

The Pizarro brothers.

mother by a different father. As soldiers all were conspicuous for bull-dog tenacity and ranked among the bravest of the brave.

It was with an ill grace that Almagro saw so many of his partner's family coming to share in the anticipated glory and booty. He instantly recognized Fernando's commanding influence and felt himself in a measure thrust into the background. Thus the seeds of a deadly feud were not long in sowing themselves.

Seeds of strife.

In December, 1531, the Pizarros started in advance, with about 200 men and 50 horses. When they arrived at Tumbez in the following spring, they learned that a civil war was raging. The conquering Inca, Huayna Capac, had died in 1523 and was succeeded by his lawful heir Huascar, son of his Coya, or only legitimate wife. The next in succession, according to Peruvian rules, seems to have been Manco, of whom we shall have more to say presently. But the late Inca had a son by one of his concubines, the daughter of a vanquished chief or tribal king of the Quitus; and this son Atahualpa had been a favourite with his father. When Huascar came to the throne, Atahualpa was made ruler of Quito, apparently in accordance with his father's wishes. Under no circumstances was Atahualpa eligible for the position of reigning Inca. He was neither the child of a Coya nor of a woman of pure Inca blood, but of a foreign woman, and was therefore an out and out bastard. About three years before the arrival of the Spaniards, however, Atahualpa, with the aid of two powerful chief

Civil war in Peru and usurpation of Atahualpa.

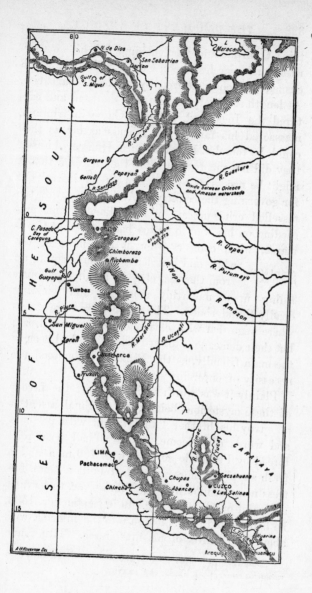

tains, Quizquiz and Chalcuchima, left his own territory and marched upon Cuzco. The war which ensued was characterized by wholesale barbarity. At length Atahualpa's chieftains defeated and captured the Inca, and, entering Cuzco in triumph, massacred his family and friends as far as they could be found. But the Inca Huascar himself they did not put to death, for they realized that it might be necessary to use him as an instrument for governing the country.[1] Atahualpa put on the tasselled crimson cap, or Inca diadem, and proceeding on his way to Cuzco had arrived at Caxamarca, when couriers brought him news of the white and bearded strangers coming up from the sea, clad in shining panoply, riding upon unearthly monsters, and wielding deadly thunderbolts. The new-comers were everywhere regarded with extreme wonder and dread, but their demeanour toward the natives had been in the main friendly, as the Pizarros understood the necessity of enforcing strict discipline.

Arrival of the Spaniards.

Plainly it was worth while to court the favour of these mysterious beings, and Atahualpa sent as an envoy his brother Titu Atauchi with presents and words of welcome. Pizarro had been reinforced by Fernando de Soto with 100 men and a fresh supply of horses; he had built a small fortress near the mouth of the Piura river, to serve as a base of operations; and late in September, 1532, he had started on his march into the interior, with about two thirds of his little force. Titu found

[1] Somewhat as Cortes used Montezuma; see Garcilasso, *Comentarios reales*, pt. i. lib. ix. cap. xxxvi.

him at Zaran, a village among the foothills of the
Andes. When Garcilasso [1] tells us that the envoy
humbled himself before Pizarro and addressed
him as " son of Viracocha," he reveals They were supposed to be " sons of Viracocha."
the theory which the Peruvians doubt-
less held concerning the new-comers.
Viracocha was the counterpart of Zeus, the sky-
god, arising from the sea-foam, the power that
gathers the clouds and delights in thunder. Like
Apollo and other Greek solar deities he was conceived as fair in complexion with bright or golden
hair. After the conquest of Peru the name *viracocha* passed into a common noun meaning " white
man," and it is still used in this sense at the present day.[2] For the red man to call the white stranger a child of Viracocha might under some circumstances be regarded as a form of ceremonious
politeness, or the phrase might even be a mere
descriptive epithet; but under the circumstances
of Titu's visit to Pizarro we can hardly doubt that
the new-comers were really invested with supernatural terrors, that the feeling of the Peruvians
was like that which had led the Mexicans at first
to take it for granted that their visitors must be
children of Quetzalcoatl. Upon any other supposition it does not seem possible to understand the
events that followed.

After receiving and dismissing the envoy with as-
surances of friendship, Pizarro pushed on through
the mountains and entered Caxamarca on the 15th
of November. It was a town of about 2,000 in-

---

[1] *Comentarios reales*, pt. ii. lib. i. cap. xix.
[2] Brinton, *Myths of the New World*, p. 180.

habitants.[1] The houses were chiefly of adobe
brick with thatched roofs, but some were built of
hewn stones laid together without cement. Around the great open square,
which might serve as market-place or mustering
ground, were what the Spaniards called capacious
barracks. Hard by was a temple of the Sun, with
a convent of vestals charged with the care of the
sacred fire. The town was overlooked by a circular tower of defence, girt with a rampart ascending spirally, somewhat, I fancy, as in old pictures
of the tower of Babel. On a rising ground some
two miles distant was encamped Atahualpa's army,
— some thousands of Indians in quilted cotton
doublets, with bucklers of stiff hide, long bronze-
pointed lances and copper-headed clubs, as well as
bows, slings, and lassos, in the use of which these
warriors were expert. Toward nightfall Fernando
Pizarro and Fernando de Soto, with five-and-thirty
horsemen, went to visit the self-styled Inca in his
quarters, and found him surrounded with chieftains
and bedizened female slaves. After introducing
themselves and inviting Atahualpa to a conference
with their commander next day in the market-
place, the cavaliers withdrew. On both sides the
extreme of ceremonious politeness had been observed.[2] Surely so strange an interview was never

Caxamarca.

---

[1] It is well described in " A True Account of the Province of
Cuzco," by Pizarro's secretary, Francisco de Xeres, in Markham's
Reports on the Discovery of Peru, London, 1872 (Hakluyt Society).

[2] Except for a moment when Soto's steed, at the malicious and
prudent touch of his rider's spur, pranced and curvetted, to the
intense dismay of half-a-dozen dusky warriors, whom Atahualpa,
after the departure of the visitors, promptly beheaded for show-

seen save when Montezuma ushered Cortes into the city of Mexico. Between the two cases there was an essential likeness. It is clear that Atahualpa and his men were paralyzed with superstitious dread, while the Spaniards on their part were well aware that according to all military principles they had thrust themselves into a very dangerous position. As they looked out that anxious night upon the mountain-slope before them, gleaming with innumerable watch-fires, we are told that many were profoundly dejected. The leaders saw that there must not be a moment's delay in taking advantage of the superstitious fears of the Indians. They must at once get possession of this Inca's person. Here, of course, the Pizarros took their cue from Cortes. In repeating the experiment they showed less subtlety and more brutality than the conqueror of Mexico; and while some allowance must be made for differences in the situation, one feels nevertheless that the native wit of Cortes had a much keener edge than that of his imitators.

Atahualpa must have passed the night in quite as much uneasiness as the Spaniards. When he came next day strongly escorted into the market-place he found no one to receive him, for Pizarro had skillfully concealed his men in the neighbouring houses. Presently a solitary white man, the priest Valverde, came forth to greet the Inca, and proceeded — through one of the interpreters here-

ing fright (Zarate, *Conquista del Peru*, ii. 4); an interesting touch of human nature! Garcilasso (pt. i. lib. ix. cap. xvi.) gives a vivid account of the uncontrollable agonies of terror with which the Peruvians regarded horses.

tofore mentioned — to read him a long-winded dis-
quisition on dogmatic theology and church history,
beginning with the creation of Adam and passing
stage by stage to the calling of St. Peter, and so
on to the bull by which Alexander VI. had given
the kingdom of the Incas (along with other realms

Capture of
Atahualpa. too numerous to mention) to the Most
Catholic King. In conclusion Ata-
hualpa was summoned, under penalty of fire and
sword, to acknowledge the papal supremacy and
pay tribute to Charles V.[1] Of this precious rig-
marole the would-be Inca probably fathomed just
enough to be convinced that the mysterious strangers, instead of being likely to lend him aid, were
an obstacle of unknown strength to be reckoned
with ; and in a fit of petulant disappointment he
threw upon the ground the Bible which the priest
had handed him. As soon as this was reported to
Pizarro the war-cry "Santiago!" resounded, the
ambushed Spaniards rushed forth and seized Atahualpa, and for two hours a butchery went on in
which some hundreds of his bewildered followers
perished.

The success of this blow was such as the wildest
imagination could not have foreseen. Here at the
crisis of the war the superhuman "sons of Viracocha" had come upon the scene and taken matters into their own hands. They held the person
of the sacrilegious usurper Atahualpa, and men

---

[1] There is a good abstract of this speech, with some eminently
sound critical remarks, in Helps's *Spanish Conquest*, vol. iii. pp.
533–541. Compare the famous *Requerimiento* of Dr. Palacios
Rubios, *id.*, vol. i. pp. 379–384.

who had rashly come too near them had been slain with unearthly weapons, struck down as if by lightning. The people were dumb and helpless. The strangers treated Atahualpa politely, and such edicts as they issued through him were obeyed in some parts of the country.

His first thought was naturally for his liberation. Confined in a room twenty-two feet in length by seventeen in width, he made a mark upon the wall as high as he could reach with his hand, and offered as ransom gold enough to fill the room up to that height. Pizarro accepted the offer, and the gold began to be collected, largely in the shape of vases and other orna- *Ransom collected for Atahualpa.* ments of temples. But it came in more slowly than Atahualpa had expected, and in June, 1533, the stipulated quantity was not yet complete. In some towns the priests dismantled the sacred edifices and hid their treasures, waiting apparently for the crisis to pass. The utter paralysis of the people in presence of the white men was scarcely matched by anything in the story of Cortes. While the treasure was collecting, Fernando Pizarro, with twenty horsemen and half-a-dozen arquebusiers, made a journey of four hundred miles through the heart of the country to the famous temple of Pachacamac, and although they boldly desecrated the sacred shrine they went and came unmolested![1]

[1] The people believed that no one but the consecrated priests of Pachacamac could enter the shrine of the wooden idol without instantly perishing. So when Fernando Pizarro coolly walked in and smashed the "graven image," and had the shrine demolished, and made the sign of the cross as "an invincible weapon against the Devil," they concluded that he must be a god who knew

Soon after Fernando's return to Caxamarca, in April, Almagro arrived at that town, with his party of 150 soldiers and 84 horses. In June the enormous spoil of gold, equivalent to more than $15,000,000 in modern reckoning, besides a vast amount of silver, was divided among the children of the sky-god. Almagro's newly arrived men wished to share equally with the others, and as they were obliged to content themselves with a much smaller portion, there was fresh occasion for ill-feeling between Almagro and the Pizarros.

Fernando Pizarro was now sent to Spain with the emperor's share of the plunder. Atahualpa placed more trust in him than in the others, and gave expression to a fear that his own safety was imperilled by his departure. The atmosphere seems to have been heavy with intrigue.

Murder of the captive Inca Huascar by Atahualpa. From Cuzco the imprisoned Inca Huascar offered the Spaniards a treasure still larger than they had as yet received, on condition that they would set him free and support him against Atahualpa. The latter heard of this, and soon afterward Huascar was secretly murdered. At the same time the Spaniards, still uneasy and suspicious, as was natural, had reason to believe that Atahualpa was privately sending forth instructions to his chieftains to arouse their parts of the country. When one is driven to despair, one is ready to fight even against sky-gods. Pizarro saw that it would not do for

what he was about, and with whom it would be unsafe to interfere. See Squier's *Peru*, p. 65; Markham, *Reports on the Discovery of Peru*, London, 1872, p. 83.

a moment to allow such proceedings. A savage display of power seemed necessary; and so Atahualpa, having been brought to trial for conspiracy against the white men, for the murder of his brother, and for divers other crimes, even including idolatry and polygamy, was duly convicted and sentenced to be burned at the stake. On his consenting to accept baptism the sentence was commuted for a milder one, and on the 29th of August, in the public square at Caxamarca, Atahualpa, was strangled with a bow-string. At this time Fernando de Soto was absent; on his return he denounced the execution as both shameful and rash. As to the shamefulness of the transaction modern historians can have but one opinion. Personal sympathy, of course, would be wasted upon such a bloodthirsty wretch as Atahualpa; but as for the Spaniards, it would seem that perfidy could no farther go than to accept an enormous ransom from a captive and then put him to death. As a question of military policy, divorced from considerations of morality, the case is not so clear. The Spaniards were taking possession of Peru by the same sort of right as that by which the lion springs upon his prey; there was nothing that was moral about it, and their consciences were at no time scrupulous as to keeping faith with heretics or with heathen. They were guided purely by considerations of their own safety and success, and they slew Atahualpa in the same spirit that Napoleon murdered the Duke d'Enghien, because they deemed it good policy to do so. In this Pizarro and Almagro

Atahualpa put to death by the Spaniards.

were agreed; Soto and a few others were of a different opinion, and it is not easy now to tell which side conceived the military situation most correctly.

In order to control the country Pizarro must control the person of the Inca, and that sovereign must understand that to conspire against the " sons of Viracocha " was simply to bring down sure and swift destruction upon himself. There was reason for believing that Atahualpa's usurped authority was not so willingly recognized by the country as that of the genuine Inca; and Pizarro had expressed an intention of bringing Huascar to Caxamarca and deciding between his claims and those of Atahualpa, when his purpose was frustrated by the assassination of the former. It thus appears that there was a valid political reason for holding Atahualpa responsible for the murder.

For the present Pizarro proclaimed Toparca, one of Atahualpa's sons, but the lad fell sick and died within a few weeks. Symptoms of anarchy were here and there manifested; in some towns there were riots, and distant chieftains prepared to throw off their allegiance. On the march to Cuzco, which began late in September, the Spaniards, now about 500 in number, were for the first time attacked. The assailants were 6,000 Indians, led by Atahualpa's brother, Titu Atauchi, but the Spaniards beat them off without serious loss. Pizarro laid the blame of this attack upon the chieftain Chalcuchima, whom he had with him, and the Indian was accordingly burned at the stake for an example. A few days afterward, Manco, already mentioned as next to Huascar in the customary line of succession, came to the Spanish camp and made his submission in due form. It was a great and decisive triumph for Pizarro. He lost no time in proclaiming the new Inca under the style of Manco Capac Yupanqui, and on the 15th of November, 1533, the sovereign and his supernatural guardians made a solemn entry into Cuzco, where the usual inaugural ceremonies and festivities took place. It was the anniversary of Pizarro's entry into Caxamarca. In that one eventful year he had overthrown the usurper, and now, as he placed the crimson cap upon the head of the legitimate Inca, might it not seem that he had completed the conquest of the golden kingdom? Relying upon the superstitious awe which had helped him to such an astounding result, he ventured in the course of the next four months to set up a Spanish municipal government in Cuzco, to seize upon divers houses and public buildings for his followers, and to convert the Temple of the Sun into a Dominican monastery.

The true Inca, Manco, makes his submission, and is inaugurated at Cuzco by Pizarro.

The chieftain Quizquiz, with a portion of Atahualpa's forces, held out against the new Inca, whereupon Almagro in a brief campaign drove him into the Quito territory and overpowered him. Meanwhile the news of all these wonderful events had reached the ears of Pedro de Alvarado in Guatemala, and not yet satiated with adventure, that cavalier, with 500 followers, sailed for the South American coast, landed in

Pedro de Alvarado.

the bay of Caraques, and after a terrible march through the wilderness, in which one fourth of the number perished, he came up with Almagro at Riobamba. After some parley, as his men showed symptoms of deserting to Almagro, Alvarado came to the conclusion that it would be wiser not to interfere in this part of the world. He consented to be bought off for a good round sum, and went back to Guatemala, leaving most of his men to recruit the Spanish forces in Peru.

The arrival of Fernando Pizarro in Spain, with his load of gold and his tale of adventure, aroused such excitement as had hardly been felt since the return of Columbus from his first voyage across the Sea of Darkness. Again Span-

Effect of the
news in Spain.

iards began flocking to the New World, and ships plied frequently between Panama and the shores of the Inca's country. For commercial purposes a seat of government on the coast was preferable to Cuzco, and accordingly on the 6th of January, 1535, Francisco Pizarro founded the city of Lima. While he was busy in laying out streets and putting up houses his brother Fernando returned from Spain. Francisco had been created a marquis and the territory subject to his government had been described in the royal patent as extending southward 270 leagues from the river Santiago, in latitude 1° 20′ north. Provision had also been made for Almagro, but in such wise as to get him as far out of the way as possible. He was appointed governor of the country to the south of Pizarro's, with the title of marshal. Pizarro's province was to be called New Castile;

Almagro's, which covered Chili, or the greater part of it, was to be called New Toledo.

Thus with fair phrases Almagro was virtually set aside; he was told that he might go and conquer a new and unknown country for himself, while the rich country already won was to be monopolized by the Pizarros. Theirs was the bird in the hand, his the bird in the bush; and no wonder that his wrath waxed hot against Fernando. In this mood he insisted that at any rate the city of Cuzco fell south of the boundary-line, and therefore within his jurisdiction. This was not really the case, though its nearness to the line afforded ground for doubt, and something might depend upon the way in which the distance from the river Santiago was measured. Almagro was a weak man, apt to be swayed by the kind of argument that happened to be poured into his ears for the moment. At first he was persuaded to abandon his claim to Cuzco, and in the autumn of 1535 he started on his march for Chili, with 200 Spaniards and a large force of Indians led by the Inca's brother Paullu, and accompanied by the high priest or Villac Umu. There were to be stirring times before his return.

Three years had now elapsed since the seizure of Atahualpa, and two since the coronation of Manco, and quiet seems to have been generally maintained. But the Inca's opinion as to the character and business of the white strangers must needs have been modified by what was going on. If at first he may have welcomed their aid in overthrowing the rival party and helping him to his throne, he could now see unmistakable signs that they had come to stay. Spaniards were arriving by the ship - load; they were building towns, seizing estates and enslaving the people, despoiling temples, and otherwise comporting themselves as odious masters. Mere familiarity must have done something toward dispelling the glamour which had at first surrounded and protected them. Æsop's fox nearly died of fright on first seeing a lion, but by and by made bold to go up to him and ask him how he did. In an emergency it might be worth while to test the power of the new tyrants and see if they were really the sacred children of Viracocha. The departure of Almagro for Chili offered a favourable moment for an insurrection, and there is no doubt that the plans of the Inca and his friends were deliberately concerted. Almagro had not proceeded many days' march when Paullu and the Villac Umu deserted him with their Indians and hurried back toward Cuzco, while at the same time the Inca succeeded in escaping from the city. Now ensued the only serious warfare between Spaniard and Indian which the conquest of Peru involved. With astonishing suddenness and vehemence the rebellion broke out in many parts of the country, so that the communication between Cuzco and Lima was cut, and for some months the Spaniards in the one town did not know whether their friends in the other were alive or dead. Francisco Pizarro at Lima was fain to call for succour from Panama, Guatemala,

Manco plans an insurrection.

and Mexico. The Inca occupied the great Sacsahuaman fortress overlooking Cuzco, and laid siege
to the city, where Fernando was in command, with his brothers Gonzalo and   The Spaniards
besieged in
Juan. For six months, from February   Cuzco.
to August, 1536, the siege was closely pressed.
There were frequent and vigorous assaults, and
how the little band of Spaniards contrived to maintain themselves against such terrible odds is one
of the marvels of history. They not only held
their own within the walls, but made effective
sorties. Such prodigies of valour have rarely
been seen except in those books of chivalry that
turned Don Quixote's brain. Juan Pizarro was
slain in an assault upon the fortress, but Fernando at length succeeded in taking it by storm.
After a while the Inca began to find it difficult to
feed so many mouths. As September   Total defeat
approached, it was necessary, in order   of the Inca.
to avoid a famine, for large numbers to go home
and attend to their planting. With his force
thus reduced the Inca retired into the valley of
Yucay, where he encountered Almagro returning
from Chili. A battle ensued, and Manco was
defeated with great slaughter.

Almagro's men, after penetrating more than
three hundred miles into Chili, and enduring the
extremes of cold and hunger, without finding
wealthy towns or such occasions for pil-
lage as they expected, had at length be-   Almagro returns and
gun to murmur, and finally they per-   seizes Cuzco.
suaded their leader to return and renew his claim
to Cuzco. He arrived in time to complete the dis-

comfiture of the Inca, and then appeared before that city. He was refused admission, and an agreement was made by which he promised to remain encamped outside until the vexed question of jurisdiction could be peaceably determined. Some months of inaction passed, but at length, in April, 1537, Almagro was led to believe, perhaps correctly, that Fernando Pizarro was secretly strengthening the works, with the intention of holding the city against him. Almagro thereupon treated the agreement as broken, seized the city by surprise, and took Fernando and Gonzalo prisoners.

This act was the beginning of a period of eleven years of civil disturbance, in the course of which all the principal actors were swept off the stage, as in some cheap blood-and-thunder tragedy. For our purposes it is not worth while to recount the petty incidents of the struggle, — how Almagro was at one moment ready to submit to arbitration and the next moment refused to abide by the decision ; how Fernando was set at liberty and Gonzalo escaped ; how Almagro's able lieutenant, Rodrigo de Orgoñez, won a victory over Pizarro's men at Abançay, but was totally defeated by Fernando Pizarro at Las Salinas and perished on the field ; how at last Fernando had Almagro tried for sedition and summarily executed. On which side was the more violence and treachery it would be hard to say. Indeed, as Sir Arthur Helps observes, " in this melancholy story it is difficult to find anybody whom the reader can sympathize much with." So far as our story of the conquest

Civil war ; execution of Almagro ; and final defeat of the Inca.

of Peru is concerned, we may observe the Spaniards once, in a leisure interval among their own
squabbles, turning their attention to it! After
his victory at Abançay in July, 1537, Orgoñez
completed the overthrow of the Inca Manco, scattered his army, and drove him to an inaccessible
fastness in the mountains.

Almagro's execution was in July, 1538, and the
next year Fernando Pizarro thought it prudent to
return to Castile, with an enormous quantity of
gold, and give his own account of the late troubles.
But, as already observed, the Spanish government
was liable to resent too summary measures on the
part of its servants in the Indies, and much de-
pended upon the kind of information it obtained
in the first place. On this occasion it How Fernan-
got its first impressions from friends of do Pizarro was
                                          received in
Almagro, and it fared ill with the other in Spain.
side. Fernando was kept under surveillance at
Medina del Campo for more than twenty years,
and was then allowed to go home to his estate in
Estremadura, where he died in 1578, at the age, it
is said, of one hundred and four years.

After his brother's departure the Marquis Pizarro had some further trouble with the Inca,
who from time to time renewed a desultory warfare among the mountains. It was but a slight
annoyance, however. Peru was really conquered,
and Pizarro was able to send out expeditions to
great distances. In March, 1540, Pedro de Valdivia set out for Chili and remained there seven
years, in the course of which he founded Valpa-
raiso (September 3, 1544) and other towns, and

for the moment seemed to have conquered the country. Nevertheless it was here that Valdivia's conquest of Chili. the Spaniards encountered more formidable opposition than anywhere else in America. On Valdivia's return to his colony in 1549 its very existence was imperilled by the assaults of the Araucanians. These valiant Indians, led by their illustrious chieftains, Caupolican and Lautaro, maintained a warfare which has been celebrated in the famous epic poem of Alonso de Ercilla, who was one of the Spanish officers engaged.[1] In this struggle Valdivia perished. Other governors until the end of the century found the Araucanians unconquerable; and, indeed, even to the present day this aboriginal American people may boast, with the Montenegrins of the Balkan peninsula, that they have never bent their necks to the yoke of the foreigner.

To return to the Marquis Pizarro: in 1539 he put his brother Gonzalo in command over the province of Quito, which had been conquered by Benalcazar, and on Christmas of that year Gonzalo started to explore the cinnamon forests to the eastward. A memorable affair it was, and placed this Pizarro in a conspicuous place among men of incredible endurance. His little army of 350 Expedition of Gonzalo Pizarro in search of El Dorado. Spaniards (attended at the outset by 4,000 Indians) crossed the Andes and plunged deeper and deeper into the wilderness, until food grew scarce. Then, lured

---

[1] Ercilla, *La Araucana*, Madrid, 1776, 2 vols. 12°. Lope de Vega wrote a play on the same subject, "Arauco Domado," in his *Comedias*, tom. xx., Madrid, 1629.

on by false reports of a rich and fruitful country ahead (mayhap, another golden kingdom! why not?) they pressed onward, with great exertion built a small vessel capable of carrying part of their company and their baggage, and so, partly on water, partly on land, made their way down the Napo river, one of the tributaries of the Amazon. Hearing now that the rich country was to be found at the confluence of the Napo with the greater river, Gonzalo sent Francisco de Orellana ahead with fifty men in the brigantine to gather supplies, and return. When Orellana reached the region in question he found scant sustenance there, and decided that it would be impossible to force his vessel back against the powerful current. It was easier to keep on down stream and see if some golden kingdom might not be found upon its banks. So Orellana basely left his comrades in the lurch, and Orellana's descent of the Amazon. sailed down the Amazon 4,000 miles to its mouth, a most astounding exploit in the navigation of an unknown and very dangerous river. Escaping the perils of starvation, shipwreck, and savages, Orellana came out upon the ocean and made his way to the island of Cubagua, whence he went soon afterward to Spain, and succeeded in raising an expedition to return and make conquests in the Amazon country,[1] but his death and the remonstrances of Portugal frustrated this attempt.

[1] "The name of river of the Amazons was given to it because Orellana and his people beheld the women on its banks fighting as valiantly as the men. . . . It is not that there are Amazons on that river, but that they said there were, by reason of the valour of the women." Garcilasso (Markham's transl.), lib. viii. cap. xxii.

One of Orellana's companions, who had boldly denounced as cowardly and treacherous his intention of deserting Pizarro, was left behind to starve in the forest, but contrived to keep himself alive till Gonzalo arrived at the mouth of the Napo, and found him, a mere skeleton. On learning his story it became evident that there was nothing to do but make the best of their way back to Quito. After

Gonzalo's return to Quito. one of the most terrible marches recorded in history, a march in which more than two thirds of the company perished, Gonzalo brought the famished survivors into Quito in June, 1542, and there he was met by unwelcome news. During the two and a half years of his absence great changes had taken place.

For a time everything had gone prosperously with Francisco Pizarro. The rage for silver and gold had brought thousands of Spaniards into the country, and by taking advantage of the system of military roads and posts already existing, they were soon better able than the Incas had ever been to hold all that territory in complete subjection. Pizarro was fond of building and gardening, and took much interest in introducing European cereals and other vegetables into Peru. While he was engaged in such occupations his enemies were lay-

The Marquis Pizarro and the " men of Chili." ing plots. His brother Fernando, on leaving the country, had warned him against the "men of Chili," as Almagro's partisans were called. But the marquis did not profit by the warning. A man of tact, like Cortes, would have won over these malcontents by extending to them judicious favours and making them feel it to be for their interest to come to his support. But Pizarro had neither the generosity nor the sagacity to adopt such a course, nor had he the prudence of his brother Fernando. He treated the men of Chili with rudeness and severity, and still was careless about guarding himself. To such straits, it is said, were some of these men reduced thrcugh persecutions that could be traced to Pizarro, that a dozen cavaliers, who happened to have their quarters in the same house, had only one cloak among them, which they used to take their turns in wearing, the cloaked man going out while the others staid at home.[1] After a while some of these ill-used men conspired to murder Pizarro, and on Sunday, June 26, 1541, nineteen of them, led by a very able officer named Juan de Rada, boldly made their way into the governor's palace at Lima just as he was finishing his mid-day dinner, and in a desperate assault, in which several of the conspirators fell under Pizarro's sword, they succeeded in killing the sturdy old man, along with his half-brother Alcántara and other friends.[2] Almagro's illegitimate half-breed son, commonly called "Almagro the lad," was now proclaimed governor of Peru by the conspirators. But his day was a short one. It happened that Charles V. had sent out a learned judge, Vaca de Castro, to advise with Pizarro concerning the government of his province, and with characteristic prudence had authorized him in case

Assassination of Pizarro.

[1] Herrera, dec. vi. lib. viii. cap. vi.
[2] The scene is most graphically described by Prescott, in his *Conquest of Peru*, bk. iv. chap. v.

of Pizarro's death to assume the government himself. Castro had just arrived at Popayan when he was met there by the news of the assassination. Finding himself sure of the allegiance of some of

The "bloody plains of Chupas."

Pizarro's principal captains, as Benalcazar and Alonso de Alvarado, he proclaimed himself governor, and in the battle of Chupas, September 16, 1542, he defeated young Almagro, who was forthwith tried for treason and beheaded in the great square at Cuzco.

Gonzalo Pizarro loyally gave in his allegiance to the new governor, and retired to his private estate in Charcas, south of Lake Titicaca. The troubles, however, were not yet over. In the next chapter we shall see how Indian slavery grew up

The New Laws, and the rebellion of Gonzalo Pizarro.

in the New World, and how through the devoted labours of Las Casas measures were taken for its abolition. It was in 1542 that Las Casas, after a quarter of a century of heroic effort, won his decisive victory in the promulgation of the edicts known as the "New Laws." These edicts, as we shall see, resulted in the gradual abolition of Indian slavery. If they had been put into operation according to their first intent they would have worked an immediate abolition, and the act of confiscation would have applied to nearly all the Spaniards in Peru. The New Laws therefore aroused furious opposition, and the matter was made still worse by the violent temper of the new viceroy, Blasco Nuñez Vela, who arrived in Lima early in 1544, charged with the duty of enforcing them. From arbitrary imprisonment Vela's vio-

lence extended to open and shameless murder, until at length the people rose in rebellion, and Gonzalo Pizarro came forth from his retirement to lead
them. After a year of turbulence a battle was
fought near Quito, January 18, 1546, in which
poor, half-crazed Vela was defeated and slain, and
Gonzalo became master of Peru.

But his triumph was short-lived. The Spanish
government sent out a wily and smooth-tongued
ecclesiastic, a military priest and member of the
Council of the Inquisition, Pedro de la Pedro de la
Gasca, armed with extensive powers for Gasca.
settling all the vexed questions. Gasca's most
effective weapon was the repeal of those clauses of
the New Laws which demanded the immediate
abolition of slavery. These clauses were repealed,
and preparations were made for the compromise
hereafter to be described. But for these preliminaries Gasca would probably have accomplished
little. As it was, his honeyed tongue found no
difficulty in winning over the captains of Pizarro's
fleet at Panama. They had been sent there to
watch the situation, and, if necessary, to prevent
Gasca from proceeding farther, or to bribe him to
join Pizarro, or perhaps to seize him and carry him
to Peru as a prisoner. But this crafty man, "this
Cortes in priestly garments," as Sir Arthur Helps
calls him, talked so well that the captains put the
fleet at his disposal and conveyed him to Tumbez,
where he landed June 13, 1547. It was still open
to Pizarro to maintain that he had not taken up
arms against the crown, but only against a tyranni-
cal viceroy and in defence of the emperor's loyal

subjects. It was rather a difficult position, but Vela's conduct had been such as to lend it strong support, and had Gonzalo Pizarro been richer in mental resources he might have carried it off successfully. As it was, he had great and not unmerited confidence in his own military ability, and unwisely decided to hold out against Gasca.

For a moment events seemed to favour Pizarro. An able captain, Diego de Centeno, who through all these vicissitudes had remained loyal to the crown, now captured Cuzco for Gasca; whereupon a campaign ensued which ended in the total overthrow of Centeno in the bloody battle of Huarina, near Lake Titicaca, October 20, 1547. This gleam of success was but momentary. Nowhere was the sword to be found that could prevail against Gasca's tongue. Such wholesale defection as suddenly ruined Gonzalo Pizarro has seldom been seen. When he encountered Gasca in person, on the plain of Sacsahuana, April 9, 1548, his soldiers began deserting by scores. As one company after another contrived to slip away and flee into the arms of the royalists, Gonzalo's quaint lieutenant, Carvajal, a weather-beaten veteran of the wars in Italy, kept humming with grim facetiousness the words of an old Spanish ditty : —

Defeat and execution of Gonzalo Pizarro.

> Estos mis cabellos, madre,
> Dos á dos me los lleva el ayre.[1]

---

[1] As Helps renders it, "These my hairs, mother, two by two the breeze carries them away." *Spanish Conquest*, vol. iv. p. 258. The best description of Gonzalo's rebellion is the one given by Helps.

After a faint pretence of fighting, in which fifteen men were killed, Pizarro, finding himself without an army, quietly rode over to Gasca's camp and surrendered himself. On the following day he was beheaded, while old Carvajal, in his eighty-fifth year, was hanged and quartered, and this was the end of the sway of the Pizarros in the land of the Incas. All except Fernando died by violence. The victorious Gasca proved himself an adept in hanging and beheading, but accomplished little else. After his bloody assizes he returned to Spain in 1550, and was rewarded with a bishopric. In 1553 there was a brief epilogue of rebellion in Peru, under the lead of Hernandez Giron, who was beheaded in 1554.

A new era began under the able administration of Andrea Hurtado de Mendoza, Marquis of Cañete, who came out in 1556. The con- Arrival of Mendoza. quest of Peru may with his viceroyalty be pronounced complete ; in other words, not only had the Indians been conquered, but their unruly conquerors were at last overcome, and into the country, thus reduced to order, more than 8,000 Spaniards had come to stay.

Considering the story of the conquest of Peru as a whole, we cannot but be · struck with the slightness of the resistance made by the people. Except for the spirited siege of Cuzco by the Inca Manco, there was no resistance worthy of the name. The conquerors turned temples into churches and enslaved the people, and yet in the midst of this large population a handful of Spaniards were able to squabble among themselves and kill each other with as little concern as if they had been in an empty country. Evidently this society in which governmental control had been so far developed at the expense of individualism was a society where it did not make much difference to the people what master they served. To conquer such a country it was only necessary to get control of the machinery of administration. I think it may have been a perception of this state of things that encouraged Atahualpa to make his attempt to overthrow the legitimate line of Incas. He doubtless hoped, with the aid of the men of Quito and other imperfectly conquered provinces, to get control of Cuzco and the system of military posts and roads radiating therefrom, believing that thus he could maintain himself in power in spite of the fact that his birth disqualified him for the position of supreme Inca. His success would have been a revolution; and it is instructive to see him trying to provide against the opposition of the Inca caste by keeping the genuine Inca a captive in his hands instead of putting him to death. By thus controlling all the machinery of government, the captive Inca included, Atahualpa evidently had no occasion to fear anything like popular insurrection. Whether his scheme would have succeeded must, of course, remain doubtful; but it is extremely curious to see the Spaniards at the critical moment step in and beat him at his own game, without more than half understanding what they were doing. In capturing Atahualpa there is no doubt that Pizarro took his cue from Cortes, but between the seizure of Atahualpa and that of Montezuma the points of difference were more important than the points of likeness. It is customary to speak of Atahualpa as "the last Inca," and I suppose the fact is commonly forgotten that he was really only governor of Quito, a victorious usurper who had just begun to call himself the Inca, but had not been formally invested with that supreme dignity. Garcilasso expressly declares that the people — by whom he means the members of his own Inca caste and their loyal dependents — were grateful to the white man for overthrowing the usurper who had first captured and finally murdered their true Inca Huascar. "They said that the Spaniards had put the tyrant to death as a punishment and to avenge the Incas; and that the god Viracocha, the father of the Spaniards, had ordered them to do it. This is the reason they called the first Spaniards by the name of Viracocha, and believing they were sons of their god, they respected them so much that they almost worshipped them, and scarcely made any resistance to the conquest." [1]

This explanation, from so high an authority as Garcilasso Inca, shows us clearly why resistance to the Spaniards did not fairly begin until three years after the seizure of Atahualpa; and then, when the legitimate Inca Manco headed the attack upon the Spaniards, not only had their numbers greatly increased, but they had already secured control of a great part of the governmental

[1] Garcilasso, pt. i. lib. v. cap. xxi., Markham's translation.

machinery, and to the mass of the people a mere change of masters was not a matter of vital importance.

After the decisive defeat of Manco Capac by Orgoñez in 1537, that Inca retired to an almost inaccessible fastness in the great fork of the Andes where the river Marañon takes its rise, and there he kept up a kind of court. From that point he now and then made a sudden descent and attacked

Fate of the Inca Manco.

the Spaniards, but accomplished little or nothing. His end was a strange one, with a touch of the comical. When Juan de Rada and his party were crossing the great square at Lima, on their way to assassinate the Marquis Pizarro, one of the company, a certain Gomez Perez, was observed to step out of the way to avoid wetting his shoes in a puddle. "What!" cried the fierce Rada, "here are we about to wade up to our knees in blood, and you are afraid of a pool of water! Go home, you silly fop, you are no fit company for the like of us!" After the overthrow of young Almagro at Chupas, this Gomez Perez, with others of that faction, took refuge at the Inca's little court in the mountains, where they were hospitably received. On the arrival of Blasco Nuñez Vela in 1544 there were negotiations between that viceroy and the Inca, which resulted in Manco's giving in his allegiance to the Emperor Charles V. Gomez Perez served as the Inca's messenger in these negotiations. He was an ill-mannered fellow, who took no pains to veil his contempt for "coloured men," and he was often rude to the Inca, who usually received his coarse words with quiet dignity. But one day, as the two were playing at ninepins some dispute arose, and the Spaniard became so abusive that Manco gave him a push, exclaiming, "Go away, you forget with whom you are speaking." Without another word Gomez, who had one of the big balls in his hand, hurled it at the Inca's head and killed him on the spot.[1] At the sight of this outrage the Indians who were present, watching the game, fell upon Gomez and slew him. The other Spaniards fled to their quarters, but the enraged Indians set fire to the building, and butchered them all as fast as they were driven out by the flames. Thus ignominiously perished the wretched remnant of the Almagro faction.

Manco was succeeded by his son Sayri Tupac, who for fourteen years continued to hold his court among the mountains. On the arrival of the Marquis of Cañete, negotiations were opened with this Inca, who consented to become a pen- End of the sioner of the Spaniards. The valley of Inca dynasty. Yucay was given him, and there he lived from 1558 until his death in 1560. His brother and successor, Titu Cusi Yupanqui, returned to Manco's mountain lair, and held court there for eleven years, resuming his practical independence. When

[1] Garcilasso, *Comentarios reales*, pt. ii. lib. iv. cap. vii. Mr. Prescott's account of this affair (*Conquest of Peru*, bk. iv. chap. iii.) is slightly misleading. Mr. Markham (in Winsor, *Narr. and Crit. Hist.*, vol. ii. p. 546) makes a strange mistake in the date, and the context shows that it is not a misprint; he says that Manco "met his death in 1553, after a disastrous reign of twenty years." Manco was crowned in 1533, and his death occurred in 1544, and in the eleventh year of his reign.

the viceroy Francisco de Toledo arrived, in **1571,** he determined to put a stop to this sort of thing, and events soon furnished him with a pretext. A missionary friar having gone to visit Titu Cusi at his court, the Inca suddenly fell sick and died, whereupon the friar was seized and put to death for sorcery. Titu Cusi was succeeded by his brother Tupac Amaru, a mere lad. Now the viceroy Toledo sent an army into the mountains, which broke up the Inca's court, slew many chieftains, and captured the Inca Tupac Amaru. The unfortunate youth was taken to Cuzco, and beheaded in revenge for the friar's death, and this was the **end of** the Inca dynasty.

CHAPTER XI.

LAS CASAS.

IT is curious to reflect that with the first arrival of civilized Europeans in this New World there should have come that plague of slavery which was so long to pollute and curse *The plague of slavery.* it, and from the complicated effects of which we shall not for long years yet succeed in fully recovering. Nor is it less curious to reflect how the fates of the continents America and Africa, with their red men and black men, became linked together, from the early time when Prince Henry of Portugal was making those exploring expeditions that prepared the way for the great discovery of Columbus. It was those expeditions upon the African coast that introduced slavery into the world in what we may distinguish as its modern form. For in the history of slavery there have been two quite distinct periods. The ancient slave was the prisoner captured in war, the αἰχμά- λωτος, in the picturesque phrase of the Greeks, which has been somewhat freely rendered as "fruit of the spear." We have observed that in the lower stage of barbarism captives *Ancient slavery.* are tortured to death; in the middle stage they are sacrificed to the gods, but as agriculture develops and society becomes settled they are more and more used as slaves; and in the upper stage of barbarism a complete system of slave-labour is developed. Doubtless this course of things was attended with some advantages in its day. Ancient slavery was a help in the coalescence of tribes into nations, and to enslave the captive was not quite so cruel as to roast him alive or cut him to pieces. With the advance of civilization ancient slavery slowly grew milder in type. The slaves of a Greek or a Roman were white men like himself, so that the element of race antipathy was absent. By slow degrees European slaves acquired customary rights and privileges and often became freemen.[1]   In general, after

[1] For a brief characterization of Roman slavery see Gibbon's *Decline and Fall*, chap. ii., with Guizot's and Milman's notes. The cruelties inflicted upon slaves in the days of the Roman republic were frightful, but in the general and remarkable improvement of Roman law in point of humanity under the emperors, the condition of the slaves was notably ameliorated. One among countless testimonies to the mildness of slavery in the fifth century of the Christian era is furnished by an interesting conversation which took place in the year 448 between the Roman historian Priscus and a certain versatile Greek who had become enamoured of wild life and was engaged in the service of the terrible Attila. Priscus says the Romans treat their slaves much more kindly than the Hunnish king treats the free warriors that follow his banner and divide the spoils of war. They deal with them as friends or brothers, teach them the Scriptures, nurse them tenderly in sickness, and are not allowed to inflict upon them cruel punishment; moreover, it is a common and highly esteemed practice to give them freedom either by last will and testament, or by deed during the master's lifetime. See Bury's *Later Roman Empire*, vol. i. p. 219. On the general subject, see Wallon, *Histoire de l'esclavage dans l'antiquité*, Paris, 1847, 3 vols.; Denis, *Histoire des théories et des idées morales dans l'antiquité*, Paris, 1856, tom. ii. pp. 55–218; Friedländer, *Mœurs romaines du règne d'Auguste à la fin des Antonins*, Paris,

making all due allowances, the face of the Christian Church was resolutely set against slavery, so that later wars and conquests created only such modified forms of it as serfdom and villenage. By the fifteenth century ancient slavery was dead in England, and moribund on the continent of Europe, when all at once and most unexpectedly modern slavery came into existence. In this modern system slavery *Modern slavery.* became an extensive branch of commerce. Men of weaker race, despised as heathen with red or black skins, were hunted and caught by thousands, and sold in places where there was a demand for cheap labour. There were features in this modern system as hideous as the worst features of the ancient system. And curiously enough, just as the progress of discovery in Africa had originated this wholesale traffic in men, the discovery of America opened up an immense field where there was soon to be a great and growing demand for cheap labour.

In 1441 Prince Henry's master of the robes, Antonio Gonçalvez, in a voyage along the Morocco coast, captured a few Moors and carried them to Portugal.[1] The next year these Moors begged Gonçalvez to take them back to *Its beginnings.* Morocco, and offered him a ransom in the shape of negro slaves. On hearing of this, Prince Henry told Gonçalvez by all means to exchange the Moors for negroes, because the former were obstinate

1865, tom. i. pp. 288–292; Ozanam, *History of Civilization in the Fifth Century,* London, 1868, vol. ii. pp. 36–43.

[1] See above, vol. i. p. 323.

infidels who would not give up their Mahometan faith, whereas the black men, being simply heathen, might more easily be persuaded to espouse Christianity.[1] Gonçalvez accordingly sailed, set free his Moors, and returned to Portugal with a small cargo of negro slaves. This transaction, in the year 1442, seems to have been the beginning of slavery in its especially modern form. After this many ship-loads of negroes were brought to Lisbon, and Prince Henry, in receiving his royal fifth of the proceeds of these expeditions, was known to take slaves along with buffalo hides and gold dust.

A graphic description of the arrival of a company of these poor creatures, brought by Lançarote in the year 1444, is given by an eye-witness, the kind-hearted Portuguese chronicler Azurara. "The other day," he says, "which was the eighth of August, very early in the morning by reason of the heat, the mariners began to bring to their vessels, and . . . to draw forth those captives . . . : whom, placed together on that plain, it was a marvellous sight to behold, for amongst them there were some of a reasonable degree of whiteness, handsome and well made; others less white, resembling leopards in their colour; others as black as Ethiopians, and so ill-formed, as well in their faces as in their bodies, that it seemed to the beholders as if they saw the forms of a lower world. But what heart was that, how hard soever, which was not pierced with sorrow,

Azurara's narrative.

---

[1] To doubt the sincerity of such an argument is to misunderstand Prince Henry and the age in which he lived.

seeing that company: for some had sunken cheeks, and their faces bathed in tears, looking at each other; others were groaning very dolorously, looking at the heights of the heavens . . . and crying out loudly, as if asking succour from the Father of nature; others struck their faces with their hands, throwing themselves on the earth; others made their lamentations in songs, according to the customs of their country, which, although we could not understand their language, we saw corresponded well to the height of their sorrow. But now . . . came those who had the charge of the distribution, and they began to put them apart one from the other, in order to equalize the portions; wherefore it was necessary to part children and parents, husbands and wives, and brethren from each other. Neither in the partition of friends and relations was any law kept, only each fell where the lot took him. . . . And while they were placing in one part the children that saw their parents in another, the children sprang up perseveringly and fled unto them; the mothers enclosed their children in their arms and threw themselves with them upon the ground, receiving wounds with little pity for their own flesh, so that their offspring might not be torn from them! And so, with labour and difficulty, they concluded the partition, for, besides the trouble they had with the captives, the plain was full of people, as well of the town as of the villages and neighbourhood around, who on that day gave rest to their hands the mainstay of their livelihood, only to see this novelty." [1]

[1] I quote from the version given by Sir Arthur Helps, in his

There we have the infernal picture, very much
as it was to be seen four hundred years later in
our own country, as so many of us can still remember. But for the discovery of America this
traffic in human beings would doubtless have been
greatly limited in extent and duration. The conditions of European agriculture and mining were
not such as to create a market for them. Natural
economic laws would have prevented slavery from
thriving in Europe, as they prevented it in New
England. But in the subtropical regions of the
New World slavery grew up quickly and sturdily,
as foul weeds sprout in a congenial soil. At first
it was a slavery of red men, and Columbus himself played an important part in establishing it.
When Columbus came to Hispaniola on his second
voyage, with 17 ships and 1,500 followers, he found
the relations between red men and white
men already hostile, and in order to
get food for so many Spaniards, foraging expeditions were undertaken, which made

Beginnings of
Indian slavery
under Colum-
bus.

Spanish Conquest, vol. i. pp. 37–39, since it would be impossible
to improve upon it. The original text is in Azurara, *Chronica
do descobrimento e conquista de Guiné*, Paris, 1841, pp. 132–134.
This chronicle was completed in 1453. Azurara goes on to give
another side to the picture, for being much interested in the poor
creatures he made careful inquiries and found that in general
they were treated with marked kindness. They became Christians, and were taught trades or engaged in domestic service;
they were also allowed to acquire property and were often set
free. This, however, was in the early days of modern slavery
and in the period of Prince Henry and his ideas. At a later date,
when Portuguese cruisers caught negroes by the hundred and
sold them at Seville, whence they were shipped to Hispaniola to
work in the mines, there was very little to relieve the blackness
of the transaction.

matters worse. This state of things led Columbus to devise a notable expedient. In some of the neighbouring islands lived the voracious Caribs. In fleets of canoes they would swoop upon the coasts of Hispaniola, capture men and women by the score, and carry them off to be cooked and eaten. Now Columbus wished to win the friendship of the Indians about him by defending them against these enemies, and so he made raids against the Caribs, took some of them captive, and sent them as slaves to Spain, to be taught Spanish and converted to Christianity, so that they might come back to the islands as interpreters, and thus be useful aids in missionary work. It was really, said Columbus, a kindness to these cannibals to enslave them and send them where they could be baptized and rescued from everlasting perdition; and then again they could be received in payment for the cargoes of cattle, seeds, wine, and other provisions which must be sent from Spain for the support of the colony. Thus quaintly did the great discoverer, like so many other good men before and since, mingle considerations of religion with those of domestic economy. It is apt to prove an unwholesome mixture. Columbus proposed such an arrangement to Ferdinand and Isabella, and it is to their credit that, straitened as they were for money, they for some time refused to accept it.

Slavery, however, sprang up in Hispaniola before any one could have fully realized the meaning of what was going on. As the Indians were unfriendly and food must be had, while foraging expeditions were apt to end in plunder and bloodshed, Columbus tried to regulate matters by prohibiting such expeditions and in lieu thereof im-

Tribute. posing a light tribute or tax upon the entire population of Hispaniola above fourteen years of age. As this population was dense, a little from each person meant a good deal in the lump. The tribute might be a small piece of gold or of cotton, and was to be paid four times a year. Every time that an Indian paid this tax, a small brass token duly stamped was to be given him to hang about his neck as a voucher. If there were Indians who felt unable to pay the tribute, they might as an alternative render a certain amount of personal service in helping to plant seeds or tend cattle for the Spaniards.

No doubt these regulations were well meant, and if the two races had been more evenly matched, perhaps they might not so speedily have developed into tyranny. As it was, they were like rules for regulating the depredations of wolves upon sheep. Two years had not elapsed before the alternative of personal service was demanded from whole villages of Indians at once. By 1499 the island had

Reparti- begun to be divided into *repartimientos,*
mientos. or shares. One or more villages would be ordered, under the direction of their native chiefs, to till the soil for the benefit of some specified Spaniard or partnership of Spaniards; and such a village or villages constituted the *repartimiento* of the person or persons to whom it was assigned. This arrangement put the Indians into a state somewhat resembling that of feudal villen-

age; and this was as far as things had gone when the administration of Columbus came abruptly to an end.

It will be remembered that in 1502 the Spanish sovereigns sent to Hispaniola a governor selected with especial care, a knight of the reli-

Ovando's treatment of white men.

gious order of Alcántara, named Nicolas de Ovando. He was a small, fair-haired man of mild and courteous manners, and had an excellent reputation for ability and integrity. We are assured on the most unimpeachable authority that he was a good governor for white men. As to what was most needed in that turbulent colony, he was a strict disciplinarian, and had his own summary way of dealing with insubordinate characters. When he wished to dispose of some such incipient Roldan he would choose a time to invite him to dinner, and then, after some polite and interested talk, whereby the guest was apt to feel highly flattered, Ovando would all at once point down to the harbour and blandly inquire, " In which of those ships, now ready to weigh anchor, would you like to go back to Spain ? " Then the dumbfoundered man would stammer, " My Lord, my Lord," and would perhaps plead that he had not money enough to pay his passage. " Pray do not let that trouble you," said this well-bred little governor, " it shall be my care to provide for that." And so without further ceremony the guest was escorted straight from dinner-table to ship.[1]

But this mild-spoken Ovando was capable of

[1] Las Casas, *Historia de las Indias*, tom. iii. p. 204.

strange deeds, and the seven years of his administration in Hispaniola were so full of horror that I
never can read his name without a shudder.   His
methods with Indians may be illustrated by his
treatment of Anacaona, wife of that chieftain Ca-
onabó who had been sent to Spain.[1]   Ovando
heard that the tribe, in which this woman exercised great authority, was meditating another attack upon the Spaniards, and he believed
that an ounce of prevention was worth
a pound of cure.   His seat of government was at the town of San Domingo, and Anacaona's territory at Xaragua was 200 miles distant.
Ovando started at once with 300 foot soldiers and
70 horse.   On reaching Xaragua he was received
in a friendly manner by the Indians, who probably
had no wish to offend so strong a force.   Games
were played, and Ovando proposed to show the
Indians a tournament, at which they were much
pleased, as their intense fear of the horse was beginning to wear off.   All the chieftains of the
neighbourhood were invited to assemble in a large
wooden house, while Ovando explained to them the
nature of the tournament that was about to take
place.   Meanwhile the Spanish soldiers surrounded
the house.   Ovando wore upon his breast the badge
of his order, a small image of God the Father,[2] and
as he stood talking with the chiefs, when he knew
the preparations to be complete, he raised his hand
and touched the image.   At this concerted signal

*Ovando's
treatment of
red men.*

---

[1] See above, vol. i. p. 482.

[2] "Un Dios Padre en abito blanco."   Marquez, *Tesoro militas
de Cavallería*, p. 24, apud Helps, vol. i. p. 207.

the soldiers rushed in and seized the chiefs, and bound them hand and foot. Then they went out and set fire to the house, and the chiefs were all burnt alive. Anacaona was hanged to a tree, several hundred Indians were put to the sword, and their country was laid waste. Ovando then founded a town in Xaragua, and called it the City of Peace, and gave it a seal on which was a dove with an olive-branch.[1]

But this was nothing to what happened in Ovando's time. There were such atrocities as would seem incredible were they not recounted by a most intelligent and faithful witness who saw with his own eyes many of the things of which he tells us. Bartolomé de Las Casas was born in Seville in 1474.[2] His family, one of the noblest

---

[1] An account of the affair is given in Herrera, dec. i. lib. vi. cap. iv., and with a pictorial illustration in Las Casas, *Indiarum devastationis et excidii narratio*, Heidelberg, 1664, p. 11. Herrera observes that the queen did not approve of Ovando's proceedings, and expressed an intention of investigating the affair, but the investigation was never made. Very likely Ovando's patron Fonseca, who cynically avowed that he cared not how many Indians perished, may have contrived to prevent it.

[2] The life of Las Casas is beautifully and faithfully told by Sir Arthur Helps, in his *History of the Spanish Conquest in America*, London, 1855–61, in 4 vols., a book which it does one's soul good to read. The most recent and elaborate biography is by Don Antonio Fabié, *Vida y escritos de Fray Bartolomé de Las Casas*, Madrid, 1879, in 2 vols. See also Llorente, *Vie de Las Casas*, prefixed to his *Œuvres de Las Casas*, Paris, 1822, tom. i. pp. ix.– cx. ; Remesal, *Historia de Chyapa y de Guatemala*, Madrid, 1619. References may also be found in Oviedo, Gomara, Herrera, Torquemada, and other historians. One should above all read the works of Las Casas himself, concerning which much information may be obtained from Sabin's *List of the Printed Editions of the Works of Fray Bartholomé de Las Casas, Bishop of Chiapa*, New

in Spain, was of French origin, descended from the viscounts of Limoges.[1] They were already in Spain before the thirteenth century, and played a distinguished part in the conquest of Seville from the Moors by Ferdinand III. of Castile, in 1252. From that time forward, members of the family were to be found in positions of trust, and among their marked traits of character were invincible courage and spotless integrity. By birth and training Bartholomew was an aristocrat to the very tips of his fingers. For the earlier part of his life dates can hardly be assigned, but the news of the triumphant return of Columbus from his first voyage across the Sea of Darkness may probably have found him at the university of Salamanca, where for several years he studied philosophy, theology, and jurisprudence, and obtained a licentiate's degree. His father, Don Francisco de Las Casas, accompanied Columbus on the second voyage, and re-

Birth and family of Las Casas.

York, 1870. The book contains also a notice of the MSS. — The *Life of Las Casas*, by Sir Arthur Helps, London, 1868, consists of passages extracted from his larger work, and suffers seriously from the removal of the context.

[1] Argote, *Nobleza de Andalucia*, fol. 210. According to Llorente (*Vie de Las Casas*, p. xcviii.) a branch of the Seville family returned to France. Don Carlos de Las Casas was one of the grandees who accompanied Blanche of Castile when she went to France in the year 1200, to marry the prince, afterward Louis VIII. From this nobleman was descended Napoleon's faithful chamberlain the Marquis de Las Cases. The migration of the French family to Spain probably antedated the custom of giving surnames, which was growing up in the eleventh and twelfth centuries. The name Las Casas was of course acquired in Spain, and afterward the branch of the family which had returned to France changed the spelling to Las Cases.

turned to Seville in 1497 with a young Indian slave whom Columbus had given him. It was on this occasion that Isabella asked, with some indignation, " Who has empowered my admiral thus to dispose of my subjects ? " The elder Las Casas gave the Indian to his son, who soon became warmly interested in him and in his race ; and as the father retained an estate in Hispaniola, the son came out with Ovando in 1502 and settled in that island.[1] He was then twenty-eight years old. Little is known of his first occupations there, except that he seems to have been more or less concerned in money-making, like all the other settlers. But about 1510 he was ordained as a priest. He seems to have been the first Christian clergyman ordained in the New World. He was a person of such immense ability and strength of character that in whatever age of the world he had lived he would undoubtedly have been one of its foremost men. As a man of business he had rare executive power ; he was a great diplomatist and an eloquent preacher, a man of Titanic *His character and writings.* energy, ardent but self-controlled, of unconquerable tenacity, warm-hearted and tender, calm in his judgments, shrewdly humorous, absolutely fearless, and absolutely true. He made many and bitter enemies, and some of them were unscrupulous enough ; but I believe no one has ever accused him of any worse sin than extreme fervour of

[1] According to Llorente, the elder Las Casas accompanied Columbus on his first voyage in 1492, and Bartholomew was with him on his third voyage in 1498, but this has been disproved. See Humboldt, *Examen critique*, tom. iii. p. 286.

temperament. His wrath could rise to a white heat, and indeed there was occasion enough for it. He was also very apt to call a spade a spade and to proclaim unpleasant truths with pungent emphasis. But his justice is conspicuously displayed in his voluminous writings. He was one of the best historians of his time, and wrote a most attractive Spanish style, quaint, pithy, and nervous, — a style which goes straight to the mark and rings like true metal.[1] It is impossible to doubt the accuracy of his statements about the matters of fact which were within the range of his personal knowledge. His larger statistics, as to the numbers of the Indian populations exterminated, have been doubted with good reason ; statistics are a complicated af-

[1] I do not mean to be understood as calling it a *literary* style. It is not graceful like that of great masters of expression such as Pascal or Voltaire. It is not seldom cumbrous and awkward, usually through trying to say too much at once. But in spite of this it is far more attractive than many a truly artistic literary style. There is a great charm in reading what comes from a man brimful of knowledge and utterly unselfish and honest. The crisp shrewdness, the gleams of gentle humour and occasional sharp flashes of wit, and the fervid earnestness in the books of Las Casas, combine to make them very delightful. It was the unfailing sense of humour, which is so often wanting in reformers, that kept Las Casas from developing into a fanatic. The judicious words of Humboldt in another connection will apply very well to the style of Las Casas : — in speaking of it, " il ne s'agit pas de discuter ce qu'on appelle vaguement le mérite littéraire d'un écrivain. Il s'agit de quelque chose de plus grave et de plus historique. Nous avons considéré le style comme expression du caractère, comme reflet de l'intérieur de l'homme. . . . C'est chez les hommes plus disposés à agir qu' à soigner leur diction, chez ceux qui demeurent étrangers à tout artifice propre à produire des émotions par le charme du langage, que la liaison si long-temps signalée entre le caractère et le style se fait sentir de préférence." *Examen critique*, tom. iii. p. 240.

fair, in which it is easy to let feelings make havoc
with figures.[1] But with regard to particular statements of fact one cannot help believing Las Casas,
because his perfect sincerity is allied with a judgment so sane and a charity so broad as to con-
strain our assent. He is almost always ready to
make allowances, and very rarely lets his hatred of
sin blind him to any redeeming qualities there
may be in the sinner. It was he that said, in his
crisp way, of Ovando, that he was a good governor,
but not for Indians. What Las Casas witnessed
under the administration of Ovando and other
governors, he published in 1552, in his "Brief Relation of the Destruction of the Indies," a book of
which there are copies in several languages, all
more or less rare now.[2] It is one of the most
grewsome books ever printed.

We have seen how by the year 1499 communities of Indians were assigned in *repartimiento* to
sundry Spaniards, and were thus reduced to a kind
of villenage. Queen Isabella had disapproved of
this, but she was persuaded to sanction The royal
it, and presently in 1503 she and Ferdi- orders of 1503.
nand issued a most disastrous order. They gave
discretionary power to Ovando to compel Indians
to work, but it must be for wages. They ordered

[1] The arithmetic of Las Casas is, however, no worse than that
of all the Spanish historians of that age. With every one of them
the nine digits seem to have gone on a glorious spree.

[2] I have never seen any of the English versions. Sabin mentions four, published in London in 1583, 1656, 1687, and 1699.
List of the Printed Editions, etc., pp. 22-24. The edition which
I use is the Latin one published at Heidelberg, 1664, small
quarto.

him, moreover, to see that Indians were duly instructed in the Christian faith, provided that they
must come to mass "as free persons, for so they
are." It was further allowed that the cannibal
Caribs, if taken in actual warfare, might be sold
into slavery. Little did the sovereigns know what
a legion of devils they were letting loose. Of
course the doings in Hispaniola always went the
full length of the authority granted from Spain,
and generally went far beyond. Of course the
Indians were compelled to work, and it was not
for wages; and of course, so long as there was no
legal machinery for protecting the natives, any
Indian might be called a cannibal and sold into
slavery. The way in which Ovando carried out
the order about missionary work was characteristic. As a member of a religious order of knights,
he was familiar with the practice of *encomienda*,
by which groups of novices were assigned to cer-

Encomiendas. tain preceptors to be disciplined and instructed in the mysteries of the order.
The word *encomienda* means "commandery" or
"preceptory," and so it came to be a nice euphe-
mism for a hateful thing. Ovando distributed Indians among the Spaniards in lots of 50 or 100 or
500, with a deed worded thus: "To you, such a
one, is given an *encomienda* of so many Indians,
and you are to teach them the things of our holy
Catholic Faith." In practice the last clause was
disregarded as a mere formality, and the effect
of the deed was simply to consign a parcel of Indians to the tender mercies of some Spaniard to
do as he pleased with them. If the system of

repartimientos was in effect serfdom or villenage, the system of *encomiendas* was unmitigated slavery.

Such a cruel and destructive slavery has seldom, if ever, been known. The work of the Indians was at first largely agricultural, but as many mines of gold were soon discovered they were driven in gangs to work in the mines. There was a rush of Spaniards to Hispaniola, like the rush of all sorts and conditions of white men in recent times to California and Australia, and we know well what kind of a population is gathered together under such circumstances. For a graphic description of it we may go to Charles Reade's "Never too Late to Mend." And here we must take care not to identify too indiscriminately the Spaniards, as such, with the horrors perpetrated in Hispaniola. It was not in the charac- *Effects of the* ter of Spaniards so much as in the char- *gold.* acter of ruffians that the perpetrators behaved, and there have been ruffians enough among people who speak English. If the worst of these slave-drivers was a Spaniard, so too was Las Casas. Many of the wretches were the offscourings of camps, the vile refuse of European wars; some of them were criminals, sent out here to disencumber Spanish jails. Of course they had no notion of working with their own hands, or of wielding any implement of industry except the lash. With such an abundant supply of cheap labour an Indian's life was counted of no value. It was cheaper to work an Indian to death and get another than to take care of him, and accordingly the slaves were worked to death without mercy. From time to time the Indians rose in rebellion, but these attempts were savagely suppressed, and a policy of terror was adopted. Indians were slaughtered by the hundred, burned alive, impaled on sharp stakes, torn to pieces by blood-hounds. In retaliation for the murder of a Spaniard it was thought proper to call up fifty or sixty Indians and chop off their hands. Little children were flung into the water to drown, with less concern than if they had been puppies. In the mingling of sacred ideas with the sheerest devilry there was a grotesqueness fit for the pencil of Doré. Once, " in honour and reverence of Christ and his twelve Apostles," they hanged thirteen Indians in a row at such a height that their toes could just touch the ground, and then pricked them to death with their sword-points, taking care not to kill them quickly. At another

Hideous cruelties.

time, when some old reprobate was broiling half-a-dozen Indians in a kind of cradle suspended over a slow fire, their shrieks awoke the Spanish captain who in a neighbouring hut was taking his afternoon nap, and he called out testily to the man to despatch those wretches at once, and stop their noise. But this demon, determined not to be baulked of his enjoyment, only gagged the poor creatures. Can it be, says Las Casas, that I really saw such things, or are they hideous dreams? Alas, they are no dreams; " all this did I behold with my bodily mortal eyes." [1]

This tyranny went on until the effect was like

[1] " Todo esto yo lo vide con mis ojos corporales mortales." *Hist. de las Indias*, tom. iii. p. 96.

that of a pestilence. The native population rapidly diminished until labour grew scarce, and it was found necessary in Hispaniola to send and kidnap Indians from other islands, and to import from Seville negroes that had been caught by the Portuguese in Africa. The first slave-hunters that went to the Lucayan islands beguiled the simple natives with pretty stories and promises, and thus enticed them on board their ships. Some thousands of Lucayans were taken to Hispaniola, and there is a touching story of one of these poor fellows, who cut down and hollowed out a pithy tree, and lashed to it smaller stems till he had made a good staunch raft. He stuffed it with corn and calabashes of fresh water, and then with two friends, a man and a woman, he put to sea one dark night, and they paddled toward the north star.[1] After many anxious days and nights they had gone more than 200 miles and were coming near to their own land, when all at once their hearts were sickened at the sight of a Spanish cruiser in the offing, and presently they were stowed beneath its deck and carried back in black despair to the land of bondage. No less pathetic is the story of the cacique Hatuey in Cuba, who had heard that the Spaniards were coming over from Hispaniola and hit upon an ingenious expedient for protecting his people. Taking a big lump of gold he called his

[1] Herrera, *Historia de las Indias*, Madrid, 1601, tom. i. p. 228. As Sir Arthur Helps observes, "there is somewhat of immortality in a stout-hearted action, and though long past it seems still young and full of life : one feels quite anxious now, as if those Indians were yet upon that sea, to know what becomes of them." *Spanish Conquest.* vol. i. p. 226.

clan-chiefs together, and said : — Behold, this is
the god of the white men ; wherefore let us dance
to it and reverence it, that if peradventure they
come hither, it may tell them to do us no harm ;
and so these simple barbarians adored the piece
of yellow metal and danced around it, and sought
to win its favour.[1]

In 1509 Ovando was recalled, and went home,
a poor man, leaving as his last act the larger part
of his property to found a hospital for needy Spaniards. Under his successor, Diego Columbus, there
was little improvement. The case had become a
hard one to deal with. There were now what are
called " vested rights," the rights of property in
Antonio   slaves, to be respected. But in 1510
Montesino.   there came a dozen Dominican monks,
and they soon decided, in defiance of vested rights,
to denounce the wickedness they saw about them.
So one Sunday in the year 1511 Father Antonio
Montesino preached a great sermon in the church
at San Domingo, from the text, "I am the voice
of one crying in the wilderness." His words, says
the chronicler, were "very piercing and terrible."
He told his dismayed hearers that they were living in mortal sin, and their greed and cruelty

---

[1] Herrera, *op. cit.* tom. i. p. 293. This propitiation of the white
man's yellow god did not avail to save the unfortunate cacique.
Soon after their arrival in Cuba the Spaniards caught him, and
he was burned alive at the stake. As he was writhing amid the
flames, a priest held up a cross before him and begged him to
"become a Christian " so that he might go to heaven. The half-
roasted Indian replied that if there were Christians in heaven he
had no desire to go to any such place. See Las Casas, *Indiarum
devastationis et excidii narratio,* p. 16.

were such that for any chance they had of going to heaven they might as well be Moors or Turks!

Startling words, indeed, to Spanish ears, — to be told that they were no better than Mahometans! The town was in an uproar, and after the noon dinner a deputation of the principal citizens went to the shed which served temporarily as a monastery, and angrily demanded an apology from Father Antonio. The prior's quiet reply was that Father Antonio's sentiments were those of the Dominican community and would on no account be retracted. The infuriated citizens then said that unless a different tone was taken in the pulpit next Sunday the monks had better pack up their goods for a sea voyage. That would be easily done, quoth the prior, and verily, says Las Casas, with his sly humour, it was so, for all they had on earth would have gone into two small trunks.[1]

Next Sunday the church was thronged with Spaniards from far and near, for the excitement was fierce. Mass was performed, and then, amid breathless silence, Father Antonio stepped into the pulpit and preached a still more terrible sermon; threatened his hearers with eternal torments, and declared that the monks would refuse confession to any man who should maltreat his Indians or engage in the slave-trade. Glorious Antonio Montesino! first of preachers on American soil to declare war to the knife against this gravest of American sins!

Loyalty to the church was too strong among .

[1] These events are related with full details by Las Casas, *Hist. de las Indias*, tom. iii. pp. 365–380.

LIBRARY OF
MUSKINGUM COLLEGE
New Concord, Ohio.

Spaniards for any violence to be offered to these monks, but the citizens made complaint to King Ferdinand. His wife Isabella, dying six years before these events, had left to him in her will one The king's half of the income to be got from the position. Indies during his lifetime. After Isabella's death the crown of Castile had passed to their daughter Joanna, and Ferdinand for a while, restricted to his own kingdom of Aragon, had little to do with American affairs. But after a couple of years, Joanna having become insane, Ferdinand had become regent of Castile, and was thus lord over America, and as half the American revenue, which was chiefly gold from the mines, was to come to him, the colonists in Hispaniola looked to him to defend their vested interests. The citizens of San Domingo got hold of an unworthy member of the Franciscan order, and sent him to Spain to complain against the Dominicans; and Antonio Montesino went over himself to forestall the Franciscan monk. Antonio saw the king and made a deep impression upon him, so that a conclave of learned priests was assembled, and various plans of relief and reform were discussed. Nothing was really accomplished, except that some seeds of reform were sown, to bear fruit at a later season.

Meanwhile the good Montesino had gained an ally upon the scene of action worth a dozen kings. Las Casas was by natural endowment a many-sided man, who looked at human affairs from various points of view. Under other circumstances he need not necessarily have developed into a philanthropist, though any career into which he might have been drawn could not have failed to be honourable and noble. At first he seems to have been what one might call worldly-minded.

But the most interesting thing about him we shall find to be his steady intellec-

Las Casas at first a slave-owner.

tual and spiritual development; from year to year he rose to higher and higher planes of thought and feeling. He was at first a slave-owner like the rest, and had seen no harm in it. But from the first his kindly sympathetic nature asserted itself, and his treatment of his slaves was such that they loved him. He was a man of striking and easily distinguishable aspect, and the Indians in general, who fled from the sight of white men, came soon to recognize him as a friend who could always be trusted. At the same time, however, as a good man of business he was disposed to make money, and, as he tells us, " he took no more heed than the other Spaniards to bethink himself that his Indians were unbelievers, and of the duty that there was on his part to give them instruction, and to bring them to the bosom of the Church of Christ." He sympathized with much that was said by Montesino, but thought at first that in his unqualified condemnation of the whole system of slavery that great preacher was going too far. We must not be wanting in charity toward slaveholders. It is hard for a man to extricate himself from the entanglements of ideas and situations prepared for him before he was born. The heart of Las Casas, however, was deeply stirred by Montesino, and he pondered much upon his words.

In the same year that those memorable sermons were preached, Diego Columbus made up his mind to conquer and colonize Cuba, and he sent Velasquez for that purpose. Las Casas presently followed. The usual tale of horrors had begun, but he succeeded in doing much to improve the situation. For the time he was the only priest on the island. The tremendous power of the church was personified in him, and he used it unflinchingly in defence of the Indians. When the island was regarded as conquered, Velasquez proceeded to give *encomiendas* of Indians to his friends, and a large village was given as an *encomienda* to two partners, Conversion of Las Casas. of whom one was Las Casas. It was the duty of Las Casas to say mass and now and then to preach, and in thinking of his sermon for Pentecost, 1514, he opened his Bible, and his eye alighted upon these verses in the 34th chapter of Ecclesiasticus: —

" The Most High is not pleased with the offerings of the wicked: neither is he pacified for sin by the multitude of sacrifices.

" The bread of the needy is their life; he that defraudeth him thereof is a man of blood.

" He that taketh away his neighbour's living slayeth him; and he that defraudeth the labourer of his hire is a shedder of blood."

As he read these words a light from heaven seemed to shine upon Las Casas. The scales fell from his eyes. He saw that the system of slavery was wrong in principle. The question whether you treated your slaves harshly or kindly did not go to the root of the matter. As soon as you took from the labourer his wages the deadly sin was committed, the monstrous evil was inaugurated. There must be a stop put to this, said Las Casas. We have started wrong. Here are vast countries which Holy Church has given to the Spaniards in trust, that the heathen may be civilized and brought into the fold of Christ; and we have begun by making Hispaniola a hell. This thing must not be suffered to grow with the growth of Spanish conquest. There was but one remedy. The axe must be put to the root of the tree. Slavery must be abolished.

Las Casas began by giving up his own slaves. He had reason enough to know that others might not treat them so well as he, but he was not the man to preach what he did not practise. His partner, Pedro de Renteria, was a man of noble nature and much under his influence, so that there was no difficulty there. Then Las Casas went into the pulpit and preached to his con- His first pro-
gregation that their souls were in dan- ceedings.
ger so long as they continued to hold their *encomiendas* of Indians. "All were amazed," he says; "some were struck with compunction; others were as much surprised to hear it called a sin to make use of the Indians, as if they had been told it were sinful to make use of the beasts of the field."

Too many were of this latter mood, and finding his people incorrigible, Las Casas sold what worldly goods he had left, and went to Spain to lay the case before King Ferdinand. First he visited Bishop Fonseca, as the most important member of the Council for the Indies. From this coarse man,

His reception by Fonseca; with his cynical contempt for philanthropists, Las Casas got such a reception as might have been expected. It will be remembered that Ovando was one of Fonseca's creatures. When Las Casas told how 7,000 children had cruelly perished in Hispaniola within three months, he doubtless overstated the case, and clearly Fonseca did not believe him. He answered roughly, "Look here, you droll fool, what is all this to me, and what is it to the king?" This fairly took our poor priest's breath away. He only exclaimed, "O great and eternal God! to whom, then, is it of any concern?" and so he turned upon his heel and left the room.

On arriving at Seville, he learned that the king had just died, January 23, 1516. Ferdinand's daughter Joanna, queen of Castile and heiress to the throne of Aragon, was still insane, and both thrones descended practically to her illustrious son Charles, a boy of sixteen, who was then in Flanders. For the present the great cardinal Ximenes was regent of Spain, and to him went Las Casas with his tale of woe. From the cardinal he obtained ready and cordial sym-

and by Cardinal Ximenes. pathy. It was a fortunate circumstance that at this juncture brought two such men together. Las Casas knew well that the enslavement of Indians was not contemplated in the royal orders of 1503, except so far as concerned cannibals taken in war; but the evil had become so firmly established that at first he hesitated about the policy of using this line of argument. He

prudently shaped his question in this wise : " With
what justice can such things be done, whether the
Indians are free or not?" Here, to his joy, the
cardinal caught him up vehemently. "With no
justice whatever : what, are not the Indians free?
who doubts about their being free?" This was a
great point gained at the start, for it put the official theory of the Spanish government on the side of
Las Casas, and made the Spaniards in America
appear in the light of transgressors. The matter
was thoroughly discussed with Ximenes First attempts
and that amiable Dutchman, Cardinal at reform.
Adrian, who was afterwards pope. A commission
of Hieronymite friars was appointed to accompany
Las Casas to the West Indies, with minute instructions and ample powers for making investigations and enforcing the laws. Ximenes appointed
Las Casas Protector of the Indians, and clothed
him with authority to impeach delinquent judges
or other public officials. The new regulations,
could they have been carried out, would have done
much to mitigate the sufferings of the Indians.
They must be paid wages, they must be humanely
treated and taught the Christian religion. But
as the Spanish government needed revenue, the
provision that Indians might be compelled to
work in the mines was not repealed. The Indians
must work, and the Spaniards must pay them.
Las Casas argued correctly that so long as this
provision was retained the work of reform would
go but little way. Somebody, however, must work
the mines ; and so the talk turned to the question
of sending out white labourers or negroes.

Here we come to the statement, often repeated, that it was Las Casas who first introduced negro slavery and the African slave-trade into the New World. The statement is a good specimen of the headlong, helter-skelter way in which things get said and believed in this superficial world. As first repeated, there was probably an agreeable tinge of paradox in representing the greatest of philanthropists as the founder of one of the vilest systems of bondage known to modern times. At length it has come to pass that people who know nothing about Las Casas, and have absolutely no other idea associated with his name, still vaguely think of him as the man who brought negro slaves to America as substitutes for Indians, — the man who sacrificed one race of his fellow-creatures to another, and thus paid Peter by robbing Paul.

The popular notion about Las Casas and negro slavery.

There could not be a grosser historical blunder than this notion, and yet, like most such blunders, it has arisen from a perversion of things that really were said if not done. In order to arrive at historical truth, it is not enough to obtain correct items of fact; it is necessary to group the items in their causal relations and to estimate the precise weight that must be accorded to each in the total result. To do this is often so difficult that half-truths are very commonly offered us in place of whole truths ; and it sometimes happens that of all forms of falsehood none is so misleading as the half-truth.

The statement about Las Casas, with which we are here concerned, properly divides itself into a pair of statements. It is alleged, in the first place, that it was Las Casas who first suggested the employment of negroes as substitutes for Indians; and in the second place, that the origin, or at any rate the steady development, of negro slavery in America was due to this suggestion. These are two different propositions and call for different comments.

With regard to the first, it is undoubtedly true that Las Casas at one time expressed the opinion that if there must be slave labour, the enslavement of blacks might perhaps be tolerated as the smaller of two evils, inasmuch as the negroes were regarded as a hardier race than the Indians and better able to support continuous labour. At one time the leading colonists of Hispaniola had told Las Casas that if they might have license to import each a dozen negroes, they would coöperate with him in his plans for setting free the Indians and improving their condition. When Las Casas at the Spanish court was confronted with the argument that there must be somebody to work the mines, he recalled this suggestion of the colonists, and proposed it as perhaps the least odious way out of the difficulty. It is therefore evident that at that period in his life he did not realize the wickedness of slavery so distinctly in the case of black men as in the case of red men. In other words, he had not yet outgrown that mediæval habit of mind which regarded the right to "life, liberty, and the pursuit of happiness," and other rights, not as common to all mankind, but as parcelled out among groups

and classes of men in a complicated way that to our minds, on the eve of the twentieth century,
has become wellnigh unintelligible. It was the great French writers of the eighteenth century who first gave distinct expression to the notion of "unalienable rights," with which mankind has been endowed by the Creator. This notion has become so familiar to our minds that we sometimes see the generalizations of Rousseau and Diderot, or whatever remains sound in them, derided as mere platitudes, as if it had never been necessary to preach such self-evident truths. But these "platitudes" about universal rights were far enough from being self-evident in the sixteenth century. On the contrary, they were extremely unfamiliar and abstruse conceptions, toward which the most enlightened minds could only grope their way by slow degrees.[1] In Las Casas it is interesting to trace such a development. He had gradually risen to the perception of the full wickedness of slavery in the form in which he had become familiar with it; but he had not yet extended his generalizations, as a modern thinker would do, to remote cases, and in order to gain a point, the supreme importance of which he keenly felt, he was ready to make concessions. In later years he blamed himself roundly for making

Mediæval and modern conceptions of rights.

Gradual development of the modern conception in Las Casas.

[1] As Mr. John Morley observes, "the doctrine of moral obligations toward the lower races had not yet taken its place in Europe." *Diderot and the Encyclopædists*, London, 1880, p. 386. Mr. Morley's remarks on the influence of Raynal's famous book, *Histoire des deux Indes* in this connection, are admirable.

any such concessions. Had he "sufficiently considered the matter," he would not for all the world
have entertained such a suggestion for a moment;
for, said he, the negroes "had been made slaves
unjustly and tyrannically, and the same reason
holds good of them as of the Indians." [1]

With regard to the second of the statements we
are considering, the question arises how far did
this suggestion, for which Las Casas afterward so
freely blamed himself, have any material
effect in setting on foot the African *His momenta-*
ry suggestion
slave-trade or in enlarging its dimen- *had no tracea-*
ble effect upon
sions? The reply is that it had no *negro slavery.*
such effect whatever. As for the beginnings, negroes had been carried to Hispaniola in small numbers as early as 1501; and in the royal instructions
drawn up at that time for Ovando, he was forbidden to take to the colony Moors, Jews, new
converts from Islam or Judaism, monks not Spanish, and the children of persons burned at the
stake for heresy, but he might take negro slaves. [2]
Official documents prove that at various times between 1500 and 1510 negroes were sent over to
work in the mines, but not in large numbers. [3]
As for the extensive development of negro slavery
in the West Indies, it did not begin for many
years after that period in the career of Las Casas
with which we are now dealing, and there is nothing to show that his suggestion or concession was
in any way concerned in bringing it about. If, on

---

[1] Las Casas, *Hist. de las Indias*, tom. iv. p. 380.

[2] Navarrete, *Coleccion de viages*, tom. ii. doc. 175.

[3] Herrera, *Hist. de las Indias*, tom. i. pp. 274–276.

the other hand, instead of confining our attention to this single incident in his life, the importance of which has been egregiously exaggerated, we consider the general effect of his life-work, that effect was clearly adverse to the development of the African slave-trade. For if the depopulation of the New World had continued, which Las Casas did so much to check, it cannot be doubted that

His life-work did much to diminish the volume of ne-gro slavery and the spirit-ual corruption attendant upon it.

the importation of negroes to Spanish America would have been immeasurably greater than it has been. The Afri-can slave-trade would have assumed much larger proportions than it has ever known, and its widely ramifying influ-ence for evil, its poisonous effects upon the character of European society in the New World, whether Spanish or English, would probably have surpassed anything that we can now realize. When the work of Las Casas is deeply considered, we cannot make him anything else but an antagonist of human slavery in all its forms, and the mightiest and most effective antagonist, withal, that has ever lived. Subtract his glorious life from the history of the past, and we might still be waiting, sick with hope deferred, for a Wilberforce, a Garrison, and a Lin-coln.

In all the work at the Spanish court the Bishop of Burgos tried by every means in his power to impede and thwart Las Casas, and agents of the colonists gained the ears of the Hieronymite friars, so that matters were very imperfectly mended, and the next year, after a stout fight, Las Casas returned to Spain to find the great cardinal on his death-bed. The loss of this powerful ally was a serious misfortune for Las Casas. He was not long, however, in winning the esteem of Charles V. The young king greatly liked him, and his grave face always lighted up with pleasure whenever he happened to meet "Master Bartholomew," as he used to call him. Las Casas now tried to enlist white emigrants for the West Indies, to labour there; but the task of getting Spaniards to work, instead of making slaves work for them, was not an encouraging one. At length, however, he devised a scheme which seemed likely to work. He undertook to select fifty Spaniards for whose characters he could vouch, to subscribe 200 ducats each and go with him to found a colony upon the mainland. That the Indians might distinguish between these men and any other Spaniards they had ever seen, they were to wear a peculiar uniform, white with a coloured cross. If their work should prosper he intended to ask the Pope to recognize them as a religious fraternity, like those of the Middle Ages, which had been of such inestimable value as civilizing agencies. He promised to make it an enterprise which should justify itself by paying its own way and yielding a steady revenue to the crown. If he could not cure the evils in the islands, he could at least set the example of a new colony founded on sound principles, and might hope that it would serve as a centre for the diffusion of a higher civilization in the New World.

In pursuance of this scheme Las Casas obtained

from Charles V. a grant of territory about Cumaná on the Pearl Coast. There were three years of hard work in these preliminaries, hindered at every step by the malignant intrigues of Bishop Fonseca. At length, in 1520, the Protector of the Indians returned to Hispaniola, and in 1521 he was ready for the Pearl Coast. Some Dominicans had already founded a small monastery there, and from them Las Casas could always look for cordial assistance. But Satan had not been asleep while these things were going on. In the neighbouring island of Cubagua, fishing for pearls,

The mischief that one miserable sinner can do.
was a young man named Alonso de Ojeda,[1] concerning whom Las Casas says, with truth, " that if he had not been born, the world would have lost nothing." Ojeda wanted slaves, and thought it a bright idea to catch a few on the mainland and pretend they were cannibals. He took a notary with his party in order to catechise some chiefs and have such answers taken down as could be made to convict them of cannibalism.[2] But having no paper about him he stopped at the Dominican monastery and asked for a sheet, which was given him. Ojeda presently changed his mind, abandoned his cate-

[1] Llorente (*Œuvres de Las Casas*, tom. i. p. 139) confounds him with the Alonso de Ojeda whose career we have already traced down to his death in 1515, five years before the time of the events we are now narrating. Curiously enough, on another page of the same volume (p. xlv.) Llorente warns the reader not to confound the two, but thinks that this younger sinner may perhaps have been the son of the other. I suspect this is a mere guess.

[2] The reader will observe that some slight progress seems to have been made, since these legal formalities were deemed necessary.

chising project as uncertain and tedious, and
adopted some other device. A few miles down the
coast he fell in with some Indians, attacked them
under circumstances of foulest treachery, slew a
great many, and carried off the rest in his vessel.
Now the Indians were always deeply impressed
with the way in which white people communicated
intelligence to one another by means of mysterious
bits of paper. Some Indians had seen the innocent
monk give the piece of paper to Ojeda, and so, as
the news of his evil deeds flew along the coast, they
naturally concluded that the Dominicans must be
his accomplices. So they not only contrived to kill
the worthless Ojeda the next time he touched upon
the coast, but they set fire to the monastery and
massacred the monks. And so fiercely was their
wrath now kindled against all Spaniards that soon
after the founding of the colony of Las Casas at
Cumaná, on an occasion when — fortunately for
him — some business had called him
back to Hispaniola, they attacked the Destruction of
the little col-
little colony in overwhelming numbers, ony.
and destroyed it. Those who escaped their javelins
were fain to flee to the neighbouring islands and
thence to San Domingo. Their incipient village
was burned to the ground, and not a white man
was left on the Pearl Coast.

Seven years had now elapsed since that memorable Pentecost of 1514, seven years of ceaseless toil
and sore perplexity, and now, just as the way was
beginning to seem clear toward some tangible result, everything was ruined by the villainy of one
scurvy knave. There is reason to suppose that

Las Casas may have somewhat overtaxed his strength. His nerves were strained beyond endur-

Grief of Las Casas; he becomes a Dominican monk.

ance, and when he heard the news of this terrible blow, he fell, for the first and only time in his life, into a fit of profound despondency. Perhaps, said he, in prophetic language, "the Spaniards are not to be saved from the commission of great wickedness and from decay of their power." Perhaps God had for some inscrutable purpose decreed that the Indians must be destroyed. Perhaps there was in his own soul some lurking sin which made him unworthy to be God's instrument for righting these grievous wrongs.[1] The Dominican monastery at San Domingo was no longer a mere shed. In its pleasant garden would Las Casas sit motionless hour after hour, absorbed in meditation upon these heart-rending mysteries of the Divine Providence. The good monks improved the situation by persuading Las Casas to join their order. He became a Dominican in 1522, and remained there at the monastery for eight years, leading the life of a close student, acquiring a profound knowledge of patristic and mediæval theology, becoming expert in the sinuosities of scholastic logic, and writing history such as the world could ill afford to spare.

During these eight years the Spanish empire in

[1] "The dignity and greatness of his cause were so predominant in the mind of Las Casas as to leave no room for influences merely personal. It does not appear that he ever expected gratitude from the Indians; nor did the terrible disaster which he suffered at Cumaná leave, apparently, the slightest rancour in his mind." Helps, *Spanish Conquest*, vol. iv. p. 334.

America was rapidly expanding. When Las Casas entered the monastery, Cortes had lately captured the great Mexican pueblo and overthrown the Aztec confederacy. Then Pedro de Alvarado conquered Guatemala, while Pedrarias and his captains devastated Nicaragua like a typhoon or a plague. Now in 1530 the Pizarros and Almagro were just starting on their final and decisive expedition for the conquest of Peru. Old Pedrarias had just died at somewhere about his ninetieth year. The horrors of Hispaniola had been repeated in Nicaragua. We may suppose that this had much to do with arousing the Dominicans of Hispaniola to renewed activity. Las Casas tells us very little about himself at this conjuncture. Indeed, his history of the Indies brings us down no farther than 1522. But we learn from Antonio de Remesal — an excellent authority for this part of his career — that he emerged from his seclusion in 1530, went over to Spain, and obtained from Charles V. a decree prohibiting the enslavement of Indians in the countries which Pizarro and Almagro were expected to conquer.[1] On returning to Hispaniola, Las Casas was sent to the new Dominican monastery in Mexico, there to take companions and proceed to Peru, for the purpose of proclaiming the imperial decree and founding a monastery there. For some reason the latter purpose was not carried out. The decree was proclaimed, but it proved impossible to enforce it. For three or four years Las Casas was kept busy in Nicaragua, putting a

[margin note: Spanish conquests, and resulting movements.]

[1] Remesal, *Historia de Chiapa*, Madrid, 1619, p. 103.

curb upon the rapacity and cruelty of the new governor. Meanwhile a friend of his was appointed Bishop of Guatemala, and thither Las Casas repaired early in 1536. A Dominican monastery, founded there somewhat prematurely, had been unoccupied for six or seven years, and Las Casas and three of his companions now took possession of it. There the first thing they did was to acquire a knowledge of the Quiché language spoken by the natives of Guatemala, a language not without some interesting native literature which modern scholarship has discovered and edited.[1] So zealously did these four monks work that it was not long before they could talk quite fluently in Quiché, and they soon found occasion to put this rare accomplishment to a practical use.

The little monastery in Guatemala.

While in the monastery at San Domingo, Las Casas had written his famous Latin treatise *De unico vocationis modo*, or the only proper method of calling men to Christianity. In these years of trial his mind had been growing in clearness and grasp. He had got beyond all sophistical distinctions between men of one colour and faith and men of another, — a wonderful progress for a Spaniard born eight years before the Moor was driven from Granada. He had come to see what was really involved in the Christian assumption of the brotherhood of men; and accordingly he main-

[1] See Brasseur de Bourbourg, *Bibliothèque Mexico-Guatémalienne; Popol Vuh, le Livre Sacré des Quichés;* and for the literature of a neighbouring people in Guatemala, see Brinton's *Annals of the Cakchiquels*, Philadelphia, 1885.

tained that to make war upon infidels or heathen, merely because they are infidels or heathen, is sinful; and that the only right and lawful way of bringing men to Christ is the way of reason and persuasion. To set

The only right way to bring men to Christ.

forth such a doctrine at that time and still keep clear of the Inquisition required consummate skilfulness in statement. This little book was never printed, but manuscript copies of the original Latin and of a Spanish translation were circulated, and called forth much comment. The illustrations drawn from American affairs exasperated the Spanish colonists, and they taunted Las Casas. He was only a vain theorizer, they said; the gospel of peace would be all very well in a world already perfect, but in our world the only practicable gospel is the gospel of kicks and

A challenge.

blows. Go to, let this apostle try himself to convert a tribe of Indians and make them keep the peace; he will soon find that something more is needed than words of love. So said the scoffers, as they wagged their heads.

Las Casas presently took them at their word. The province of Tuzulutlan, just to the north of Guatemala and bordering upon the peninsula of Yucatan, was called by the Spaniards the "Land of War." It was an inac-

The Land of War.

cessible country of beetling crags, abysmal gorges, raging torrents, and impenetrable forest. In their grade of culture the inhabitants seem to have resembled the Aztecs. They had idols and human sacrifices, and were desperate fighters. The Spaniards had three times invaded this country, and three times had been hurled back in a very dilapidated condition. It could hardly be called a promising field, but this it was that Las Casas chose for his experiment.[1]

Tuzulutlan, or the "Land of War."

Let us note well his manner of proceeding, for there are those to-day who maintain that the type of character which Victor Hugo has sketched in Monseigneur Bienvenu is not calculated to achieve success in the world. The example of Las Casas, however, tends to confirm us in the opinion that when combined

The highest type of manhood.

---

[1] A full account of the work of Las Casas in Tuzulutlan is given in Remesal's *Historia de Chiapa*, lib. iii. cap. ix.-xi., xv.-xviii.

with sufficient intelligence, that type of character is the most indomitable and masterful of all. And in this I seem to see good promise for the future of humanity. The wisdom of the serpent, when wedded to the innocence of the dove, is of all things the most winning and irresistible, as Las Casas now proceeded to prove.

Alvarado, the fierce governor of Guatemala, was absent in Spain. Las Casas talked with the temporary governor, Alonzo de Maldonado, and the result of their talk was the following agreement, signed May 2, 1537. It was agreed that Diplomacy of "if Las Casas, or any of his monks, Las Casas. can bring these Indians into conditions of peace, so that they should recognize the Spanish monarch for their lord paramount, and pay him any moderate tribute, he, the governor, would place those provinces under his majesty in chief, and would not give them to any private Spaniard in *encomienda*. Moreover, no lay Spaniard, under heavy penalties, except the governor himself in person, should be allowed for five years to enter into that territory." [1] Ojedas and other such sinners were now, if possible, to be kept at a distance. No doubt Maldonado smiled in his sleeve when he signed his name to this agreement. Of course it could never come to anything.

Thus guaranteed against interference, the good monks went to work, and after a due amount of preliminary fasting and prayer they began by putting into Quiché verses an epitome of Christian doctrine simple enough for children to apprehend,

[1] Helps, *Spanish Conquest*, iii. 337.

— the story of the fall of man, the life and death
of Christ, the resurrection of the dead, and the

Preparations
for a peaceful
invasion of the
Land of War.

final judgment. It is a pity that these
verses have not been preserved, but no
doubt Las Casas, whose great heart
knew so well how to touch the secret springs of
the Indian mind, knew how to make the story as
attractive and as moving as possible. The verses
were nicely balanced in couplets, so as to aid the
memory, and were set to music so that they might
be chanted to the accompaniment of the rude Indian instruments. Then the monks found four
Indian traders, who were in the habit of travelling
now and then through the "Land of War" with
goods to barter. They spent many weeks in winning the affection of these Indians and teaching
them their sacred poem, explaining everything with
endless patience, until the new converts knew it
all by heart and felt able to answer simple questions
about it. When the monks felt sure that the work
was thoroughly done, they despatched the four
traders on their missionary errand to the pueblo of
the most powerful cacique in that country, taking
care to provide them with an ample store of mir-
rors, bells, Spanish knives, and other stuff attractive to barbarians.

When the traders arrived at their destination
they were hospitably received, and, ac-

cording to custom, were lodged in the
tecpan.[1] They were zealous in their
work, and obeyed their instructions faithfully. After vending their wares as usual, they called for

[1] See Bandelier, in *Peabody Museum Reports*, vol. ii. p. 673.

Ancient Nahuatl Flute Melodies.

some Mexican drums or timbrels, and proceeded
to chant their sacred couplets.[1] They were well
received.   Indians uttering such strange sweet
words must have seemed miraculously inspired, and
so the audience thought.   For several days the
performance was repeated, and the traders were
beset with questions.   After a while they drew
pictures of the tonsured monks, and said that they
learned these mysteries from these holy men, who,
although white men, were not like other Spaniards,
for they spent their lives in doing good, they had
no wives, they treated all women with respect, they

[1] As a specimen of the kind of music likely to have been employed on this occasion, I give a page of ancient Nahuatl flute
melodies, taken from Dr. Brinton's *The Güegüence; a Comedy Bal-
let in the Nahuatl-Spanish Dialect of Nicaragua*, Philadelphia,
1883.   In the introduction to that interesting work there is a
section on the music and musical instruments of the natives of
Nicaragua, who were and are an outlying branch of the great
Nahua people.   From statements of Oviedo, Father Duran, Benzoni, and other old writers, further illustrated by the investigations of modern travellers, Dr. Brinton has made a learned and
valuable essay.   If the reader who is familiar with the history of
music will take the trouble to compare the melodies here cited
from page xxxiv. of Dr. Brinton's work with the melodies from the
Güegüence itself, given by Dr. Brinton on page xl., he will recognize at once that the latter have been produced under Spanish
influences, while the former show no trace of such influence and
are undoubtedly genuine aboriginal music.   The reader will observe the monotony and the limited range of the melodies here
cited, and can imagine the lugubrious but perhaps not wholly unpleasant effect of such tunes when chanted in the open air to the
accompaniment of the *teponaztli* or old Mexican timbrels.   For
some account of the ancient Peruvian music, see Garcilasso, *Comentarios reales*, pt. i. lib. ii. cap. xxvi.   An interesting collection
of Zuñi melodies, recorded upon phonographic cylinders by Dr.
Fewkes, of the Hemenway Archæological Expedition, may be
found in the *Journal of American Ethnology and Archæology*,
vol. i. pp. 63–92.

cared nothing for gold, and they taught that the time had come for abolishing human sacrifices. The cacique became so interested as to send his younger brother back to Guatemala with the Indian traders, charging him to watch the Dominicans narrowly, and if he should find them answering to the description that had been given of them he might invite them to visit Tuzulutlan.

Thus the ice was broken. It is needless to say that the young chieftain was well received, or that he was satisfied with what he saw. The invitation was given, and one of the Dominicans, the noble Luis de Barbastro, who was the most fluent of the four in the Quiché language, now made his way into the inaccessible fastnesses of Tuzulutlan, escorted by the young chief and the Indian traders. By the first of November, six months after the beginning of the enterprise, Father Luis had converted the cacique and several clan chiefs, a rude church had been built, and human sacrifices prohibited by vote of the tribal council.[1] Then Las Casas, with another monk, arrived upon the scene. There was much excitement among the tawny people of Tuzulutlan. The hideous priests of the war-god were wild with rage. They reminded the people, says Remesal, that the flesh of these white men, dressed with chile sauce, would make a dainty dish. Some secret incendiary burned the church, but as the cacique

The first positions carried.

[1] As already observed, there are many indications in the history of the conquest of Mexico and Central America that a considerable portion of the people were by no means unwilling to bid farewell to their cruel religions.

and so many clan chiefs had been gained, there was no open rebellion. Before another year had elapsed the Indians had voluntarily destroyed their idols, renounced cannibalism, and promised to desist from warfare unless actually invaded. And now were to be seen the fruits of the masterly diplomacy of Las Casas. Though the cacique had thrice defeated the Spaniards, he knew well how formidable they were. By acknowledging the supremacy of Charles V. — a sovereign as far off as

The victory won.   the sky — and paying a merely nominal tribute, he had the word of Las Casas, which no Indian ever doubted, that not a Spaniard, without the express permission of the Dominicans, should set foot upon his territory. This arrangement was made, the peaceful victory was won, and Las Casas returned to Guatemala, taking with him the cacique, to visit Alvarado, who had just returned from Spain.

This rough soldier, it will be remembered, was the man who by his ill-judged brutality had precipitated the catastrophe of the Spaniards in the city of Mexico on the May festival of 1520. In his hard heart there was, however, a gallant spot. He knew a hero when he saw him, and he well knew that, with all his military qualities, he could never have done what Las Casas had just done. So when the stern conqueror and lord of Guatemala, coming forth to greet Las Casas and the Indian king, took off his plumed and jewelled cap, and bent his head in reverence, it seems to me one of the beautiful moments in history, one of the moments that comfort us with the thought of

what may yet be done with frail humanity when
the spirit of Christ shall have come to be better
understood. Of course Alvarado confirmed the
agreement that no lay Spaniard should be allowed
to enter Tuzulutlan; was he not glad enough thus
to secure peace on this difficult and dangerous
frontier?

Las Casas now, in 1539, went to Spain and had
the agreement confirmed in a most solemn and peremptory order from Charles V. The order was
obeyed. The "Land of War" was left unmolested and became thenceforth a land of The "Land of
peace.[1] Not only did it cease to trouble True Peace."
the Spaniards, but it became a potent centre for
missionary work and a valuable means of diffusing Christian influences among other Indian communities. The work was permanent. Las Casas
had come, he had seen, and he had conquered;
and not a drop of human blood had been shed!

Meanwhile he had not been idle in other directions, and at length had gained the most powerful
of allies. That reformation within the Papacy,
which was one of the consequences of Luther's
revolt, was beginning. Paul III. was a pope of
different type from either the wretched Borgia or
the elegant and worldly Medici. In the summer
of 1537, while Las Casas and his monks Enslavement
were preparing their mission to the of Indians
"Land of War," the Pope issued a brief the Pope.
forbidding the further enslavement of Indians,
under penalty of excommunication. Henceforth

---

[1] A part of this region has ever since borne the name Vera Paz,
or "True Peace," and thus upon every map is this noblest of conquests recorded.

any governor who should give, or any settler who
should receive, a new *encomienda* of Indians, or
who should forcibly deprive them of their goods,
was to be refused the sacraments of the Church.
Thus the further spread of slavery was to be
stopped.   Before leaving Guatemala for Spain,
Las Casas had the pleasure of translating this
decree into Spanish and sending it to all parts of
the Indies.[1]   He was detained five years in Spain,
as the emperor needed his advice, and it was during this period that he wrote his " Destruction of
the Indies " and other famous books.   In 1542 he
won his grand and decisive triumph in the promulgation of the New Laws by Charles V.
The decisive clause was as follows : —
" Item.   We order and command that hencefor-
ward for no cause whatever, whether of war, rebellion, ransom, or in any other manner, can any
Indian be made a slave."   This clause was never
repealed, and it stopped the spread of slavery.
Other clauses went further, and made such sweeping provisions for immediate abolition that it proved
to be impossible to enforce them.[2]   The rebellion

The New
Laws.

---

[1] A copy of the text of this papal brief is given in Remesal,
lib. iii. cap. xvii.

[2] " It is well known that the liberation of the Indians from
personal servitude was a measure, not only of humanity and justice, but also of policy, on the part of the Spanish government,
to weaken the growing power of the conquerors and early colonists.   The troubles in Peru give a good example of the state of
affairs."   Bandelier, in *Peabody Museum Reports*, vol. ii. p. 445.
There is some reason for believing that at the time of Gasca's
arrival in Peru, Gonzalo Pizarro was intending to throw off his
allegiance to Spain entirely and make himself king, in which he
would doubtless have been upheld by the settlers had not Gasca

in Peru, which ended in bringing Gonzalo Pizarro's head to the block, was chiefly a rebellion against the New Laws, and as will be inferred from our account of Gasca's proceedings, it was suppressed chiefly by repealing those clauses that operated as a confiscation of property in slaves already existing. The matter was at last compromised by an arrangement that *encomiendas* should be inheritable during two lives, and should then escheat to the crown. This reversion to the crown meant the emancipation of the slaves.

The final compromise.

Meanwhile such provisions were made, and by degrees more and more stringently enforced, as to protect the lives of the Indians and keep them together in their own communities, so that the dreadful *encomienda* reverted to the milder form of the *repartimiento*. Absolute slavery was transformed into villenage. In this ameliorated form the system continued. As generations passed from the scene, the Spanish crown was persuaded to extend the inheritance of the *encomienda* to a third and a fourth life, but without surrendering the reversion. Moreover, there were always some reversions falling in for want of heirs, so that there was gradual emancipation from the first. In this way Indian slavery was tethered and restricted

been able to bring the news of the modification in the New Laws. See the letter from Carvajal to Pizarro, dated March 17, 1547: — " Y esto suplico á vuestra Señoria, que se hierre por mi cabeça; porque para la corona de Rey, con que, en tan breves dias, emos de coronar á vuestra Señoria, avra muy gran concurso de gente. Y para entonces, yo quiero tener cargo de aderecerlas, y tenerlas como conviene." Fernandez, *Historia del Peru*, pt. i. lib. ii. cap. xlix.

until, after the middle of the eighteenth century, under the enlightened administration of Count Florida Blanca, it was annulled.

Though it took so long to reap the full result of the heroic labours of Las Casas, the triumph was none the less his triumph. It was he that, in despite of all harrowing rebuffs and disappointments, brought pope and emperor to his side in the unconquerable determination that the enslavement of Indians must be stopped. He arrested the evil, and though he did not live to see it eradicated, he gave such a direction to things that their further course was upward and not downward. Before he died there was in every part of Spanish America a staff of crown officers charged with the duty of protecting the interests of the crown in the reversion of the *encomiendas*.[1] Then it was no longer possible with impunity to repeat the horrors of Hispaniola and of Nicaragua. It was Las Casas that saved the greater part of Spanish America from such a fate.[2]

Immense results of his labours.

[1] The contemporary testimony of one of the greatest and noblest of Spanish historians to the improvement already wrought in Peru through the work of Las Casas is worth citing : — "In the audiences there are learned men of great piety, who punish those Spaniards that oppress the Indians in any way ; so that now there is no one who can ill treat them, and, in the greater part of these kingdoms, they are as much masters of their own estates and persons as are the Spaniards themselves. Each village is moderately assessed with the amount to be paid as tribute. I remember that, when I was in the province of Xauxa a few years ago, the Indians said to me with much satisfaction : 'This is a happy time, like the days of Tupac Inca Yupanqui ; ' a king of ancient times, whose memory they hold in great veneration." Cieza de Leon, ed. Markham, vol. i. p. 13.

[2] The words of Sir Arthur Helps are strictly just and true : —

The remaining years of this noble life, full as they are of interest, must be passed over briefly. After refusing the bishopric of Cuzco, Las Casas was persuaded to accept the humbler position of bishop of Chiapa near Guatemala. He never could be prevailed upon to accept a reward or present of any sort, but he took the see of Chiapa, as a soldier would undertake to storm a redoubt. He knew there was hard work in store for him there in enforcing the New Laws. When he arrived upon the scene in 1544, it was much as if Garrison in 1860 had se- Las Casas made Bishop of Chiapa. cured from the United States government a decree of emancipation, and then had gone to Charleston with authority to enforce it. The new bishop was greeted with howls of rage. In any other than a Spanish community it might have gone hard with him, but the fiercest Spaniard would always be pretty sure to stop short of laying violent hands upon a prince of the church.[1]

" His was one of those few lives that are beyond biography, and require a history to be written in order to illustrate them. His career affords perhaps a solitary instance of a man who, being neither a conqueror, a discoverer, nor an inventor, has by the pure force of benevolence become so notable a figure that large portions of history cannot be written, or at least cannot be understood, without the narrative of his deeds and efforts being made one of the principal threads upon which the history is strung." *Spanish Conquest*, vol. iv. p. 350.

[1] " For such is the reverence they bear to the Church here, and so holy a conceit they have of all ecclesiastics, that the greatest Don in Spain will tremble to offer the meanest of them any outrage or affront." Letter of August 15, 1623, referring to the death of Thomas Washington, page to Prince Charles on his visit with Buckingham to Spain, discovered by Mr. Henry FitzGilbert Waters, in the British Museum. See *The Visitor*, Salem, Mass.. February 11, 1891.

The dignity, the commanding tact, of Las Casas was moreover such that a terrible mob at Ciudad Real ended in the rioters throwing themselves in tears at his feet, kissing the hem of his robe, and begging his forgiveness.[1] After three years Las Casas resigned his bishopric and returned to Spain. It was a time when the New Laws were imperilled, and he felt that his steadying hand was needed at the Spanish court, while he had now in the New World so many Dominicans devoted to the good work that he could afford to leave it to the care of these faithful lieutenants.[2] During the vicissitudes of his long struggle he had crossed the Atlantic not less than fourteen times; he had once, it appears, sailed down the Pacific to Peru; he had four times travelled far into Germany to get the emperor's ear at some critical moment. Now his journeyings were to cease. After leaving America in 1547 he returned no more, but lived for the remaining nineteen years of his life at the Dominican college of San Gregorio at Valladolid.

His final return to Spain.

In 1550 he took part in a great controversy with Juan de Sepulveda, one of the most celebrated scholars of that time. Sepulveda wrote a book in which he maintained the right of the pope and the king of Spain to make war upon the heathen people of the New World and bring them forcibly into the fold

His controversy with Sepulveda.

---

[1] See the thrilling accounts in Remesal, lib. vii. cap. viii.–x.; Helps, iv. 303–312.

[2] I would by no means be understood as wanting in appreciation of the glorious work of Motolinia and other noble Franciscans, but our subject has its limitations.

of Christ. This was contrary to the doctrine
which Las Casas had set forth fifteen years before
in the Latin treatise above mentioned. He felt
that it was dangerous, and determined to answer
Sepulveda. After the fashion of those days,
Charles V. convoked at Valladolid a council of
learned theologians, and the cause was argued before them at great length by Las Casas and Sepulveda. The doughty champions assailed each
other with texts from the Bible and Aquinas, scholastic logic and patristic history, and every other
weapon known in the mediæval armory. For a
man of such fervour as Las Casas it was a delicate
situation. In maintaining his ground that persuasion is the only lawful method for making men
Christians, extreme nicety of statement was required, for the least slip might bring him within
the purview of the Inquisition. Men were burning at the stake for heresy while this discussion
was going on, and the controversy more than once
came terribly near home. But as Sepulveda said
afterwards, with unfeigned admiration of his antagonist, he was "the most crafty and vigilant
of mortals, and so ready with his tongue that in
comparison with him Homer's Ulysses was a thick-
witted stutterer." [1] When it came to a judgment
the council did not dare to occupy the position of
Las Casas, and so they gave a hesitating judgment
in favour of Sepulveda ; but the emperor, doubt-

[1] "Longum esset præstigias, artes et machinamenta comme-
morare, quibus me deprimere, et veritatem atque justitiam ob-
scurare conatus est artifex ille versutissimus, et idem vigilantis-
simus et loquacissimus, cui Ulysses Homericus collatus iners erat
et balbus." Sepulveda, *Opera*, Madrid, 1780, tom. iii. p. 241.

less with a pleasant smile for Master Bartholomew, proceeded forthwith to suppress Sepulveda's book, and sent stringent orders to America to have any copies of it found there seized and burned.

In 1555 Charles V. retired to the monastery of Yuste, and his son Philip II. became king of Spain. Las Casas and Philip's plans, as all know, were so vast Philip II. and so impossible that he wrecked himself and Spain with them. At the outset he was short of money, and there were advisers at hand to remind him that the colonists in America would jump at the chance of buying in the reversion of their *encomiendas* at a handsome price in hard cash. This would at once put a very large sum of money into Philip's hands, and it would put the Indians back into absolute slavery, as in the old days in Hispaniola. The temptation was great, and against such a frightful disaster Las Casas, now in his eighty-second year, came forth to contend. Fortunately the power of the Church, reinforced by political considerations already mentioned, was firmly enlisted on his side, and he prevailed. This was the last of his triumphs, and it is worth remembering that pretty much the only praiseworthy thing Philip II. ever did was done under his influence.

In his eighty-seventh year, in the peaceful seclusion of the college at Valladolid, Las Casas brought to a close the great " History of the In-The History dies," which he seems to have begun in of the Indies. the monastery at San Domingo more than thirty years before. A remark of Remesal's makes it probable that the book was begun, per-

haps in so far as the sketching of its general outline was concerned, as early as 1527, but its knowledge of contemporary writers and events proves
that it was for the most part written between 1552
and 1561. In a formal note dated November,
1559, Las Casas consigned the book in trust to the
College of San Gregorio, expressing his wish that
it should not be made public before the end of
that century. Partly from the inertia attendant
upon all human things, partly because of the plain-
ness with which it told such terrible truths, the
book was allowed to lie in manuscript for more
than three hundred years. During the present
century such writers as Irving, Helps, and a few
others, read it to good purpose in the manuscript,
and at length in 1875 it was published. In a far
truer sense than any other book, it may be called
the corner-stone of the history of the American continent. It stops at 1522, when Las Casas became
a Dominican monk. One wishes that it might
have been continued to 1547, when he took his
last leave of the New World. But there are limits
even to what the longest and strongest life can do.
After finishing his work upon this book, and in
his ninetieth year, Las Casas wrote a valuable
treatise on the affairs of Peru. His last act was
to go to Madrid and secure a royal decree promot-
ing in certain ways the welfare of the natives of
Guatemala. Having accomplished this, he died
at Madrid, after a few days' illness, at Death of Las
the age of ninety-two. In all this long Casas.
and arduous life — except for a moment, perhaps,
on the crushing news of the destruction of his

colony upon the Pearl Coast — we find no record of work interrupted by sickness, and to the very last his sight was not dim nor his natural force abated.

In contemplating such a life as that of Las Casas, all words of eulogy seem weak and frivolous. The historian can only bow in reverent awe before a figure which is in some respects the most beautiful and sublime in the annals of Christianity since the Apostolic age. When now and then in the course of the centuries God's providence brings such a life into this world, the memory of it must be cherished by mankind as one of its most precious and sacred possessions. For the thoughts, the words, the deeds of such a man, there is no death. The sphere of their influence goes on widening forever. They bud, they blossom, they bear fruit, from age to age.

CHAPTER XII.

THE WORK OF TWO CENTURIES.

THE wreck of the Admiral's flagship on the Christmas of 1492 determined the site of the first European colony in the New World, and perhaps it is not too much to say that by this accident the fortunes of Columbus were from that day forth linked to the island of Hispaniola. There the Spanish colonial society assumed its earliest type. From that island we have seen the lines of discovery and conquest radiating westward with Velasquez and Cortes, and southward with Balboa and the Pizarros. To Hispaniola we returned in order to trace the beginnings of Indian slavery and the marvellous career of Las Casas. From Hispaniola we must now again take our start, but to return no more. We have to follow the lines of discovery northward with Ponce de Leon and Pineda, and far beyond them, until we have obtained a sketch of the development of the knowledge of the huge continental mass of North America. This development was the Work of Two Centuries, and during that period much other work of cardinal importance was going on in the world, which had resulted before its close in the transfer of maritime supremacy and the lead in colonial enterprise

Hispaniola the centre of Spanish colonization.

from Spain and Portugal to France and England.
In completing our geographical story, therefore,
we shall return no more to Hispaniola, but shall
be led farther and farther away from that earliest
A change of   centre, under the guidance of various
scene.   leaders with various aims, until the
epilogue will take us into the frozen zone which
was visited in our prologue, and once more we
shall see a stout Scandinavian captain land upon
the shores of North America, coming this time,
however, from the Siberian coast with Russian
ships, to sever the last link that in men's minds
continued to connect the New World with the
continent of Asia. In covering so much ground
in a single chapter, we must be content with a
mere sketch of the outlines ; for that will be most
conducive to clearness and will best harmonize
with the general plan upon which this work has
been from the outset conceived.

As we have already seen, it is in a high degree
probable that the peninsula of Florida was circumnavigated, and a portion of the Atlantic coast
First voyage   to the northward visited, in the spring
of Vespucius.   and summer of 1498, by an expedition
in which Pinzon and Solis were the commanders,
with Vespucius and Ledesma assisting as pilots.
Reasons have also been given why that voyage was
not followed up and came to be wellnigh forgotten,
as was also the case, though to a less extent, with
the voyages of John Cabot and the Cortereals.
The Indian ocean, with its spices, being the region
toward which men's eager eyes were turned, the

wild coasts of North America were hastily glanced at and abandoned, very much as your dog sniffs at an unpromising bone, and turns away. As already observed, the only probable effect of a voyage around Florida at that moment would be to throw more or less discredit upon Marco Polo.

Stories from eastern Asia had not, however, lost their charm for adventurers. In Mandeville's multifarious ragout there is mention of a Fountain of Youth at a place called Polombe. The author cribbed it from a spurious letter purporting to come from Prester John, which made its way through Europe in the latter part of the twelfth century. Those that drink The Fountain of Youth. of this fountain, says the old rogue, seem always young, as he knows because he has tried it himself![1] Now this Fons Juventutis had its remote

---

[1] " At the heued of þis ilk forest es þe citee of Polombe ; and besyde þat citee es a mountayne, wharoff þe citee takeȝ þe name, for men calleȝ þe mountayne Polombe. And at þe fote of þis mountayne es a well, noble and faire ; and þe water þeroff has a swete sauour and reflaire, as it ware of diuerse maner of spicery. And ilke houre of þe day þe water chaungeȝ diuersely his sauour and his smell. And wha so drinkes fastand thryes of þat well, he sall be hale of what maner of malady þat he hase. And forþi þat wonneȝ nere þat well drynkeȝ þeroff ofter, and þerfore þai hafe neuermore sekeness, bot euermore þai seme yung. I, John Maundeuill, sawe þis well and drank þeroff thrys and all my felawes, and euermore sen þat tyme I fele me þe better and þe haler and supposeȝ for to do till þe tyme þat Godd of his grace will make me to passe oute of þis dedly lyf. Sum men calleȝ þat well *Fons iuuentutis*, þat es for to say, þe well of yowthehede ; for þai þat drinkeȝ þeroff semeȝ all way yung. And þai say þis well commeȝ fra Paradys terrestre, for it es so vertuous. Thurghe oute all þis cuntree þer growes þe best gynger þat es ower whare ; and marchaundes commeȝ þider fra ferre cuntreeȝ for to bye it." Roxburgh Club's *Buke of Mandeuill*, p. 84.

origin in folk-lore, and there is nothing strange in the Spaniards hearing things said by the Indians that reminded them of it. From something thus said by the Indians they got the idea that upon an island called Bimini, northward from Hispaniola, this famous fountain was situated ; [1] and in 1512 the brave Juan Ponce de Leon, who had come out with Columbus in his second voyage, obtained King Ferdinand's permission to go and conquer Bimini. He sailed with three caravels from Porto Rico in March, 1513, and on the 27th of that month, being Easter Sunday, which in Spanish is called Pascua Florida, he came within sight of the coast ever since known as that of Florida. On the 2d of April Ponce de Leon landed a little north of the site of St. Augustine, and then turned back and followed the coast of the peninsula around to its west side in latitude 27° 30'. Further exploration was prevented at that time by the breaking out of war with the Caribs. It was not until 1521 that Ponce de Leon was able to take a colony to the Land of Easter. His party was attacked with great fury by the Indians, and instead of finding his fountain of youth he received a wound in the thigh from a flint arrow, which caused him to abandon the enterprise and retreat to Cuba, where he died after prolonged suffering.

The Land of Easter.

Proof was already at hand that Florida was not an island, for in 1519 Alvarez de Pineda had followed that coast as far as the site of Tampico

---

[1] Peter Martyr, dec. ii. lib. x. ; cf. Oviedo, pt. i. lib. xix. cap. xv.

in Mexico, where he found Cortes and his men in
the course of their preliminary wanderings before
founding Vera Cruz. Pineda then turned back,
and after a while entered the mouth of Pineda's dis-
the Mississippi, which he called Rio de covery of the
Mississippi,
Santo Espiritu. He seems to have 1519.
been the first European to sail upon this great
river. How far he ascended it is not clear, but
he spent six weeks upon its waters and its banks,
trading with the Indians, who seemed friendly
and doubtless laboured under the usual first impression as to the supernatural character of the
white men. Pineda said that he saw one considerable Indian town and no less than forty hamlets,
and that the Indians wore gold ornaments.[1]

This voyage increased the interest in exploration to the northward, and another cause now began to operate in the same direction. When the
remnant of Magellan's expedition returned to
Spain in 1522, after its three years' voyage, it first
began to be dimly realized in Europe that there
was an immense ocean between Mundus Novus
and Asia. It now became an object to find ways
of getting past or through this barrier of land
which we now call America, in order to make the
voyage to Asia. In 1525 Garcia de Loaysa was
sent by the Spanish government to the strait of
Magellan, and arrived there. Early in 1526 one
of Loaysa's ships was caught by a storm in the

[1] See Navarrete, *Coleccion*, tom. iii. pp. 147–153; Herrera,
dec. ii. lib. x. cap. xviii.; Peter Martyr, dec. v. cap. i. In his
visit to Tampico, Pineda was preceded by Diego de Camargo,
who sailed thither in 1518. See Las Casas, *Hist. de las Indias,*
tom. iv. p. 466.

Atlantic, near the strait, and driven southward as far as Cape Horn, but this fact did not attract general attention. The voyage of Magellan did not end the controversy between Spain and Portugal as to the ownership of the Moluccas, for their longitude was variously reckoned. Did they lie west or east of the meridian antipodal to Pope Alexander's dividing line on the Atlantic? With the best of intentions, the problem of longitude was in those days very difficult, and a discrepancy of a thousand miles or more between the Spanish and Portuguese reckonings was likely enough to occur, even had there been no bias on the part of the reckoners. As it was, there was no hope of agreement between the two powers, except through some political compromise. In 1524 the question was submitted to what is known as the Congress of Badajos, an assembly of cosmographers, pilots, and lawyers, including such famous names as Ferdinand Columbus and Sebastian Cabot, with Estevan Gomez, Sebastian Elcano, Diego Ribeiro, and others. "They were empowered to send for persons and papers, and did in reality have before them pilots, papal bulls, treaties, royal grants and patents, log books, maps, charts, globes, itineraries, astronomical tables, the fathers of the church, ancient geographies and modern geographers, navigators with their compasses, quadrants, astrolabes, etc. For two months they fenced, ciphered, debated, argued, protested, discussed, grumbled, quarrelled, and almost fought, yet they

[marginal notes:] Cape Horn.   Congress of Badajos.

could agree upon nothing."[1] The congress broke up without any definite result, and Spain retained her hold upon the Spiceries. The Philippine archipelago, which equally with the Moluccas lies on the Portuguese side of the dividing line, remains in Spanish hands to this day. But in 1529 Charles V. ceded his claim upon the Moluccas to Portugal for 350,000 gold ducats. His original intention was merely to grant a long lease, but by some oversight no precise period was mentioned, and the lease was suffered to become perpetual. In 1548 the emperor was urged by his legal advisers to recall the lease, but would not; whereat " some marvelled and others grieved, but all held their peace."[2]

Now since the Portuguese used their own route across the Indian ocean to the Spiceries, many years elapsed before much attention was paid to the southern extremity of South America. The next person to see Cape Horn was Sir Francis Drake in 1578, and the first person to sail around it was the Dutch navigator Schouten van Horn, after whom it was named. This was not until 1616.

. It was the excessive length of the voyage from Europe to Asia by this southwestern route that prevented activity in this direction. Sailors began trying to find shorter routes. As it was now

[1] Stevens, *Historical and Geographical Notes*, p. 42. " Estuvieron muchos dias mirando globos, cartas y relaciones, y alegando cada qual de su derecho, y porfiando terribilissimamente." Gomara, *Historia general de las Indias*, Antwerp, 1554, fol. 131 verso.

[2] Guillemard's *Magellan*, p. 16.

proved that there was a continuous coast-line all
the way from the strait of Magellan
to the St. John's river in Florida, one
immediate effect of Magellan's voyage
was to turn people's attention to the northward
in the hope of finding a northwest passage from
Europe to Asia. A most pathetic and thrilling
story is that of the persistent search for the
Northwest Passage, kept up for 330 years, and
gradually pushed farther and farther up among
Arctic ice-floes, until at length in 1854 the passage was made from Bering strait to Davis strait
by Sir Robert McClure. For more than a century
after Magellan did navigators anxiously scan the
North American coast and sail into the mouths of
great rivers, hoping to find them straits or channels
leading into the western ocean; for it began to
be plain that this coast was not Asia, but a barrier
in the way thither, and until long inland expeditions had been made, how was anybody to know
anything about the mass of the northern continent, or that it was so many times wider than
Central America?

Search for a Northwest Passage, 1524-1854.

The first of these navigators was Lucas Vasquez
d'Ayllon, who came up in 1524 from Hispaniola
and tried the James river and Chesapeake bay.
Not finding a northwest passage, but liking the
country, he obtained a grant of it from Charles V.,
and in 1526 began to build a town called San Miguel, about where the English founded
Jamestown eighty-one years afterward.
Negro slaves were employed by the
Spaniards in this work, and this would seem

*Spanish col-
ony on James
river, 1526.*

to be the first instance of slave labour on the part of negroes within the territory since covered by the United States. Ayllon had 600 people with him, both men and women, besides 100 horses ; and Antonio Montesino accompanied him as missionary preacher. If this enterprise had succeeded, the future course of American history might have been strangely modified. But Ayllon died of a fever, and under the combined effects of hunger and sickness, internecine quarrels, negro insurrection, and attacks from the Indians, the little colony soon succumbed; and of the survivors the greater part were shipwrecked on the way back to Hispaniola. Antonio Montesino was sent in 1528 to Venezuela, where he disappears from history. When or where he died we do not know, save that in the register of the Dominican monastery of San Estevan, in Salamanca, against the honoured name of Antonio Montesino there is written in some unknown hand this marginal note, *Obiit martyr in Indiis*, " died a martyr in the Indies," which must probably mean that he was somewhere slain by poor stupid red men unable to recognize their best friends.

While Ayllon was losing his own life and those of his people on the bank of the James river, another navigator was searching for a new route for the ships of Charles V. to the Moluccas. In the course of the year 1525 Estevan Gomez, Voyage of Gomez, 1525. the pilot who had so basely deserted Magellan, coasted from Labrador to Florida, taking notice of Cape Cod, Narragansett bay, and the mouths of the Connecticut, Hudson, and Delaware rivers. The comment of Peter Martyr upon this voyage of Gomez is very significant, as illustrating the small favour with which such voyages as those of the Cabots and the first of Vespucius had been regarded. "Stephanus Gomez, . . . neither finding the straight, nor Gaitaia [Cathay] which he promised, returned backe within tenn monethes after his departure. I always thought and presupposed this good man's imaginations were vayn and friuolous. Yet wanted he no suffrages and voyces in his fauour and defence. Notwithstanding he found pleasant and profitable countries, agreeable with our parallels and degrees of the pole. . . . *But what need haue we of these things which are common with all the people of Europe?* To the South, to the South for the great and exceeding riches of the Equinoctiall : they that seek riches must not go vnto the cold and frosen North." [1]

Gomez seems to have been preceded on these coasts by more than one navigator sailing in the service of France. We have already observed Norman and Breton sailors taking their share in the fisheries upon the banks of Newfoundland from the beginning of the century.[2] Francis I. of

[1] Martyr, dec. viii. cap. x. ; Herrera, dec. iii. lib. viii. cap. viii. ; Gomara, cap. xl. ; Oviedo, cap. x. In Diego Ribeiro's map, made in 1529, the regions about Virginia are called " land of Ayllon," and the regions from New Jersey to Rhode Island are called " land of Estevan Gomez." The name given by Gomez to what was afterwards called Hudson's river was Rio de San Antonio. See De Costa, *Sailing Directions of Henry Hudson*, Albany, 1869, p. 44.

[2] For Léry's attempt to found a colony at Cape Breton in 1518, see Sixte Le Tac, *Histoire chronologique de la Nouvelle France*, pp. 40, 58.

France manifested but slight reverence for Pope Alexander VI. and his bulls. According to Bernal Diaz he sent word to his great rival Charles V., asking him by what right he and the king of Portugal undertook to monopolize the earth. Had our first father Adam made them his sole heirs? If so it would be no more than proper for them to produce a copy of the will; and meanwhile he should feel at liberty to seize upon all he could get. Among the corsairs active at that time in the French marine was one known to the Spaniards as Juan Florin or Florentin. His name was Giovanni da Verrazano, and he seems to have been born about 1480 at Florence, where his family had attained distinction. In 1523 he captured the treasure on its way from Cortes, in Mexico, to the Emperor Charles V.; and early in the next year he crossed the Atlantic with one ship and about fifty men. The first land sighted was probably near Cape Fear, in North Carolina. From that point Verrazano skirted the coast northward as far as latitude 50°, and seems to have discovered the Hudson river, and to have landed upon Rhode Island and at some point not far from the mouth of the Piscataqua. Little or nothing is known of Verrazano after this voyage.[1]

Voyage of Verrazano, 1524.

[1] It has been doubted whether Verrazano ever made any such voyage. See Murphy, *The Voyage of Verrazano*, New York, 1875. Mr. Murphy's conclusions have not been generally sustained. For further discussions see Brevoort, *Verrazano the Navigator*, New York, 1874; Asher's *Henry Hudson*, London, 1860, pp. 197–228; Kohl's *Discovery of Maine*, chap. viii.; De Costa, *Verrazano the Explorer*, New York, 1881, with a full bibliographical note; Winsor, *Narr. and Crit. Hist.*, iv. 1–30.

It has been said that he was caught by the Spaniards in 1527 and hanged for piracy, and there is another story that he was roasted and eaten by the Indians in that year, but all this is quite doubtful.

The staggering blows inflicted upon Francis I. by Charles V. in the Italian campaign of 1525 prevented any further activity in following up the voyage of Verrazano. Ten years later came Jacques Cartier, who explored the lower portion of the river St. Lawrence, and found an Iroquois town, named Hochelaga, on an eminence which he called Montreal. Before Champlain's arrival, seventy years later, the Iroquois had been driven from this region. In 1540–43 an unsuccessful attempt was made by the Sieur de Roberval, aided by Cartier, to establish a French colony in Canada. Connected with this expedition was the voyage of the pilot Jehan Allefonsce, of Saintonge, in which he seems to have visited the coast between Cape Cod and Cape Ann.[1] Little more was done by the French in this direction until the time of Champlain.

Cartier and Roberval, 1534–43.

The maps made about this time reflect the strong desire for a northwest passage to Cathay in the extreme slimness which they assign to a part of the North American mainland. In 1529 Hieronimo da Verrazano made a map in which he undertook to represent his brother's discoveries;[2] and upon

[1] For a discussion of this voyage, see De Costa, *Northmen in Maine*, pp. 80–122; and his chapter in Winsor, *Narr. and Crit. Hist.*, vol. iv. chap. ii.; see also Weise, *Discoveries of America*, New York, 1884, chap. xi.

[2] For a reduced copy of the map see Winsor, *Narr. and Crit.*

this map we find Florida connected with the Verrazano region by a slender isthmus. The   The "Sea of
imaginary sea washing the western shore Verrazano."
of this isthmus was commonly known as the Sea of
Verrazano. Possibly the notion may have arisen
from a misinterpretation of some small neck of land
with a bay or sound beyond it somewhere upon the
Atlantic coast explored in the voyage of 1524. But,
in whatever misconception it may have had its origin, the Sea of Verrazano continued to be reproduced on maps for many years, until inland exploration expelled it. Two interesting illustrations,
toward the middle of the sixteenth century, show
respectively the wet and the dry theories of the relation of the North American coast to Asia. The
first of these maps, made at Venice in 1536, by
Baptista Agnese, cuts off the hypothetical unvisited
coasts to the south of Peru [1] and to the west and
north of Mexico with a dotted line, but gives the
equally hypothetical coast of the Verrazano sea as
if its existence were quite undoubted. According
to this map the voyage to Cathay by the Verrazano
route would be at least as simple as the voyage to
Peru by way of Panama. A very different view is
given upon the "Carta Marina" by Jacopo Gastaldi, published in the Ptolemy of 1548. Here
Florida and Mexico appear as parts of Asia, and
the general conception is not unlike that of the
globe of Orontius Finæus; but the Verrazano sea

Hist., iv. 26. The original is in the College of the Propaganda at
Rome.

[1] The coast from the strait of Magellan northward to Peru was
first explored by Alonso de Camargo in 1539–40.

appears to the north of Florida. Here, therefore, it does not afford a ready means of access to China, but to some northern ocean washing the shores of an "Upper India," concerning which it may be suspected that the map-maker's ideas were not of the clearest.

Sketch of Agnese's map, Venice, 1536.[1]

From this chart of Gastaldi's the position of the Verrazano sea naturally leads us to the map by

[1] KEY: — "1. Terra de bacalaos.   2. (*dotted line*) El viage de France.   3. (*dotted line*) El viage de Peru.   4. (*dotted line*) El viago a maluche.   5. Temistetan.   6. Iucatan.   7. Nombre de dios.   8. Panama.   9. La provintia del peru.   10. La provintia de chinagua.   11. S. paulo.   12. Mundus novus.   13. Brazil.   14. Rio de la plata.   15. El Streto de ferdinando de Magallanas." Winsor, *Narr. and Crit. Hist.*, iv. 40.

Sebastian Münster, published in the Ptolemy of
1540. Though thus published eight years earlier
than Gastaldi, this map represents in some respects

Gastaldi's Carta Marina, 1548.[1]

a later development toward the more correct views
heralded by Mercator.[2] There is an approach to-

[1] KEY: — "1. Norvegia. 2. Laponia. 3. Gronlandia. 4. Tierra
del Labrador. 5. Tierra del Bacalaos. 6. La Florida. 7. Nueva
Hispania. 8. Mexico. 9. India Superior. 10. La China. 11.
Ganges. 12. Samatra. 13. Java. 14. Panama. 15. Mar del Sur.
16. El Brasil. 17. El Peru. 18. Strecho de Fernande Magalhaes.
19. Tierra del Fuego." Winsor, *Narr. and Crit. Hist.*, iv. 43.
Observe that Gastaldi retains the mediæval notion of Greenland
as connected with Norway.

[2] See above, p. 153.

INDIA superior

Terra florida

Chamaho   Panuco Inf. Tortucard

CVBA

Incatara

Iamic

Berragua

Nouus

Catigara   out Iula At
                         ent Brasil

Inf. infortu
nate

Mare pacificum

Münster's

map, 1540.[1]

Winsor, *Narr. and Crit. Hist.*, iv. 41.

ward the conception of the western hemisphere as a distinct and integral whole, though the Pacific is still very narrow and Zipangri (Japan) still comes very near to Mexico, as in the Stobnicza map of 1512. The reader will also observe the New World with its Catigara, the significant mark of a Ptolemaic pedigree, although now quite torn asunder from Asia. Pizarro and his pilots would, I suspect, have laughed somewhat rudely at the promontory on which this Catigara is placed, — an imaginary fragment of Asia that happened to stay on this side when the tear came. As to the Verrazano sea, when we compare it upon this map and that of Agnese, as well as upon Michael Lok's map more than forty years later, we can understand how it was that even as late as the seventeenth century such a navigator as Henry Hudson should try to get through his river into the Pacific.

The only means of correcting these inadequate and fluctuating views were to be found in expeditions into the interior of the continent, and here the beginnings were slow and painful. The first Spaniard to avail himself of Pineda's discoveries was Panfilo de Narvaez, the man who had been sent to Mexico to arrest and supersede Cortes, and had so ingloriously failed in that attempt. Pineda's mention of gold ornaments on the Mississippi Indians was enough to set Narvaez in motion. If there was so much glory and plunder in one direction, why not in another? He obtained permission to conquer and govern all the northern coast of the gulf of Mexico, and started

Expedition of Narvaez.

from Cuba in March, 1528, with four ships, carrying 400 men and 80 horses. Landing at Apalache
bay, he made a bootless excursion into the country,
and on his return to the seashore was unable to find
his ships, which were sailing to and fro on the watch
for him. After travelling westward on foot for a
month, Narvaez and his men, with desperate exer-
tions, built five frail boats and pursued their journey by water. After six weeks of coasting they
came to the mouth of a river so great that it fresh-
ened the sea so that they could drink the sea-water.
At the mouth of this river, the Mississippi, two of
the boats, one of them containing Narvaez himself,
were capsized, and all their company lost. The
other three boats were thrown ashore, probably
somewhere in eastern Texas, and such of their
crews as escaped starvation were murdered by the
natives. Four men, however, the treasurer Cabeza
de Vaca, with two Spanish comrades, Dorantes and
Castillo, and a negro called Estevánico, or "Little
Steve," had a wonderful course of adventures.
They were captured by different parties
of Indians and carried about in various   Adventures of
                                            Cabeza de
directions in the wilderness of western   Vaca.
Louisiana and eastern Texas. Cabeza de Vaca
achieved some success as a trader, bartering shells
and wampum from the coast for "flint flakes, red
clay, hides and skins, and other products of the regions inland." [1] A reputation early acquired as a

[1] The journey of Cabeza de Vaca and his comrades is ably described and their route traced by Mr. Bandelier, *Contributions to
the History of the Southwestern Portion of the United States*, Cambridge, 1890 (Papers of the Archæological Institute of America
— American Series. V. Hemenway Southwestern Archæological
Expedition).

medicine-man or sorcerer proved helpful to him, and may very likely have preserved his life. After strange vicissitudes and terrible sufferings the four comrades were thrown together again at some point west of the Sabine river in Texas. Circumstances happened to give them all a reputation for skilful sorcery, and by degrees they made use of this singular power to induce the parties of Indians with them to move in certain directions rather than others. With a vague hope of finding the seashore they kept in the main a westerly course, and presently their fame grew to such a height that Indians came to them in throngs bringing gifts. Proceeding in this way they presently crossed the Rio Pecos near its junction with the Rio Grande; then ascending the latter river they made their way across Chihuahua and Sonora to the gulf of California, and then turning southward at length in May, 1536, reached Culiacan, then an extreme frontier of the Spaniards, after this wonderful pilgrimage of nearly 2,000 miles.

The reports of this journey aroused much interest among the Spaniards in Mexico. Not less than four attempts at exploration upon the Pacific coasts had been made by Cortes, but not much had been accomplished beyond the discovery of Lower California. Now there were reasons that made the idea Legend of the of an inland expedition to the northward Seven Cities. seem attractive. There was a tradition afloat in Europe, that on the occasion of the conquest of the Spanish peninsula by the Arabs in the eighth century, a certain bishop of Lisbon with a goodly company of followers took refuge upon an

island or group of islands far out on the Sea of
Darkness, and founded seven cities there. With
the fabulous Antilia, which was commonly regarded
as the island of the Seven Cities, we have already
made acquaintance. Its name, slightly modified
into "Antilles," came to be applied to the West
Indies. Its seven cities were curiously transferred
into the very heart of the American continent.
Among the Nahuatl tribes there was a legend of
Chicomoztoc, or the Seven Caves from which at
some period in the past their ancestors issued. As
soon as the Spaniards got hold of this legend they
contrived to mix up these Seven Caves with their
Seven Cities. They were supposed to be somewhere to the northward, and when Cabeza de Vaca
and his comrades had disclosed the existence of
such a vast territory north of Mexico, it was resolved to search for the Seven Cities in that direction. The work was entrusted to Fray Marcos of
Nizza, or Nice, as we now call it since it
has been "reunited" — that is the or- Fray Marcos.
thodox French way of expressing it — to France.
He was a Franciscan monk of great ability, who
had accompanied Pizarro on the first march to Caxamarca to meet Atahualpa. He had afterward gone
to Quito and thence seems to have accompanied Alvarado on his return to Guatemala. He had lately
found his way to Mexico, and was selected by the
great viceroy Antonio de Mendoza to go and find
the Seven Cities.[1] He was attended on the journey

[1] Like so many other travellers and explorers Fray Marcos has
been charged with falsehood; but his case has been to a considerable extent cleared up in Bandelier's excellent monograph
already cited, *Contributions to the History of the Southwestern Portion of the United States.*

by the negro Estevánico and a few Pima Indians who
had been educated at Mexico; and their reception
by the natives along the route was extremely hospitable. At Matape, an Indian village in Sonora,
they heard definite news of a country situated
thirty days' march to the northward, where there
were seven large cities, "with houses of stone and
lime, . . . the smallest ones of two
The Seven
Cities of
Cibola.
stories and a flat roof, and others of
three and four stories, and that of the
lord with five, all placed together in order; and on
the door-sills and lintels of the principal houses
many figures of turquoise stones . . . and [it was
said] that the people of these cities are very well
clothed," etc.[1] The name of the first of these
cities was said to be Cibola. And from that time
forth this became a common name for the group,
and we hear much of the Seven Cities of Cibola.

These were the seven pueblos of Zuñi, in New
Mexico, of which six were still inhabited at the
end of the sixteenth century. The name Cibola was
properly applied to the group, as it referred to the
whole extent of territory occupied by the Zuñis.
Zuñi.
The surviving pueblo which we know
to-day as Zuñi will probably serve as an
excellent sample of the pueblo towns visited by
the Spaniards in their first wanderings in North
America. As Fray Marcos drew near to it he
heard much of the power and glory of Cibola, and
began to feel that his most romantic anticipations
were about to be verified; but now came his first
misfortune on this journey, and it was a sharp one.

[1] Bandelier, *op. cit.* p. 130.

Hitherto the white man and the black man had been treated with the reverence due to supernatural beings, or to persons who at least were mighty wizards. But at Kiakima, the first of the Zuñi pueblos, the negro's " medicine " was not accepted. Estevánico travelled some miles in advance of Fray Marcos. When he arrived at the first of the cities of Cibola, flaunting the turquoises and the handsome Indian girls, with whom he had been presented in the course of the journey, — much to the disgust of the Franciscan friar, — the elders and chiefs of the pueblo would not grant him admittance. He was lodged in a small house outside the enclosure, and was cautiously catechised. When he announced himself as the envoy and forerunner of a white man, sent by a mighty prince beyond the sky to instruct them in heavenly things, the Zuñi elders were struck with a sense of incongruity. How could black represent white, or be the envoy and forerunner of white? To the metaphysics of the

Murder of Estevánico and retreat of Fray Marcos.

middle status of barbarism the question wore a very uncanny look, and to the common sense of the middle status of barbarism the self-complacent Estevánico appeared to be simply a spy from some chieftain or tribe that wanted to conquer the Zuñis. A Cortes might easily have dealt with such a situation, but most men would consider it very uncomfortable, and so did poor silly " Little Steve." While the elders were debating whether they should do reverence to him as a wizard, or butcher him as a spy, he stole out of his lodging and sought safety in flight ; and this act, being promptly de-

A street in Zuñi.

tected, robbed him of all dignity and sealed his fate. A hue and cry went after him, and an arrow soon found its way to his heart. The news of this catastrophe checked the advance of Fray Marcos. His Indian comrades were discouraged, and the most he could do was to keep them with him while he climbed a hill whence he could get a Pisgah sight of the glories of Cibola. After he had accomplished this, the party returned with all possible haste to Culiacan, and arrived there in August, 1539, after an absence of five months.

As an instance of the tenacious vitality of tradition, and its substantial accuracy in dealing with a very simple and striking fact, it is interesting to find that to this day the Zuñis remember the fate of Estevánico. In one of the folk - tales taken down by Mr. Cushing from the lips of Zuñi priests, it is said that " previous to the first coming of the *Mexicans* (the Zuñi Indian calls all the Spanish-speaking people Mexicans), a *black Mexican* made his appearance at the Zuñi village of Kiakima. He was very greedy, voracious, and bold, and the people killed him for it. After his death the Mexicans [i. e. Spaniards] made their appearance in numbers for the first time, and made war upon the Zuñis, conquering them in the end." [1]

Zuñi recollection of the affair.

---

[1] Bandelier, *op. cit.* p. 154. I think I never spent a pleasanter afternoon than once at Manchester-by-the-sea, with Mr. Cushing and three Zuñi priests who had come thither for the summer to assist him in his work. These Indians of the middle status told me their delightful yarns in exchange for Norse and Russian folk-tales which I told them, and Mr. Cushing served as a lively and dramatic interpreter. These Zuñis were very handsome men,

It was indeed only the next year that the Spaniards made their appearance, accompanied by their
terrible horses.   Six months after the return of
Fray Marcos to Culiacan, an army of 300 Spaniards and 800 Mexican Indians, under
Francisco de Coronado, started for Cibola.   They visited the Zuñi and Moqui pueblos,
discovered the grand cañon of the Colorado, and
marched northward as far as a village called Quivira, concerning the site of which there is some
diversity of opinion.   The farthest point reached
by Coronado may have been somewhere near the
boundary between the states of Kansas and Ne-
braska, or perhaps farther west at some point on
the south fork of the Platte river.[1]   He passed quite
beyond the semi-civilized region of the pueblos, and
was disgusted at finding Quivira only a rude village of thatched wigwams instead of the fine city
for which he had been looking.   The supply of
maize and bison-meat prevented the famine which
so commonly overwhelmed such long expeditions,
and Coronado took excellent care of his men.
Many subordinate explorations were undertaken by
detached parties, and a vast extent of country was
visited.   At length, in the spring of 1542, the
army returned to Mexico, greatly vexed and cha-

Expedition of Coronado.

abounding in kindliness and droll humour, while their refined
grace of manner impressed me as hardly inferior to that of Japa-
nese gentlemen. The combination of this civilized demeanour
with the primeval naïveté of their thoughts was in a high degree
piquant and interesting.

[1] A detailed account of Coronado's expedition is given in the
chapter on " Early Explorations of New Mexico," by H. W.
Haynes, in Winsor, *Narr. and Crit. Hist.*, vol. ii. chap. vii.

grined at having discovered no gold nor any
wealthy kingdom, and this disappointment found a
vent in anathemas vented upon Fray Marcos, which
have ever since been echoed by historians.

Not only in the far west, but also in the east,
did the experience of Cabeza de Vaca serve to
stimulate the desire to explore the interior of the
continent. To Fernando de Soto, no less than to
the viceroy Mendoza, it seemed as if in such a wide
extent of territory there must be king- Expedition of
doms worth plundering. We have al- Soto.
ready met with Soto serving under Pizarro in
Peru. In 1537 he was appointed governor of
Cuba, and was authorized to conquer and occupy
the country embraced within the patent of Narvaez.
He started from Havana in May, 1539, with nine
vessels, containing 570 men and 223 horses. Landing about thirty miles west of the bay of Juan
Ponce, he marched laboriously as far northward as
the Savannah river, and then turned westward.
The golden country for which he was seeking did
not appear, but the Indians on the route were very
hostile. Though Soto had roundly blamed Pizarro
for his treatment of Atahualpa, his own conduct
toward Indians seems to have been at once cruel
and foolish. The Spaniards had to fight their way
across the country, and the tribes of the Creek
confederacy were no mean antagonists. At a palisaded village called Mauvila, a few miles above
the junction of the Tombigbee and Alabama
rivers,[1] there was a desperate fight, in the autumn

[1] It was probably *Mauvila*, or *Maubila*, that gave the name
Mobile to the river formed by the junction of these two. See
Charlevoix, *Journal historique*, p. 452.

of 1541, in which Soto lost 170 of his men, while
from the Spanish estimate of 2,500 as the loss of
the Indians it would perhaps be safe to strike off
a cipher.[1] In December the Spaniards reached
the Yazoo, and spent the winter in that neighbourhood. In the spring they crossed the Mississippi
at the lowest of the Chickasaw bluffs, and ascended
the western bank of the great river as far, perhaps,
as New Madrid. Finding no signs of El Dorado
in that direction, they turned southward. On the
21st of May, 1542, Soto died of a fever, and was
buried in the Mississippi. His men, commanded
by Luis de Moscoso, built boats in which they descended the river and coasted westward along the
shores of Texas. On the 10th of September,
1543, the survivors of the expedition, 311 in number, reached Tampico.[2]

The work of founding colonies in North America
languished. In 1546–49 a party of Dominican
friars, led by the noble Luis de Barbastro, who

[1] The later experiences of American backwoodsmen in fighting
these formidable barbarians should make us distrust all stories of
battles attended with great disparity of loss. If Soto killed 250
of them without losing more than 170 of his own men, he came
off remarkably well. Compare Roosevelt's *Winning of the West*,
vol. i. p. 83 ; vol. ii. 123.

[2] An excellent account of Soto's expedition by one of the survivors was translated into English in 1611, by Richard Hakluyt,
and is now among the publications of the Hakluyt Society : — *The
Discovery and Conquest of Florida*, London, 1851. A brief relation by Luis de Biedma is appended to this book. Garcilasso de
la Vega also wrote a narrative (*La Florida del Ynca*, Lisbon,
1605) based upon reports of survivors, but uncritically treated.
See also Pickett's *History of Alabama*, pp. 25–41. In this connection the reader will find much that is instructive in Jones's
Antiquities of the Southern Indians, New York, 1873.

had been with Las Casas in Tuzulutlan, made an attempt to found a missionary settle- Dominicans in ment in Florida, but they were all mas- Florida. sacred by the Indians. The work was then taken up by Guido de Labazares and Tristan de Luna, under the auspices of Luis de Velasco, the humane and enlightened viceroy of New Spain. Their little colony was barely rescued from destruction by Angelo de Villafañe in 1561, and in the autumn of that year Philip II. announced that there would be no further attempts to colonize that country. As no gold was to be found, the chief reason for occupying Florida was to keep the French from getting hold of it, and it was thought there was no danger of the French coming for the present.

Curiously enough, however, just about this time the French did come to Florida. Two French attempts at colonization grew directly out of the wars of religion. The illustrious Coligny was one of the first men, if not the very first, to conceive the plan of founding a Protestant state in America. In 1555 a small expedition, under Nicholas de Villegagnon, was sent to the coast of Huguenots in Brazil. A landing was made on the Brazil. site of Rio de Janeiro, huts were built, and earthworks thrown up. A large reinforcement of Huguenots, with several zealous ministers from Geneva, arrived on the scene in 1557. But fierce theological disputes combined with want of food to ruin the little community. Villegagnon returned to France to carry on his controversy with the clergy, and the next year the miserable survivors of the colony were slaughtered by the Portuguese.[1]

Coligny's next attempt was made upon the coast of Florida, under the lead of Jean Ribaut, a hardy Huguenot of Dieppe. On May day, 1562, Ribaut, with a small advance party, reached the St. John's river, whence they coasted northward as far as the spot to which they gave the name Port Royal, in what is now South Carolina. Here they built a small fortress, and thirty men were left in charge of it while Ribaut returned to France to bring out his colony. For a while the little garrison lived on the hospitality of the Indians, until the latter, who had at first revered them as children of the Sun, began to despise them as sturdy beggars. Then as hunger began to pinch them, they mutinied and slew their commander. The time wore on, and nothing was heard of Ribaut. At last, in sheer despair, they contrived to patch together a crazy brigantine and set sail for France. Their scanty stock of food gave out while they were in mid-ocean, and one of the party had been devoured by his comrades, when they were picked up by an English cruiser and carried off to London.

Huguenots in Florida; Ribaut.

The return of Ribaut had been delayed by the breaking out of war between the Huguenots and the Guise party; but in 1563 the truce of Amboise made things quiet for a while, and in the following year a new expedition set out for Florida, under the leadership of Ribaut's friend

Laudonnière.

---

[1] The story of the Huguenots in Brazil is fully told by Lescarbot, *Histoire de la Nouvelle France*, Paris, 1612, livre ii.

René de Laudonnière, a pious and valiant knight and a kinsman of Coligny. This company was much larger and better equipped than the former, but there was an essential vice in its composition. There were plenty of soldiers and gentlemen un-used to labour, and a few clever mechanics and tradesmen, but no tillers of the soil. In France, indeed, the rural population remained wedded to the old faith, and there were no Protestant yeomen as in England. The new expedition landed at the St. John's river, and built a fort near its mouth, which, in honour of Charles IX., was called Fort Caroline. This work off their hands, they devoted themselves to injudicious intrigues with the Indian potentates of the neighbourhood, explored the coun-try for gold, and sent home to France for more assistance. Then they began to be mutinous, and presently resorted to buccaneering, with what fatal consequences will presently be seen. A gang of malcontents stole two of the pinnaces, and set out for the coast of Cuba, where, after capturing a small Spanish vessel, they were obliged to go ashore for food, and were thereupon arrested. Carried before the authorities at Havana, they sought to make things right for themselves by giving full information of the settlement at Fort Caroline, and this ill-omened news was not slow in finding its way to the ears of the king of Spain. It came at an opportune moment for Philip II. He had just found a man after his own heart, Pedro Menendez de Avilès, an admirable soldier and matchless liar, brave as a mastiff and savage as a wolf. This man had persuaded Philip to change his mind and let him go and try to found a colony in Florida, whereby the Indians might be converted to Christianity.

Just as Menendez was getting ready to start, there came from Havana the news of the ill-fated Laudonnière and his enterprise. These heretics were trespassers on the territory which Holy Church had assigned to the Spanish crown, and, both as trespassers and as heretics, they must be summarily dealt with. Rumour had added that Ribaut was expected from France with a large armament, so that no time was to be lost. The force at Menendez's disposal was largely increased, and on the 29th of June, 1565, he set sail from Cadiz, with eleven ships and more than 1,000 fighting men, hoping to forestall the arrival of the French commander. The mood in which Menendez started was calculated to make him an ugly customer. He was going on a *crusade*. The original crusades were undertaken for a worthy purpose, and helped to save the Cross from being subdued by the Crescent. But after a while, when heresy became rife, the pope would proclaim a crusade against heretics, and a bloody affair this was apt to be, as the towns of southern France once had reason to know. We may fitly call Menendez the Last of the Crusaders.

Things had fared badly with the colony at Fort Caroline. Mutiny had been checked by the summary execution of a few ringleaders, but famine had set in, and they had come to blows with the Indians. Events succeeded each other curiously. On the 3d of August, in the depth of their distress, Elizabeth's doughty sea-king Sir John Haw-

Menendez, the Last of the Crusaders.

kins touched at the mouth of the St. John's, gave
them food and wine, and offered them a free passage to France in his own ships, and on Laudonnière's refusal left with them a ship with which to
make the voyage for themselves if they should see
fit. On the 28th of August Ribaut at last arrived
with seven ships, bringing 300 men and ample
supplies. On the 4th of September, toward mid-
night, appeared the Spanish fleet !

The squadron of Menendez had undergone great
hardships, and several of the vessels had been
wrecked. Five ships now arrived, but after exchanging defiances with the French, Menendez
concluded not to risk a direct attack, and crept off
down the coast until he came to the site Beginnings of
of St. Augustine. Some 500 negroes St. Augustine.
had been brought on the fleet, and were at once
set to work throwing up entrenchments. One of
the French ships, hanging in the rear, had taken
note of these proceedings, and hurried back to
Fort Caroline with the information. It was then
decided to leave Laudonnière with a small force to
hold the fort, while Ribaut by a sudden naval attack should overwhelm the Spanish fleet and then
pounce upon the troops at St. Augustine before
their entrenchments were completed. This plan
seemed to combine caution with boldness, but the
treachery of wind and weather defeated it. On
the 10th of September Ribaut set sail, and early
next morning his whole fleet bore down upon the
Spaniards. But before they could come to action
there sprang up an equinoctial gale which drove
the French vessels out to sea, and raged so fiercely

for several days as to render it morally certain that, wherever they might be, they could not have effected a return to their fort. It was now the turn of Menendez to take the offensive. On the morning of the 17th, with the storm still raging, he started forth, with 500 men and a couple of Indian guides, to force his way through the forest. For thrice twenty-four hours they waded through swamps and forded swollen brooks, struggling with tall grass and fighting with hatchets the tangled underbrush, — until just before dawn of the 20th, drenched with rain, covered from head to foot with mud, torn with briars, fainting with hunger and weariness, but more than ever maddened with bigotry and hate, this wolfish company swept down the slope before Fort Caroline. The surprise was complete, and the defences, which might barely have sufficed against an Indian assault, were of no avail to keep out these more deadly foes. Resistance was short and feeble. Laudonnière and a few others escaped into the woods, whence, some time afterward, they sought the shore, and were picked up by a friendly ship and carried home to France. Of those who staid in the fort, men, women, and children, to the number of 142, were slaughtered. A few were spared, though Menendez afterward, in his letter to the king, sought to excuse himself for such unwarranted clemency.

Slaughter of the people in Fort Caroline.

Meanwhile the ships of Jean Ribaut were hopelessly buffeting the waves. One after another they were all wrecked somewhere below Matanzas Inlet, a dozen miles south of St. Augustine. Most of the

crews and troops were saved, and, collecting in two
bodies, began to work their way back toward Fort
Caroline. On the 28th of September the first body,
some 200 in number, had halted at Ma- First massa-
tanzas Inlet, which they had no means of cre at Matan-
zas Inlet.
crossing, when they encountered Me-
nendez, who with about 70 men was on the lookout
for them. The two parties were on opposite sides
of this arm of the sea, and the Spaniard so disposed his force among the bushes that the enemy
could not estimate their real number. A boat was
then sent out, and three or four French officers
were decoyed across the river under promise of
safety. They now learned that their fort was destroyed, and their wives and comrades murdered.
At the same time they were requested, in courteous
terms, to lay down their arms and entrust themselves to the clemency of Menendez. Hard as it
seemed, starvation stared them in the face as the
only alternative, and so after some discussion it
was deemed most prudent to surrender. The arms
were first sent across the river, and then the prisoners were brought over, ten at a time, each party
being escorted by twenty Spaniards. As each party
of ten arrived, they were led behind a sand-hill
some distance from the bank, and their hands were
tied behind their backs. A great part of the day
was consumed in these proceedings, and at sunset,
when the whole company of Huguenots had thus
been delivered defenceless into the hands of their
enemy, they were all murdered in cold blood. Not
one was left alive to tell the tale.

A day or two later Ribaut himself, with 350 men,

his entire remaining force, arrived at the inlet, and found Menendez duly ambushed to receive him. Once more the odious scene was acted out. The Frenchmen were judiciously informed of what had been done, but were treated with much courtesy,

Second massacre at Matanzas Inlet.

regaled with bread and wine, and coaxed to surrender. This time there was a difference of opinion. Some 200 swore they would rather be devoured by the Indians than trust to the clemency of such a Spaniard ; and they contrived to slip away into the forest. The remaining 150, with Ribaut himself, were ferried across in small detachments, disarmed and bound, as had been done to their comrades, and when all had been collected together, all but five were put to death. That is to say, five were spared, but besides these, one sailor, who was not quite killed, contrived to crawl away, and after many adventures returned to France, to tell the harrowing tale. From this sailor, and from one of the five who were spared, we get the French account of the affair. The Spanish account we have from Menendez himself, who makes his official report to the king as coolly as a farmer would write about killing pigs or chickens. The two accounts substantially agree, except as regards the promise of safety by which the Frenchmen were induced to surrender. Menendez represents himself as resorting to a pious fraud in using an equivocal form of words, but the Frenchman declares that he promised most explicitly to spare them, and even swore it upon the cross. I am inclined to think that the two statements may be reconciled, in view of the acknowledged skill of Menendez and all his kith and kin as adroit dissemblers. After all said and done, it was a foul affair, and the name Matanzas, which means " slaughterings," came naturally enough to attach itself to that inlet, and remains to this day a me- mento of that momentary fury of a New World crusade.

It used to be said in the days of Philip II. that wherever in any country there turned up a really first-class job of murder, you might be sure the king of Spain had something to do with it. The St. Bartholomew affair, for example, was a case in point. The job done by Menendez, though small in scale, was certainly a thorough one, for it ended the Huguenot colony in Florida. Of the remnant of Ribaut's force which did not surrender, some disappeared among the In- dians. Some were captured by Menendez, and the lives of these he spared, inasmuch as from the glut of slaughter some of his own men recoiled and called him cruel. From his master, however, Me- nendez received hearty approval for his ferocity, relieved by a slight hint of disapprobation for his scant and tardy humanity. " Tell him," said Philip, " that as to those he has killed, he has done well, and as to those he has saved, they shall be sent to the galleys."

This massacre of Frenchmen by Spaniards was perpetrated in a season of peace between the two governments. It was clearly an insult to France, inasmuch as the Huguenot expeditions had been undertaken with the royal commission. But the court of Catherine de' Medici was not likely to call

Philip II. to account for anything he might take it into his head to do. Redress was not far off, but it came in a most unexpected way and at the hands of a private gentleman.

Dominique de Gourgues was a Gascon of noble birth, who had won high distinction in the Italian wars. It is not clear whether he was Catholic or Dominique de Gourgues. Protestant, but he bore a grudge against the Spaniards, by whom he had once been taken prisoner and made to work in the galleys. He made up his mind to avenge the fate of his fellow-countrymen; it should be an eye for an eye and a tooth for a tooth. So he sold his family estate and borrowed money besides, and fitted up three small ships and enlisted about 200 men. In August, 1567, he sailed to the Guinea coast, armed with a royal commission to kidnap negroes. After an autumn and winter of random cruising he crossed the ocean, and it was when approaching Cuba that he first revealed to his followers his purpose. Little persuasion was required. With eager enthusiasm they turned their prows toward the Land of Easter, and soon came to anchor a few miles to the north of the Spanish fort. The Indians were overjoyed at their arrival. At first they had admired Menendez for his craft and the thoroughness with which he disposed of his enemies. But they had since found ample cause to regret their change of neighbours. On the arrival of Gourgues they flocked to his standard in such numbers that he undertook at once to surprise and overwhelm the Spanish garrison of 400 men. The march was conducted with secrecy and despatch.

The Spaniards, not dreaming that there could be such a thing as a Frenchman within three thousand miles of Florida, had grown careless about their watch, and were completely surprised. At mid-day, just as they had finished their dinner, the French and Indians came swarming upon them from all points of the compass. A wild panic en-sred, the works were carried and the defenders slaughtered. Of the whole Spanish force not a man escaped the sword, save some fifteen or twenty whom Gourgues reserved for a more ignominious fate, and to point a moral to this ferocious tale. At the capture of Fort Caroline, it is said that Menendez hanged several of his prisoners to trees near by, and nailed above them a board with the inscription, — "Not as to Frenchmen, but as to Lutherans." Gourgues now *Quid pro quo.* led his fifteen or twenty surviving captives to these same trees, and after reading them a severe lecture hanged them all, and nailed above them the inscription, — "Not as to Spaniards, but as to liars and murderers." The fort was then totally de-molished, so that not a beam or a stone was left in place. And so, having done his work in a thorough and business-like way, the redoubtable avenger of blood set sail for France.

In the matter of repartee it cannot be denied that Gourgues was successful. The retort would have had still more point if Menendez had been one of the hanged. But — unfortunately for the require-ments of poetic justice — the principal liar and murderer was then in Spain, whence he returned a couple of years later, to rebuild his fort and go on converting the Indians.

These sanguinary events were doubtless of real historic importance.   Unpromising as was the be-ginning of the Florida colony, it was no more so than the earliest attempts to settle Canada and Louisiana.   In the brief glimpses that we get of Ribaut we can discern the outlines of a steadfast character that would have been likely to persevere until a solid result had been accomplished. So Menendez seems to have thought when he wrote to the king that by killing this man he believed himself to have dealt a heavier blow to France than if he had beaten an army.   No doubt the affair of Matanzas removed what might have become an additional and serious obstacle in the way of the English, when France and England came to struggle for the mastery over North Amer-ica.[1]

Historic im-portance of the affair.

As for Spain herself, owing to causes presently to be mentioned, she had about reached the limit of her work in the discovery and conquest of Amer-ica.   For the brief remainder of our story we have to deal chiefly with Frenchmen on land and with Englishmen on sea.   The work of demonstrating the character of the continental mass of North

[1] The story of the Huguenots in Florida is superbly told by Francis Parkman, in his *Pioneers of France in the New World*, Boston, 1865.   The chief primary sources are Ribaut's *Whole and True Discovery of Terra Florida*, englished and reprinted by Hakluyt in 1582; Basanier, *L'histoire notable de la Floride*, Paris, 1586; Challeux, *Discours de l'histoire de la Floride*, Dieppe, 1566; *La reprinse de la Floride par le Cappitaine Gourgues*, printed in the collection of Ternaux-Compans; the Spanish chaplain Men-doza's narrative, contained in the same collection; and the MS. letters of Menendez to Philip II., preserved in the archives of Seville and first made public by Mr. Parkman.

America and its internal configuration was mostly done by Frenchmen. The expeditions of Soto and Coronado had made a goodly beginning, but as they were not followed up they did not yield so much increase of geographical knowledge as one might suppose. Two interesting maps made in England early in the last quarter of the sixteenth century represent respectively the wet and dry styles of interpreting the facts as they looked to cartographers at that time. The map dedicated to Sir Philip Sidney by Michael Lok, and published in Hakluyt's "Divers Voyages" in 1582,[1] retains the "Sea of Verrazano," but gives enough continent to include the journeys of Soto and Coronado. In one respect it is interesting as showing just about the extent of North America that was known in 1582, ninety years after the first crossing of the Atlantic by Columbus. The reader will observe that the imaginary islands of Brazil and St. Brandon have not disappeared, but are shifted in position, while the Frislanda of the Zeno narrative appears to the south of Greenland. A conspicuous feature is the large island of Norombega (equivalent to New England with Acadia), separated from the mainland by what is apparently the Hudson river figured as a strait communicating with the St. Lawrence.[2]

Beyond the limits of the known land, and in the

[1] The copy here given is photographed from the reduced copy in Winsor, *Narr. and Crit. Hist.*, iv. 44.

[2] It was very commonly believed at that time that the river discovered by Verrazano and afterward to be named for Hudson was such a strait.

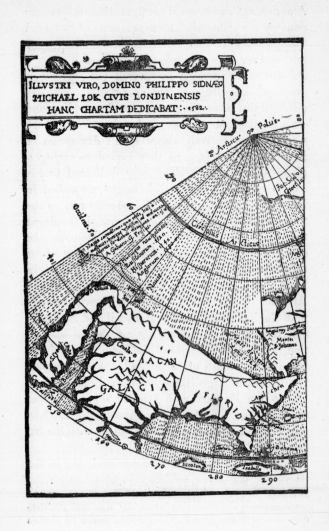

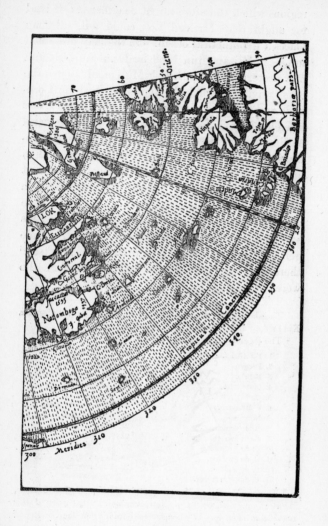

regions which therefore might be either sea or land for aught that Michael Lok could tell, his map places a hypothetical ocean. On the map presented to Queen Elizabeth in 1580 by Dr. John Dee, and now preserved in the British Museum, it is just the other way.[1] Beyond the limits reached by Coronado and Soto and Cartier, this map indicates a vast stretch of unvisited continent, and in its general outline it seems to come nearer to an adequate conception of the dimensions of North America than any of its predecessors.[2] It is noticeable, too, that although this is a " dry " map there is no indication of a connection between America and Asia. The western hemisphere was emerging in men's minds as a distinct and integral whole. Though people generally were not as yet enlightened to this extent,[3] there were many navigators and geographers who were.

[1] The sketch here given is taken from Winsor (iv. 98) after Dr. Kohl's copy in his Washington Collection.

[2] The legends on Dee's map are as follows : —

1. Estotiland.	14. C. de S. Roman.
2. Drogeo.	15. C. de Sta Hellena.
3. Belisle.	16. La Bermuda.
4. C. de Raso.	17. La Emperada.
5. C. de Bryton.	18. Terra Florida.
6. S. Brandan.	19. Rio de Spirito Santo.
7. Norombega.	20. Rio de Palmas.
8. R. de Gamas.	21. Mexico.
9. R. de San Antonio.	22. S. Thoma.
10. C. de Arenas.	23. C. California.
11. C. de St. Iago.	24. Ys de Cedri.
12. C. de S. John.	25. Y del reparo.
13. C. de terra falgar.	

[3] Thomas Morton, of Merrymount, in his *New English Canaan*, Amsterdam, 1637, writes of New England, " what part of this mane continent may be thought to border upon the Country of the Tartars, it is yet unknowne."

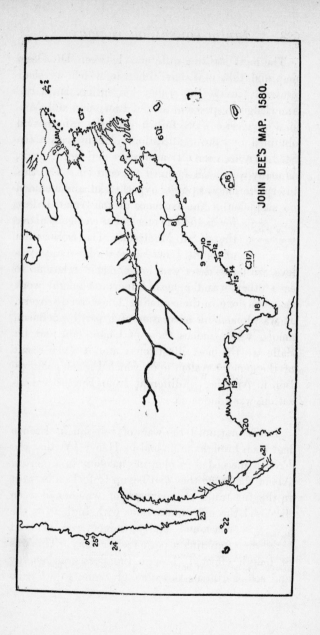

JOHN DEE'S MAP. 1580.

The most striking difference between Dr. Dee's map and that of Louis Joliet, to which we shall presently invite the reader's attention, is in the knowledge respecting the St. Lawrence and Mississippi rivers. Dee fails to give the information obtained by Soto's expedition. He interprets the St. Lawrence correctly as a river and not a strait, as many were still inclined to regard it. But this interpretation was purely hypothetical, and included no suspicion of the existence of the Great Lakes,

Work of the great French explorers.

for in 1580 no one had as yet gone above the site of Montreal. The exploration of the St. Lawrence and Mississippi valleys, with the determination of their relations to each other, was the most important inland work that was done in the course of American discovery. It was done by a succession of great Frenchmen, among whose names those of Champlain and La Salle are the most illustrious; and it was a result of the general system upon which French colonization in America, so different from English colonization, was conducted.

It was not until the wars of religion in France had been brought to an end by Henry IV. that the French succeeded in planting a colony in America. About that time they had begun to feel an interest in the fur trade, the existence of which had been disclosed through transactions with Indians on the

Samuel de Champlain.

coast, and sundry attempts were made at founding a permanent colony. This was at length effected through the persistent energy and self-sacrificing devotion of Samuel de Champlain, who made a settlement at Quebec in 1608 and became the founder of Canada. Champlain was one of the most remarkable Frenchmen of his day, — a beautiful character, devout and high-minded, brave and tender. Like Columbus and Magellan, like Livingstone in our own time, he had the scientific temperament. He was a good naturalist, and has left us the best descriptions we have of the Indians as they appeared before they had been affected by contact with white men. Champlain explored our northeastern coast quite carefully, and gave to many places the names by which they are still known.[1] He was the first white man to sail on the beautiful lake which now bears his name, and he pushed his explorations so far inland as to discover lakes Ontario and Huron.

It was the peculiar features of French policy in colonization that led to this long stride into the interior of the continent. Those features were developed during the lifetime of Champlain and largely under the influence of his romantic personality. The quaint alliance of missionary and merchant, the black-robed Jesuit and the dealer in peltries; the attempt to reproduce in this uncongenial soil the institutions of a feudalism already doomed in the Old World; the policy of fraternization with the Indians and participation in their everlasting quarrels; the policy of far-reaching exploration and the occupation of vast areas of territory by means of well-chosen military posts; all these features, which

Features of French colonization.

[1] As, for example, Mount Desert, which retains a vestige of its old French pronunciation in accenting the final syllable.

give to early Canadian history such fascinating interest,[1] were by no means accidental. They were parts of a deliberate system originating chiefly with Champlain, and representing the romantic notions of empire that were a natural outgrowth of the state of French society in the days of Henry IV. For Champlain to succeed at all, it became necessary for him to accept the alliance of the Jesuits, although his own sympathies were with the national party in France rather than with the Spanish and ultramontane policy of the followers of Loyola. As another condition of success he deemed it necessary to secure the friendship of the Algonquin tribes in the valley of the St. Lawrence, and with this end in view he aided them in defeating the Mohawks near Ticonderoga in July, 1609. The result was that permanent alliance of the Five Nations, first with the Dutch settlers in the valley of the Hudson and afterward with the English, which is one of the great cardinal facts of American history down to 1763. The deadly hostility of the strongest Indian power upon the continent was a feature of the situation with

Causes which drew the French into the interior.

---

[1] It is full of romantic incident, and abounds in instructive material for the philosophical student of history. It has been fortunate in finding such a narrator as Mr. Francis Parkman, who is not only one of the most picturesque historians since the days of Herodotus, but likewise an investigator of the highest order for thoroughness and accuracy. The presence of a sound political philosophy, moreover, is felt in all his works. The reader who wishes to pursue the subject of French exploration in North America should begin with Mr. Parkman's *Pioneers of France, Jesuits in North America,* and *La Salle.* A great mass of bibliographical information may be found in Winsor, *Narr. and Crit. Hist.,* vol. iv. chaps. iii.–vi.

which the French had to reckon from the very start, and the consequences were for them in many ways disastrous.[1] But what here concerns us is chiefly the effect of these circumstances in drawing the French at once into the interior of the continent. The hostile Iroquois could and sometimes did effectually cut off the fur trade between the northwestern forests and the lower St. Lawrence; so that for commercial reasons it was necessary for the French to occupy positions flanking the Long House, and this military necessity soon carried their operations forward as far as Lake Huron. As religion and commerce went hand in hand, it was there that those heroic Jesuits, Brébeuf and Lalemant, did their noble work and suffered their frightful martyrdom; and it was in the destruction of this Huron mission that the Iroquois dealt their first staggering blow against the French power in America.

Somewhat later, when it became apparent that at sundry centres between the seashore and the Alleghany mountains a formidable English power was growing up, French schemes involving military control of the interior of the continent assumed still larger dimensions, and a far-reaching work of exploration was undertaken by that man of iron, if ever there was one, Robert Cavelier de La Salle. As Champlain had laid the foundations of Canada and led the way to the

Robert de La Salle.

---

[1] For example, it was the Iroquois who in 1689 defeated the scheme of Louis XIV. for capturing New York and securing to the French the valley of the Hudson. The success of that scheme might have changed the whole current of American history and prevented the formation of our Federal Union.

Great Lakes, so La Salle completed the discovery of the Mississippi and carried the empire of France in theory from the crest of the Alleghanies to that of the unvisited Rocky mountains. In the long interval since 1542 the work of Soto and Coronado had almost lapsed into oblivion. Of the few who remembered their names there were fewer who could have told you where they went or what they did, so that the work of the French explorers from Canada had all the characteristics of novelty. In 1639 Jean Nicollet reached the Wisconsin river, and heard of a great water beyond, which he supposed must be the Pacific ocean, but which was really the Mississippi river. In the following years Jesuit missionaries penetrated as far as Lake Superior, and settlements were made at Sault Sainte Marie and Michillimackinac. In 1669 La Salle made his first western journey, hoping somewhere or somehow to find a key to the solution of the problem of a northwest passage. In the course of this expedition he discovered the Ohio river and perhaps also the Illinois. La Salle's feudal domain of Saint Sulpice, near Montreal, bears to this day the name of La Chine (China), which is said to have been applied to it in derision of this fruitless attempt to find the Pacific and the way to Cathay.[1] By this time the French had heard much about the Mississippi, but so far from recognizing its identity with the Rio de Espiritu Santo of the Spaniards, they were inclined to regard it as flowing into the Pacific, or into the " Vermilion Sea," as they called the narrow gulf between Mexico and Old Califor-

[1] Parkman's *La Salle*, p. 21.

nia. In 1673 this view was practically refuted by
the priest Marquette and the fur trader Marquette and Joliet.
Joliet, who reached the Mississippi by
way of the Wisconsin, and sailed down the great
river as far as the mouth of the Arkansas.

La Salle now undertook to explore the Mississippi to its mouth, and prepare for the establish-
ment of such military posts as would effectually
confirm the authority of Louis XIV. throughout
the heart of the continent, and permanently check
the northward advance of New Spain and the westward progress of the English colonies. La Salle
was a man of cold and haughty demeanour, and had
made many enemies by the uncompromising way
in which he pushed his schemes. There was a
widespread fear that their success might result in
a gigantic commercial monopoly. For these and
other reasons he drew upon himself the enmity of
both fur traders and Jesuits ; and, as so often happens with men of vast projects, he had but little
ready money. But he found a powerful friend in
the viceroy Count Frontenac, and like that picturesque and masterful personage he had rare skill in
managing Indians. At length, in 1679, after countless vexations, a vessel was built and launched on
the Niagara river, a small party of thirty or forty
men were gathered together, and La Salle, having
just recovered from a treacherous dose of poison,
embarked on his great enterprise. His departure
was clouded by the news that his impatient creditors had laid hands upon his Canadian estates, but,
nothing daunted, he pushed on through the lakes
Erie and Huron, and after many disasters reached

the southern extremity of Lake Michigan. The vessel was now sent back with half the party to Niagara, carrying furs to appease the creditors and purchase additional supplies for the remainder of the journey, while La Salle with his diminished company pushed on to the Illinois, where a fort Fort Crève-cœur. was built and appropriately named Fort Crèvecœur. It was indeed at a heart-breaking moment that it was finished, for so much time had elapsed since the departure of their little ship that all had come to despair of her return. No word ever came from her. Either she foundered on the way, or perhaps her crew may have deserted and scuttled her, carrying off her goods to trade with on their own account.

After a winter of misery, in March, 1680, La Salle started to walk to Montreal. Leaving Fort Crèvecœur and its little garrison under the command of the brave Henri de Tonty, a A thousand miles in the wilderness. lieutenant who could always be trusted, he set out, with four Frenchmen and one Mohegan guide; and these six men fought their way eastward through the wilderness, now floundering through melting snow, now bivouacking in clothes stiff with frost, now stopping to make a bark canoe, now leaping across streams on floating ice-cakes, like the runaway slave-girl in "Uncle Tom's Cabin;" in such plight did they make their way across Michigan and Ontario to the little log-fortress at Niagara Falls. All but La Salle had given out on reaching Lake Erie, and the five sick men were ferried across by him in a canoe. Thus because of the sustaining power of wide-ranging thoughts and a lofty purpose, the gentleman reared in luxury and trained at college surpassed in endurance the Indian and the hunters inured to the forest. He had need of all this sustaining power, for at Niagara he learned that a ship from France, freighted for him with a cargo worth 20,000 livres, had been wrecked and totally lost in the St. Lawrence. Nothing daunted by this blow he took three fresh men, and completed his march of a thousand miles to Montreal.

There he collected supplies and reinforcements and had returned as far as Fort Frontenac, at the lower end of Lake Ontario, when further woful tidings greeted him. A message from the fort so well named " Heartbreak " arrived in July. The garrison had mutinied and pulled that blockhouse to pieces, and made their way back through Michigan. Recruiting their ranks with other worthless freebooters, they had plundered the station at Niagara, and their canoes were now cruising Defeat of the on Lake Ontario in the hope of crown- mutineers. ing their work with the murder of La Salle. These wretches, however, fell into their own pit. The indomitable commander's canoes were soon swarming on the lake, and he was not long in overtaking and capturing the mutineers, whom he sent in chains to the viceroy. La Salle now kept on his way to the Illinois river, intending to rebuild his fort and hoping to rescue Tonty with the few faithful followers who had survived the mutiny. That little party had found shelter among the Illinois Indians; but during the summer of 1680 the great village of the Illinois was sacked by the

Iroquois, and the hard-pressed Frenchmen retreated
Sack of the Illinois town. up the western shore of Lake Michigan
as far as Green Bay. When La Salle
reached the Illinois he found nothing but the horrible vestiges of fiery torments and cannibal feasts.
Without delay he set to work to secure the friendship and alliance of the western tribes, on the
basis of their common enmity to the Iroquois.
After thus spending the winter to good purpose,
he set out again for Canada, in May, 1681, to
arrange his affairs and obtain fresh resources. At
the outlet of Lake Michigan he fell in with his
friend Tonty, and together they paddled their canoes a thousand miles, and so came to Fort Frontenac.

The enemies of the great explorer had grown
merry over his apparent discomfiture, but his stub-
born courage at length vanquished the adverse
fates, and on the next venture things went
smoothly. In the autumn he started with a fleet
of canoes, passed up the lakes from Ontario to
the head of Michigan, crossed the narrow portage
Descent of the Mississippi, 1682. from the Chicago river to the Illinois,
and thence coming out upon the Mis-
sissippi glided down to its mouth. On
the 9th of April, 1682, the fleurs-de-lis were duly
planted, and all the country drained by the great
river and its tributaries, a country vaster than La
Salle imagined, was declared to be the property of
the king of France, and named for him Louisiana.

Returning up the Mississippi after this triumph,
La Salle established a small fortified post on the
Illinois river, which he called St. Louis. Leaving

Tonty in command there, he lost no time in returning to France for means to complete his far-reaching scheme. A colony was to be founded at or near the mouth of the Mississippi, and a line of military posts was to connect it with Canada. La Salle was well received by the king, and a fine expedition was fitted out, but everything was ruined by the incompetence or ill fortune of the naval commander, Beaujeu. The intention was to sail directly to the mouth of the Mississippi, but the pilots missed it and passed beyond; some of the ships were wrecked on the coast of Texas; the captain, beset by foul weather and pirates, disappeared with the rest, and was seen no more; and two years of misery followed. At last, in March, 1687, La Salle started on foot in search of the Mississippi, hoping to ascend it and find succour at Tonty's fort; but he had scarcely set out with this forlorn hope when two or three mutinous wretches skulked in ambush and shot him dead.

La Salle's last expedition, 1687.

These explorations of Joliet, Marquette, and La Salle opened up the centre of the continent, and in the map dedicated by Joliet to Count Frontenac, in 1673,[1] we see a marked advance be-

---

[1] The sketch here given is reduced from the sketch in Winsor, iv. 208, after the coloured facsimile accompanying Gravier's *Étude sur une carte inconnue*, Paris, 1879. There is another coloured facsimile in the *Magazine of American History*, vol. ix. p. 273, in connection with the excellent bibliographical articles by Mr. Appleton Griffin, of the Boston Public Library, on the discovery of the Mississippi, pp. 190–199, 273–280. This is the earliest map of the Mississippi valley that is based upon real knowledge. The legends are as follows: —

yond Dr. Dee's map of 1580. The known part of the continent of North America represented has come to be very large, but Joliet has no suspicion of the huge dimensions of the portion west of the Mississippi, and his style of theorizing is oceanic in so far as he fills up the unknown spaces with water rather than land. A freezing ocean usurps the place of northwestern British America, and Hudson Bay appears as an open gulf in this ocean. From this great inland sea, forever memorable for Henry Hudson's wild and tragic fate, and from the shores of Lake Superior, rival lines of fur trade were presently to carry the knowledge and influence of the white men still farther into the unknown West. About the time that La Salle was starting from Fort Crèvecœur for Montreal, the Recollet friar, Louis de Hennepin, with two companions, set out from the same point with La Salle's directions

Hennepin in the Minnesota country.

1. Mer Glaciale.
2. Les sauvages habitent cette isle.
3. Baye d'Hudson.
4. Labrador.
5. Le fleuve de St. Laurent.
6. Tadoussac.
7. Le Saguenay.
8. Quebec.
9. Montroyal.
10. Acadie.
11. Baston [i. e. Boston].
12. Nouvelle Suède.
13. La Virginie.
14. La Floride.
15. Cap de la Floride.
16. Fort de Frontenac.
17. Lac Frontenac ou Ontario.
18. Lac Erie.
19. Lac Huron.
20. Le Sault Ste Marie.
21. Lac Supérieur.
22. Lac des Illinois ou Missihiganin.
23. Riviere Miskonsing.
24. Riviere de Buade.
25. Paoutet, Maha, Atontauka, Illinois, Peouaria, 300 cabanes, 180 canots de bois de 50 pieds de long.
26. Minongio, Pani, Ouchagé, Kansa, Missouri.
27. Riviere de la Divine ou l'Outrelaize.
28. Riv. Ouabouskigou [i. e. Ohio].
29. Akansea sauvages.
30. Riviere Basire.
31. Tapensa sauvages.
32. Le Sein de Mexique.
33. Le Mexique.
34. La Nouvelle Granade.
35. Mer Vermeille, ou est la Califournie, par ou on peut aller au Perou, au Japon, et à la Chine.

to explore the Illinois river to its mouth. The
little party were captured by Sioux Indians and
carried off into the Minnesota country as far as

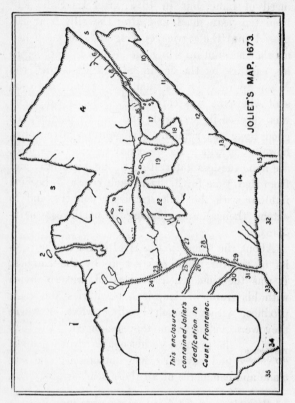

the falls of St. Anthony and beyond. Hennepin's
pocket compass was regarded by these redskins as
potent medicine, so that he was adopted by an
old chief and held in high esteem. After many
romantic adventures he found his way back to

Montreal, and indeed to Paris, where in 1683 he published a narrative of his experiences.[1] What he had done and suffered entitled him to a fair meed of fame, but in 1697, after La Salle had been ten years dead, and after the silly friar had passed into the service of England, he published another account in which he declared that before his capture by the Sioux he had descended the Mississippi river to its mouth and returned to the spot where he was captured.[2] The impudent lie was very easily exposed, and Father Hennepin's good fame was ruined. His genuine adventures, however, in which the descriptions can be verified, are none the less interesting to the historian; and from that time forth the French began to become familiar with the Lake Superior country, and to extend their alliances among the northwestern Indians.

About the same time a rival claim to the profits of the fur trade was set up by the English. It was the time when Charles II. was so lavish with his grants of American territories and their produce, without much heeding what or where they were, or to whom they belonged. In 1670 he granted to his cousin Prince Rupert and several other noblemen "the sole trade and commerce of all those seas, straits, bays,

The Hudson Bay Company.

[1] Hennepin, *Description de la Louisiane, nouvellement découverte*, Paris, 1683.

[2] Hennepin, *Nouvelle découverte d'un très grand pays situé dans l'Amérique, entre le Nouveau Mexique et la Mer Glaciale*, Utrecht, 1697 [dedicated to King William III.]. It has the earliest known engraved plate showing Niagara Falls, and a fine map containing results of explorations north of Lake Superior

rivers, lakes, creeks, and sounds lying within the
entrance of Hudson's Straits, with all the lands,
countries, and territories upon the coasts and confines" of the same. This was the beginning of
the Hudson Bay Company, and from that day until
lately the vast and vaguely defined country which
has been the scene of its operations has been
known as "Rupert's Land." From that day to
this it has been a huge "preserve for fur-bearing
animals and for Indians who might hunt and trap
them," a natural home for beavers, "otters, mar-
tens, musk-rats, and all the other species of amphibious creatures, with countless herds of buffa-
loes, moose, bears, deer, foxes, and wolves." In
the time of which we are treating, these beasts had
freely multiplied, "the aborigines killing only
enough of them for their clothing and subsistence
till the greed of traffic threatened their complete
extirpation."[1] Upon the shores of Hudson Bay
the agents of the company set up fortified trading
stations and dealt with the tribes in the interior.
These proceedings aroused the jealous wrath of
the French, and furnished occasions for scrim-
mages in the wilderness and diplomatic wrangling
at Westminster and Versailles. More than once
in those overbearing days of Louis XIV. the English forts were knocked to pieces by war parties
from Canada; but after the treaty of Utrecht this
sort of thing became less common.

In the great war which that treaty of Utrecht
ended, a brave young lieutenant, named Pierre

[1] See the admirable description of Rupert's Land by Dr.
George Ellis, in Winsor, *Narr. and Crit. Hist.*, viii. 12.

Gaultier de Varennes, was wounded and left for
dead on the field of Malplaquet, but recovered and
lived to play a part in American his-
La Vérendrye.
tory.   He was a native of Three Rivers
in Canada, and returned thither after the war,
assuming for some reason the name of La Vérendrye, by which he has since been known.   About
1728 La Vérendrye, being in command of a fort
to the north of Lake Superior, was led by Indian
reports to believe that the western ocean could be
reached by journeys in canoes and on foot from
that point.   He was empowered to make the experiment at his own expense and risk, and was
promised a monopoly of the fur trade in the countries he should discover.   This arrangement set
all the traders against him, and the problem assumed very much the same form as that with
which La Salle had struggled.   Nine years were
consumed in preliminary work, in the course of
which a wide territory was explored and a chain
of forts erected from the Lake of the Woods to
the mouth of the river Saskatchewan.   From this
region La Vérendrye made his way to the Mandan
villages on the Missouri ; and thence
French dis-
covery of the   his two sons, taking up the work while
Rocky moun-
tains, 1743.   he was temporarily disabled, succeeded
in reaching the Bighorn range of the Rocky mountains on New Year's day, 1743.   At this point,
marvelling at the interminable extent of the continent and believing that they must at last be
near the Pacific, though they were scarcely within
a thousand miles of it, they felt obliged to turn
back.   Another expedition was contemplated, but

by this time so many jealousies had been aroused that the remaining energies of the family La Vérendrye were frittered away. The Hudson Bay Company incited the Indians of the Saskatchewan region to hostilities against the French; and it was not long before all their romantic schemes were swallowed up in the English conquest of Canada.[1]

The crossing of the continent was not completed until the beginning of the nineteenth century. After President Jefferson's purchase of the Louisiana territory from France had carried the western frontier of the United States up to the crests of the Rocky mountains, the question as to what power belonged the Oregon territory beyond remained undecided. It is not necessary to encumber our narrative with a statement of this complicated question.[2] *Discovery of the Columbia river, 1792.* It is enough to observe that in 1792 Captain Robert Gray, in the ship Columbia, of Boston, in the course of a voyage around the world, ascended for some distance the magnificent river to which he gave the name of his vessel. It was only fourteen years since that part of the North American coast had been mapped out by the famous Captain Cook, but neither he nor Vancouver, who was on that coast in the same year with Gray, discovered the Columbia river. Gray was unquestionably the first white man to enter it and to recognize it as

[1] In writing this paragraph I am under obligations to Mr. Parkman's paper on "The Discovery of the Rocky Mountains," *Atlantic Monthly*, June, 1888.

[2] For a statement of it, see Hubert Bancroft's *Northwest Coast*, vol. i.; Barrows's *Oregon;* Vancouver's *Voyage of Discovery*, London, 1798; Winsor, *Narr. and Crit. Hist.*, vii. 555–562.

LIBRARY OF MUSKINGUM COLLEGE

New Concord, Ohio.

an immense river and not a mere arm of the sea ; and upon the strength of this discovery the United States laid claim to the area drained by the Columbia. To support this claim by the further exploration of the valley, and possibly also to determine by inspection of the country what bearings, if any, the purchase of Louisiana might have upon the question, Captains Meriwether Lewis and William Clark[1] were sent out, with thirty-two men, upon the same enterprise that had been attempted by La Vérendrye and his sons. Lewis and Clark, like the Frenchmen, took their final start from one

First crossing of the continent, 1806.

of the Mandan villages. From April 7 till August 11, 1806, they worked up the Missouri river and its Jefferson fork in boats and canoes, and then made their way through the mountains to the headwaters of the Columbia, down which they sailed to its mouth, and came out upon the Pacific on the 7th of November, after a journey of nearly 4,000 miles from the confluence of the Mississippi with the Missouri. The progress across the continent, begun by Champlain, was thus completed, two hundred years later, by Lewis and Clark.   •

The final proof of the separation of North America from Asia by Vitus Bering was an incident in the general history of arctic exploration. When the new continent from Patagonia to Labrador came to be recognized as a barrier in the way to the Indies, the search for a northwest passage

---

[1] He was brother to George Rogers Clark, conqueror of the Northwest Territory.

necessarily became restricted to the arctic regions,
and attempts were also made to find a
northeast passage around Siberia into Search for a
Northwest
Passage.
the Pacific. This work was begun by
the English and Dutch, at about the time when
Spanish activity in discovery and colonization was
coming to a standstill. There is much meaning in
the simultaneous expeditions of Drake and Frobisher, just at the time of Queen Elizabeth's alliance with the revolted Netherlands. In the reign
of Elizabeth's grandfather England had for a moment laid a hand upon North America ; she now
went far toward encompassing it, and in the voyage of Drake, as in that of Cabot, a note of prophecy was sounded. In the years 1577–80 Drake
passed the strait of Magellan, followed the coast
northward as far as some point in northern California or southern Oregon, and took formal possession of that region, calling it New Al- Drake and
Frobisher.
bion. Thence he crossed the Pacific
directly to the Moluccas, a much shorter transit than
that of Magellan, and thence returned to England
by way of the Cape of Good Hope. This was the
second circumnavigation of the earth. Its effect
upon the geographical knowledge of North America was to sustain the continental theory indicated
upon Dr. Dee's map of 1580.[1] About the same
time, in 1576–78, Sir Martin Frobisher in three

[1] See Drake's *World Encompassed*, ed. Vaux, London, 1854
(Hakluyt Soc.). There is a story that a Greek sailor, Apostolos
Valerianos, who had served in the Spanish marine under the name
of Juan de la Fuca, came after Drake in 1592, and discovered the
strait which bears that name. See Peschel, *Geschichte der Erd-
kunde*, bd. i. p. 273.

voyages entered the strait which bears his name and that which is called after Hudson, in search of a passage to Cathay.[1]

The second attempt in these arctic waters was made by that scientific sailor, John Davis, who in 1585–87 penetrated as far as latitude 72° 12′ and discovered the Cumberland islands.[2] Attention was at the same time paid to the ocean between Greenland and Norway, both by the Muscovy Company in London, of which Dr. Dee was now one of the official advisers, and by Dutch navigators, under the impulse and guidance of the eminent Flemish merchant, Balthasar Moucheron. In 1594–96 William Barentz discovered Spitzbergen and thoroughly explored Nova Zembla, but found little promise of a route to Cathay in that direction.[3] Then came Henry Hudson, grandson of one of the founders of the Muscovy Company. In 1607 and 1608 he made two voyages in the service of that company. In the first he tried to penetrate between Greenland and Spitzbergen and strike boldly across the North Pole; in the second he tried to pass between Spitzbergen and Nova Zembla. His third voyage was made in 1609, in that famous little eighty-ton craft the Half-Moon, and in the service of the Dutch East India Company.

Davis and Barentz.

Henry Hudson.

[1] See Frobisher's *Three Voyages*, ed. Collinson, London, 1867 (Hakluyt Soc.).

[2] See Davis's *Voyages and Works on Navigation*, ed. A. H. Markham, London, 1880 (Hakluyt Soc.).

[3] See Motley's *United Netherlands*, vol. iii. pp. 552–576; Gerrit de Veer, *Three Voyages to the Northeast*, ed. Koolemans Beynen, London, 1876 (Hakluyt Soc.).

He had with him some letters which his friend
Captain John Smith had sent him from Virginia,
in which allusion was made to the great river
which, as we now know, had already been visited
by Verrazano and Gomez, and probably also by
sporadic French traders, who may have ascended
it as far as the mouth of the Mohawk in quest of
peltries.[1] It seemed to Smith, from what he had
heard, that this water might be a strait leading
into a western ocean. When Hudson reached
Nova Zembla, he found the sea as full of ice as before, and thereupon, in excess of his instructions,
he faced about and stood across the Atlantic, in
the hope of finding his northwest passage at about
the fortieth parallel. His exploration of the river
which has since borne his name served to turn
the attention of Dutch merchants to the fur trade,
and thus led to the settlement of New Netherland,
while at the same time it proved that no passage
to Cathay was to be found in that direction. In
the following year Hudson had returned to the
English service, and in a further search for the

---

[1] See Weise's *Discoveries of America*, New York, 1884, chap.
xi. Mr. Weise suggests that the name *Terre de Norumbega* may
be a corruption of *Terre d'Anormée Berge*, i. e. "Land of the
Grand Scarp," from the escarpment of palisaded cliffs which is
the most striking feature as one passes by the upper part of Man-
hattan island. See the name Anorumbega on Mercator's map,
1541, above, p. 153. Thevet (1556) says that *Norombègue* is a
name given to the Grand River by the French. Laudonnière
(1564) has it *Norumberge*. The more common opinion is that the
Norumbega river was the Penobscot, and that the name is a presumed Indian word *Aranbega*, but this is doubtful. In the loose
nomenclature of the time the name Norumbega may have been
applied now to the Penobscot and now to the Hudson, as it was
sometimes to the whole country between them.

passage he found his way into that vast inland sea which is at once "his tomb and his monument." In midsummer of 1611 he was turned adrift in an open boat by his mutinous crew and abandoned on that gloomy waste of waters.[1]

The result of this memorable career, embraced as it was within four short years, was to dispel illusory hopes in many directions, and limit the search to the only really available route — the one which Hudson would probably have tried next — William Baffin. by way of the strait discovered by Davis. This route was resumed in 1615 by William Baffin, who left his name upon a long stretch of sea beyond that explored by Davis, and reached the 78th parallel, discovering Jones and Lancaster sounds, as well as the sound which commemorates the name of the merchant prince, Sir Thomas Smith, first governor of the East India Company.[2] Nothing more was accomplished in this direction until Sir John Ross, in 1818, opened the modern era of arctic exploration.[3]

[1] See Asher's *Henry Hudson the Navigator*, London, 1860 (Hakluyt Soc.); Read's *Historical Inquiry concerning Henry Hudson*, Albany, 1866; De Costa, *Sailing Directions of Henry Hudson*, Albany, 1869. Portuguese sailors seem to have entered the bay called after Hudson as early as 1558–69; see Asher, p. cxliv.

[2] See Markham's *Voyages of William Baffin*, London, 1881 (Hakluyt Soc.). For a brief account of Sir Thomas Smith (or Smythe) see Fox-Bourne, *English Merchants*, vol. i. pp. 315–317; there is a portrait of him in Winsor, *Narr. and Crit. Hist.*, vol. iii. p. 94.

[3] Just as this final chapter goes to press I have received the sheets of Winsor's *Christopher Columbus*, a few days in advance of publication. On page 651 he cites the unsuccessful voyages of Luke Fox and Thomas James in Hudson's Bay in 1631 as checking further efforts in this direction.

One consequence of these voyages was to abolish the notion of a connection between Greenland and Europe, and to establish the outlines of the northeastern coast of North America, in such wise as to suggest, in the minds of the few northern scholars who knew anything about the Vinland traditions, the correct association of the idea of Vinland with the idea of America. As I have already observed, there was nothing to suggest any such association of ideas until the period of the four great navigators, Frobisher, Davis, Hudson, and Baffin; at that period we begin to catch glimpses of it, dimly and dubiously in 1570 with Stephanius, briefly but distinctly in 1610 with Arngrim Jonsson;[1] and at last in 1705 a general interest in the subject was awakened by Torfæus.

Effect upon the conception of Vinland.

While Frobisher and his successors were groping for a northwest passage to Cathay, the Russians were steadily advancing by overland conquests toward that land of promise. Between 1560 and 1580 the Cossack Irmak crossed the Ural mountains and conquered Siberia as far as the Obi river. Thence, urged on by the quest for gold and peltries, and the need for subduing unruly neighbours, the Russian arms pressed eastward, until in 1706 the peninsula of Kamtchatka was added to their domains.

Russian conquest of Siberia.

At that period the northern Pacific and the wild coasts on either side of it were still a region of mystery. On the American side nothing was known north of Drake's " New Albion," on the

[1] See above, vol. i. p. 394.

Asiatic side nothing north of Japan. Some still believed that the two continents were joined together; others held that they were separated by a strait, for how else could there be a Northwest Passage?[1] Peter the Great wished to settle such questions and ascertain the metes and bounds of his empire, and in 1724, shortly before his death, he appointed the Danish captain Vitus Bering[2] to

Vitus Bering.

the command of an expedition for exploring the eastern shores of the Kamtchatka and Chukchi peninsulas, to see if any strait could be found there. In one respect this was an enterprise of unparalleled difficulty, for the starting point of the navigation was some 5,000 miles distant from St. Petersburg, and more than half this distance was through a howling wilderness. Many were the obstacles that had to be surmounted before Bering could build and launch his stout little ship, the Gabriel, in the early summer of 1728. The point from which he started was not far from Cape Kamtchatka. He bore to the northward, keeping in sight of the coast, and on the 11th of August sighted on the starboard the island which he named St. Lawrence. On the 14th he

---

[1] The wish was father to the thought, and the so-called strait of Anian appears on many old maps, beginning with Mercator's chart of 1569. Some maps have also a gulf of Anian; possibly from a misunderstanding of the gulf of An-nan (i. e. Tongking) mentioned in a passage interpolated into Marco Polo, bk. iii. chap. iv. See Lauridsen's *Vitus Bering*, p. 202. But this explanation is doubtful.

[2] Until lately the Danish name has appeared in English with a German and incorrect spelling, as *Behring*. The best book on this navigator is Lauridsen's *Vitus Bering*, Chicago, 1889, translated by Professor Julius Olson, of the University of Wisconsin.

left East Cape receding astern, and seemed to have open sea on both sides of him, for he did not descry the American coast about forty miles distant. After a day's Discovery of Bering strait, 1728. sail into the Arctic ocean, he turned and passed back through the strait without seeing the opposite coast. He believed, and rightly as it happened, that he had found an end to Asia, and completed the proof of the existence of a continuous sea-coast from the mouth of the Lena river to Kamtchatka. A gigantic enterprise was now set on foot. The Siberian coast was to be charted from Nova Zembla to the Lena; Japan was to be reached from the north; and the western shore of America was to be discovered and explored. As to the latter part, with which we are here concerned, a Russian officer, Gvosdjeff, sailed into Bering's strait in 1732 and saw the American coast.[1] Before more extensive work could be done it was necessary to build the town of Petropavlovsk, in Kamtchatka, as a base of operations. From that point the two ships St. Peter and St. Paul, under Bering's command, set sail in the summer of 1741. At first they took a south- Bering's discovery of Alaska, 1741. easterly course in order to find an imaginary "Gamaland," which was by a few theorizers supposed to lie in mid-Pacific, east of Japan. Thus they missed the Aleutian islands. After reaching latitude 46°, not far from the 180th meridian, they gave up the search for this figment of fancy, and steering northeasterly at length reached the Alaska coast under the volcano St. Elias. On the more

[1] Lauridsen, *op. cit.* p. 130.

direct return voyage, which took them through the
Aleutian archipelago, they encountered fierce
storms, with the added horrors of famine and
scurvy. When they came to the island known as
Bering's, not more than a hundred miles from the
Kamtchatka coast, they were cast ashore, and there
the gallant Bering succumbed to scurvy and ague,
and died in his sixtieth year. Such were the expeditions that completed the discovery of North
America as a distinct and separate continent, and
gave to Russia for a time an American territory as
spacious as France and Germany together.

The work of Vitus Bering may be regarded as
the natural conclusion of that long chapter in the
history of discovery which began with Ponce de
Leon's first visit to the Land of Easter. When
Bering and Gvosdjeff saw the two sides of the
strait that separates America from Asia, quite
enough had been done to reveal the general outlines and to suggest the broadness of the former
continent, although many years were still to elapse
before anybody crossed it from ocean
to ocean. The discovery of the whole
length of the Mississippi, with its voluminous tributaries, indicating an extensive drain-
age area to the west of that river, the information gained in the course of trade by the Hudson
Bay Company, the stretch of arctic coast explored
by Baffin, and finally the discovery of Bering
strait, furnished points enough to give one a fairly
correct idea of North America as a distinct and
integral mass of land, even though there was still

The discovery
of America
was a gradual
development.

room for error, here and there, with regard to its
dimensions. Our story impresses upon us quite
forcibly the fact that the work of discovery has
been a gradual and orderly development. Such
must necessarily be the case. Facts newly presented to the mind must be assimilated to the pre-
existing stock of knowledge, and in the process an
extensive destruction of wrong or inadequate conceptions takes place; and this sort of thing takes
a great deal of time, especially since the new facts
can be obtained only by long voyages in unknown
seas, or tramps through the trackless wilderness, at
great cost of life and treasure. The Discovery of
America may be regarded in one sense as a unique
event, but it must likewise be regarded as a long
and multifarious process. The unique event was the
crossing of the Sea of Darkness in 1492. It established a true and permanent contact between
the eastern and western halves of our planet, and
brought together the two streams of human life
that had flowed in separate channels ever since the
Glacial period. No ingenuity of argument can
take from Columbus the glory of an achievement
which has, and can have, no parallel in the whole
career of mankind. It was a thing that could be
done but once. On the other hand, when we regard the Discovery as a long and multifarious process, it is only by a decision more or less arbitrary
that we can say when it began or when it ended.
It emerged from a complex group of facts and
theories, and was accomplished through a multitude of enterprises in all quarters of the globe.
We cannot understand its beginnings without pay-

ing due heed to the speculations of Claudius Ptolemy at Alexandria in the second century of our
era, and to the wanderings of Rubruquis in Tar-
tary in the thirteenth; nor can we describe its
consummation without recalling to memory the
motives and results of cruises in the Malay archipelago and journeys through the snows of
Siberia. For our general purpose, however, it is
enough to observe that a period of two hundred
years just about carries us from Dias and Columbus to Joliet and La Salle, or from Ponce de Leon
to Vitus Bering. The sixteenth and seventeenth
centuries carried far toward completion the work
of 1492.

In our brief survey of the work of discovery
during those two centuries, one striking contrast
forces itself upon our attention. We began this
chapter in company with Spaniards; toward its
close our comrades have been chiefly Frenchmen
and Englishmen. In the days of Cortes
and Magellan, the Spain of Charles V.
was the foremost power in the world;
in the days of La Salle the France of
Louis XIV. was the foremost power. The last
years of Louis XIV. saw Spain, far sunken from
her old preëminence, furnishing the bone of con-
tention between France and England in the first
of the two great struggles which won for England
the foremost place. As regards America, it may
be observed that from 1492 until about 1570 the
exploring and colonizing activity of Spain was
immense, insomuch that upon the southern half of

*Cessation of
Spanish ex-
ploring and
colonizing ac-
tivity after
about 1570.*

the New World it has left its stamp forever, so that to-day the Spanish is one of the few imperial languages. After 1570 this wonderful manifestation of Spanish energy practically ceased, and this is a fact of supreme importance in the history of North America. But for this abrupt cessation of Spanish energy the English settlements at Jamestown and Plymouth would have been in quite as dangerous a position as Ribaut's colony in Florida. It is worth while, therefore, to notice one or two eloquent items of chronology. In 1492 Spain was relieved of a task which had long absorbed all her vital energies, the work of freeing her soil from the dominion of the Moors. In 1570 she was entering upon another task which not only absorbed but wellnigh exhausted her energies, the attempt to suppress Protestantism in Europe and to subdue the revolted Netherlands. When she had once put her hand to this work, Spain had no surplus vitality left for extending her sway in America. She was scarcely able to maintain the ground she had already occupied; she could not defend the West Indies against the buccaneers, and the end of the seventeenth century saw Hispaniola in the hands of France and Jamaica in the hands of England, and various lesser Antilles seized by the one or the other of these two powers.

It is furthermore worthy of notice that there was a clear causal connection between the task which Spain finished in 1492 and that upon which she entered a little before 1570. The transition from the crusade against the infidel to the crusade against the heretic was easy, and in her case almost inevitable.   The effects of the long Moorish war

The long
struggle be-
tween Span-
iards and
Moors.

upon Spanish character and Spanish policy have often been pointed out. The Spaniard of the sixteenth century was what eight hundred years of terrible warfare, for home and for religion, had made him. During a period as long as that which in English history has now elapsed since the death of William the Conqueror, the Mussulman invaders held sway in some part of the Spanish peninsula ; yet they never succeeded in entering into any sort of political union with the native inhabitants.   From first to last they behaved as invaders and were treated as invaders, their career in this respect forming a curious and instructive parallel to that of the Turks in eastern Europe, though as a people the Arab-Moors were of far higher type than Turks.   Entering Spain in 711, they soon conquered the whole peninsula.   From this deluge about a century later the Christian kingdom of Leon began to emerge. By the middle of the eleventh century the Spaniards had regained half their country, and the Mahometans were placed upon the defensive. By the middle of the thirteenth, the Moorish dominion became restricted to the kingdom of Granada ; and finally we have seen Granada subdued in the same year in which Columbus discovered America.   During all this period, from 711 to 1492, the years when warfare was not going on along the fluctuating frontier between Spaniard and Moor were few indeed.   Among the Spaniards industrial life was almost destroyed.   The way to obtain the necessaries of life was to make raids

upon the Mussulmans, and the career of the bandit
became glorified. In the central and southern
provinces, on the other hand, the Moors developed
a remarkable industrial civilization, surpassing
anything to be seen in Christian Europe except
in Constantinople down to the end of the twelfth
century. As the frontier moved gradually southward, with the advance of the Christians, the in-
dustrious Mussulman population in large part
became converted to Christianity, and went on cultivating the arts of life. These converts,
who were known as Moriscoes, were always despised and ill-treated by the
Spaniards. Such a state of things continued to
throw discredit upon labour. Spinning and weav-
ing and tilling the soil were regarded as fit occupations for unclean Moriscoes. It was the prerogative of a Christian Spaniard to appropriate the
fruits of other people's labour; and we have seen
this feeling at work in many details of the Spanish conquest in America. Not that it was at all
peculiar to Spaniards. Devices for appropriating
the fruits of other people's labour have in all countries been multifarious, from tomahawks to tariffs.
But the circumstances of Spanish history were
such as to cast upon labour a stigma especially
strong by associating it with men of alien race and
faith who were scarcely regarded as possessing any
rights that Christians should feel bound to respect.

This prolonged warfare had other effects. It
combined the features of a crusade with those of
a fight for the recovery of one's patrimony. The
general effect of the great Crusades, which brought

Its effect in throwing discredit upon labour.

different Christian peoples in contact with each other and opened their eyes to many excellent features in eastern civilization, was an education for Europe. From these liberalizing experiences the Spanish peninsula was in great measure cut off. It was absorbed in its own private crusade, and there was altogether too much of it. While other nations occasionally turned their attention to wars of religion, Spain had no attention left for anything else. It was one long agony through five-and-twenty generations, until the intruder was ousted. Thus, although Visigothic institutions smacked of sturdy freedom as much as those of any other Germanic people, nevertheless this unceasing militancy trained the Spaniards for despotism. For the same reason the church acquired more overweening power than anywhere else in Europe. To the mediæval Spaniard orthodoxy was practically synonymous with patriotism, while heresy like manual industry was a mark of the hated race. Unity in faith came to be regarded as an object to secure which no sacrifices whatever could be deemed too great. When, therefore, the Protestant Reformation came in the sixteenth century, its ideas and its methods were less intelligible to Spaniards than to any other European people. By nature this land of mediæval ideas was thus marked out as the chief antagonist of the Reformation ; and when it was attempted to extend to the Netherlands the odious measures that were endured in Spain, the ensuing revolt called forth all the power that Philip II. could summon to suppress it. To overthrow the rebellious heretic seemed as

Its effect in strengthening religious bigotry.

sacred a duty as to expel the Moslem. A crusade against heresy, headed by Pope Innocent III. and Philip Augustus of France, had once been crowned with success, and one of the most grewsome chapters in human Spain's crusade in the Netherlands. history had been written in blood at Beziers and Carcassonne. Such a crusade did Spain attempt against the Netherlands, until England, too, was drawn into the lists against her, and the crisis was reached in 1588, in the destruction of the Invincible Armada, a military overthrow scarcely paralleled until the wreck of Napoleon's army in Russia.

The defeat of the Armada was such a blow to Spain's prestige that France, England, and the Netherlands soon proceeded to their work of colonization in North America with little fear of hindrance. But while France and England paid much attention to America, the Dutch paid comparatively little, and for a reason that is closely linked with our general subject. The attention of the Dutch was chiefly concentrated upon the East Indies. After Effects of oceanic discovery in developing Dutch trade. the Turks had cut off the Mediterranean routes, and Portugal had gained control of the Asiatic trade, the great Netherland towns began to have relatively fewer overland dealings with Venice and Genoa, and more and more maritime dealings with Lisbon. The change favoured the Dutch more than the Flemish provinces, by reason of the greater length of the Dutch coast line. By dint of marvellous energy and skill the coast of Holland and Zealand became virtually one vast seaport, a distributing centre for the whole north of Europe, and during the sixteenth century the volume of Dutch merchant shipping was rapidly and steadily increased. Now it happened in 1578 that the King Sebastian of Portugal, who has furnished a theme for so many romantic legends, led an army into Morocco, and there was killed in battle. Philip II. forthwith declared the throne of Portugal vacant, and in 1580 seized the kingdom for himself. This act abruptly cut off the East India trade of the Dutch, and at the same time it made all the Portuguese colonies dependencies of Spain, and thus left the Dutch free to attack them wherever they saw fit. Borgia's meridian was thus at last wiped out.

After 1588 the Dutch proceeded at once to invade the colonial world of Portugal. They soon established themselves in Java and Sumatra, and by 1607 they had gained complete possession of the Molucca islands. This was the beginning of the empire which Holland possesses to-day in the East Indies, with a rich territory four times as large as France, a population of 30,000,000, and a lucrative trade. From this blow Portugal never recovered. She regained her independence in 1640, but has never since shown the buoyant vigour that made the days of Prince Henry the Navigator and of Albuquerque so remarkable.

Conquest of the Portuguese Indies by the Dutch.

The overthrow of the Invincible Armada thus marks the downfall of maritime power for both the rival nations of the Iberian peninsula. It would be wrong, however, to attribute such an enduring calamity to a single great naval defeat, or even to the exhausting effects of the unsuccessful war against the Dutch. A healthy nation quickly repairs the damage wrought by a military catastrophe, but Spain was not in a healthy condition. The overmastering desire to put down heresy, to expel the "accursed thing," possessed her. The struggle with the Moors had brought this semi-suicidal craving to a height which it never reached with any other European nation. In the present narrative we have had occasion to observe that as soon as Ferdinand and Isabella had finished the conquest of Granada, they tried to add to the completeness of their triumph by driving all Jews from their homes and seizing their goods. In times past, the conquered Moors had in great numbers embraced Christianity, but it was with difficulty that the Spaniards tolerated the presence of these Moriscoes in their country.[1] In 1568, the Moriscoes, goaded by ill treatment, rose in rebellion among the mountains of Granada, and it took three years of obstinate fighting to bring them to terms. Their defeat was so crushing that they ceased to be dangerous politically, but their orthodoxy was gravely suspected. In 1602 the archbishop of Valencia proposed that

Disastrous results of persecuting heretics.

---

[1] On the rich and important subject of the Moors in Spain, see Al Makkari, *History of the Mohammedan Dynasties in Spain*, transl. by Gayangos, London, 1840, 2 vols. in quarto; Conde, *Dominacion de los Arabes en España*, Paris, 1840 (to be read with caution); Coppée, *Conquest of Spain by the Arab-Moors*, Boston, 1881, 2 vols.; Reinaud, *Invasions des Sarrazins en France*, Paris, 1836; Chénier, *Recnerches historiques sur les Maures*, Paris, 1787, 3 vols.; Circourt, *Histoire des Mores Mudejares et des Morisques*, Paris, 1846, 3 vols.; see, also, with reference to the Jews, Grætz, *Les Juifs d'Espagne*, Paris, 1872.

all the Moriscoes in the kingdom, except children under seven years of age, should be driven into exile, that Spain might no longer be polluted by the merest suspicion of unbelief. The archbishop of Toledo, primate of Spain, wished to banish the children also. It is said that Friar Ble-da, the Dominican, urged that all Moris-coes, even to the new-born babe, should be massacred, since it was impossible to tell whether they were Christians at heart or not, and it might safely be left to God to select his own. The views of the primate prevailed, and in 1609, about a million people were turned out of doors and hustled off to Morocco. These proceedings involved an amount of murder that has been estimated as about equivalent to the massacre of St. Bartholomew. Of the unfortunate people who reached Africa, thousands perished of hunger, or were slain by robbers, or kidnapped into slavery.

Expulsion of the Moriscoes from Spain, 1609.

These Moriscoes, thus driven from the land by ecclesiastical bigotry, joined with hatred of their race, were the most skilful labourers Spain possessed. By their expulsion the manufacture of silk and paper was destroyed, the cultivation of sugar, rice, and cotton came to an end, the wool-trade stopped short, and irrigation of the soil was discontinued. The disturbance of industry, and the consequent distress, were so far-reaching that in the course of the next seventy years the population of Madrid was decreased by one half, and that of Seville by three quarters; whole villages were deserted, large portions of arable land went out of cultivation; and

Terrible consequences.

brigandage gained a foothold which it has kept almost down to the present day. The economic ruin of Spain may be said to date from the expulsion of the Moriscoes. Yet no deed in history was ever done with clearer conscience or more unanimous self-approval on the part of the perpetrators than this. Even the high-minded and gentle-hearted Cervantes applauded it, while Davila characterized it as the crowning glory of Spanish history. This approval was the outcome of a feeling so deeply ingrained in the Spanish mind that we sometimes see curious remnants of it to-day, even among Spaniards of much liberality and enlightenment. Thus the eminent historian Lafuente, writing in 1856, freely confessed that the destruction of Moorish industries was economically a disaster of the first magnitude; but after all, he says, just think what an " immense advantage " it was to establish " religious unity " throughout the nation and get rid of differences in opinion.[1] Just so: to insure that from the Pyrenees to Gibraltar all people should appear to think exactly alike about questions confessedly unfathomable by human intelligence, — this seemed to the Spaniards an end of such supreme importance as to justify the destruction of a hundred thousand lives and the overthrow of some of the chief industries of the kingdom. It was a terrible delusion, but perhaps we are not entitled to blame the Spaniards too severely when we reflect that even among ourselves, in spite of all the liberalizing influences to which the English race

[1] Lafuente, *Historia de España*, Madrid, 1856, tom. xvii. p. 340.

has so long been subjected, the lesson is only just beginning to be learned that variety in religious beliefs is not an evil, but a positive benefit to a civilized community, whereas uniformity in belief should be dreaded as tending toward Chinese narrowness and stagnation. This is the true lesson of Protestantism, and it is through this lesson, however imperfectly learned, that Protestantism has done so much to save the world from torpor and paralysis.

Uniformity in religious beliefs is not desirable.

But it was not merely in the expulsion of the Moriscoes that the Spanish policy of enforcing uniformity was suicidal. Indeed, the disastrous effects which we are wont to attribute to that striking catastrophe cannot really be explained without taking into account another and still more potent cause. The deadly Inquisition, working steadily and quietly year after year while fourteen generations lived and died, wrought an amount of disaster which it is difficult for the mind to grasp. Some eight or ten years ago an excavation happened to be made in the Plaza Cruz del Quemadero in Madrid, the scene of the most terrible part of Victor Hugo's " Torquemada." Just below the surface the workmen came upon a thick stratum of black earth 150 feet long. On further digging it was found to consist chiefly of calcined human bones, with here and there a fragment of burnt clothing. Dark layers varying from three to nine inches in thickness were here and there interrupted by very thin strata of clay or sand.[1] A singular kind of geological problem

Dreadful work of the Inquisition.

[1] This deposit was examined by men of science and antiqua-

was thus suggested: how many men and women must have died in excruciating torments in order to build up that infernal deposit? During the fifteen years when Torquemada was inquisitor-general, from 1483 to 1498, about 10,000 persons were burned alive. The rate was probably not much diminished during the sixteenth century, and the practice was kept up until late in the eighteenth; the last burning of a heretic was in 1781. From the outset the germs of Protestantism were steadily and completely extirpated. We sometimes hear it said that persecution cannot kill a good cause, but that "the blood of the martyrs is the seed of the church." This is apt to be true because it is seldom that sufficient unanimity of public opinion is enlisted in support of persecution to make it thorough. It was not true in Spain. The Inquisition there did suppress free thought most effectively. It was a machine for winnowing out and destroying all such individuals as surpassed the average in quickness of wit, earnestness of purpose, and strength of character, in so far as to entertain opinions of their own and boldly declare them. The more closely people approached an elevated standard of intelligence and moral courage, the more likely was the machine to reach them. It worked with such fiendish efficiency that it was next to impossible for such people to escape it; they were strangled

It was a device for insuring the survival of the unfittest.

rians, and the newspapers began publishing the details of their investigations, whereat the clergy grew uneasy, and persuaded the government to have the whole stratum dug away and removed as quickly as possible, so as to avoid further scandal. See *The Nation*, New York, 1883, vol. xxxvi. p. 470.

and burned by tens of thousands, and as the inevitable result, the average character of the Spanish people was lowered.[1]   The brightest and boldest were cut off in their early prime, while duller and weaker ones were spared to propagate the race; until the Spaniard of the eighteenth century was a much less intelligent and less enterprising person than the Spaniard of the sixteenth.   Such damage is not easily repaired; the competition among nations is so constant and so keen, that when a people have once clearly lost their hold upon the foremost position they are not likely to regain it.

Under this blighting rule of the Inquisition the general atmosphere of thought in Spain remained mediæval.   Ideas and methods which other nations were devising, to meet the new exigencies of modern life, were denied admission to that unfortunate country.   In manufactures, in commerce, in the control of the various sources of wealth, Spain was soon left behind by nations in which the popular intelligence was more flexibly wielded, and from which the minds hospitable toward new ideas had not been so carefully weeded out.   It was not in

The Spanish policy of crushing out individualism resulted in universal stagnation.

---

[1] In this connection the reader should carefully study the admirable book lately published by our great historian of mediæval institutions, Henry Charles Lea, *Chapters from the Religious History of Spain*, Philadelphia, 1890.   I have been especially struck with the chapter on the "Censorship of the Press," where the subject is treated with a prodigious wealth of learning.   We are apt to sigh over popular ignorance even in these days of elaborate educational appliances and untrammelled freedom of discussion. Under the rule of the Spanish Inquisition all the zeal and energy which we now devote to developing and stimulating popular intelligence was devoted to stunting and repressing it.

religious matters only, but in all the affairs of life, that the dull and rigid conservatism was shown. Amid the general stagnation and lack of enterprise, and with the universal discredit of labour, the stream of gold and silver poured into Spain from the New World did more harm than good, inasmuch as its chief effect was to diminish the purchasing power of the precious metals. Economically, perhaps, the whole situation might be summed up by saying that Spanish expenditure was not productive but unproductive, and not simply unproductive but destructive. It was devoted to checking the activities of the human mind, to doing precisely the reverse of what we are trying to do in these days with books and newspapers, schools and lectures, copyrights and patents.

It is profoundly significant that the people who have acquired by far the greater part of the maritime empire to which Spain once aspired, and who have supplanted her in the best part of the territories to which she once felt entitled in virtue of Borgia's bulls, should be the people who have differed most widely from the Spaniards in their attitude toward novelties of doctrine and independence of thought. The policy of England, in giving full play to individualism, has developed a type of national character unsurpassed for buoyancy. No class of people in England ever acquired such *It has been the policy of England to give full scope to individualism.* control of the whole society as the clergy acquired in Spain. In the worst days of English history attempts have been made to crush individuality of thought and to put a stop to the free discussion of religious and political questions.   But such attempts have been feeble and sporadic; no such policy has ever prevailed.   The history of religious persecution in England affords a most suggestive illustration.   The burning of heretics began in 1401, and the last instance occurred in 1611. During that time the total number of executions for heresy was about 400.   Of these about 300 occurred in the brief spasm of 1555–57 under Mary Tudor, daughter of a Spanish princess, and wife of the worst of Spain's persecuting monarchs. The total of 100 victims scattered through the rest of that period of two centuries makes a startling contrast to what was going on in other countries. As no type of character has thus been sedulously winnowed out by violent methods, neither has any set of people ever been expelled from England, like the Moriscoes from Spain or the Huguenots from France.   On the contrary, ever since the days of the Plantagenets it has been a maxim of English law that whosoever among the hunted and oppressed of other realms should set his foot on the soil of Britain became forthwith free and entitled to all the protection that England's stout arm could afford.   On that hospitable soil all types of character, all varieties of temperament, all shades of belief, have flourished side by side, and have interacted upon one another until there

That policy has been the chief cause of the success of English people in founding new nations.

has been evolved a race of men in the highest degree original and enterprising, plastic and cosmopolitan.   It is chiefly this circumstance, combined with their successful preservation of self-government, that has

won for men of English speech their imperial position in the modern world. When we contrast
the elastic buoyancy of spirit in Shakespeare's
England with the gloom and heaviness that were
then creeping over Spain, we find nothing strange
in the fact that the most populous and powerful
nations of the New World speak English and not
Spanish. It was the people of Great Britain that,
with flexible and self-reliant intelligence, came to
be foremost in devising methods adapted to the
growth of an industrial civilization, leaving the
Middle Ages far behind. Wherever, in any of
the regions open to colonization, this race has come
into competition with other European races, it has
either vanquished or absorbed them, always proving its superior capacity. Sometimes the contest
has assumed the form of strife between a civilization based upon wholesome private enterprise and
a civilization based upon government patronage.
Such was the form of the seventy years' conflict
that came to a final decision upon the Heights of
Abraham, and not the least interesting circumstance connected with the discovery of this broad
continent is the fact that the struggle for the possession of it has revealed the superior vitality of
institutions and methods that first came to matu-
rity in England and now seem destined to shape
the future of the world.

APPENDIX A.

THE Latin is the original text, for an account of which see
above, vol. i. p. 356, note 3. The Italian is from the version in
the *Vita dell' Ammiraglio*, concerning which M. Harrisse says that
it is "très-inexact et interpolée." I have here italicised the portions of either text which do not occur in the other, so that the
reader may judge for himself how far such a charge is justified.

A Cristoforo Colombo
Paolo fisico salute. Io veg-
go il nobile e gran desiderio
tuo di voler passar là, dove
nascono le spezerie, onde
per risposta d' una tua lettera ti mando la copia d' un'
altra lettera, che alquanti
giorni fa io scrissi ad un
mio amico, domestico del
serenissimo re di Porto-
gallo, avanti le guerre di
Castiglia, in risposta d' un'
altra, che per commissione
di Sua Altezza egli mi
scrisse sopra detto caso : e
ti mando un' altra carta
navigatoria, simile a quella
ch' io mandai a lui, per
la qual resteranno soddis-

fatte le tue dimande. La copia di quella mia lettera è questa.

Copia misa christofaro colonbo per paulum fisicum cum una carta navigacionis.

Ferdinando martini canonico vlixiponensi paulus phisicus salutem. a tua valitudine de gracia et familiaritate cum rege vestro genero[siss]imo [et] magnificentissimo principe iocundum mihi fuit intelligere. cum tecum allias locutus sum de breuiori via ad loca aromatum per maritimam navigacionem quam sit ea quam facitis per guineam, querit nunc S[erenissimus] rex a me quandam declaracionem ymo potius ad occulum ostensionem vt *etiam mediocriter doti* illam viam caperent et intelligerent. Ego autem quamvis cognoscam posse hoc ostendi per formam spericam ut est mundus tamen determinaui, pro faciliori intelligencia ac etiam pro faciliori opera, ostendere, viam illam per quam carte navigacionis fiunt illud de-

A Fernando Martinez canonico di Lisbona Paolo fisico salute. Molto mi piacque intendere la domestichezza che tu hai col tuo sereniss. e magnificentiss. re, e quantunque volte io abbia ragionato del *brevissimo* cammino che è di qua all' *Indie*, dove nascono le spezerie, per la via del mare, il quale io tengo più breve di quel che voi fate per Guinea, tu mi dici che Sua Altezza vorrebbe ora da me alcuna dichiarazione, o dimostrazione, acciocchè si intenda e si possa prendere detto cammino. Laonde, come ch' io sappia di poter ciò mostrarle con la sfera in mano, e farle veder come sta il mondo; nondimeno ho deliberato per più facilità e per maggiore intelligenza dimostrar detto cammino per una carta simile a quelle che si fanno per navigare, e così

clarare. Mito ergo sue Maiestati cartam manibus meis factam in qua designantur

litora vestra et insule ex quibus incipiatis iter facere verius occasum senper

et loca ad que debeatis peruenire et quantum a polo vel a linea equinotiali debeatis . declinare et per quantum spacium siue per quot miliaria debeatis peruenire ad loca fertilissima omnium aromatum et gemarum, et non miremini si voco occidentales partes vbi sunt aromata cum communiter dicantur orientales,

quia nauigantibus ad occidentem senper ille partes inueniuntur *per subterraneas nauigaciones.* Si enim per terram et per superiora itinera, ad orientem senper reperrientur [1] linee ergo recte in longitudine

la mando a Sua Maestà. fatta e disegnata di mia mano : nella quale è dipinto *tutto il fine del ponente, pigliando da Irlanda all' austro insino al fin di Guinea,* con *tutte* le isole *che in tutto questo cammino giacciono ;* per fronte alle quali dritto per ponente *giace dipinto il principio dell' Indie* con le isole e luoghi dove potete andare, e quanto dal polo *artico* vi potete discostare per la linea equinoziale, e per quanto spazio, cioè in quante leghe potete giungere a quei luoghi fertilissimi d' ogni sorte di spezeria, e di gemme e pietre preziose. E non abbiate a maraviglia, se io chiamo Ponente il paese ove nasce la spezeria, la qual comunemente dicesi che nasce in Levanti ; perciocchè coloro, che navigheranno al ponente, sempre troveranno detti luoghi in ponente ; e quelli, che anderanno per terra al levante, sempre troveranno detti luoghi in levante. Le linee dritte,

[1] Read *reperientur.*

carte signate ostendunt distanciam ab orientem [1] versus occidens, que autem transuerse sunt, ostendunt spacia a meridie versus septentrionem. notaui autem in carta diuersa loca ad que peruenire potestis pro maiori noticia nauigancium siue ventis vel casu aliquo alibi quam existimarent venirent; *partin* [2] *autem vt ostendant incolis ipsos habere noticiam aliquam patrie illius, quod debebit esse iocundum satis.*

non considant [3] autem in insulis nisi mercatores aserit.[4] ibi enim tanta copia nauigancium est cum mercimoniis vt in toto reliquo orbe non sint sicuti in vno portu nobilisimo vocato zaiton. aserunt enim cen-

che giacciono al lungo in detta carta, dimostrano la distanza che è dal ponente al levante; le altre, che sono per obliquo, dimostrano la distanza che è dalla tramontana al mezzogiorno. Ancora io dipinsi in detta carta molti luoghi nelle parte *dell' India* dove si potrebbe andare, avvenendo alcun caso di fortuna o di venti contrari, o qualunque altro caso, che non si aspettasse, che dovesse avvenire.

E appresso, per darvi piena informazione di tutit quei luoghi, i quali desiderate molto conoscere, sappiate, che in tutte quelle isole non abitano nè praticano altri che mercatanti; avvertendovi quivi essere così gran quantità di navi e di marinari con mercatanzie, come in ogni altra parte del mondo, specialmente in un porto

---

[1] Read *oriente.*

[2] Read *partim.*

[3] Read *considunt.*

[4] Perhaps meant for *asseritur,* "it is related." Columbus may have forgotten to finish the word. Or perhaps Toscanelli may have inadvertently used the active *asserit,* "he relates," meaning Marco Polo.

tum naues piperis magne in eo portu singulis annis deferri, sine aliis nauibus portantibus allia aromata. patria illa est populatisima *ditisima* multitudine prouinciarum et regnorum et ciuitatum sine numero, sub vno principe qui dicitur magnus Kan quod nomen significat in latino rex regum, cuius sedes et residencia est vt plurimum in provincia Katay. antiqui sui desiderabant consorcium christianorum iam sunt .200. annis,[1] miscerunt[2] ad papam et postulabant plurimos dotos in fide vt illuminarentur; sed qui missi sunt, inpediti in itinere redierunt. etiam

tempore Eugenii venit vnus ad eugenium qui de beniuolentia magna erga christianos afirmabat et ego

nobilissimo, chiamato Zaiton, dove caricano e discaricano ogni anno cento navi grosse di pepe, oltre alle molte altre navi, che caricano altre spezerie. Questo paese è popolatissimo, e sono molte provincie e molti regni e città senza numero sotto il dominio di un principe chiamato il gran Cane, il qual nome vuol dire re de' re, la residenza del quale la maggior parte del tempo è nella provincia del Cataio. I suoi antecessori desiderarono molto aver pratica e amicizia con cristiani, e già dugento anni mandarono ambasciatori al sommo pontefice, supplicandolo che gli mandasse molti savij e dottori, che gl' insegnassero la nostra fede, ma per gl' impedimenti ch' ebbero detti ambasciatori, tornarono indietro senza arrivare a Roma. E ancora a papa Eugenio IV. venne uno ambasciatore, il quale gli raccontò la grande amicizia che quei principi e i

---

[1] Read *anni.*
[2] Read *miserunt.*

secum longo sermone locutus sum de multis, de magnitudine edificiorum regalium et de magnitudine fluuium[1] in latitudine et longitudine mirabili et de multitudine ciuitatum in ripis fluuium,[1] vt in vno flumine .200. circiter ciuitates sint constitute, et pontes marmorei magne latitudinis et longitudinis vndique colonpnis ornati. hec patria digna est vt per latinos queratur, non solum quia lucra ingencia ex ea capi posunt auri argenti gemarum omnis generis et aromatum que nunquam ad nos deferuntur, verum propter doctos viros philosofos et astrologos peritos et quibus ingeniis et artibus ita potens et magnifica prouincia gubernentur[2] ac etiam bella conducant. hec pro aliquantula satisfactione ad suam peticionem, quantum breuitas temporis dedit et occupaciones mee conscepscerunt,[3] paratus in futurum regie maiestati quan-

loro popoli hanno coi cristiani; e io parlai lungamente con lui di molte cose, e delle grandezze delle fabriche regalè, e della grossezza de' fiumi in larghezza e in lunghezza, ed ei mi disse molte cose maravigliose della moltitudine delle città e luoghi che son fondati nelle rive loro; e che solamente in un fiume si trovava dugento città edificate con ponte di pietre di marmo, molto larghi e lunghi, adornati di molte colonne. Questo paese è degno tanto, quanto ogni altro, che si abbia trovato; e non solamente vi si può trovar grandissimo guadagno, e molte cose ricche; ma ancora oro, e argento, e pietre preziose, e di ogni sorte di spezieria in grande quantità, della quale mai non si porta in queste nostre parti. Ed è il vero, che molti uomini dotti, filosofi, e astrologi, e altri grandi savij in tutte le arti, e di grande ingegno governano quella gran pro-

[1] Read *fluminum.*
[3] Read *concesserunt.*

[2] Read *gubernetur.*

tum volet latius satisfacere. data florencie 25 iunii 1474.

A ciuitate vlixiponis per occidentem in directo sunt .26. spacia in carta signata quorum quodlibet habet miliaria .250. vsque ad nobilisim[am] et maximam ciuitatem quinsay. circuit enim centum miliaria et habet pontes decem et nomen eius sonat cita del ciclo ciuitas celi et multa miranda de ea narrantur, de multitudine artificium et de reditibus. hoc spacium est fere tercia pars tocius spere, que ciuitas est in prouincia mangi, siue vicina prouincie Katay

vincia, e ordinano le battaglie. ‖ E questo [1] sia per sodisfazione delle vostre richieste, quanto la brevità del tempo, e le mie occupazioni mi hanno concesso. E così io resto prontissimo a soddisfare e servir sua altezza, compiutamente in tutto quello che mi comanderà. Da Fiorenza, ai 25 giugno dell' anno 1474. ‖ Dalla città di Lisbona per dritto verso ponente sono in detta carta ventisei spazj, ciascun de' quali contien dugento e cinquanta miglia, fino alla nobilissima e gran città di Quisai, la quale gira cento miglia *che sono trentacinque leghe;* ove sono dieci ponti di pietra di marmore. Il nome di questa città significa Città del Cielo, della qual si narrano cose maravigliose intorno alla grandezza degli ingegni, e fabriche, e rendite. Questo spazio è quasi la terza parte della sfera. Giace

[1] In the Italian arrangement this passage is transposed to the end of the letter, and the passage " Dalla città di Lisbona," etc. (which in the Latin arrangement forms a postscript) follows immediately after "battaglie."

in qua residencia terre regia est. Sed ab insula antilia vobis

nota ad insulam nobilisimam cippangu sunt decem spacia. est enim

illa insula fertilissima aur[o] margaritis et gemmis, et auro solido cooperiunt tenpla et domos regias, *itaque per ygnota*

itinera non magna maris spacia transeundum. multa fortasse essent aperitus[1] *declaranda, sed diligens*

considerator per hec poterit ex se ipso reliqua prospicere. vale dilectisime.

questa città nella prouincia di Mango, vicina alla provincia del Cataio, nella quale sta la maggior parte del tempo il re. E dall' isola di Antilia, *che voi chiamate di Sette Città,* della quale avete notizia, fino alla nobilissima isola di Cipango sono dieci spazj, *che fanno due mila e cinquecento miglia, cioè dugento e venticinque leghe;* la quale Isola è fertilissima di oro, di perle, e di pietre preziose. E sappiate, che con piastre d' oro fino coprono i tempj e le case regali. *Di modo che, per non esser conosciuto il cammino, tutte queste cose si ritrovano nascoste e coperte; e ad essa si può andar sicuramente. Molte altre cose si potrebbono dire; ma, come io vi ho già detto a bocca, e voi siete prudente e di buon giudicio, mi rendo certo che non vi resta cosa alcuna da intendere: e però non sarò più lungo.*

---

[1] Read *apertius.*

THE Latin text of this letter is preserved in the handwriting of Columbus upon the fly-leaf of one of his books in the Colombina at Seville. See above, vol. i. p. 356, note 3. I here subjoin a specimen of the handwriting of Columbus, from a MS. in the Colombina, reproduced in Harrisse's *Notes on Columbus*.

APPENDIX B.

THE BULL *Inter Cetera.*

EXEMPLAR BVLLAE SEV
DONATIONIS, AVTORITATE
CVIVS, EPISCOPVS ROMANVS

Alexander eius nominis fextus, con-
cefsit et donauit Caftellæ regibus
et fuis fuccefforibus, regiones
et Infulas noui orbis in
Oceano occidentali His-
panorum nauigationi-
bus repertas.·.

LEXANDER EPISCOPVS, feruus feruo-
rum Dei, Charifsimo in Chrifto filio Ferdinando Regi, et Charifsimæ in Chrifto
filiæ Elizabeth Reginæ Caftellæ, Legionis,
Aragonum, Siciliæ, et Granatæ, illuftribus, falutem et
Apoftolicam benedictionem.

Inter cætera Diuinæ maieftati beneplacita opera
et cordis noftri defiderabilia, illud profecto potifimum
exiftit vt fides catholica et Chriftiana religio noftris
præfertim temporibus exaltetur ac vbilibet amplietur

APPENDIX B.

¶ THE COPPIE OF THE BULL
OR DONATION, BY TH[E]AU-
TORITIE WHEROF, POPE
Alexander the fyxte of that name,
gaue and graunted to the kynges of
Caſtyle and theyr ſucceſſours the
Regions and Ilandes founde in
the Weſte Ocean ſea by
the nauigations of the
Spanyardes.

Lexander byſhoppe, the ſeruaunte of the ſer-
uantes of God : To owre moſte deare beloued ſonne in Chriſt Kynge Ferdinande,
And to owre deare beloued doughter in
Chryſte Elyzabeth Queene of Caſtyle, Legion, Aragon,
Sicilie, and Granata, moſt noble Princes, Gretynge
and Apoſtolical benediction.

Amonge other woorkes acceptable to the diuine
maieſtie and accordynge to owre hartes deſyre, this
certeinely is the chiefe, that the Catholyke fayth and
Chriſtian religion, ſpecially in this owre tyme may in
all places bee exalted, amplified, and enlarged, wherby

ac dilatetur, animarumque falus procuretur, ac barbaricæ
nationes deprimantur et ad fidem ipfam reducantur.
Vnde cum ad hanc facram Petri fedem Diuina fauente
clementia (meritis licet imparibus) euocati fuerimus,
cognofcentes vos tanquam veros catholicos reges et
principes : quales femper fuiffe nouimus, et a vobis
præclare gefta, toti pene orbi notifsima demonftrant,
nedum id exoptare, fed omni conatu, ftudio et diligentia, nullis laboribus, nullis impenfis, nullifque par-
cendo periculis, etiam proprium fanguinem effundendo
efficere, ac omnem animum veftrum, omnefque conatus
ad hoc iam dudum dedicafse, quemadmodum recupe-
ratio regni Granatæ a tyrannide Saracenorum hodier-
nis temporibus per vos, cum tanta Diuini nominis
gloria facta teftatur. Digne ducimur non immerito,
et debemus illa vobis etiam fponte, ac fauorabiliter
concedere, per quæ huiufmodi fanctum ac laudabile
ab immortali deo acceptum propofitum, in dies feruen-
tiori animo ad ipfius dei honorem et Imperij Chriftiani propagationem, profequi valeatis. Sane accepi-
mus quod vos qui dudum animum propofueratis aliquas
infulas et terras firmas remotas et incognitas, ac per
alios hactenus non repertas, quærere et inuenire, vt
illarum incolas et habitatores ad colendum Redemp-
torem noftrum et fidem catholicam profitendum re-
duceretis, hactenus in expugnatione et recuperatione
ipfius regni Granatæ plurimum occupati, huiufmodi
fanctum et laudabile propofitum veftrum ad optatum
finem perducere nequiuiftis : Sed tamen ficut Domino
placuit, regno predicto recuperato, volentes defiderium
veftrum adimplere. dilectum filium Chriftophorum Co-

the health of ſoules may be procured, and the Barbarous nations ſubdued and brought to the fayth.   And
therefore wheras by the fauoure of gods clemencie
(although not with equall deſertes) we are cauled to
this holy ſeate of Peter, and vnderſtandynge you to bee
trewe Catholyke Princes as we haue euer knowen you,
and as youre noble and woorthy factes haue declared
in maner to the hole worlde in that with all your
ſtudie, diligence, and induſtrye, you haue ſpared no
trauayles, charges, or perels, aduenturynge euen the
ſhedynge of your owne bludde, with applyinge yowre
hole myndes and endeuours here vnto, as your noble
expeditions achyued in recoueryng the kyngdome of
Granata from the tyrannie of the Sarracens in theſe
our dayes, doo playnely declare your factes with ſo
great glorye of the diuine name.   For the whiche as
we thinke you woorthy, ſo owght we of owre owne free
wyl fauorably to graunt all thynges whereby you maye
dayely with more feruent myndes to the honoure of god
and enlargynge the Chriſtian empire, proſecute your
deuoute and laudable purpoſe moſt acceptable to the
immortall God.   We are credably informed that wheras
of late you were determyned to ſeeke and fynde certeyne
Ilandes and firme landes farre remote and vnknowen
(and not heretofore found by any other) to th[e]in-
tent to bringe th[e]inhabitauntes of the ſame to honoure owre redemer and to profeſſe the catholyke fayth,
you haue hetherto byn much occupied in th[e]expug-
nation and recouerie of the kyngedome of Granata,
by reaſon whereof yowe coulde not brynge yowre ſayde
laudable purpoſe to th[e]ende deſyred.   Neuertheleſſe
as it hath pleaſed almyghty god, the foreſayde kyngedome beinge recouered, wylling t[o]accomplyſhe your
ſayde deſyre, you haue, not without great laboure,
perelles, and charges, appoynted owre welbeloued

lonum virum vtique dignum et plurimum commendatum
ac tanto negotio aptum, cum nauigijs et hominibus ad
fimilia inftructis, non fine maximis laboribus, ac periculis, et expenfis deftinaftis vt terras firmas et Infulas
remotas et incognitas, huiufmodi per mare vbi hactenus
nauigatum non fuerat, diligenter inquireret. Qui tandem
(Diuino auxilio facta extrema diligentia in mari Oceano
nauigantes) certas infulas remotifsimas et etiam terras
firmas, quæ per alios hactenus repertæ non fuerant,
inuenerunt. In quibus plurimæ gentes pacifice vi-
uentes, et (vt afferitur) nudi incedentes, nec carnibus
vefcentes, inhabitant : Et vt præfati nuncij veftri pof-
sunt opinari, gentes ipfæ in Infulis et terris prædictis
habitantes credunt vnum deum creatorem in Cœlis
efse, ac ad fidem catholicam amplexandum et bonis
moribus imbuendum fatis apti videntur : Spefque
habetur, quod fi erudirentur, nomen Saluatoris Domini
noftri Iefu Chrifti in terris et infulis prædicts facile
induceretur. Ac præfatus Chriftophorus in vna ex
principalibus Infulis prædictis, iam vnam turrim fatis
munitam, in qua certos Chriftianos qui fecum inerant,
in cuftodiam et vt alias Infulas ac terras firmas remotas
et incognitas inquirerent pofuit, conftrui et ædificari
fecit. In quibus quidem Infulis et terris iam repertis,
aurum, aromata, et aliæ quamplurimæ res præciofæ
diuerfi generis et diuerfæ qualitatis reperiuntur. Vnde
omnibus diligenter, et præfertim fidei catholicæ exal-
tatione et dilatatione (prout decet Catholicos Reges et
Principes) confideratis, more progenitorum veftrorum
claræ memoriæ Regum, terras firmas et infulas prædictas, illarumque incolas et habitatores, vobis diuina

ſonne Chriſtopher Colonus (a man certes wel com-
mended as moſte worthy and apte for ſo great a matter) well furnyſhed with men and ſhippes and other
neceſſaries, to ſeeke (by the ſea where hetherto no
manne hath ſayled) ſuche firme landes and Ilandes
farre remote and hitherto vnknowen. Who (by gods
helpe) makynge diligente ſearche in the Ocean ſea,
haue founde certeyne remote Ilandes and firme landes
whiche were not heretofore founde by any other. In
the which (as is ſayde) many nations inhabite lyu-
inge peaceably and goinge naked, not accuſtomed to
eate fleſhe. And as farre as yowre meſſengers can con-
iecture, the nations inhabitynge the foreſayde landes
and Ilandes, beleue that there is one god creatoure in
heauen : and ſeeme apte to be brought to th[e]imbraſ-
inge of the catholyke faythe and to be imbued with
good maners : by reaſon whereof, we may hope that if
they well be inſtructed, they may eaſely bee induced
to receaue the name of owre ſauiour Ieſu Chriſt. We
are further aduertiſed that the forenamed Chriſtopher
hathe nowe builded and erected a fortreſſe with good
munition in one of the foreſayde principall Ilandes in
the which he hath placed a garriſon of certeine of the
Chriſtian men that wente thyther with him : aſwell to
th[e]intent to defende the ſame, as alſo to ſearche
other Ilandes and firme landes farre remote and yet
vnknowen. We alſo vnderſtande, that in theſe landes
and Ilandes lately founde, is great plentie of golde and
ſpices, with dyuers and many other precious thynges
of ſundry kyndes and qualities. Therfore al thinges
diligently conſidered (eſpecially th[e]amplifyinge and
enlargyng of the catholike fayth, as it behoueth catholike Princes folowyng th[e]exemples of yowre
noble progenitours of famous memorie) wheras yowe
are determyned by the fauour of almightie god to ſub•

fauente clementia fubiicere et ad fidem Catholicam reducere propofuiftis.

Nos itaque huiufmodi veftrum fanctum et laudabile propofitum plurimum in Domino commendantes, ac cupientes vt illud ad debitum finem perducatur, et ipfum nomen Saluatoris noftri in partibus illis inducatur, hortamur vos quamplurimum in Domino, et per facri lauacri fufceptionem, qua mandatis Apoftolicis obligati eftis, et per vifcera mifericordiæ Domini noftri Iefu Chrifti attente requirimus, vt cum expeditionem huiufmodi omnino profequi et affumere prona mente orthodoxæ fidei zelo intendatis, populos in huiufmodi Infulis et terris degentes, ad Chriftianam religionem fufcipiendam inducere velitis et debeatis, nec pericula nec labores vllo vnquam tempore vos deterreant, firma fpe fiduciaque conceptis quod Deus omnipotens conatus veftros fœliciter profequetur. Et vt tanti negotij prouintiam Apoftolicæ gratiæ largitate donati, liberius et audacius affumatis, motu proprio non ad veftram vel alterius pro vobis fuper hoc nobis oblatæ petitionis inftantiam, fed de noftra mera liberalitate, et ex certa fcientia, ac de Apoftolicæ poteftatis plenitudine, omnes Infulas et terras firmas inuentas et inueniendas, detectas et detegendas verfus Occidentem et Meridiem, fabricando et conftruendo vnam lineam a polo Arctico, fcilicet Septemtrione, ad polum Antarcticum, fcilicet Meridiem fiue terræ firmæ et infulæ inuentæ et inueniendæ fint verfus Indiam aut verfus aliam quamcunque partem quæ linea diftet a qualibet Infularum quæ vulgariter nuncupantur de los Azores et Cabo Verde centum leucis verfus Occidentem et Meridiem.

due and brynge to the catholyke fayth th[e]inhabi-
tauntes of the forefayde landes and Ilandes.

Wee greatly commendynge this yowre° godly and
laudable purpofe in owr lorde, and defirous to haue
the fame brought to a dewe ende, and the name of
owre fauioure to be knowen in thofe partes, doo
exhorte yowe in owre Lorde and by the receauynge
of yowre holy baptifme wherby yowe are bounde to
Apoftolicall obedience, and erneftely require yowe by
the bowels of mercy of owre Lorde Iefu Chrift, that
when yowe intende for the zeale of the Catholyke
faythe to profecute the fayde expedition to reduce the
people of the forefayde landes and Ilandes to the
Chriftian religion, yowe fhall fpare no labours at any
tyme, or bee deterred with any perels, conceauynge
firme hope and confidence that the omnipotent godde
wyll gyue good fucceffe to yowre godly attemptes.
And that beinge autoryfed by the priuilege of the
Apoftolycall grace, yowe may the more freely and
bouldly take vpon yowe th[e]enterpryfe of fo greate a
matter, we of owre owne motion, and not eyther at
yowre requeft or at the inftant peticion of any other
perfon, but of owre owne mere liberalitie and certeyne
fcience, and by the fulneffe of Apoftolycall power, doo
gyue, graunt, and affigne to yowe, yowre heyres and
fucceffours, al the firme landes and Ilandes found or
to be found, difcouered or to be difcouered toward the
Weft and South, drawyng a line from the pole Artike
to the pole Antartike (that is) from the north to the
Southe : Conteynynge in this donation, what fo euer
firme landes or Ilandes are founde or to bee founde
towarde *India*, or towarde any other parte what fo
euer it bee, beinge diftant from, or without the fore-
fayd lyne drawen a hundreth leaques towarde the
Wefte and South from any of the Ilandes which are
commonly cauled *De los Azores* and *Cabo Verde*.

Itaque omnes Infulæ et terræ firmæ repertæ et re
periendæ, detectæ et detegendæ a præfata linea verfis
Occidentem et Meridiem, quæ per alium Regem aut
Principem Chriftianum non fuerint actualiter poffeffæ
vfque ad diem natiuitatis Domini noftri Iefu Chrifti
proxime præteritum, a quo incipit annus præfens
Milleffimus Quadringenteffimus Nonageffimus tercius
quando fuerunt per nuncios et capitaneos veftros inuentæ aliquæ prædictarum Infularum, auctoritate omnipotentis Dei nobis in beato Petro concefsa, ac vicariatus
Iefu Chrifti qua fungimur in terris, cum omnibus illarum
dominijs, ciuitatibus, caftris, locis, et villis, iuribufque
et iurifdictionibus ac pertinentijs vniuerfis, vobis here-
dibufque et fuccefforibus veftris (Caftellæ et Legionis
regibus) in perpetuum tenore præfentium donamus
concedimus, et affignamus : Vofque et hæredes ac
fuccefsores præfatos illarum Dominos, cum plena, libera,
et omnimoda poteftate, autoritate, et iurifdictione,
facimus, conftituimus, et deputamus. Decernentes ni-
hilo minus per huiufmodi donationem, concefsionem, et
affignationem noftram, nullo Chriftiano Principi qui
actualiter præfatas Infulas et terras firmas poffederit
vfque ad prædictum diem natiuitatis Domini noftri
Iefu Chrifti ius quæsitum, fublatum intelligi pofse aut
auferri debere.

Et infuper mandamus vobis in virtutæ fanctæ obedi-
entiæ (vt ficut pollicemini et non dubitamus pro veftra
maxima deuotione et regia magnanimitate vos efse factu-
ros) ad terras firmas et Infulas prædictas, viros probos
et Deum timentes, doctos, peritos, et expertos, ad in-

All the Ilandes therfore and firme landes, founde
and to be founde, difcouered and to be difcouered
from the fayde lyne towarde the Weft and South, fuch
as haue not actually bin heretofore poffeffed by any
other Chriftian kynge or prynce vntyll the daye of the
natiuitie of owre Lorde Iefu Chryfte lafte pafte, from
the which begynneth this prefent yeare beinge the
yeare of owre Lorde. M. CCCC. lxxxxiii. when fo euer
any fuch fhalbe founde by your meffingers and capy-
taines, Wee by the autoritie of almyghtie God graunted
vnto vs in faynt Peter, and by the office which we beare
on the earth in the fteede of Iefu Chrifte, doo for euer
by the tenoure of thefe prefentes, gyue, graunte, affigne,
vnto yowe, yowre heyres, and fucceffoures (the kynges
of Caftyle and Legion) all thofe landes and Ilandes,
with theyr dominions, territories, cities, caftels, towres,
places, and vyllages, with all the ryght, and iurifdic-
tions therunto perteynynge : conftitutynge, affignynge,
and deputynge, yowe, yowre heyres, and fucceffours
the lordes thereof, with full and free poure, autoritie,
and iurifdiction. Decreeinge neuertheleffe by this
owre donation, graunt, and affignation, that from no
Chriftian Prince whiche actually hath poffeffed the
forefayde Ilandes and firme landes vnto the day of
the natiuitie of owre lorde beforefayde theyr ryght
obteyned to bee vnderftoode hereby to be taken away,
or that it owght to be taken away.

Furthermore wee commaunde yowe in the vertue
of holy obedience (as yowe haue promyfed, and as wee
doubte not you wyll doo vppon mere deuotion and
princely magnanimitie) to fende to the fayde firme
landes and Ilandes, honefte, vertuous, and lerned men,
fuche as feare God, and are able to inftructe th[e]in-

ftruendum incolas et habitatores præfatos in fide Catholica et bonis moribus imbuendum, deftinare debeatis, omnem debitam diligentiam in præmifsis adhibentes.

Ac quibufcumque perfonis, cuiufcunque dignitatis, etiam imperialis et regalis ftatus, gradus, ordinis vel conditionis, fub excommunicationis latæ fententiæ pœna quam eo ipfo fi contra fecerint incurrant, diftrictius inhibemus ne ad Infulas et terras firmas inuentas et inueniendas, detectas et detegendas verfus Occidentem et Meridiem, fabricando et conftruendo lineam a polo Arctico ad polum Antarcticum, fiue terræ firmæ et Infulæ inuentæ et inueniendæ fint verfus Indiam aut verfus aliam quamcunque partem quæ linea diftet a qualibet Infularum quæ vulgariter nuncupantur de los Azores et Cabo Verde centum leucis verfus Occidentem et Meridiem vt præfertur, pro mercibus habendis vel quauis alia caufa accedere præfumat abfque veftra ac hæredum et fuccefsorum veftrorum prædictorum licentia fpeciali : Non obftantibus conftitutionibus et ordinationibus Apoftolicis, cæterifque contrariis quibufcunque, in illo a quo imperia et dominationes et bona cuncta procedunt : Confidentes quod dirigente Domino actus veftros, fi huiufmodi fanctum ac laudabile propofitum profequamini, breui tempore cum fœlicitate et gloria totius populi Chriftiani, veftri labores et conatus exitum fœlicifsimum confequentur. Verum quia difficile foret præfentes literas ad fingula quæque loca in quibus expediens fuerit deferri, volumus ac motu et fcientia fimilibus decernimus, quod illarum tranffumptis manu publici notarij inderogati fubfcriptis, et figillo alicuius per-

habitauntes in the Catholyke fayth and good maners, applyinge all theyr poffible diligence in the premiffes.

We furthermore ftreightly inhibite all maner of perfons, of what ftate, degree, order, or condition fo euer they bee, although of Imperiall and regall dignitie, vnder the peyne of the fentence of excommunication whiche they fhall incurre yf they doo to the contrary, that they in nó cafe prefume without fpeciall lycence of yowe, yowre heyres, and fucceffours, to trauayle for marchaundies or for any other caufe, to the fayde landes or Ilandes, founde or to bee found, difcouered, or to bee difcouered, toward the weft and fouth, drawing a line from the pole Artyke to the pole Antartike, whether the firme lands and Ilandes found and to be found, be fituate toward *India* or towarde any other parte beinge diftant from the lyne drawen a hundreth leagues towarde the weft from any of the Ilandes commonly cauled *De los Azores* and *Cabo Verde* : Notwithftandynge conftitutions, decrees, and Apoftolycall ordinaunces what fo euer they are to the contrary : In him from whom Empyres, dominions, and all good thynges doo procede : Truftynge that almyghtie god directynge yowre enterprifes, yf yowe followe yowre godly and laudable attemptes, yowre laboures and trauayles herein, fhall in fhorte tyme obteyne a happy ende with felicitie and glorie of all Chriftian people. But forafmuch as it fhulde bee a thynge of great difficultie for thefe letters to bee caryed to all fuche places as fhuld bee expedient, we wyll, and of lyke motion and knowleage doo decree that whyther fo euer the fame fhalbe fent, or wher fo euer they fhalbe receaued with the fubfcription of a common notarie therunto requyred, with the feale of any perfon conftitute in ecclefiafticall dignitie, or fuche as are autoryfed by the ecclefiafticall courte, the fame fayth and credite to bee

fonæ in ecclefiaftica dignitate çonftitutæ, feu curiæ ecclefiafticæ munitis, ea prorfus fides in iudicio et extra ac alias vbilibet adhibeatur, quæ præfentibus adhiberetur fi efsent exhibitæ vel oftenfæ.

Nulli ergo omnino hominum liceat hanc paginam noftræ commendationis, hortationis, requifitionis, donationis, concefsionis, afsignationis, conftitutionis, deputationis, decreti, mandati, inhibitionis, et voluntatis, infringere vel ei aufu temerario contraire. Si quis autem hoc attentare præfumpferit, indignationem omnipotentis Dei, ac beatorum Petri et Pauli Apoftolorum eius, fe nouerit incurfurum.·.

Datum Romæ apud fanctum Petrum : Anno incarnationis Dominicæ. 1493. quarto nonas Maij : Pontificatus noftri anno primo.·.

gyuen thereunto in iudgement or els where, as fhulde bee exhibyted to thefe prefentes.

It fhall therefore bee lawefull for no man to infringe or rafhely to contrarie this letter of owre commenda-tion, exhortacion, requefte, donation, graunt, affigna-tion, conftitution, deputation, decree, commaundement, inhibition, and determination. And yf any fhall pre-fume to attempte the fame, he owght to knowe that he fhall thereby incurre the indignation of almyghtie God and his holye Apoftles Peter and Paule. (∴) (:) (∵)

℃ Gyuen at Rome at faynt Peters : In the yeare of th[e]incarnation of owre Lord M. CCCC. LXXXXIII. The fourth day of the nones of Maye, the fyrfte yeare of owre feate. ( ) ( ) ( )

APPENDIX C.

1. *Those who went out in the Santa Maria, and returned in the Niña:* —

Christopher Columbus, captain-general.
Juan de La Cosa, of Santoña, master, and owner of
the vessel.
Sancho Ruiz, pilot.
Maestre Alonso, of Moguer, physician.
Maestre Diego, boatswain (*contramaestre*).
Rodrigo Sanchez, of Segovia, inspector (*veedor*).
Terreros, steward (*maestresala*).
Rodrigo de Jerez, of Ayamonte.
Ruiz Garcia, of Santoña.
Rodrigo de Escobar.
Francisco de Huelva, of Huelva.
Rui Fernandez, of Huelva.
Pedro de Bilbao, of Larrabezua.
Pedro de Villa, of Santoña.
Diego de Salcedo, servant of Columbus.
Pedro de Acevedo, cabin boy.
Luis de Torres, converted Jew, interpreter.

2. *Those who went and returned in the Pinta:* —

Martin Alonso Pinzon, of Palos, captain.
Francisco Martin Pinzon, of Palos, master.
Cristóbal Garcia Xalmiento, pilot.

Juan de Jerez, of Palos, mariner.

Bartolomé Garcia, of Palos, boatswain.

Juan Perez Vizcaino, of Palos, caulker.

Rodrigo de Triana, of Lepe.

Juan Rodríguez Bermejo, of Molinos.

Juan de Sevilla.

Garcia Hernández, of Palos, steward (*despensero*).

Garcia Alonso, of Palos.

Gomez Rascon, of Palos, ⎱
Cristóbal Quintero, of Palos, ⎰ owners of the vessel.

Juan Quintero, of Palos.

Diego Bermudez, of Palos.

Juan Bermudez, of Palos.

Francisco Garcia Gallego, of Moguer.

Francisco Garcia Vallejo, of Moguer.

Pedro de Arcos, of Palos.

3. *Those who went and returned in the Niña:* —

Vicente Yañez Pinzon, of Palos, captain.

Juan Niño, of Moguer, master.

Pero Alonso Niño, of Moguer, pilot.

Bartolomé Roldan, of Palos, pilot.

Francisco Niño, of Moguer.

Gutierre Perez, of Palos.

Juan Ortiz, of Palos.

Alonso Gutierrez Querido, of Palos.

4. *Those who were left in Hispaniola, and perished, most of them murdered by the natives:* —

Pedro Gutierrez, keeper of the king's drawing room.

Rodrigo de Escobedo, of Segovia, notary.

Diego de Arana, of Cordova, high constable (*alguazil mayor*).

Alonso Velez de Mendoza, of Seville.

Alvar Perez Osorio, of Castrojeriz.

Antonio de Jaen, of Jaen.

The bachelor Bernardino de Tapia, of Ledesma.

Cristóbal del Alamo, of Niebla.

Castillo, silversmith and assayer, of Seville.

Diego Garcia, of Jerez.

Diego de Tordoya, of Cabeza de Buey, in Estremadura.

Diego de Capilla, of Almaden.

Diego de Torpa.

Diego de Mables, of Mables.

Diego de Mendoza, of Guadalajara.

Diego de Montalban, of Jaen.

Domingo de Bermeo.

Francisco Fernandez.

Francisco de Godoy, of Seville.

Francisco de Aranda, of Aranda.

Francisco de Henao, of Avila.

Francisco Ximénez, of Seville.

Gabriel Baraona, of Belmonte.

Gonzalo Fernandez de Segovia, of Leon.

Gonzalo Fernandez de Segovia, of Segovia.

Guillermo Ires, [qy. William Irish, or William Harris?], of Galney [i. e. Galway], Ireland.

Fernando de Porcuna.

Jorge Gonzalez, of Trigueros.

Maestre Juan, surgeon.

Juan de Urniga.

Juan Morcillo, of Villanueva de la Serena.

Juan de Cueva, of Castuera.

Juan Patiño, of La Serena.

Juan del Barco, of Barco de Ávila.

Juan de Villar, of Villar.

Juan de Mendoza.

Martin de Logrosa, of Logrosa.

Pedro Corbacho, of Cáceres.

Pedro de Talavera.

Pedro de Foronda.

Sebastian de Mayorga, of Majorca.

Tristan de San Jorge.

Tallarte de Lages [qy. Arthur Laws, or Larkins?], of England.

This list is taken from Captain Cesáreo Fernández Duro's learned monograph, *Colon y Pinzon. Informe relativo á los pormenores de descubrimiento del Nuevo Mundo,* Madrid, 1883.

Juan de La Cosa is usually spoken of as having accompanied Columbus on his second voyage but not on his first. An ordinance of the sovereigns, however, dated February 28, 1494, and preserved among the Simancas MSS., thus addresses La Cosa : — " Fuistes por maestre de una nao vuestra á las mares del océano, donde en aquel viaje fueron descubiertas las tierras ó islas de la parte de las Indias, é vos perdistes la dicha nao," *anglicè,* " You went as master of a ship of your own to the ocean seas where in that voyage were discovered the lands and islands of the Indies, and you lost the said ship." Navarrete, *Biblioteca maritima española,* tom. ii. p. 209. Mr. Winsor (*Christopher Columbus,* p. 184) seems to think that this La Cosa was a different person from the great pilot and cosmographer, who was a native of Santoña and resident of Puerto de Santa Maria ; but Captain Duro (p. 292) makes him the same person. Cf. Harrisse, *Christophe Colomb,* i. 406.

APPENDIX D.

(After the corrected lists in Guillemard's *Magellan*.)

1. *The eighteen who returned to Seville in the Victoria.*

   Juan Sebastian Elcano, captain-general.

   Miguel de Rodas, boatswain (*contramaestre*) of the Victoria.

   Francisco Albo, of Axio, boatswain of the Trinidad.

   Juan de Acurio, of Bermeo, boatswain of the Concepcion.

   Martin de Judicibus, of Genoa, superintendent of the Concepcion.

   Hernando de Bustamante, of Alcántara, barber of the Concepcion.

   Juan de Zuvileta, of Baracaldo, page of the Victoria.

   Miguel Sanchez, of Rodas, skilled seaman (*marinero*) of the Victoria.

   Nicholas the Greek, of Naples, *marinero* of the Victoria.

   Diego Gallego, of Bayonne, *marinero* of the Victoria.

   Juan Rodriguez, of Seville, *marinero* of the Trinidad.

   Antonio Rodriguez, of Huelva, *marinero* of the Trinidad.

   Francisco Rodriguez, of Seville (a Portuguese), *marinero* of the Concepcion.

Juan de Arratia, of Bilbao, common sailor (*grumete*) of the Victoria.

Vasco Gomez Gallego (a Portuguese), *grumete* of the Trinidad.

Juan de Santandres, of Cueto, *grumete* of the Trinidad.

Martin de Isaurraga, of Bermeo, *grumete* of the Concepcion.

The Chevalier Antonio Pigafetta, of Vicenza, passenger.

2. *The thirteen who were arrested at the Cape Verde islands.*

Pedro de Indarchi, of Teneriffe, master of the Santiago.

Richard, from Normandy, carpenter of the Santiago.

Simon de Burgos (a Portuguese), servant of Mendoza, the traitor captain of the Victoria.

Juan Martin, of Aguilar de Campo, servant of the same Mendoza.

Roldan de Argote, of Bruges, bombardier of the Concepcion.

Martin Mendez, of Seville, accountant of the Victoria.

Juan Ortiz de Gopega, of Bilbao, steward of the San Antonio.

Pedro Gasco, of Bordeaux, *marinero* of the Santiago.

Alfonso Domingo, *marinero* of the Santiago.

Ocacio Alonso, of Bollullos, *marinero* of the Santiago.

Gomez Hernandez, of Huelva, *marinero* of the Concepcion.

Felipe de Rodas, of Rodas, *marinero* of the Victoria.

Pedro de Tolosa, from Guipuzcoa, *grumete* of the Victoria.

3. *The four survivors of the Trinidad, who returned to Spain long after their comrades.*

Gonzalo Gomez de Espinosa, constable (*alguazil*) of the fleet.

Juan Rodriguez, of Seville (called " the deaf "), *marinero* of the Concepcion.

Ginez de Mafra, of Xeres, *marinero*.

Leon Pancaldo, of Savona near Genoa, *marinero*.

INDEX.

Estotiland, Antonio Zeno's description of, i. 244.

Estufas, or council-houses of the pueblo Indians, i. 89.

Eudoxus, his voyages on the coast of Africa, i. 302; Strabo and Pliny on, i. 302.

Eugenius IV., pope, grants heathen countries to Portugal, i. 324, 457.

Europe, why the voyages of the Northmen produced so little effect in, i. 257, 258; state of, in the year 1000, i. 258; and Asia, i. 261; the inhabited world of mediæval, i. 261; her trade with Asia, i. 262; the dark ages of, i. 269; and the Turks, i. 271; in the fourteenth century, i. 276; origin of the name, ii. 136.

Exogamy, in Australia, i. 60; in the phratry, i. 70.

Eyrbyggja Saga, mentions Vinland, i. 203.

Færoe islands, Nicolò Zeno wrecked upon, i. 227; Sinclair's conquest of, i. 228; Antonio Zeno returns to, i. 230; the name, on Nicolò Zeno's map, i. 236.

Family, patriarchal, not primitive, i. 53; "mother-right," i. 54; in the lower status of savagery, i. 58; the clan, i. 60; change of kinship from female to male line, and its results, i. 61–63; family life, i. 66, 67; in Mexico at the time of the discovery, i. 122.

Faria y Sousa, on Magellan offering his services to Spain, ii. 191.

Females, kinship reckoned through, i. 56, 57; power in domestic life, i. 68; councils of squaws among the Wyandots, i. 70; results of kinship through, i. 77; among the Zuñis, i. 89; succession through, in Peru, ii. 346.

Fenton, his "Early Hebrew Life," i. 63.

Ferdinand, king of Aragon, his relation to Columbus's enterprise, i. 419; and Pinzon's expedition in 1497, i. 487, ii. 86; his position in 1511, ii. 448; death, ii. 452.

Fernandez, Garcia, his testimony relating to Columbus, i. 412.

Feudalism, unknown to aboriginal society in America, i. 98, 100.

Fewkes, Dr., his collection of Zuñi melodies, ii. 470.

Fiji, cannibalism in, i. 120.

Finæus, Orontius, his globe in 1531, ii. 122; influenced by Ptolemy and Mela, ii. 126.

Finn M'Cumhail, the Irish legends of, and Homer, i. 196.

Five Nations, joined in a confederacy, i. 45. *See also* Iroquois; Iroquois Confederacy.

Flateyar-bók version of Eric the Red's Saga, i. 199.

Florida, on Cantino's map, 1502, ii. 74; before the exploration of Ponce de Leon, ii. 79; Ponce de Leon's voyage on the coast of, ii. 486; Dominicans in, ii. 511; Huguenots in, ii. 512; vengeance of Gourgues, ii. 520.

Folk-lore, of the red men, i. 51; Journal of, i. 52.

Fonseca, Juan Rodriguez de, at the head of the department of Indian affairs in Spain, i. 460; he quarrels with Columbus, i. 462; delays Columbus, i. 487; his machinations at the court, i. 497; his creature Bobadilla, i. 499; on the return of Columbus, i. 503; voyage of Ojeda instigated by, ii. 93; and Cortes, ii. 290; and Pedrarias Dávila, ii. 378; and Indian slavery, ii. 452; hinders Las Casas, ii. 460.

Fort Caroline, built by Laudonnière, ii. 513; slaughter of the people by Menendez, ii. 516.

Fox, Captain Gustavus, his identification of Guanahani, i. 433.

France, in the year 1000, i. 258.

French, the, their policy in colonization, ii. 529; drawn into the interior, ii. 530; result of their hostility to the Five Nations, ii. 530.

Freydis, daughter of Eric the Red, and her evil deeds in Vinland, i. 169–171.

Fries, Lorenz, his edition of Ptolemy, ii. 145.

Frislanda, on Nicolò Zeno's map and in Columbus's letter, i. 236; proved the same as the Færoe islands, i. 238; described by Columbus, i. 382.

Frobisher, Sir Martin, his explorations, ii. 545, 546.

Fródhi, founder of historical writing in Iceland, i. 204. *See also* Ari Fródhi.

Frontenac, Count, helps La Salle, ii. 533.

Fuca, Juan de la, and the strait which bears his name, ii. 545.

Fuegians, status of, ii. 298.

Fusang, the country discovered by the Chinese, i. 148, 149.

Fustel de Coulanges, on early kingship, i. 112.

Gaffarel, Paul, on the Sargasso sea, i. 427.

Gallatin, Albert, on the danger of trusting the Spanish narratives, i. 101.

Gallo, declares that Columbus's brother suggested the route to the Indies, i. 395.

Gallo, island of, Pizarro awaits Almagro and supplies at, ii. 393.

Gama, Vasco da, his voyage to Hindu-

Religious and Philosophical

THE DESTINY OF MAN

Viewed in the Light of His Origin.   16mo, gilt top, $1.00.

Of one thing we may be sure : that none are leading us more surely or rapidly to the full truth than men like the author of this little book, who reverently study the works of God for the lessons which He would teach his children. — *Christian Union* (New York).

THE IDEA OF GOD

As Affected by Modern Knowledge.   16mo, gilt top, $1.00,

The vigor, the earnestness, the honesty, and the freedom from cant and subtlety in his writings are exceedingly refreshing. He is a scholar, a critic, and a thinker of the first order. — *Christian Register* (Boston).

THROUGH NATURE TO GOD

16mo, gilt top, $1.00.

CONTENTS. — *The Mystery of Evil ; The Cosmic Roots of Love and Self-Sacrifice ; The Everlasting Reality of Religion.*

The little volume has a reasonableness and a persuasiveness that cannot fail to commend its arguments to all. — *Public Ledger* (Philadelphia).

LIFE EVERLASTING

16mo, gilt top, $1.00 net.   Postage 7 cents.

This brief work is a contribution to the evolution of the theory of evolution on lines which are full of the deepest suggestiveness to Christian thinkers. — *The Congregationalist.*

OUTLINES OF COSMIC PHILOSOPHY

Based on the Doctrine of Evolution, with Criticisms on the Positive Philosophy.   In 4 volumes, 8vo, $8.00.

You must allow me to thank you for the very great interest with which I have at last slowly read the whole of your work. . . . I never in my life read so lucid an expositor (and therefore thinker) as you are. — CHARLES DARWIN.

DARWINISM, AND OTHER ESSAYS

Crown 8vo, gilt top, $2.00.

MYTHS AND MYTH-MAKERS

Old Tales and Superstitions interpreted by Comparative Mythology.   Crown 8vo, gilt top, $2.00.

THE UNSEEN WORLD

And Other Essays.   Crown 8vo, gilt top, $2.00.

EXCURSIONS OF AN EVOLUTIONIST

Crown 8vo, gilt top, $2.00.

𝔐iscellaneous ·

A CENTURY OF SCIENCE

And Other Essays.   Crown 8vo, $2.00.

Among our thoughtful essayists there are none more brilliant than Mr. John Fiske.   His pure style suits his clear thought. — *The Nation* (New York).

CIVIL GOVERNMENT IN THE UNITED STATES

Considered with some Reference to its Origins.   With Questions on the Text by Frank A. Hill, and Bibliographical Notes by Mr. Fiske.   Crown 8vo, $1.00, net; postpaid.

It is most admirable, alike in plan and execution, and will do a vast amount of good in teaching our people the principles and forms of our civil institutions. — MOSES COIT TYLER, *Professor of American Constitutional History and Law, Cornell University.*

HOUGHTON MIFFLIN COMPANY

BOSTON: 4 PARK STREET; NEW YORK: 85 FIFTH AVENUE

WRITINGS OF JOHN FISKE

Historical

THE DISCOVERY OF AMERICA

With some Account of Ancient America and the Spanish Conquest. With a Steel Portrait of Mr. Fiske, many maps, facsimiles, etc. 2 vols. crown 8vo, gilt top, $4.00.

The book brings together a great deal of information hitherto accessible only in special treatises, and elucidates with care and judgment some of the most perplexing problems in the history of discovery. — *The Speaker* (London).

OLD VIRGINIA AND HER NEIGHBOURS

2 vols. crown 8vo, gilt top, $4.00.
Illustrated Edition, 2 vols. 8vo, $8.00, net.

History has rarely been invested with such interest and charm as in these volumes. — *The Outlook* (New York).

THE BEGINNINGS OF NEW ENGLAND

Or, the Puritan Theocracy in its Relations to Civil and Religious Liberty. Crown 8vo, $2.00. Illustrated Edition. Containing Portraits, Maps, Facsimiles, Contemporary Views, Prints, and other Historic Materials. 8vo, gilt top, $4.00, net.

Having in the first chapters strikingly and convincingly shown that New England's history was the birth of centuries of travail, and having prepared his readers to estimate at their true importance the events of our early colonial life, Mr. Fiske is ready to take up his task as the historian of the New England of the Puritans. — *Advertiser* (Boston).

THE DUTCH AND QUAKER COLONIES IN AMERICA

With 8 Maps. 2 vols. crown 8vo, gilt top, $4.00
Illustrated Edition, 2 vols. 8vo, $8.00, net.

The work is a lucid summary of the events of a changeful and important time, carefully examined by a conscientious scholar, who is master of his subject. — *Daily News* (London).

NEW FRANCE AND NEW ENGLAND

With Maps. Crown 8vo. $2.00.
Illustrated edition. *Containing about 200 Illustrations. 8vo, gilt top, $4.00, net.*

This volume presents in broad and philosophic manner the causes and events which marked the victory on this continent of the English civilization over the French.

THE AMERICAN REVOLUTION

With Plans of Battles, and a Steel Portrait of Washington. 2 vols. crown 8vo, gilt top, $4.00. Illustrated Edition. Containing about 300 Illustrations. 2 vols. 8vo, gilt top, $8.00, net.

Beneath his sympathetic and illuminating touch the familiar story comes out in fresh and vivid colors. — *New Orleans Times-Democrat.*

THE CRITICAL PERIOD OF AMERICAN HISTORY, 1783-1789

With Map, Notes, etc. Crown 8vo, gilt top, $2.00. Illustrated Edition. Containing about 170 Illustrations. 8vo, gilt top, $4.00, net.

The author combines in an unusual degree the impartiality of the trained scholar with the fervor of the interested narrator. — *The Congregationalist* (Boston).

THE WAR OF INDEPENDENCE

In Riverside Library for Young People. With Maps. 16mo, 75 cents.

THE MISSISSIPPI VALLEY IN THE CIVIL WAR

With 20 Maps and Plans. 1 vol. crown 8vo, $2.00.

A HISTORY OF THE UNITED STATES FOR SCHOOLS

With Topical Analysis, Suggestive Questions, and Directions for Teachers, by F. A. Hill, and Illustrations and Maps. Crown 8vo, $1.00, net, postpaid.

Controversary